Reading and Learning in Content Areas

Second Edition

Randall J. Ryder
University of Wisconsin, Milwaukee

Michael F. Graves
University of Minnesota

JOHN WILEY & SONS, INC.
New York • Chichester • Weinheim • Brisbane • Singapore • Toronto

Cover art: Charles Ransier/Franklin County board of MR/DD, Southeast School, Columbus, Ohio

Library of Congress Cataloging-in-Publication Data
Ryder, Randall J.
    Reading and learning in content areas / Randall J. Ryder, Michael
F. Graves, — 2nd ed.
      p. cm.
    Includes bibliographical references and index.
    ISBN 0-471-36558-0
    1. Content area reading—United States.   2. Communication in education—
United States.   3. Learning.   I. Graves, Michael F.
II. Title.
LB1050.455.R93   1998
428.4′0712—dc21   97–22988
                                         CIP

Printed in the United States of America

10 9 8 7 6 5

Preface

The second edition of *Reading and Learning in Content Areas* continues with many of the basic themes of the first edition, but also advances numerous new and exciting ideas for ways content teachers can facilitate students' ability to gain understanding through reading, thinking, and communicating in subject matter areas. Our goal in writing this edition was not only to update the content of the text, but also to refine and modify the book's format and style to make it more meaningful and relevant to our readers. The following provides a brief description of the book's themes, organization, and application.

THEMATIC EMPHASES

The content of the chapters of this book is based on two overriding themes that focus on the process and artifacts of learning in subject matter areas. The first is that instruction and learning require a variety of communication processes. We view reading as one of numerous elements of an integrated approach to learning. Writing, discussion, observation, and engagement in demonstrations are integral to learning from text. So too are videotapes and a multitude of technological innovations such as CDs, digital sound, and video, and of course the multimedia environment of the Internet. A second theme is that the classroom provides a rich and dynamic context for constructing meaning. We recognize the importance of instruction that focuses on the active nature of human learning, the wealth of knowledge, views, and backgrounds that students bring to the classroom, and the potential of the classroom to extend itself into an increasingly connected global community. In classrooms of the sort we envision, teachers help students locate information and create and manage learning environments in which students communicate with one another, collaborate and assume responsibility, and acquire strategies for learning that extend beyond a given lesson or classroom. Throughout this book we describe activities that (1) draw upon students' ability to collectively engage in authentic learning that acknowledges the students' knowledge, (2) recognize students' cultural and linguistic diversity in a manner that allows students to gain a better awareness of that diversity, and (3) encourage students to engage in learning activities that are meaningful and provide the opportunity for higher-level thinking and understanding. Finally, we would note that in revising this book for the second edition, we have devoted considerable effort to conveying our thematic emphasis through a format that encourages your active participation in the book, and which is both informative and presented in an easily accessible style.

CHAPTER ORGANIZATION

A number of organizational features have been incorporated in this book. Chapters begin with a concept map and written narrative that overviews the chapter's content. Interspersed in each chapter are practice exercises and classroom vignettes. The exercises allow you to engage in or reflect on the concepts. Answers for the exercises are located at the end of the book. Classroom vignettes provide either insights from teachers or our comments from observing instructional activities in classroom settings. Additionally, where appropriate, we have provided commentaries on the use of certain instructional activities in an effort to highlight some of the strengths and limitations we have noted from our experiences as well as those of our students and our academic colleagues. Finally, each chapter concludes with a summary of the major points presented in the chapter and a Reflections section that gives you the opportunity to engage in some extended and personal application of strategies or topics addressed throughout the chapter. We would also note that we have provided a brief annotation of the references that appear at the end of each chapter. Hopefully, these will assist you in identifying materials that may be of interest.

APPLICATION OF THE BOOK'S CONTENT

One of the greatest strengths of our schools is the innovative and diverse instructional practice of teachers. Due to a teacher's style of instruction and personality, some degree of adaptation in presentation or format of a given instructional strategy is likely to be observed from classroom to classroom. Similarly, the variation of student characteristics between classrooms in a school or between schools will necessitate adaptation. Therefore we encourage you to consider how the instructional activities or topics presented throughout this book may require some modification to meet your needs as well as those of your students. However, we are also confident that we have limited our focus to activities and classroom practice that are functional, effective, and adaptable to a wide variety of educational settings and styles of instruction. No doubt some of the instructional ideas you may acquire from this book may be new to you. Some may even appear initially to be a radical departure from more traditional instructional approaches. We encourage you, therefore, to consider carefully the potential merit of these new ideas, apply them to your classroom, and reflect on their effect on students' learning. You may, for example, consider explaining a new instructional idea to your students, asking them for their assistance in engaging in this approach, and requesting them to evaluate its effectiveness.

ACKNOWLEDGMENTS

We would like to acknowledge five groups of individuals who have assisted us in the preparation of this book. First, we would like to extend our appreciation to the numerous graduate and undergraduate students, teachers, administrators, and parents who have provided us the opportunity to gain a better understanding of the process of educating children. Without their ideas, viewpoints, and [comments], our ability to sharpen our own vision of instruction would [be] severely lessened. Second, we would like to acknowledge the numerous st[udents in] elementary, middle, and high schools who have allowed us to observe the us[e of] many of the activities presented in this book and who have provided us feedback on the effectiveness of these activities. Their ideas and comments have sharpened our appreciation of the importance of focusing instruction on the needs of the learner. Third, we would like to thank the numerous scholars who, over the past several decades, have enriched the knowledge base that has informed this book. Through their efforts, the teaching profession has acquired a much better understanding of learning and instruction. Fourth, we would like to thank the many talented professionals at Prentice Hall who have assisted us in the preparation of this book. In particular we would like to acknowledge the efforts of Jeff Johnston and Brad Potthoff, who were steadfast in their commitment to our efforts and unwavering in their encouragement during the process of writing. Moreover, we would like to thank the following reviewers whose insights and suggestions provided us with innovative and thoughtful ideas that we have incorporated in this second edition: Mary Ann Gray-Schlegel, Millersville University of Pennsylvania; Betty McEady, California State University–Monterey Bay; James McGlinn, University of North Carolina–Asheville; Harry B. Miller, Northeast Louisiana University; Sue R. Mohrmann, Texas A & M University–Kingsville; and Lana Smith, The University of Memphis.

Finally, we would like to thank our wives, Pamela and Bonnie. Writing this revision was for the most part a very pleasant and rewarding experience. Revising gave us an opportunity to think through our original ideas, add the best of new thinking we have come across since the first edition, and present our ideas in ways we believe will be most useful to our readers. Occasionally, though, the going did get rough and time consuming. In these instances, Pam and Bonnie provided the patience, support, and occasional prodding that we needed to sustain our efforts and move our work forward.

thoughtful com-
certainly be
dents in
of

Contents

Chapter 10   Assessment   326

Answers to Practice Activities   363

Index   377

C H A P T E R

1

Introduction

CHAPTER OVERVIEW

This chapter is divided into four sections. In the first section, we provide a brief historical overview of content area reading instruction. In the second section, we present our guiding principles of content area reading instruction that serve as the underlying conceptual foundation for the topics presented throughout this book. In the third section, we discuss the concept of functional literacy and the incidence of illiteracy from a historical perspective. Also in this section, we present a discussion of how well our students are learning in school, noting in particular detail historical data on students' academic achievement. In the fourth and final section we provide a general model of the reading process.

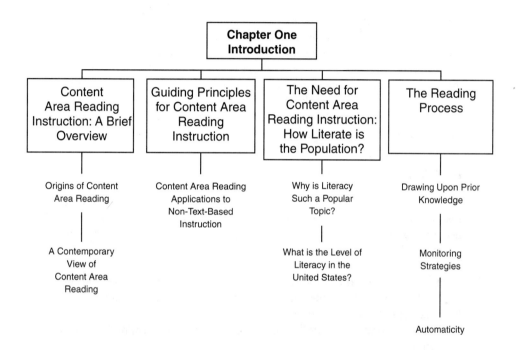

CONTENT AREA READING
INSTRUCTION: A BRIEF OVERVIEW

This section contains a brief history of content area reading instruction as well as a discussion of the contemporary view of the role of content area reading instruction in the subject matter classroom and the impact that the content of this book may have on the way you view learning. The section concludes with a set of guiding principles for content area reading instruction.

Whether you are engaged in an educational program leading to certification as a teacher or an experienced classroom teacher, you may be unfamiliar with the purpose of content area reading instruction. It is not unusual, for example, for an individual seeking certification in social studies or science to question the merits of taking a "reading" course when one's area of emphasis is seemingly far removed from the instruction of reading. In other words, why should anyone other than a reading teacher be interested in content area reading? Before we respond to that question, consider two instructional scenarios that follow, then respond to the four statements appearing after the second scenario.

Scenario One

Mr. Johnston's ninth-grade civics class adheres to a traditional form of instruction four days of the week. He lectures for thirty minutes directly on the content of the textbook as the students sit passively taking notes, then provides students a list of ten short-answer questions focusing on the content of his lectures. Students respond to these questions individually, the questions are corrected by the class, and the results of the students' performance are entered into Mr. Johnston's grade book. On the fifth day of the week, students are asked to read from their textbook, then answer questions similar in format to those presented following the lecture.

Scenario Two

Ms. Jones's ninth-grade civics class does not adhere to a traditional instructional routine. At present, her class is studying the form and function of the legislative branch of the federal government. To engage students in this content, Ms. Jones has instructed students to track the origin of four recent pieces of federal legislation. In doing so, students are asked to identify the originator of the bill, the supporters of the bill, the political action committees' positions on the bill, and the contributions that these political action committees directed to those legislators backing the legislation. Students then email legislators to determine their position on the legislation.

Clearly the instructional style of these two teachers is dramatically different. Mr. Johnston adheres to a rather traditional approach of providing students with information, engaging the students in passive learning activities, and relying upon a single text to direct his instruction. Ms. Jones, on the other hand, engages students in rather global tasks that allow students to acquire knowledge of a topic as they are engaged in a problem-solving task. She makes extensive use of technology and cooperative learning, and promotes the idea that students should assume ownership of their learning through meaningful and direct involvement.

Below are some statements related to the teaching styles of Mr. Johnston and Ms. Jones. Take a moment to consider your position on the following statements by responding whether you agree or disagree with the statement.

1. The nature of gaining information and making sense of the world around us is changing rapidly as we apply greater amounts of technology.

  ___ Agree   ___ Disagree

2. Classroom learning occurs through the integration of reading, writing, speaking, and viewing.

     ___ Agree   ___ Disagree

3. Learning should be limited to information provided either by the teacher or from a textbook.

     ___ Agree   ___ Disagree

4. In the world around us we often need to examine problems or issues from multiple perspectives and from different backgrounds of experience.

     ___ Agree   ___ Disagree

Now that you have considered these statements, let's return to the question of why knowledge of content area reading can benefit the teaching of subject matter content. In our view, statements one, two, and four address some of the key elements of content area reading. First, content area reading is not a static process where students see their primary responsibility as memorizing information from a text, a video, or a lecture. Rather, it is a dynamic process involving the students' ability to listen to others, entertain various points of view or sources on a given topic, and then to construct meaning. Second, we don't view reading as being distinct from other forms of communication. In fact, the students' ability to acquire meaning from text can be enhanced when the teacher integrates writing, listening, and viewing activities. Finally, learning increasingly is dependent upon the use of technology. Use of the Internet, computers, video recorders, telephones, and other forms of technology provide rich resources to promote learning. Thus, we view content area reading as the process of making meaning from content in a manner that uses technology, integrates reading, writing, speaking, viewing, and listening, and allows students to learn in a social context that promotes their ability to construct their understanding from multiple perspectives and multiple sources of information. Certainly many of these ideas are not new.

Origins of Content Area Reading

The origins of content area reading instruction can be traced back to the 1920s when the U.S. Bureau of Education acknowledged that each subject matter area contributes directly to the development of reading competency (Gray, 1925), leading to the slogan "every teacher should be, to a certain extent, a teacher of reading." During the past twenty years content area reading instruction has evolved in its instructional practice and its importance in teacher training. The first book dedicated exclusively to content reading, *Teaching Reading in the Content Areas* (Herber, 1970), helped to distinguish instruction to aid students in the reading of subject matter text from the instruction of reading within the confines of the basal reader program (the self-contained reading instruction from kindergarten through eighth grade consisting of graded student books and teacher instructional manuals). At the same time that the importance of content area reading instruction was being recognized by educators, attention was drawn to the observation that test results on advanced skills in reading were showing small, yet consistent, declines (Eckland, 1982; Harnischfeger & Wiley, 1975).

No doubt the increased awareness of students' reading performance had some influence on efforts to improve teacher preparation in reading. In 1973 eight states required course work in content area reading instruction for secondary teacher certification (Estes & Piercey, 1973). Approximately a decade later, thirty-one states required course work in content area reading instruction for all secondary teacher certification programs, and an additional five states required content reading course work solely for English and language arts teachers (Farrell & Cirrincione, 1984). These preservice teacher training efforts directed at content area reading strategies have produced some measurable results on teachers' perceptions of their own teaching. Teachers who integrated these strategies into their instruction report greater confidence in their teaching (Pearce & Bader, 1986), and a sense that their lessons are more organized (Conley, 1986). Additionally a number of strategies have had a positive effect on students' achievement (Alvermann & Swafford, 1989; Bean, Singer, & Frazee, 1986) as well as their attitude toward the subject matter (Bean, 1981).

While the effect of content area reading strategies on students' learning is encouraging, obstacles remain. Students enrolled in secondary teacher certification programs display resistance to content reading course work requirements (Memory, 1983; O'Brien, 1988), they often have preconceived ideas about the nature of teaching in their respective subject matter areas (Holt-Reynolds, 1992), and in-service programs directed at improving teachers' knowledge of content reading strategies have a limited effect on classroom instruction (Gehrke, Schaefer, & Schlick, 1982; Smith & Feathers, 1983).

A Contemporary View of Content Area Reading

For many years reading instruction was based on the assumption that readers were passive. As a more thorough understanding of the reading process developed from research conducted during the 1970s and 1980s, reading was no longer viewed as a passive activity whereby the reader memorized information from the text. Reading was now seen as a process whereby the reader independently draws upon strategies to construct meaning. The distinction between a passive reading activity and an active reading activity is determined by the degree a reader can retrieve and utilize prior knowledge. Passive reading requires the reader to commit text information to memory, and to prepare for recall of that information in its original form. Active reading requires the reader to have a purpose for reading, to activate available knowledge that is related to that purpose, to read for additional information, and finally to restructure their knowledge on the basis of the new information. An example of an interdisciplinary lesson to construct knowledge through active learning observed by one of us focused on the development and movement of tornadoes. A group of middle school students and their English, social studies, and science specialists decided to determine how to predict where tornadoes might occur in the United States, how those tornadoes could be tracked, and to what extent tornadoes reoccurred in a storm system. Using WeatherNet, a comprehensive meteorological site on the Internet, one class of students began to monitor radar and satellite images as well as group reports of tornado activity throughout the United States. Once a tornado was observed, the group closely monitored the climatic conditions in the area that produced the storm (humidity, wind direction, barometric pressure, temperature, etc). Another group obtained a CD-ROM that explained the formation and occurrence of tornadoes. And yet another group used email to set up an observational network of schools in Kansas and Oklahoma to monitor and report on weather conditions in their area. Based on information from the group studying the causes and development of tornadoes, students began to observe certain areas of the plains states when specific weather conditions were present. Using data provided from the cooperating observational network and information obtained on the Internet, students began to generate their own forecasts of tornadic activity. Finally, all students wrote a multimedia book containing radar images, text, and graphic images to describe the development, occurrence, and tracking of tornadoes across the central plains.

Creating a learning environment for a lesson like the one on tornadoes requires considerable planning and flexibility on behalf of the teacher. It also recognizes the importance of the students' ability to consciously apply strategies to construct meaning from the subject matter curriculum. In our view of classroom learning, teachers and students jointly assume the responsibility for learning. To more fully describe the nature of learning in the content area classroom, we provide the following set of guiding principles. These principles serve as an instructional and conceptual foundation for the topics and instructional activities addressed throughout this book.

GUIDING PRINCIPLES FOR CONTENT AREA READING INSTRUCTION

The guiding principles presented in this section stress the importance of allowing the teacher to assist students in constructing knowledge, and the importance of recognizing the diverse intellectual, social, and cultural contributions that students bring to class. Additionally these principles reflect a view that content reading is functional, and that it should recognize the various constraints (e.g., class size, available instructional time, student ability, and motivation) that exist in the classroom.

1. Content area reading instruction is based on the assumption that students acquire meaning through the application of strategies, skills, and prior knowledge to text material. Content reading, therefore, is functional and driven by the learner's need to acquire knowledge. The goal of the teacher is to create and direct an instructional sequence using activities and strategies that will enhance the students' acquisition of knowledge. To the student, content reading is a strategic process to acquire meaning, not a set of skills or exercises taught in isolation of content. To the teacher, content reading instruction consists of employing teaching strategies and instructional designs that direct students through the curriculum to accomplish the instructional objectives.

2. The classroom is a dynamic social, cultural, and intellectual environment where students acquire information and construct knowledge. Content area reading instruction draws upon the teacher's ability to evaluate the diverse social elements involved in classroom learning and the sources of information that contribute to that intellectual environment. Instruction within this environment draws upon the students' knowledge individually and collectively. Similarly, instruction should present learning activities similar to those encountered in everyday problem-solving tasks that demand social interactions among individuals of various educational and social backgrounds. The complex and diverse nature of the social environments in school is characterized by Greene (1989, p. 144):

> Teachers must somehow conceptualize the scale and anonymity of society today, the pulsations of city streets, the protected enclaves of the suburbs, the persisting homogeneities in certain villages and towns. They must be aware of the privileged young's claims of entitlement, the complaint postures of those seeking upward mobility, the apathy and wariness of the disinterested.

Although the diverse needs and social backgrounds of students can pose a considerable challenge to teachers, unchallenged beliefs and stereotypes can interfere with learning (Oakes, 1986). The way students learn and the social patterns they follow in the classroom may reflect their cultural background (Garcia, 1993). We believe teachers should acknowledge the cultural and social diversity of the classroom on an ongoing basis. And we advance instructional methods that incorporate the social, cultural, and cognitive diversity of the classroom in the confines of subject matter instruction.

3. Content area reading instruction provides a context for students to apply their knowledge of information literacy. Although the primary source of classroom information is a single textbook, students are more likely to become actively involved in learning when they make use of multiple text sources, as well as visual media such as videotapes, films, slides, transparencies, audiotapes, and compact diskettes. We believe learning from sources of information made available through computer technology (such as the videodisc and CD-ROM) will be increasingly evident in classroom instruction. Content area reading instruction should draw upon new instructional technology and existing text-based sources of information to promote learning.

4. Content area reading instruction aims to facilitate active learning. Instruction in the subject matter areas traditionally has proceeded on the assumption that curriculum is shaped by the objectives and content identified in curriculum guides, textbooks, and state and local educational agencies. As a result, many teachers attend primarily to the content to be delivered rather than the process of delivering that content. A likely outcome of this emphasis is that beginning teachers view the function of teaching as telling students what they need to know (Vosniadou & Brewer, 1987). And seasoned teachers, pressured by measures of accountability, focus their efforts at communicating the constructs of their subject matter area rather than on the process that allows the learner to use the constructs to acquire knowledge. As a result, the needs of the learner may not be addressed until the teacher has dealt with the problems of management and their own evaluation of their teaching competencies (Fuller, 1969). Some teachers, unable to meet the complex demands in the classroom, never address the needs of the students. Instead, their efforts are directed toward behavioral management.

Active processing of information requires much more than committing information to memory, because individuals differ in the way they organize and interpret information. Acknowledging the students' diverse interpretations of information, the content area teacher can draw upon the students' ability to describe their strategies for constructing meaning, as well as model strategies that allow students to monitor their own processing of information. These strategies are *functional*. Over time the teacher gradually reduces the amount of direct instruction to promote the students' ability to independently monitor and direct their learning.

5. Instructional strategies and activities in the content areas are adaptable to the constraints of the classroom. Teachers experience considerable demands on their time. Faced with frequent additions to the curriculum, the pressure of accountability, the frustrations of balancing the students' needs with the curriculum mandated by the district, and the increasing responsibility of the school to address innumerable societal ills, teachers are severely restricted in the amount of time they can devote to learning or applying new instructional strategies. Content area reading instruction acknowledges these constraints by advancing instructional strategies that are practical, readily adaptable to a variety of instructional contexts, and which promote an effective learning environment for teachers and students.

To summarize, the purpose of content area reading instruction is to improve the students' learning through the integration of instructional strategies in the subject matter curriculum, rather than the presentation of strategies in isolation. Content area reading instruction is functional, directed by the students' academic needs as well as their cultural and social background. Content reading is **a process** to facilitate learning. The locus of control is the teacher, who serves to provide information, to present strategies that facilitate learning, and to direct the students' ability to become independent learners. To accomplish these goals the teacher assumes much more than the role of information provider. The teacher now assumes the role of a coach, a maestro, and a navigator. As a coach, the teacher models learning strategies in an effort to enhance the students' insight into their own cognitive processes. And as a coach, the teacher must recognize the individual and aggregate characteristics of the learners, providing feedback and direction to both individuals and the group. As a maestro, the teacher must assess the students' knowledge of the content and assist them as they engage in activities centered around classroom instruction. And as a navigator, the teacher facilitates discussions, questioning activities, demonstrations, and hands-on projects and authentic learning tasks designed for the whole class, cooperative groups, or independent learning.

Content Area Reading Applications to Non-Text-Based Instruction

While the term *content reading* would seem to be limited to instruction centered around text, most of the topics and activities discussed throughout this book apply equally as well to subject matter areas where texts are used infrequently or are absent altogether. Teachers of mathematics, art, industrial or physical education, foreign languages, and

English as a second language can improve non-text-based instruction by applying content area reading strategies. For example, applying the strategies presented in Chapter 3, "Preparing Students to Learn," a physical education teacher could begin a unit on basketball by first presenting students with a graphic display of the various positions and their functions, then asking them to observe a film, videotape, or CD displaying a group of professional basketball players. Similarly, an art teacher may consider having students engage in a cooperative learning activity (Chapter 7) in which they generate written summaries (Chapter 6) of the process for firing ceramics in a kiln. This activity would allow students to reflect on their learning, share their insights with their peers, and provide closure on the process and technique of firing clay. Activities such as these provide students with the background information necessary for learning, increase the likelihood that students will connect the lesson content to their everyday lives (either watching or playing sports or more closely examining a ceramic cup or mug), and provide the teacher a means to assess the students' understanding of a lesson's objectives prior to the instruction of that content.

▼ PRACTICE ACTIVITY 1.1

Imagine that you are about to present a forty-minute lesson in your subject matter area. List the types of activities you would use to help students understand this content. In responding, consider the degree to which you will involve the students in the lesson. This lesson does not have to be based on a text selection. Some possible answers can be found at the end of the chapter.

▼▼

THE NEED FOR CONTENT AREA READING INSTRUCTION: HOW LITERATE IS THE POPULATION?

This section contains a brief overview of the concept of literacy, a discussion of historical trends in the levels of literacy in the United States, and a description of recent assessment data on students' ability to read and write. Before reading the following section, carefully read and then respond to the following statements. Answers to these statements can be found at the end of this section.

1. Adults read and write about as well now as they did 100 years ago.

   _____ Agree   _____ Disagree

2. How we define literacy depends on the social and economic needs at a given point in time.

   _____ Agree   _____ Disagree

3. During the past fifteen years the school-age population has significantly improved in its ability to perform higher-level reading tasks.

   _____ Agree   _____ Disagree

4. With technological advances, the need to be literate will actually decrease by the year 2000.

_____ Agree   _____ Disagree

Why is Literacy Such a Popular Topic?

During the past decade, Americans increasingly have become aware of the importance of literacy. This heightened awareness has been fueled by economic, educational, and social factors. Economically, business has shifted from the production of capital goods to the delivery of services, which in turn has required a higher level of reading and writing skills. The need for literate workers to meet the increased demands of the workplace of the twenty-first century and the finding that most students at grades 4, 8, and 12 possess basic competencies, but that few have reached levels likely to be required for the twenty-first century workplace (Mullis, Campbell, & Farstrup, 1993), has generated considerable debate among politicians, business leaders, and educators. According to the Department of Labor's Goals 2000 report (Johnston & Packer, 1987), in the year 2000 below-average skills will be good enough for only 27% of the jobs created between 1985 and 2000. This compares with 40% of the jobs in the mid-1980s. Although these projections have been questioned (Flynn, 1988; Rumberger and Levin, 1989), it is apparent that there will be a steady increase in the number of occupations requiring individuals with higher levels of training and education prior to entering the workplace (Council of Chief State School Officers, 1995; Lee et al., 1994; McCarthy, 1994). The absence of comprehensive assessments of the nature and development of the thinking skills necessary in the workplace make it difficult to assess changes in the total distribution of jobs. However, certain segments of the workforce do serve as examples of these changes. In the textile industry, for example, generations of low-skilled workers who previously worked on mechanical looms are now required to function with sophisticated machinery run by computers. Operators of this new equipment are required to read and comprehend complex manuals and apply higher-level thinking skills to conceptualize the equipment's operation. Similar examples can be found in the utilities, the automobile industry, and manufacturers that have retooled factories with technology. The disparity between the level of literacy skills required in the workplace and the level of literacy skills available to the worker has raised serious concerns from the private sector. This sentiment is evident in the following statement by Louis Gerstner, CEO of IBM:

> The problem is stark; for as far as we can see into the future—certainly. during the next ten years—the U.S. economy will create virtually no new jobs for those who lack basic skills. Put simply, it takes more human capital to earn a decent living today, to make a real contribution to a business, or for a firm to make a world-competitive product. As a result, we are paying our well-educated people more, and our uneducated people relatively less (Gerstner, Semerad, Doyle, & Johnston, 1994, p. 9).

What is the Level of Literacy in the United States?

The criteria for "being literate" depends upon the type of reading and writing tasks required in society at any given point in time. While one was considered literate in

1979 if one had completed six years of education (Irwin, 1987), a twelfth-grade standard has been suggested as more appropriate for the tasks required in today's society (Aaron, Chall, Durkin, Goodman & Strickland, 1990). Unfortunately, as indicated in the National Adult Literacy Study (Kirsch, Jungeblut, Jenkins, & Kolstad, 1993), large percentages of adults demonstrate limited skills that may restrict their opportunities for gaining access to and achieving in many occupations. With 21% of the adult population having only rudimentary reading and writing skills (Kirsch et al.) and difficulty with common reading materials (Stedman & Kaestle, 1987), our awareness of the incidence of illiteracy is heightened and educational institutions are called upon to narrow the gap between the literacy tasks required in everyday life and the level of reading performance acquired in school. In the workplace the level of competency with reading, writing, and mathematic skills has increased as part of an attempt to maintain our competitiveness in a global economy where numerous countries are converging upon the level of productivity in the United States (Klerman and Karoly, 1995).

Functional Literacy

Functional literacy is the ability to engage in reading tasks encountered in the workplace, as part of our civic responsibility, or during leisure activities. Generally it has been equated with school attainment levels. Students that have more education are assumed to be better readers. The level of school attainment required to be functionally literate has risen rather dramatically over the past sixty years. In 1930 one was functionally literate if one had completed three or more years of schooling; in 1950 the criteria was five or more years; in 1960 the criteria was eight or more years; and in 1980 the criteria was graduation from high school (Stedman & Kaestle, 1987).

There is, of course, some question as to the usefulness of school attainment as a measure of literacy. Years of school may not be a good measure of an individual's ability to engage in and succeed with essential reading material. Functional literacy is not an "all or nothing" human condition. If, for example, the criteria for functional literacy is the completion of twelve years of education, it would be unreasonable to assume that an individual with eleven years of schooling would be unable to read material generally encountered in society such as newspapers, common periodicals, household information, and job-related materials. Furthermore, individuals in the workplace receive considerable assistance with literacy tasks from peers or coworkers that could enhance their functional literacy skills over time. Therefore, level of school attainment cannot necessarily be equated with how well one actually engages in tasks requiring reading competency.

Many of the materials commonly encountered in our daily lives require a high level of understanding. Figure 1.1 displays a portion of the Internal Revenue Service's directions for completing the miscellaneous deductions portion of itemized deductions on Schedule A. Direct your attention to the question presented in Figure 1.1 to engage in a functional literacy task.

Understanding written instructions for federal tax returns can be a difficult task. Certainly the information describing the conditions where uniforms or special clothing can be deducted as a miscellaneous expense is open to interpretation. In fact, our conversations with two CPAs and two individuals providing telephone assistance at the

Figure 1.1
Example of a Reading Task from the Internal Revenue Service

Question: Could a member of a professional rock band who wears a neon blue leather jacket and green leather pants emblazoned with silver spiked grommets deduct the cost of this clothing under miscellaneous deductions?

Work Clothes and Uniforms
You can deduct the cost of upkeep and work clothes only if they are required as a condition of your employment and are not suitable for everyday wear. To qualify for the deduction, both conditions must be met. It is not enough that you wear distinctive clothing; it must be specifically required by your employer. Nor is it enough that you do not in fact wear your work clothes away from work; the clothing must not be suitable for taking the place of your regular clothing.

Examples of occupations in which you may be required to wear uniforms which qualify are: delivery workers, firefighters, health care workers, law enforcement officers, letter carriers, professional athletes, and transportation workers (air, rail, bus, etc.).

Musicians and entertainers can deduct the cost of theatrical clothing and accessories if they are not suitable for ordinary use.

However, work clothing consisting of white cap, white shirt or white jacket, white bib overalls, and standard work shoes, which a painter is required by his union to wear on the job, is not distinctive in character or in the nature of the uniform. Similarly, the cost and maintenance of blue work clothes worn by a welder at the request of a foreman are not deductible.

(Department of the Treasury, Internal Revenue Service, Catalog Number 10560, Publication 529, Miscellaneous Deductions)

Internal Revenue Service produced a variety of responses to our original question. Clearly not all functional reading tasks demand the degree of understanding required for IRS publications. Yet many common tasks can present problems for an individual who has inadequate reading skills or who lacks background knowledge of the topic being read.

Criteria for functional literacy have increased steadily during the past 100 years, with some of the largest increases occurring during the past twenty to thirty years. A century ago one was considered to be functionally literate if one could write his or her name. Current standards of functional literacy require the reader to read text containing unfamiliar information and to acquire both the stated and the inferred information available from the text. The standards have reached levels that not long ago were achieved only by an elite, highly educated segment of society (Resnick & Resnick, 1977). Certainly technological advances will demand wider dissemination of information, thus creating what Calfee (1994) refers to as "critical literacy"—the use of language for thinking, problem solving, and communicating. Although international comparisons of students' reading ability indicate American students perform better than their counterparts in countries selected throughout the world (U.S.

Department of Education, 1996), the need to maintain our competitive edge will likely maintain efforts to improve the literacy skills required in the workplace.

How Well Do Our Students Learn the Basic Skills?

This section presents a brief overview of how students' level of achievement has changed over the past twenty-five years. It begins with a presentation of the concerns that have gained widespread recognition in the media, then examines the results of two major sources of achievement test data that have been gathered over the past quarter century.

Since the mid-1960s a number of publications have addressed a purported crisis of learning in the schools. One of the most widely cited reports at that time, *Equality of Educational Opportunity* (Coleman et al., 1966), sponsored by the U.S. Office of Education, claimed that differences in school quality were not closely related to the differences in students' level of achievement. On the basis of this report, Jencks et al. (1972) concluded that school reform would do little to effect the inequality between students' academic achievement, and that teachers or schools had little influence on students' learning.

In the years following the Coleman report, a rather widespread decline in junior and senior high school students' standardized achievement test results gained widespread attention. For example, in 1978, scores of tenth and twelfth graders on the Iowa Test of Educational Development fell below those obtained in 1962 (Science Research Associates, 1978). At the same time, results of the Comprehensive Test of Basic Skills reading test showed declines from one-third year to one year, depending upon the grade level examined (CTB/McGraw-Hill, 1982). Similar declines were evident among students completing college entrance exams. With the publication of A *Nation at Risk* (National Commission on Excellence in Education, 1983), and approximately twelve additional reports critical of education that followed, politicians and the public were led to believe that the decline in test scores was of such significance that it threatened the economic security of the nation. These reports brought sustained attention by the media to the condition of education. Critics of the educational system attributed the cause of the decline in test scores to poor instruction (Cooperman, 1979; Ravitch, 1985), and many states enacted legislation for greater accountability through teacher competency testing and greater assessment of students' academic progress.

Was all this attention to students' academic progress justified? What evidence is there to substantiate the widespread belief that students' academic abilities were declining? In answering these questions we draw upon two sources of test results of students' academic achievement over the past twenty-five years. What follows is a description of the test results of the National Assessment of Educational Progress (NAEP) and those of the Scholastic Aptitude Test (SAT).

National Assessment of Educational Progress

The NAEP is a congressionally mandated program that began in 1969–70 for the purpose of assessing students' performance in reading, writing, mathematics, history/geography, and other academic disciplines. It is the only ongoing national assessment of academic performance, conducting regular assessment of fourth, eighth, and twelfth graders attending both public and private schools. A review of achievement trends from 1970 to 1990 (Mullis, Owen, & Phillips, 1991) and subsequent examinations of reading achievement (U.S. Department of Education, 1996) conclude that students' academic performance has been rather stable.

The reading performance of U.S. students is related to student characteristics such as race/ethnicity, parental education, and family structure. At both the fourth- and ninth-grade level, white students read better, on average, than black and Hispanic students, and students with at least one parent having a college degree read better, on average, than students whose parents have not finished high school. Students whose families are poor do not read as well as those students whose families are better off.

Scholastic Aptitude Test

A second source of achievement test data collected over the past twenty-five years is the SAT, which is administered primarily to college-bound students. Some individuals interpret the SAT scores, therefore, as a measure of our best and brightest students. The drop of scores from 1966–67 to 1974–75 raised speculation that academic achievement was falling. However, this decline in scores was more likely the result of both changes in the composition of individuals taking the test, as well as the age of the students being tested. The College Entrance Examination Board (1977) estimated that changes in the population of students taking the exam contributed to a 20% to 30% decline in scores. Stedman and Kaestle (1987) attribute the effects to fewer dropouts in the 1970s and a drop in the age at which students completed the exam as accounting for 24% to 40% of the 1970s decline. More recent test results of college-bound students fail to provide support for the perception of eroding college entrance examination scores. Scores on the College Board's achievement tests, completed by the same students who took the SAT, indicate an improvement in the 1970s in English, science, and foreign languages. And scores on the SAT (College Entrance Examination Board, 1994) and the ACT (American College Test, 1985) have either held steady or increased since 1980 (National Center for Education Statistics, 1996).

Examination of academic achievement scores over the past twenty-five years provides some solace in the finding that the school-age populations' academic performance has been rather steady. Similarly, measures obtained on the academic achievement of students planning to enter institutions of higher education indicate a slight improvement in scores from those obtained a decade earlier. Comparisons of academic performance are useful in providing a global measure of trends in how well our students are learning basic concepts taught in the school curriculum. Somewhat disturbing, however, is students' performance on higher-level thinking tasks. Results obtained from the 1988 NAEP reading assessment (Mullis, Owen, & Phillips, 1991), which have been adapted in Figure 1.2, indicate that the majority of students nationwide are capable of performing simple, discrete reading tasks. As we examine more complex levels of reading proficiency a rather dramatic decline in performance is noted. The finding that only 4.8% of twelfth graders can synthesize and learn from specialized reading materials could portend profound economic and political consequences. American business groups have expressed the need for workers who possess reasoning and problem-solving skills (National Center on Education and the Economy, 1990), the need for at-risk populations to possess skills needed in the

Figure 1.2
Percentage of Students Performing at or above Certain Reading Proficiency Levels as
Reported on the "1994 Reading Report Card for the Nation and the States"

Task	Percent of Students at Level		
	Grade 4	Grade 8	Grade 12
Can analyze and explicitly support analyses with specific examples from the text.	7%	3%	4%
Shows an understanding that includes inferential information. Students can make inferences, draw conclusions, and connect personal experiences with the text.	30%	30%	36%
Can make simple inferences from the text.	60%	70%	75%

workplace (National Alliance of Business, 1987), and the need for employees to have much higher math, language, and reasoning skills (Rumberger & Levin, 1989). If our students are going to be required to apply higher-level thinking and reasoning skills in tomorrow's workforce, then our efforts should be directed at the necessary instructional and curricular modifications to accomplish this goal.

At the beginning of this section you were presented with four statements addressing literacy. These statements and their answers are as follows:

1. Levels of literacy have been relatively static over the past 100 years.

   Disagree (Literacy is a fluid term: it changes to meet the needs of society at a given time.)

2. Standards applied to literacy are primarily motivated by social and economic considerations.

   Agree

3. During the past fifteen years the school-age population has significantly improved in its ability to perform higher-level reading tasks.

   Disagree (The level of performance on higher-level reading tasks has remained relatively static.)

4. With technological advances, the need to be literate will actually decrease by the year 2000.

   Disagree (If present trends continue, technological advances will demand workers and citizens with a higher level of literacy.)

THE READING PROCESS

Throughout this book are numerous instructional activities to enhance students' learning and their ability to construct knowledge as independent learners. These activities become more meaningful and relevant when they are examined in the context of the current thought regarding the nature of the reading process. In what follows, we present an overview of this process and, where appropriate, note some of the instructional implications of this process.

Reading can be described as an interactive process that allows the reader to construct meaning by using information obtained from various knowledge structures. These knowledge structures include knowledge of letters, knowledge of letter-sound relationships, knowledge of words, knowledge of syntax (grammar), and schematic knowledge (chunks of knowledge you possess). The interactive process allows the reader to move in two directions. Comprehension can be accomplished through an interaction between information provided from the reader's prior knowledge and information gleaned from the text (Rumelhart, 1977). This interaction can be demonstrated by reading the following.

> The man wearing the mask was at home waiting for the other man to arrive. The other man was afraid of the man with the mask.

Interpretation of these sentences draws primarily upon your ability to activate prior knowledge since the context of the situation is somewhat ill-defined. Most likely you constructed an image of a robber in someone's home, or of a physician or dentist waiting for a patient at a home office. Yet, if you are now instructed to read this passage with the understanding that you are observing the behavior of these two men in your box seat behind home plate at the World Series, the context is more clearly defined, and your comprehension of the passage now shifts to the relationship between a catcher and base runner.

Constructing meaning from text requires the reader to draw upon prior knowledge, to draw upon and monitor strategies directed toward gaining meaning, and to process information in an efficient manner. Lacking proficiency with these three elements of the reading process, the reader often fails to comprehend the text, or processes the information at a level that is limited to gaining facts or other surface-level information. What follows is a more thorough description of these three elements and a discussion of their importance in learning from text in the subject matter classroom.

Drawing Upon Prior Knowledge

One of the most important constructs influencing our understanding of reading has been schemata. As described by Rumelhart (1980), schemata are chunks of knowledge that exist in our head. All of our knowledge is packed into these units, and the units are activated in our attempts to make sense of the world. We use them in interpretation of information gained from sensory input, to construct actions we may take, to determine goals, and in general to direct the flow of information to the mind.

Schematic units contain our knowledge of objects, situations, events, actions, and sequences of actions (Rumelhart, 1980). You have a schema for the color blue, the concept of a practical joke, and junkfood, and a schema for peace, beauty, and respect. An interesting characteristic of schema is that the variables or characteristics of a particular schema can be given different values for a different individual's interpretation. Consider your schema for the concept of greed in the following.

> The Talk Show Host had decided to profit from his notoriety by writing a book full of lies, innuendoes, and misrepresentations. Exploiting the trust of his Best Friend, who was a reporter for a national newspaper, he secretly obtained various appointment books and records from the reporter's office. He then doctored these documents to include the names of Hollywood Stars and to associate these individuals in various scandals. His book became an instant success and quickly vaulted to the top of the *New York Times* bestsellers list. His greed eventually caught up with him, however, when his Best Friend produced videotapes of the Talk Show Host's entry into the office.

There are a number of interpretations of this greed schema; that is, there are a number of ways in which the characters can vary. The Talk Show Host can be young, intelligent, or overbearing. The Best Friend can be male or female. And the Hollywood Stars could be present day or former stars in movies, television, or the recording industry. But regardless of how these variables are interpreted, they have to be realized if the schema is to be interpreted.

Schemata are active processes. They are more than something that is there, readily available for use. They are recognition devices that actively work to evaluate the fit between the information perceived and themselves. In other words, schemata are actively involved in the process of determining whether or not the information perceived can be interpreted in terms of a particular schema. Schemata direct the process by which the mind takes a particular piece of information presented to our senses, calls up a particular schema in terms of which the information can potentially be interpreted, checks for congruence between the incoming information and the variables of the schema, and either determines that the information can be interpreted in terms of the schema or calls up another schema to be tested. Comprehending the following paragraph is relatively easy because of the congruence with the information and your available schema.

> It is truly amazing that our attention is drawn to those tabloids as we wait in the checkout lane at the grocery store. How can we be so gullible as to believe headlines like "Man Finds Alien Spacecraft Under Toenail," or "Massive NASA Cover-up: Moon Actually Found to be Made of Green Cheese."

The information presented is congruent with our available schema of grocery stores and checkout lines. Interpretation of the variables in the passage comes readily and without a great deal of study. As the variables become less distinct, however, we experience increased dissonance between the schema we activate and our interpretation of the information presented. Take, for example, the following paragraph:

> The joint had been presenting problems for a number of years. He discussed the problem with his neighbor. He glanced out the window. How could one corner be so pristine and the other so dilapidated? Certainly its appearance could be enhanced by nailing the culprit. Or he could gradually chisel away at the problem to remove the decay.

The congruence between information in this paragraph and one's schema is not as obvious as the first example. The words *joint, corner, chisel,* and *decay* could invoke different interpretations depending upon the schema activated. Drawing upon your schema of urban blight or neighborhood problems, you could construct a scenario of a dilapidated structure presenting problems to the quality of a neighborhood. On the other hand, if you are familiar with woodworking it would be likely that you would construct a scenario of a wood joint that was in need of repair. In either case, available schema directed your interpretation of the text information. Schemata do change. As the learner acquires more information, schemata are refined, reshaped, corrected, and restructured. A child's schema for beach is not the same as an adult's; a teenager's schema for telephone is not the same as that of a second grader. It is important to note that a reader can sometimes find an interpretation of the text that allows him or her to make sense out of the passage, yet it is not the interpretation intended by the author. Accordingly, as you engage students in questions or activities it is important to consider the variety of responses or products that students are likely to produce on the basis of their personal knowledge. But what happens when schema cannot be activated? The following excerpt from *Scientific American* provides a vivid example of the importance of available schema.

> The superconducting accelerator magnets posed major technical challenges. The magnets must confine particles within a one-centimeter region in the center of the vacuum tube as they steer the particles around a 6.3 kilometer orbit, 50,000 times a second. The accelerator magnets generate a field as electric currents flow through superconducting wires. The quality of the field depends on the precision with which the superconducting wires are placed around the vacuum tube. (Lederman, 1991, p. 51)

Unless one is familiar with the Tevatron and the process by which it first produces antiprotons and then smashes them against protons through the use of superconductivity, our schemata do not direct our mind's interpretation of the information.

Acceptance of the notion of schemata and of the importance of schemata to the process of comprehending what one reads leads to a myriad of instructional applications. First, how can we draw upon our knowledge of schemata to improve the students' ability to comprehend text? It is apparent that readers who have knowledge of different types of texts are more likely to comprehend the material contained in those texts (Meyer & Rice, 1984; Stein & Trabasso, 1982). If children, for example, have little experience listening to or reading stories, their lack of knowledge of story structures (story schemata) will lessen comprehension. Similarly, in math, children lacking well-defined schemata for math problems will experience difficulty determining what factors or variables are relevant to problem solving. And in science it has been noted that the limited schemata for scientific concepts acquired from everyday experiences limits students' understanding of scientific concepts (Anderson & Smith, 1987). In the classroom, teachers can find ways to build readers' schemata or background knowledge in order to help them interpret specific texts. Activities that provide information prior to reading, such as presenting films, videotapes, demonstrations, experiments, reading sections of a text aloud to students, previewing important concepts or vocabulary, and presenting students with specific objectives as they read, will either activate available schemata or contribute additional information to those schemata. A thorough discussion and samples of activities to increase students' prior knowledge are discussed in Chapter 3.

Our knowledge of the importance of schemata in the reading process have made a significant contribution to our understanding of the reading process. More than any other factor, the reader's ability to draw upon prior knowledge will affect whether a text is comprehended and how efficiently it is comprehended. Poor readers often are unable to draw upon schemata when they read, or when they do draw upon schemata, they are poorly organized. Schemata are mental representations of information. The reader must direct his or her attention to that information and to the information in the text to construct meaning. This awareness and regulation during reading is the second element in the reading process.

Monitoring Strategies

Reading requires conscious attention to the comprehension of a text as well as the regulation of the processes that lead to accomplishing a goal (Flavell, Miller, & Miller, 1993). This process is termed metacognition, or one's thinking about their own thinking. The importance of metacognition is based on the view that good readers exhibit metacognitive behavior, while poor readers do not (Garner, 1988; Smith, 1991), and that good readers are better able to detect ambiguous or inconsistent, or material that is otherwise ill structured (Garner & Kraus, 1982). The characteristics of a good reader involved in thinking about their thinking as they read is described by Whimbey (1975, p. 91).

> A good reader proceeds smoothly and quickly as long as his understanding of the material is complete. But as soon as he senses that he has missed an idea, that the track has been lost, he brings smooth progress to a grinding halt. Advancing more slowly, he seeks clarification in the subsequent material, examining it for the light it can throw on the earlier trouble spot. If still dissatisfied with his grasp, he returns to the point where the difficulty began and rereads the section more carefully. He probes and analyzes phrases and sentences for their exact meaning; he tries to visualize abstruse descriptions; and through a series of approximations, deductions, and corrections he translates scientific and technical terms into concrete examples.

Metacognitive strategies involve more than applying what one knows to the reading in a conscious manner. The reader must recognize how they learn, but they must also recognize factors related to their knowledge of the content being studied, the procedures or strategies to apply in that instance, and why a particular strategy is suited to one instance rather than another. It has been suggested that the learner must activate an executive control center, a conscious cognitive effort directed at planning strategies in accordance with perceived goals, and regulating progress toward the goals as one is engaged in reading (Paris, Lipson, & Wixson, 1983). Metacognition involves knowledge, control of the cognitive process, and self-control (Paris & Winograd, 1989). Self-control involves the reader's ability to commit to the task, to acknowledge his or her attitude toward the task itself, and the attention directed to the task. It is important to note that a reader may possess adequate knowledge and skillful application of cognitive strategies, but lacking self-control, metacognition is not realized. Teachers themselves, therefore, need to become aware of the importance of metacognitive behavior and its importance as a monitoring device as students assess their comprehension, and to apply fix-up strategies when comprehension fails. Additionally students should be told the importance of metacognitive behavior, and they should be taught metacognitive strategies (Miner & Reder, 1996).

PRACTICE ACTIVITY 1.2

To better understand the metacognitive process, imagine the following instructional scenario. Assume that your goal in reading the following information is to define the advantages and risks of being inoculated for influenza. As you read for that goal, note what information you attend to, how you fill in "gaps" in the text with prior knowledge, and note any rereading that you may engage in.

Influenza Vaccine

Much of the illness and death caused by influenza can be prevented by an annual influenza vaccination. Influenza vaccine is specifically recommended for those who are at high risk for developing serious complications as a result of influenza infection. These high-risk groups include all people aged 65 years or older and people of any age with chronic diseases of the heart, lung, or kidneys; diabetes; immunosuppression; or severe forms of anemia. Other groups for whom vaccine is specifically recommended are residents of nursing homes and other chronic-care facilities housing patients of any age with chronic medical conditions, and children and teenagers who are receiving long-term aspirin therapy and who may therefore be at risk for developing Reye syndrome after an influenza virus infection. Influenza vaccine is also recommended for people who are in close or frequent contact with anyone in the high-risk groups defined above. These people include health care personnel and volunteers who work with high-risk patients and people who live in a household with a high-risk person.

Although annual influenza vaccination has long been recommended for people in the high-risk groups, many still do not receive the vaccine. Some people are not vaccinated because of misperceptions about influenza and the vaccine. They mistakenly perceive influenza as merely a nuisance and believe that the vaccine causes unpleasant side effects or that it may even cause the flu. The truth is that influenza vaccine causes no side effects in most people. The most serious side effect that can occur after influenza vaccination is an allergic reaction in people who have severe allergies to eggs, since the viruses used in the vaccine are grown in hens' eggs. For this reason, people who have an allergy to eggs should not receive influenza vaccine.

Less than one-third of those who receive the vaccine have some soreness at the vaccination site, and about 5% to 10% experience mild side effects, such as headache or low-grade fever for about a day after vaccination. These side effects are most likely to occur in children who have not been exposed to influenza virus in the past.

Some people do not receive influenza vaccine because they believe it is not very effective. There are several different reasons for this belief. People who have received influenza vaccine may subsequently have an illness that is mistaken for influenza, and they believe that the vaccine failed to protect them. In other cases, people who have received vaccine may indeed have an influenza infection. Overall vaccine effectiveness varies from year to year, depending upon the degree of similarity between the influenza virus strains included in the vaccine and the strain or strains that circulate during the influenza season. Because the vaccine strains must be chosen 9 to 10 months before the influenza season, and because influenza viruses mutate over time, sometimes mutations occur in the circulating strains between the time vaccine strains are chosen and the next influenza season is over. These mutations sometimes reduce the ability of the vaccine-induced antibody to inhibit the newly mutated virus, thereby reducing vaccine efficacy.

(Centers for Disease Control and Prevention. Influenza Prevention and Control. [Online] Available http://www.cdc.gov/ncidod/diseases/flu/fluvirus.htm#part1b, May 29, 1996)

▼ ▼

Automaticity

An automatic activity is an activity that can be performed instantaneously and without conscious attention. At least some of the subprocesses that are part of the overall process of reading must be automatic if the reader is to construct meaning from text. There are a number of processes that occur as one reads. The reader must simultaneously process information at the letter, word, phrase, sentence, and several other levels. This creates a potential problem, however. The mind's capacity to process information is limited. We simply cannot attend to too many things at once. In fact, we can only really attend to one thing at a time. Getting meaning out of sentences and longer units of discourse requires attention. If the reader must attend to other processes while reading, understanding will be restricted.

Two closely related subprocesses must be automatic. One of these is recognizing words (Haenggi & Perfetti, 1994; Laberge & Samuels, 1974; Perfetti, 1977). Readers must automatically recognize the vast majority of words they encounter. They cannot afford any sort of mental processes such as, "Oh. Let's see. Yes, this word is *consternation*." The other process that must be automatic is that of assigning meaning to words. Readers must develop rapid access to word meanings. This means that in addition to recognizing words automatically, they must automatically—instantly and without conscious attention—assign meanings to words. Many words encountered by students are at a near-automatic level; a moment of reflection is required to recall the word's meaning. *Ubiquitous* might be such a word for many seventh graders. Some seventh graders can probably recognize the word in print, might even recognize it automatically, but then would need to go through a mental process such as, "Let's see. U*biquitous*? Oh, yes. That means something is everywhere." Readers cannot afford to go through such a process with very many words they encounter. If they do, text is processed slowly and comprehension is fragmented.

There are a number of instructional implications stemming from the notion of automaticity. First, students need to have ready access to word meanings (Perfetti & Zhang, 1995). It is reasonable to assume that students should be encouraged to read widely, and teachers should be encouraged to teach word meanings directly and to teach students strategies for learning word meanings independently (Ryder & Graves, 1994). The reader must recognize and readily access the meanings of the vast majority of words they encounter in an automatic manner. Lacking that automaticity, cognitive effort is devoted to the recognition of words, reducing the likelihood that the reader will have complete comprehension.

▼ Practice Activity 1.3

The importance of automaticity in the reading process can be seen in the following example. Read the directions carefully to complete the exercise. Answers can be found at the end of the chapter.

Directions: *Read the following inverted text three times aloud. Use a tape recorder to record each reading or have someone listen to you read. For each reading note the time, in seconds, that was required to read the selection and note the number of errors. Do not invert the text to make it "normal."*

Vitamin C

Forms and Sources. Ascorbic acid, the chemical name of vitamin C, is a shortened form of antiscorbutic (scurvy-preventing) factor. A relatively simple organic acid, vitamin C, having six carbon atoms in each molecule, is structurally similar to the six-carbon sugars such as glucose. It is the least stable of all vitamins, being easily oxidized to dehydroascorbic acid. (*Dehydro* means minus hydrogen; in oxidation, the ascorbic acid loses two hydrogen atoms per molecule.) Both ascorbic acid and dehydroascorbic acid are found in foods.

Wenck, D.A., Maren, M., & Dewan, S.A. (1980). *Nutrition.* Reston, Va: Reston Publishing.

▼▼

In summary, reading can be viewed as an interactive process whereby information is obtained simultaneously from knowledge sources. These sources include letter-level knowledge, word-level knowledge, syntactic knowledge, and knowledge of the meaning of sentences and larger units of meaning. This interactive view of reading is also a compensatory model whereby inefficiencies at one level in processing text can be compensated for by using greater amounts of information from other levels (Stanovich, West, & Freeman, 1981). Thus a reader who has difficulty decoding a text can, to some extent, use background knowledge to make the content more meaningful despite difficulty with the pronunciation of certain words. Similarly, if a reader lacks specific background knowledge, metacognitive strategies may allow for the establishment of specific goals as one reads and constant monitoring to enact fix-up strategies that will enhance the accomplishment of the reading goals. Instructionally the subject matter teacher must recognize that students' reading ability is not static. Comprehension and thinking strategies can be improved by teaching difficult vocabulary, establishing reading goals, and building background knowledge.

CONCLUDING REMARKS

In this chapter we have addressed a number of topics that provide the need, the intent, and the focus of content area reading instruction. The goal of content area reading instruction today has changed little since the early 1900s: to facilitate students' ability to learn from subject matter text and nonprint sources of information. However, today's students and teachers are faced with challenges that are unprecedented in American education. The level of reading and writing ability required to be functionally literate has increased dramatically over the past twenty years, yet tests of student achievement over the past twenty-five years indicate the level of performance on many basic skills has remained relatively stable. And in the workplace, today's workers are required to be effective in expressing their thoughts in print, obtaining information and constructing knowledge from text, solving everyday work-related problems that require critical thinking, and they are required to work cooperatively with their peers. Therefore, today's high school graduates must attain a high level of literacy, must be capable of making decisions that require higher-level thinking skills, and they must be able to effectively work and communicate with their peers. With these increased literacy and academic skills have come numerous calls for educational reform. At the same time, subject matter teachers are confronted with the demands of students with increasingly divergent social, economic, and intellectual backgrounds. And teachers are required to cover more content than in the past, to integrate their content with that of other subject matter areas, and they are being held accountable for ensuring that students learn that content. To suggest that education is in a state of flux would clearly be an understatement.

This book presents the content area teacher with practical activities to allow students to better comprehend the subject matter content presented in print or through such nonprint media as demonstrations, discussions, hands-on activities, and visual presentations. Additionally this book presents activities to engage in learning activities that promote cooperative learning and to assist students in becoming more independent in their acquisition of information and their ability to construct knowledge.

REFLECTIONS

▼▼▼

This section of the chapter provides you with some activities to reflect on some of the major topics presented in the chapter, how these topics apply to literacy tasks you engage in, as well as those literacy tasks that occur in the classroom.

1. Interview a subject matter teacher to determine what steps are taken in the classroom to meet the demands of (1) students who read at various levels of ability, (2) a multicultural classroom, (3) a constructivist form of instruction whereby students are actively involved in the learning environment, (4) an integrated curriculum involving interdisciplinary instruction, multiple sources of information, or cooperative learning environments.

2. Select a text you would read for an academic course. From this source select five to ten pages of text to read. Prior to reading the selection, examine the title and headings to obtain a "gist" of the content. In an attempt to become aware of your prior knowledge, write down facts, concepts, or generalizations that come to mind from the gist of the selection. Next read the selection with the intent of becoming more aware of your own study strategies. Attend to and write down the various strategies that you use as you engage in reading, such as summarizing, questioning, reviewing, notetaking, etc.

3. Monitor for a twenty-four-hour period the types of literacy tasks you engage in outside of those involved with your schooling. Note these tasks, then rate each task on a scale of one to ten to identify the level of difficulty of the task (ten being the most difficult). Discuss your findings with your colleagues, then discuss and hypothesize how well the population at large may engage in these various types of functional literacy tasks.

4. Examine a curriculum guide, textbook, or other form of instructional material that could be used in a subject matter classroom. Survey this material and complete the following questions:

▼ To what extent does this material draw upon the reader's background knowledge? Is the student allowed to form conclusions or generalizations by using prior knowledge?

▼ To what extent does the material seem to focus on the needs of the learner? Does the instructional material consider the needs, interests, and background of the students?

▼ Does the material allow the students to apply the content in a manner that has applications in one's daily life or in the workplace?

REFERENCES

▼▼▼

Aaron, I. E., Chall, J. S., Durkin, D., Goodman, K., & Strickland, D. S. (1990). The past, present, and future of literacy education: Comments from a panel of distinguished educators, part I. *The Reading Teacher*, 43, 302–311. An interesting article for teachers describing trends in literacy instruction and the role of reading educators.

Alvermann, D. E., & Swafford, J. (1989). Do content area strategies have a research base? *Journal of Reading*, 32, 388–394. Reviews research studies that have attempted to examine the usefulness of numerous strategies that have been recommended to classroom teachers and identifies those that have been shown to be effective.

American College Test. (1985). Table: ACT score means and SDs for successive years of ACT-tested college-bound students. Iowa City: Author. Describes the results of ACT test scores during the 1980s.

Anderson, C. W., & Smith, E. L. (1987). Teaching science. In V. Richardson-Koehler (Ed.), *Educators handbook: A research perspective* (pp. 84–111). New York: Longman. Reviews the state of knowledge regarding effective science instruction.

Bean, T. W. (1981). *Improving teaching and learning from texts in history and philosophy* (Final report). Fullerton: California State University Chancellor's Office for Educational Development and Innovation (ERIC Document Production Service No. ED 205 925). Discusses application of specific content area reading strategies to the study of social science textbooks.

Bean, T. W., Singer, H., & Frazee, C. (1986). The effect of metacognitive instruction in outlining and graphic organizer construction on students' comprehension in a tenth-grade world history class. *Journal of Reading Behavior*, 18, 153–169. Examines the effect of having students engage in monitoring strategies as they engage in the construction of outlining and concept maps.

Calfee, R. C. (1994). Critical literacy: Reading and writing for a new millennium. In N. L. Ellsworth, C. N. Hedley, & A. N. Baratta (Eds.), Literacy: A redefinition. Hillsdale, NJ: Erlbaum. Presents a rather compelling argument for the need to change our literacy expectations in an information age.

Coleman, J. S., et al. (1966). *Equality of educational opportunity*, Washington, DC: U.S. Government Printing Office. A widely cited book outlining the failure of the public schools to advance students' academic achievement.

College Board Admission Testing Program. (1994). *Schlastic Aptitude Test*. Princeton, NJ: Author.

College Entrance Examination Board, Advisory Panel on the Scholastic Aptitude Test Score Decline. (1977). On *further examination*. New York: Author. Reports on SAT score declines during the 1970s.

Conley, M. W. (1986). Teacher's conceptions, decisions, and changes during initial classroom lessons containing content area reading strategies. In J. A. Niles and R. V. Lalik (Eds.), *Solving problems in literacy: Learners, teachers, and searchers* (pp. 120–126). Rochester, NY: National Reading Conference. Reports on how the use of content area reading strategies affects teachers' instruction and their perception of the use of these strategies.

Cooperman, P. (1979). The achievement decline of the 1970's. *Phi Delta Kappan*, 60, 736–739. Reviews test score data and reasons for the purported decline in college entrance exam scores during the early 1970s.

Council of Chief State School Officers. (1995). Consensus framework of workplace readiness, 1995 revision. Washington, DC: Author. Outlines the need for workers with higher levels of literacy and describes the nature of skills required for the twenty-first century.

CTB/McGraw-Hill. (1982). *Comprehensive tests of basic skills. Preliminary technical report*, Forms U and V. Monterey, CA: Author. Technical manual for the CTBS exam.

Eckland, B. K. (1982). College entrance examination trends. In G. R. Austin & H. Garber (Eds.), *The rise and fall of national test scores*. New York: Academic Press. Reviews trends in college entrance exam scores during the 1970s and offers explanations for the purported decline in test scores.

Estes, T. H., & Piercey, D. (1973). Secondary reading requirements: Report on the states. *Journal of Reading*, 17, 20–24. Reviews the results of survey reading requirements required for state licensure during the early 1970s.

Farrell, R. T., & Cirrincione, J. M. (1984). State certification requirements in reading for content area teachers. *Journal of Reading*, 28, 152–158. Reports on the survey of state requirements for content area reading courses required for teaching licensure.

Flavell, J. H., Miller, P. H., & Miller, S. A. (1993). *Cognitive development* (3rd ed.). Englewood Cliffs, NJ: Prentice-Hall. Provides an in-depth review and analysis of cognitive theories and development.

Flynn, P. M. (1988). *Facilitating technological change: The human resource challenge.* Cambridge, MA: Ballinger. Reports on the level of knowledge and literacy competencies required for workers in the twenty-first century.

Fuller, F. F. (1969). Concerns for teachers: A developmental characterization. *American Educational Research Journal, 6,* 207–226. Reports on teacher reflections and observations during classroom instruction and those variables that affect a teacher's attention to providing instruction in the classroom.

Garcia, E. E. (1993). Language, culture, and education. In L. Darling-Hammond (Ed.), *Review of research in education* (Vol. 19). Washington, DC: American Educational Research Association. Reviews the state of knowledge regarding the role of culture and language on the school learning environment and outlines how we may facilitate learning in a culturally and linguistically diverse classroom.

Garner, R. (1988). *Metacognition and reading comprehension.* Norwood, NJ: Ablex. Provides a comprehensive review of the state of our knowledge regarding the role of metacognition in the reading process.

Garner, R., & Kraus, C. (1982). Good and poor comprehender differences in knowing and regulating reading behaviors. *Educational Research Quarterly, 6,* 5–12. Examines differences in metacognitive behaviors of good and poor readers.

Gehrke, N. J., Schaefer, C., and Schlick, K. (1982). *Reading in content areas: A comparative study of attitudes, perceptions, practices of preservice and inservice secondary teachers.* Arlington, VA: ERIC Document Production Service ED 251 331. Reports on the results of a survey examining the effect of content area reading courses on in-service and preservice teachers.

Gerstner, L. V., Semerad, R. D., Doyle, D. P., & Johnston, W. B. (1994). *Reinventing education: Entrepreneurship in America's public schools.* New York: Dutton. Presents the view of business on the need and the process for restructuring the public schools.

Gray, W. S. (1925). *Summary of investigations relating to reading,* Supplementary Educational Monographs No. 28. Chicago: University of Chicago Press. Summarizes the knowledge base of reading instruction and reading in the 1920s.

Greene, M. (1989). Social and political contexts. In M. C. Reynolds (Ed.), *Knowledge base for the beginning teacher* (pp. 143–154). New York: Pergamon. Outlines the role of culture and home environment on students' learning.

Haenggi, D., & Perfetti, C. A. (1994). Processing components of college-level reading comprehension. *Discourse Processes, 17,* 83–104. Examines the role of phonology and automaticity in college students' ability to comprehend text.

Harnischfeger, A., & Wiley, D. E. (1975). *Achievement test scores decline: Do we need to worry?* Chicago: CEMEREL. Summarizes trends of achievement test scores in the early 1970s and offers conclusions accounting for the variance in scores.

Herber, H. L. (1970). *Teaching reading in content areas.* Englewood Cliffs, NJ: Prentice-Hall. This methods text addresses issues and strategies to integrate reading in the subject matter classroom.

Holt-Reynolds, D. (1992). Personal history-based beliefs as relevant prior knowledge in course work. *American Educational Research Journal, 29,* 325–349. Reports on an assessment of in-service teachers' perceptions on coursework required for licensure.

Irwin, P. M. (1987). *Adult literacy issues, programs, and options.* Issues Brief. Washington, DC: Education and Public Welfare Division, Congressional Search Service. Reviews various options for literacy programs for adults.

Jencks, C., Smith, M., Ackland, H., Bane, M. J., Cohen, D., Gintis, B., & Michelson, S. (1972). *Inequality: A reassessment of the effect of family and schooling in America.* New York: Basic Books. Reports on a reassessment of the information contained in the Coleman report and draws conclusions on the poor state of education in America.

Johnston, W. B., & Packer, A. H. (1987). *Workforce 2000: Work and workers for the 21st century.* Indianapolis, IN: Hudson Institute. A report written from a business perspective noting the educational training and competencies that will be required for workers in the twenty-first century.

Kirsch, I. S., Jungeblut, A., Jenkins, L., and Kolstad, A. (1993). Adult literacy in America: A first look at the results of the national adult literacy survey. Washington, DC: U.S. Government Printing

Office. Reviews general findings and provides an in-depth analysis of the results of the 1992 assessment of the literacy among adults.

Klerman, J. A., & Karoly, L. A. (1995). The transition of stable employment: The experience of U.S. youth in their early labor market career. Santa Monica, CA: Rand Corporation. Examines the nature of job attainment and the stability among teenage youth in full-time jobs.

Laberge, D., & Samuels, S. J. (1974). Toward a theory of automatic information processing in reading. *Cognitive Psychology*, 6, 293–323. Presents a theoretical model of automaticity and its role and importance in the reading process.

Lee, C., Casello, J., May, T., Bryant, C., Foster, R., Goodwin, W., & Meeham, M. (1994). *Occupational skill standards projects*. Washington, DC: U.S. Department of Education and U.S. Department of Labor. Reports on the nature of skills and competencies required for various jobs in the workplace.

McCarthy, K. (1994). School-to-work. A guide for state policymakers. National Conference of State Legislatures and Jobs for the Future. Investing in People Project, Issue Paper no. 3. Reviews school-to-work programs and provides an overview of their importance in providing a better-trained workforce.

Memory, D. M. (1983). Implementing a practicum in a required content area reading course. *Reading World*, 23, 116–123. Describes students' attitudes toward their participation in a content area reading practicum and their views toward the importance of content area reading instruction.

Meyer, B., & Rice, E. (1984). The structure of text. In P. D. Pearson (Ed.), *Handbook of reading research* (pp. 319–351). New York: Longman. Reports on the influence of text structure knowledge on students' comprehension of text.

Miner, A. C., & Reder, L. M. (1996). A new look at feeling of knowing: Its metacognitive role in regulating question answering. In J. Metcalfe & A. P. Shimamura (Eds.), Metacognition: Knowing about knowing. Cambridge, MA: MIT Press. Examines the role of metacognition in a reader's ability to respond to various types of questions.

Mullis, I. V. S., Campbell, J. R., and Farstrup, A. E. (1993). NAEP 1992 reading report card for the nation and the states: Data from the national and trial state assessments. Washington, DC: U.S. Government Printing Office. Summarizes the findings of the 1992 national assessment of students' reading ability.

Mullis, V. S., Owen, E. H., & Phillips, G.W. (1991). *Accelerating academic achievement: A summary of findings from 20 years of NAEP*. Princeton, NJ: National Assessment of Educational Progress, Educational Testing Service. Reviews the findings of the NAEP testing results from 1970 to 1990.

National Alliance of Business. (1987). *The fourth R: Workforce readiness*. New York: Author. Overviews the need for students to acquire higher-level competencies in communication and thinking skills prior to entering the workforce.

National Center on Education and the Economy. (1990). *America's choice: High skills or low wages*. Rochester, NY: Author. Reports on the need for better-educated workers and the problems inherent in providing jobs for undereducated youth in a service-oriented economy.

National Center for Education Statistics. (1996). |Online| Available http://gopher.ed.gov/NCES/pubs/ce/c9622a01.html. A concise report of national performance on students who completed the SAT in 1995.

National Commission on Excellence in Education. (1983). A *nation at risk: The imperative for educational form*. Washington, DC: U.S. Government Printing Office. A widely noted and controversial report noting the shortcomings of our schools and the implications of the perceived decline in students' academic achievement.

Oakes, J. (1986). Keeping track, part 1: The policy and practice of curriculum inequality. *Phi Delta Kappan*, 68, 12–17. An interesting review of the effect of academic tracking and suggestions for replacing this form of grouping.

O'Brien, D. G. (1988). Preservice teachers' resistance to content reading instruction: A proposal for a broader rationale. In J. E. Readence & R. S. Baldwin (Eds.), *Twenty-Seventh Yearbook of the National Reading Conference*. Chicago, IL: National Reading Conference. Reports on students' attitudes in teacher training programs toward required course work in content area reading.

Paris, S. G., Lipson, M. Y., & Wixson, K. K. (1983). Becoming a strategic reader. *Contemporary*

Educational Psychology, 8, 293–316. Discusses the importance of strategic processing in the reading process and the importance of strategic processing in instructional settings.

Paris, S. G., & Winograd, P. (1989). How metacognition can promote academic learning and instruction. In B. F. Jones & L. Idol (Eds.), *Dimensions of thinking and cognitive instruction* (Vol. 1). Hillsdale, NJ: Erlbaum. Reviews the importance of self-monitoring in learning and its importance in classroom instruction.

Pearce, D. L., & Bader, L. A. (1986). The effect of unit construction upon teachers' use of content area reading and writing strategies. *Journal of Reading*, 30, 130–135. Describes a study examining teachers' views on the effect of content area reading strategies in their classrooms.

Perfetti, C. A. (1977). Language comprehension and fast decoding: Some psycholinguistic prerequisites for skilled reading comprehension. In J. T. Guthrie (Ed.), *Cognition, curriculum, and comprehension*. Newark, DE: International Reading Association. Addresses the role of decoding in the reading process from the perspective that phonological processing is a prerequisite to proficient reading.

Perfetti, C. A., & Zhang, S. (1995). The universal word identification reflex. In D. L. Medin (Ed.), *The psychology of learning and motivation* (Vol. 33). San Diego, CA: Academic Press. Examines the importance of word recognition in the reading process.

Ravitch, D. (1985). *The schools we deserve*. New York: Basic Books. Addresses the need for school reform and outlines measures for improving schools.

Resnick, D. P., & Resnick, L. B. (1977). The nature of literacy: An historical exploration. *Harvard Educational Review*, 47, 370–385. An interesting historical overview of how basic literacy skills have changed in accordance with societal need.

Rumberger, R. W., & Levin, H. M. (1989). Schooling for the modern workplace. *Investing in people: A strategy to address America's workforce crisis* (Vol. I, pp. 85–143). Washington, DC: Commission on Workforce Quality and Labor Market Efficiency, U.S. Department of Labor. Outlines the type of basic literacy skills demanded in a technological society and the workplace.

Rumelhart, D. E. (1977). Toward an interactive model of reading. In S Dornic (Ed.), *Attention and performance* (Vol. 6, pp. 573–603). Hillsdale, NJ: Erlbaum. Describes a model of reading that involves the reader's ability to draw upon both phonological and graphemic clues as well as contextual information in the process of constructing understanding.

———(1980). Schemata: The building blocks of cognition. In R. J. Spiro, B. C. Bruce, & W. F. Brewer (Eds.), *Theoretical issues in reading comprehension: Perspectives from cognitive psychology, linguistics, artificial intelligence, and education*. Hillsdale, NJ: Erlbaum. A thorough description of what schema are, how they function in reading comprehension, and their importance in the process of learning to read.

Ryder, R. J., & Graves, M. F. (1994). Vocabulary instruction presented prior to reading in two basal series. *Elementary School Journal*, 95, 139–153. Reports on findings of a study examining the nature of vocabulary instruction appearing in two widely used basal reading programs.

Science Research Associates. (1978). *Iowa tests of educational development* (Technical report). Chicago: Author. Technical manual for the Iowa Tests of Educational Development.

Smith, F. R., & Feathers, K. M. (1983). Teacher and student perceptions of content area reading. *Journal of Reading*, 1, 384–354. Describes the acceptance of content area reading strategies as reported by teachers and students.

Smith, M. (1991). Constructing meaning from text: An analysis of ninth-grade reader responses. *Journal of Educational Research*, 84, 263–271. Describes ninth-grade readers' reflections on their reading and the strategies and processes used to understand text.

Stanovich, K. E., West, R. F., & Freeman, D. V. (1981). A longitudinal study of sentence context effects in second grade children: Test of an interactive-compensatory model. *Journal of Experimental Child Psychology*, 32, 185–199. Describes the compensatory process of reading with a group of second graders whereby deficiencies in one area of the reading process can be overcome by strengths in others.

Stedman, L. C., & Kaestle, C. F. (1987). Literacy and reading in the United States, from 1880 to the present. *Reading Research Quarterly*, 21, 8–46. A rather comprehensive historical review of the nature of literacy skills and the factors that have influenced changes in these skills.

Stein, N. L., & Trabasso, T. (1982). What's in a story: An approach to verbal comprehension and instruction. In R. Glaser (Ed.), *Advances in instructional psychology* (Vol. 2, pp. 213–267). Hillsdale, NJ: Erlbaum. Discusses the role of story structures on students' reading comprehension.

U.S. Department of Education, National Center for Education Statistics. (1996). Reading literacy in the United States: Findings from the IEA reading literacy study. Washington, DC: U.S. Government Printing Office. Summarizes the findings of an international study of literacy as well as a study examining the nature of reading instruction in the United States.

Vosniadou, S., & Brewer, W. (1987). Theories of knowledge structuring in development. *Review of Educational Search*, 57, 51–67. Reports on the nature of instructional pedagogy whereby teachers act as dispensers of knowledge.

Whimbey, A. (1975). Intelligence can be taught. *New York: Dutton*. Addresses the nature of learning and reading and strategies that may enhance one's learning.

2

Vocabulary

CHAPTER OVERVIEW

In this chapter we describe ways of directly teaching vocabulary and ways of teaching students strategies they can use in improving their own vocabularies. We begin with a brief section on the importance of vocabulary in which we consider how vital words are to success in and out of school and the huge store of words that students need to learn to become proficient readers. Next come the two major sections of the chapter, "Teaching Specific Words" and "Preparing Students to Learn Words Independently." In the section on teaching specific words, we discuss various word learning tasks that students face, consider different levels of word knowledge students can achieve, suggest ways to select vocabulary to teach, and describe a variety of methods for teaching specific words. In the section on preparing students to become independent word learners, we discuss teaching students to use context and word parts to unlock the meanings of new words and using the dictionary and thesaurus. The last section in the chapter describes approaches to fostering word consciousness—a disposition to notice words, value them, and use them in precise and effective ways.

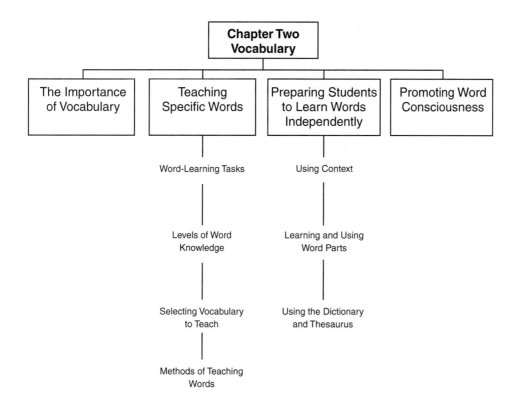

THE IMPORTANCE OF VOCABULARY

Students' vocabularies are tremendously important to their success in school and in the larger world outside of school (Graves, 1994). Measurement experts have noted that vocabulary knowledge is one of the best predictors of verbal ability and that a vocabulary test might well be substituted for an intelligence test (Anderson & Freebody, 1981). Readability researchers have contended that vocabulary strongly influences the difficulty of texts (Klare, 1984), and even those who argue that readability formulas provide inadequate assessments of the difficulty of texts recognize that vocabulary is one important factor to take into account when considering whether or not a particular text is appropriate for a particular group of students (Ryder, Graves, & Graves, 1989).

Educators have shown that teaching vocabulary can improve students' comprehension and memory of selections containing the vocabulary taught (Beck, Perfetti, & McKeown, 1982). Educators have also shown that teaching vocabulary can improve students' writing on topics related to the words taught (Duin & Graves, 1987). Speech and writing researchers have shown that the vocabulary a person uses influences others' perceptions of his or her speech and writing as well as their judgments about the person (Bradac, Bowers, & Courtright, 1982; Neilsen & Piché, 1981).

Not only are students' vocabularies very important, they are also very large. Conservative estimates based on the research of Anderson and Nagy (1992), Anglin (1993), Nagy and Anderson (1984), and White, Graves, and Slater (1990) suggest the following figures: The average first grader enters school with a listening vocabulary in excess of 5,000 words, and by the end of the first grade this same first grader can read approximately 4,000 words. By the time students reach junior high school, many of them can read 20,000 words, and by the time they complete high school many of them can read 40,000 words, making the annual rate of growth 3,000 to 4,000 words. At the same time, estimates indicate that the texts and other materials used by secondary school students contain over 100,000 different words (Nagy & Anderson, 1984) and that students might encounter 15 to 55 unknown words in a typical 1,000-word text (Nagy, Herman, & Anderson, 1985) (See Figure 2.1).

Clearly there are a lot of words to be learned. Fortunately a large number of research studies (see Baumann & Kameenui, 1991; Beck & McKeown, 1991) have suggested powerful instructional approaches. Additionally, teachers do not need to teach all the new words students encounter because students can usually understand selections even though they contain a number of unknown words (Freebody & Anderson, 1983), and students can learn many words on their own. In fact, wide reading has been shown to be an extremely effective approach to promoting vocabulary growth for both first- and second-language learners (Anderson, 1996; Elley, 1991).

Figure 2.1
Conservative Estimate of the Size and Growth of Students' Reading Vocabularies

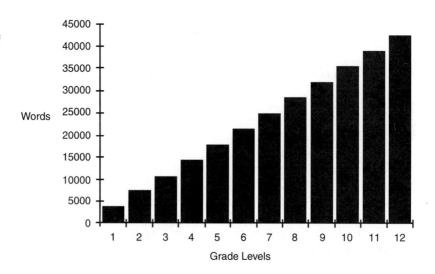

However, some of the words students need to learn should be taught directly. Additionally, teachers need to help students develop more powerful strategies for learning words independently. In the next two sections of the chapter, we consider these two major goals of vocabulary instruction—teaching specific words and preparing students to become independent word learners—and describe specific instructional procedures for accomplishing each of these goals.

TEACHING SPECIFIC WORDS

Teaching specific words is the goal that currently receives the most attention in schools. Yet instruction in specific words is often not as effective as it might be because vocabulary learning is frequently thought of as a single task for which there is a single instructional method. In reality, the task of learning words is a series of tasks that vary markedly depending on the word being taught, the learner's knowledge of the word and the concept it represents, and the depth and precision of meaning the student needs to acquire. Importantly, the sort of instruction appropriate for accomplishing one of these tasks is often inappropriate for accomplishing others; teaching methods need to be matched with the learning tasks and with the students who are doing the learning. Ensuring this match is particularly important in multicultural classrooms, where students from different backgrounds may have different vocabularies.

In the remainder of this section, we first describe four word-learning tasks. Next, we discuss levels of word knowledge. Following that, we make some suggestions for choosing words to teach. Finally, we describe teaching procedures appropriate for each of the four word-learning tasks. Together, these sections prepare you to make informed decisions about which words to teach and how to teach them.

Word-Learning Tasks

The word-learning tasks we discuss here are shown below.

Four Word-Learning Tasks

1. Learning to read words in their oral vocabularies

2. Learning new labels for known concepts

3. Learning words representing new and difficult concepts

4. Clarifying and enriching the meanings of known words

These tasks vary a great deal depending on such factors as whether the words to be learned are already in students' oral vocabularies, students' prior knowledge of the concepts represented by the words, and how thoroughly students need to know the words (Graves, 1992; Scott & Nagy, 1994).

Learning to Read Words in Their Oral Vocabularies

Learning to read words that are already part of their oral vocabularies is the principal task of primary-grade students as they begin learning to read. Familiar words such as *picnic, circle,* and *laughter* are ones that students might learn to read during their first three years of school. By about the time they reach fourth grade, good readers can read nearly all the words in their oral vocabularies (Graves, 1992). However, learning to read words in their oral vocabularies remains a task that poor readers may face even in the secondary grades. They know the words when they hear them, but they don't recognize them in print. For example, poor readers might not recognize words such as *ache* or *wrench* because of their unusual spelling.

Learning New Labels for Known Concepts

Learning new labels for concepts they already know is a word-learning task all students face. For example, the word *heterogeneous* would be unknown to most junior and senior high students, but these same students would have internalized the concept of "dissimilar parts" or of "not being the same."

Learning Words Representing New and Difficult Concepts

Learning to read words that are in neither their oral nor their reading vocabularies and for which they do not have an available concept is one of the most challenging word-learning tasks students face. Learning the full meanings of such words as *fusion, anarchism,* and *proteins* is likely to require the development of new concepts for even senior high students. In fact, in many ways learning words representing new and challenging concepts is more demanding than and quite different from any of the other word learning tasks considered here. The learner's task is to master a new idea, not just a new label for a familiar idea. Learning a new concept is likely to involve a host of subtasks—defining the new concept, recognizing instances of the new concept, distinguishing between the new concept and other similar concepts, and dealing with a great deal of information about the contexts in which the new concept is imbedded. As later sections in the chapter will illustrate, it takes very robust instruction to fully teach new and challenging concepts.

Clarifying and Enriching the Meanings of Known Words

The last word-learning task we consider here is that of refining the meanings of already known words. The meanings students originally give to words are often vague and imprecise. Initially, for example, students might not recognize any difference between *sad* and *morose,* be able to distinguish a *trumpet* from a *cornet,* or understand that the term *watershed* is usually applied to a critical point that serves as a dividing line in some historic event. As students repeatedly encounter words they know in a variety of contexts, they will gradually expand and enrich their knowledge of them. However, more direct approaches can help guarantee that students add to the depth of their word knowledge.

PRACTICE ACTIVITY 2.1

Listed below are two sets of words that present students with various word-learning tasks. Assume that you are considering teaching the first set to a class of average eighth-grade students and the second set to a class of average eleventh-grade students. Consider each word, and identify the word-learning task that it probably represents. We say *probably* because the learning task represented by a particular word may not be the same for all students even in a fairly homogeneous class. Moreover, identifying the word-learning task particular words represent requires a judgment, a hypothesis. Because doing this exercise requires you to hypothesize, it's a good one to do with a colleague so that you can talk over your decisions. Our judgments about the word-learning task each word represents are listed at the end of the book.

▼▼▼

Words for Eighth Graders

fling (a wild time)   _____ a new concept

                                 _____ a new meaning

rationale number   _____ a word in students'
                                          oral vocabularies

                                 _____ a new word for a
                                          known concept

pneumonia   _____ a word in students'
                                          oral vocabularies

                                 _____ a new concept

finite   _____ a new concept

                                 _____ a new word

Words for Eleventh Graders

fluke   _____ a new concept

                                 _____ a new word

languish   _____ a word in students'
                                          oral vocabularies

                                 _____ a new word for a
                                          known concept

fugue   _____ a word in students'
                               oral vocabularies

                             _____ a new concept

taxonomy   _____ a new concept

                             _____ a new word

Levels of Word Knowledge

Not only are there different word-learning tasks, there are also different degrees to which students can know words. Beck and McKeown (1991) identify three levels of word knowledge: _unknown_, _acquainted_, and _established_. An _unknown_ word is obviously just that—unknown. The word _levorotatory_ (an adjective pertaining to a chemical solution that rotates the plane of polarized light counterclockwise) is almost certainly unknown to both junior and senior high students. A word at the _acquainted_ level is one that students need to deliberately think about to recall its meaning. The word _fiesta_ is probably at the acquainted level for many junior high students, and the word _raucous_ is likely to be at the acquainted level for many senior high students. Finally, a word at the _established_ level is one students recognize and assign a meaning to easily and rapidly. The word _library_ is at the established level for nearly all secondary students. Here are the sorts of responses you might expect to two of these words in an eighth-grade class.

> **Ms. Ramiriz:** OK class, there are several words in the chapter we're going to read that you may not be familiar with. Let's see what you know about them. The first one is _levorotatory_. Has anyone heard that word?
>
> **Ted:** Do you mean _laboratory_, Ms. Ramiriz?
>
> **Ms. Ramiriz:** No, the word is _levorotatory_. (She writes it on the board).
>
> **Class:** Dead silence. (_Levorotatory_ is clearly unknown to these eighth graders.)
>
> **Ms. Ramiriz:** OK, what about _fiesta_?
>
> **Helen:** A party.
>
> **Gerard:** A large, noisy party.
>
> **Ramon:** A party with music. A Mexican party.
>
> **Ms. Ramiriz:** You're certainly right. Now, what else do you know about fiestas? Could you have a fiesta without music? Could a party be a fiesta if only Anglos went to it?
>
> **Class:** Some discussion, but no very definite answers. (These students' understanding of _fiesta_ is at the acquainted level.)

Any vocabulary instruction is likely to move students' knowledge of the words taught beyond the unknown level. But to learn a word thoroughly requires that students are exposed to that word in a variety of contexts (Beck & McKeown, 1983). Thus students' first encounter with a word can best be viewed as one of a series of encounters with the word that will eventually lead the students to full understanding of it.

▼ **PRACTICE ACTIVITY 2.2**

Listed below are four words for junior high students and four words for senior high students. Classify each as likely to be at the unknown, acquainted, established, or in-depth level. Our classifications are shown at the end of the book.

▼▼▼

Words for Junior High Students

> harmony, languid, fast food, and triangle

Words for Senior High Students

> examinations, pi, erstwhile, and aerobic

Selecting Vocabulary to Teach

Once you are familiar with the various word-learning tasks students face and the sorts of word knowledge that you want them to gain, you still have the task of selecting specific words to teach. Two steps are helpful here. The first is to find out just which words students are likely to know, and the second is to set up criteria for selecting words to teach.

The best source of information about what words students know is the students themselves. Research (White, Slater, & Graves, 1989) suggests that students can be quite accurate in checking words on a list to indicate those that they do and do not know. Giving students a list of words and having them indicate whether or not they know each word is an efficient and effective way of finding out the sorts of words that your students do and do not know. After you have had students identify difficult words several times, you will have a better overall understanding of which words might cause them difficulty.

Another option is to have groups of students skim through upcoming selections and pick out important words they see as difficult. Recent research indicates that students can become quite adept at this task (Dole, Sloan, & Trathen, 1995), and this is an excellent opportunity for the sort of cooperative work we describe in Chapter 7. Heterogeneous groups of four work well for this task. Divide students into groups and then explain that each group's task is to skim through a part of the upcoming selection looking for difficult words that seem important to understanding the selection. When they find such words, they are to define them and explain why they are important to understanding the selection and present the sentences in which the words occurred and their definitions to the class. At this point it, would be helpful if you modeled the selection process, thinking aloud as you identify difficult words and consider their importance in the selection.

Next, assign each group member a definite role. One student can skim the passage searching for difficult words and writing down those selected. Another can explain their importance in the selection. A third can look up the words in the dictionary and write down an appropriate definition, and the fourth can check to see that the definitions given are appropriate for the way the words are used in the passage. Each group is then assigned one section of the selection, selecting the words and definitions to be taught, and then teaching their words and explaining their importance to the class.

The job of selecting vocabulary to be learned does not end with initially selecting the words because there are often more difficult words than there is time to teach. Thus, once potentially difficult vocabulary is identified, criteria for identifying the most important words to teach need to be established. The following three guidelines will help you and your students select the most beneficial words to teach.

Guidelines for Selecting Words to Teach

1. Understanding the word is important to understanding the selection in which it appears.

2. If students can use their context or structural analysis skills to glean a meaning for the word, they ought to be allowed to do so. Having students use their word-learning skills whenever possible will both help them solidify these skills and reduce the number of words you need to teach.

3. If the word is likely to be useful outside of the selection currently being taught, if students are likely to come across it in other reading, then it is more important to teach. *Incumbent,* for example, is a fairly frequent word that some students would not know but that they are likely to encounter again. On the other hand, such words as *ganister* and *laches* are infrequent words, and students may never encounter them again.

Still another matter to consider in choosing words to teach is that of how many can reasonably be taught for a single selection. For a chapter, article, or short story of ten to twenty pages, ten words is about as many as should generally be taught. This does not mean that you need always teach this number of words for a selection. Sometimes you will teach none, and when teaching a word representing a difficult new concept, you may teach only the single word.

PRACTICE ACTIVITY 2.3

Select a text for the subject and grade level you teach and get a copy of it for a colleague too. Then, go through a section of the text and pick out words that are important and might cause students difficulty. Your colleague should do the same thing independently. Finally, get together with your colleague and discuss the words you chose, the amount of agreement you had, and the extent to which you need to continue to hone your skills at selecting vocabulary and some ways you might do that.

▼ ▼

Methods of Teaching Words

In this section, we suggest teaching procedures that can be used for each of the word-learning tasks we have described.

Learning to Read Known Words

In order to learn to read words that are in their oral vocabularies, students need to associate what is unknown—the written word—with what is already known—the spoken word. To make this happen, they need to see the word at the same time they hear it, and once the association is established, they need to rehearse it until the association becomes automatic. These steps for learning to read known words are listed below.

Steps in Learning to Read Known Words

1. Student sees the word.

2. Student hears the word pronounced.

3. Student rehearses that association numerous times.

There are many ways to accomplish each of these steps. Students can initially *see* the word in the context of their reading material, on a handout, on the board, on a screen, or on a computer. They can *hear* the word when a teacher says it, another student says it, or a speech synthesizer in a computer says it. Students can *rehearse* the association by seeing and pronouncing the word in a variety of contexts, using it in their writing, and playing games that require them to recognize printed versions of it. The best form of rehearsal for these words and an essential part of students' mastering them, however, is their reading materials that contain numerous repetitions of such words. In fact, wide reading is almost certainly the most powerful force in developing students' vocabularies, and it would be difficult to overestimate the value of getting students to do as much reading as possible. Finally, remember that these are words students already know; there is no need to teach their meanings.

Learning New Labels for Known Concepts

Here we consider two quite different sorts of instruction. First, we describe methods appropriate for introductory instruction, relatively brief instruction that teaches the basic meanings of words. Then, we describe methods appropriate for intensive instruction, relatively lengthy instruction that teaches deep and full word meanings.

Introductory Instruction   Described below are two approaches to teaching new words representing known concepts. These require different amounts of teacher preparation time and different amounts of student time and effort; and they are likely to yield different results. Both, however, include some sort of interaction and feedback from you, and both include a definition and the presentation of the word in context, two features strongly supported by recent research (Nagy, 1988; Stahl & Fairbanks, 1986).

The first form of introductory instruction, the context/dictionary/discussion procedure (Graves & Slater, 1996), consists of three simple steps.

Context/Dictionary/Discussion Procedure

Give students the word in context, ask them to look it up in the dictionary, and discuss the definitions they come up with.

subscript

Nicole, a student in Ms. Green's third-hour mathematics class, had used the term x to refer to three different quantities, and thus she added *subscripts* to distinguish the three terms.

The second form of introductory instruction, the context/relationship procedure (Graves & Slater, 1996), involves students in reading a paragraph and answering a multiple-choice question.

Context/Relationship Procedure

This procedure presents the target word three or four times in a brief paragraph, followed by a multiple-choice item designed to check students' understanding of the word. Below are a sample paragraph, a multiple-choice item, and a method for presenting each word.

Rationale

The *rationale* for my wanting to expose students to a variety of words and their meanings is partially that this will help them become better thinkers who are able to express their ideas more clearly. Part of that *rationale* also includes my belief that words themselves are fascinating objects of study. My *rationale* for doing something means my fundamental reasons for doing it.

Continued

Rationale means

_____ A. a deliberate error.

_____ B. the basis for doing something.

_____ C. a main idea for an essay.

   In presenting each word, explain the procedure's purpose, pronounce the target word, read the paragraph containing the word, and read the multiple-choice items and ask students to select the best definition by putting a check next to their choice. Finally, give students the correct answer and answer any questions they have.

Again, we want to stress that each approach involves some interaction between you and your students—a discussion that allows students to explain their understanding of the word and gives you an opportunity to shape and refine their understanding as necessary—and involves both a definition and some context.

Intensive Instruction   Here we present two forms of intensive instruction—rich and thorough instruction that provides rich and thorough understanding of the words taught.

The first form of intensive instruction considered is called semantic mapping (Heimlich & Pittelman, 1986). The steps typically followed in using semantic mapping are shown below.

Semantic Mapping Procedure

- Put a word representing a central concept on the board.
- Ask students to volunteer words related to the central concept.
- Write these on the board and group them in broad categories.
- Have students name the categories.
- Conclude the session with a discussion of the central concept, the related words, the categories, and the relationships among these elements.

Semantic mapping is particularly appropriate for selections that have a single central concept and when students have fairly substantial prior knowledge relevant to the central concept. Following are parts of a semantic mapping discussion on *telecommunications*, and the map itself is shown in Figure 2.2. This is a tenth-grade class, and they're familiar with semantic mapping.

> **Mr. Gains:** This week we'll be turning our attention to *telecommunications*, something I know many of you know quite a bit about. Let's begin by brainstorming what we know about telecommunications and creating a semantic map to show what we know. What comes to mind when you think of telecommunications?
>
> **Andrea:** The Internet, the web, email.
>
> **Samone:** TV, cable, Direct TV.
>
> **Henry:** That pretty soon, we're all going to be linked. Our school, our home, our car. Pretty soon we'll be hooked up anyplace we go. I even saw a guy on TV yesterday who wears a camera that transmits all the time. When he goes shopping, he shows his wife what he is going to buy, and she tells him whether or not it's OK.

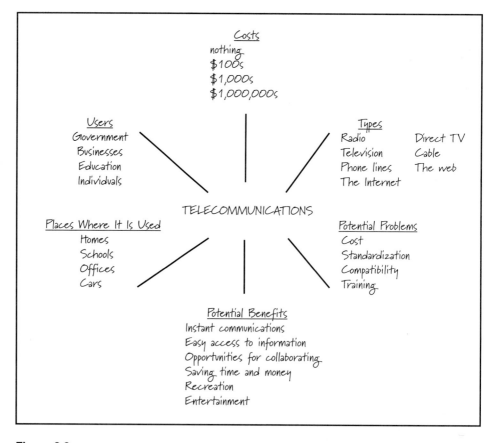

Figure 2.2
Semantic Map for the Word *Telecommunications*

Students do know a lot about telecommunications, and the conversation continues for some time, with Mr. Gains both asking questions and occasionally saying something to keep the discussion on track. As responses lag, it's time to begin grouping responses.

> **Mr. Gains:** Well, you do indeed know a lot about telecommunications. Now we need to group our responses in a map. What are some categories?
>
> **Maynard:** What about Places Where Telecommunications Is Used? And what about What It Costs to hook up all those places?
>
> **Susan:** And what about Different Users, that's something to think about.

Again, the conversation continues for some time, with Mr. Gains gradually seeking agreement and constructing the map. As the class continues its work on telecommunications, students will add to the map, and eventually it will serve as a record of what they've learned and a tool to use in reviewing.

The second type of intensive instruction suggested here is called student activated vocabulary instruction (Ryder, 1985). As described here, the procedure has four steps.

Student Activated Vocabulary Instruction

1. **Select five to ten important words that are probably unknown to students from the upcoming selection.** Words from a multicultural lesson in art and social studies dealing with the Dias de los Muertos (Day of the Dead) might include *conquistadors, secularized, evangelizing, colonialism, mosaics,* and s*erapes.*

2. **Construct four word cards for each word.** On the first card, write the word phonetically. On the second card, write the word and its definition. On the third card, write a sentence that presents the word in a rich context. On the fourth card, write the word itself. For example, the cards for *secularized* might look like this:

   - Card 1: SEC • yuh • lar • ize

   - Card 2: secularized = to have separated from religious connections or influences

   - Card 3: Urban Hispanics today tend to be somewhat secularized. They have removed themselves from many of the traditional observances of the Day of the Dead.

   - Card 4: Secularized

3. **Have students create lists of words related to each of the words to be learned.** Give each student a single card, and have students check with each other and form groups made up of the four students whose cards form a set. Have each group create a list of words related to the word being studied. At first you will probably want to model listing these sets of related words. Once

   Continued

the group has completed their list, they should put the new word, its definition, and the related words on the board or an overhead. An example for the word *secularized* is shown below:

secularized = to be separated from religious influence

spiritual   nonreligious   priest

churches   worship   parishioners

4. **Have one member of each group teach the group's word to the class.** The student should present the word, its definition, and the list of related words on the board or overhead. After reading the word and its definition, he or she should then call on class members to indicate whether each related word is either an attribute or synonym, or a nonattribute or antonym.

When considering using any form of intensive instruction it is important to realize that intensive instruction takes a good deal of time and is not something that can or should be used all the time. However, it is certainly worth the time on some occasions. Results of several studies (Beck & McKeown, 1983; Nagy, 1988) have indicated that students working with intensive instruction gain deep understanding and mastery of the words taught and that this in-depth knowledge enables them to better comprehend materials containing the words.

Learning New Words Representing New Concepts

As we said earlier, learning new words representing new concepts is a very demanding task. Just how demanding the task is depends on the difficulty of the new concept and on just how unfamiliar students are with the concept and those surrounding it. For example, in the area of literary analysis, the concept *plot* will be understood by most upper-elementary students and the concept *characterization* will be understood by most secondary students, while the concept *theme* will continue to prove difficult to pin down for many college students. Similarly, in the area of physics, the concept of *weight* will be understood by many elementary students and the concept of *volume* by many secondary students, while the concept *mass* will continue to puzzle many college students.

Note that one of the intensive instruction methods just described—semantic mapping—can also be used to teach new concepts, particularly if students have some knowledge related to the new concepts. Here we describe one additional procedure, a procedure particularly appropriate for very challenging concept learning.

The procedure was originally developed by Frayer and her colleagues (see Frayer, Frederick, & Klausmeier, 1969) and is sometimes referred to as the Frayer method. The major steps of our version of the method as it might be used to teach the concept *perseverance* are shown on the following page.

Frayer Method

1. **Define the concept, giving its attributes.**

   Perseverance is a trait that a person might possess. A person demonstrates *perseverance* when he or she remains constant to some purpose or task over some extended period despite obstacles.

2. **Distinguish between the concept and similar concepts with which it might be confused. When doing this, you may need to point out some of the nonessential features of the new concept that might falsely be considered necessary features.**

   Perseverance differs from *stubbornness* in that *perseverance* is typically seen as a positive quality and the goal toward which one perseveres is typically a worthwhile one. Conversely, *stubbornness* is usually seen as a negative quality, and the goal pursued by a person who is being stubborn is often not a worthwhile one.

3. **Provide examples of the concept and reasons explaining why they are examples.**

   A person who graduates from college despite financial responsibilities that require him or her to work full time while in college would be demonstrating *perseverance* because the goal is worthwhile and it takes a long and steady effort to reach it.

   A person who learns to ski after losing a leg in an accident is demonstrating *perseverance* for similar reasons.

4. **Provide nonexamples of the concept and reasons explaining why they are nonexamples.**

   Someone who goes fishing a lot just because he or she enjoys it is not demonstrating *perseverance* because there is no particular purpose here and no obstacles.

   Someone who waters his or her lawn once a week is not demonstrating *perseverance* because there is no particular challenge in doing so.

5. **Present examples and nonexamples to students. Ask them to identify which are and are not instances of the concept and to explain why. Give them feedback on their responses.**

   - Reading an interesting book that you thoroughly enjoy (nonexample)
   - Completing a canoe trip from the headwaters of the Mississippi to New Orleans (example)
   - Eating a dozen donuts because you are really hungry (nonexample)
   - Completing a three-mile cross-country race even though you were out of breath and dead tired after less than a mile (example)

6. **Ask the students to generate their own examples and nonexamples, let them talk about why they are examples or nonexamples, and give them feedback.**

Using the Frayer method obviously takes a substantial amount of the instructor's time and effort and a substantial amount of the students' time and effort. However, the time and effort expended yield rich rewards. This method provides students with rich understandings of important concepts.

Clarifying and Enriching the Meanings of Known Words

Two of the procedures already described—semantic mapping and the Frayer method—are appropriate for clarifying and extending word meanings as well as for providing in-depth instruction and teaching new concepts. The procedure described here, semantic feature analysis (Pittelman, Heimlich, Berglund, & French, 1991) can also be used to teach in-depth meanings and new concepts. However, it is particularly suited to refining word meanings.

Semantic Feature Analysis

1. Present students with a grid that contains a set of related words on one axis and a list of features that each of the words may or may not have on the other axis. Figure 2.3 shows a typical grid.

2. In their first work with semantic feature analysis, show students a completed grid and discuss how the minuses and pluses show whether or not a particular feature applies to each word.

3. In later work with the procedure, show students grids with the terms and attributes filled in, but without the pluses and minuses, and ask them to insert them.

4. Later still, show grids with some terms and some attributes and ask students to add to both the list of related words and the list of attributes and then to fill in the pluses and minuses.

5. Finally, after students are proficient in working with partially completed grids you supply, have them create their own grids for sets of related words they suggest.

An example illustrating the semantic feature analysis procedure with words describing roads and walkways is shown in Figure 2.3.

TYPICAL CHARACTERISTICS						
Roads and Walkways	Narrow	Wide	Paved	Unpaved	For walking	For driving
Path	+	–	–	+	+	–
Trail	+	–	–	+	+	–
Road	+	+	+	+	–	+
Lane	+	–	+	+	+	+
Boulevard	–	+	+	–	–	+
Freeway	–	+	+	–	–	+
Turnpike	–	+	+	–	–	+

Figure 2.3
Semantic Feature Analysis Grid for Roads and Walkways

Whenever semantic feature analysis is used, there should be a good deal of discussion, for the power of the procedure lies in the discussion. With the above grid, for example, discussion of the fact that *boulevards*, *freeways*, and *turnpikes* share the same features should lead to a discussion of whether additional attributes should be added in order to distinguish among these or if the three terms are synonymous.

Some Inappropriate Techniques for Teaching Vocabulary

We close this section of the chapter on teaching specific words by briefly discussing some inappropriate techniques, some quite common approaches that we do not recommend because they are generally ineffective (see Figure 2.4).

Probably the most frequently used inappropriate technique is that of giving students a list of words out of context and telling them to look up their meanings in the dictionary. Three facts argue against this. First, most words have several meanings and many shades of meaning. Taken out of context, there is no way for students to decide which dictionary definition is most appropriate. Second, unless a learner has some knowledge of a word and its meaning already, dictionary definitions are often inadequate. In general, dictionaries are more useful for students to use in checking on the meaning of a word they think they know than for determining the meaning of a totally unfamiliar word. Finally, asking students to do something does not constitute instruction; before students are asked to look up words in the dictionary, they need to be taught how to do so. Such instruction in described later in this chapter.

Another frequently suggested technique is giving students the words in context and asking them to figure out the words' meanings. This, like the previous technique, is a practice activity rather than an instructional activity; students are being asked to use context, not taught how to use it. Before you ask students to use context to discern word meanings, be sure you teach them how to do so. Teaching students to use

Figure 2.4
Inappropriate Vocabulary
Teaching Techniques

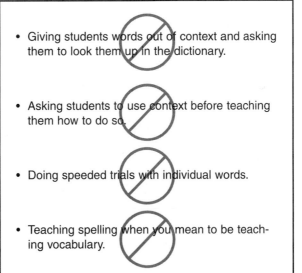

- Giving students words out of context and asking them to look them up in the dictionary.

- Asking students to use context before teaching them how to do so.

- Doing speeded trials with individual words.

- Teaching spelling when you mean to be teaching vocabulary.

context cues is discussed in the next section of this chapter. Also, although context by itself reveals some meaning and is certainly something that students need to learn to use in unlocking word meanings, a single occurrence in context seldom reveals the whole of a word's meaning. Students will usually need rich context and a definition to master a word's full meaning.

Still another frequently suggested technique is doing speeded trials with flash cards or some device that rapidly displays a word. Students need to learn to make rapid and automatic responses to words, but for the most part they learn to do this by repeatedly reading the words in the context of fairly easy and enjoyable reading. Somewhat related to the technique of doing speeded trials is that of having students search letter mazes (rows and columns filled with letters) or anagrams for words. This resembles no realistic reading task and is simply busy work.

Finally, there is the matter of teaching spelling. Learning to spell is something that students certainly need to do. However, teaching spelling and teaching vocabulary are two different tasks. In teaching vocabulary, the task is to teach students the meanings of words they don't know or (but not very frequently in secondary school) to teach students to read words that are already in their oral vocabularies. In teaching spelling, the task is to teach students to spell words they can already read. Therefore, when you teach vocabulary, you are teaching students words that are in one way or another unknown to them. When you teach spelling, you are generally teaching students to spell words they already know; the words students need to know how to spell are those words they actively use in speech and writing. Of course, if you are attempting to move words into students' writing vocabularies, you will need to be sure that students can spell the words.

▼ PRACTICE ACTIVITY 2.4

1. Construct a semantic map for the word *fear* using the categories *Reactions*, *Fearful Places*, *Antonyms*, and *Synonyms*. Our response, which is based on a semantic map presented by Nagy (1988), is shown in the answers section.

2. Create Frayer model material for teaching the concept *textbook*. Your material will look much like the sample of the Frayer method shown on page 47.

▼▼

PREPARING STUDENTS TO LEARN WORDS INDEPENDENTLY

As noted at the beginning of this chapter, students learn something like 3,000 to 4,000 words each year, many more words than could be directly taught. Thus, even if instruction in individual words were as widespread and rich as one could possibly make it, students still need to learn much of their vocabulary independently. In this section we consider three areas in which students need to develop proficiencies that will make them independent word learners: using context, learning and using word parts, and using the dictionary and thesaurus.

Using Context

Most words are learned from context; no other explanation can account for students' learning 3,000 to 4,000 words each year (Sternberg, 1987). At the same time, wrestling a word's meaning from most contexts is often very challenging. Still, it has been estimated that average students might acquire over 1,000 words—roughly one-third of the words learned during the year—from meeting them in the context of their reading (Nagy, Anderson, & Herman, 1987). If students can develop better-than-average skills in learning words from context, they can learn even more words from their reading.

Given the importance of using context, it is useful to help students learn to use context more effectively. In the remainder of this section, we present a plan for introducing the notion of context cues and suggest that you periodically embed brief lessons on context cues when challenging words come up in your content area lessons.

Introducing the Notion of Context Cues

Almost all secondary students have had some instruction in using context cues, and so introducing the notion of context cues generally means reminding students of something they have already had some experience with.

An Introduction/Review of Context Cues

1. **Tell students that they need to become adept at using context cues because most words are learned from context.** Also explain that while most of the time context will not give them a precise definition of a word, it will often give them hints to its meaning.

2. **Tell students that context cues include the words, phrases, and sentences that surround an unknown word.** Point out that context cues can come before or after an unknown word.

3. **Suggest that when they are reading a passage and come to a word they do not immediately know, they should consider the words, phrases, and sentences that surround the word and see if they can deduce enough of the word's meaning to understand its use in the passage.**

4. **Select a few sentences that include difficult words and some informative cues and explain how these cues help reveal the difficult words' meanings.** For example, you could present the sentence, "The defendant was *exonerated* by the judge because there was not enough evidence," and think aloud as follows:

   > Let's see. *Exonerated.* It is something a judge does, and it's something that happens to a defendant. Maybe it means *convicted.* But no, that's not right because the defendant got exonerated because there *wasn't* enough evidence. I think *exonerated* means something like *let off* because when there isn't enough evidence a judge is likely to let the defendant off.

5. **After you have given a few examples, let students find a few examples and explain how the context cues help reveal the meanings of difficult words.**

Further Work with Context

After this introductory lesson, further work with context should come at times when students need to figure out unknown words in their reading and the material contains some revealing context cues. Here again, you might briefly talk through the way context provides cues to one word's meaning, and let students talk through the way it provides cues to a few other words' meanings. These periodic mini-lessons will keep students conscious of the value of context cues and gradually extend their ability to use context to uncover word meanings.

PRACTICE ACTIVITY 2.5

To get some practice in identifying context cues, get together with a colleague, select a text representative of those you and your colleague use in your classes, select a half dozen sentences or sets of sentences that contain difficult words and some cues to their meanings, and discuss the cues and how they suggest the words' meanings.

▼ ▼

Learning and Using Word Parts

Using word parts—prefixes, suffixes, and roots—is another approach that can aid students in learning the thousands of words they need to learn independently. In fact, recent evidence (White, Power, & White, 1989) suggests that by the time they enter junior high and are reading material that contains a large proportion of affixed words, students are likely to learn a very substantial number of words from structural analysis. In this section, we discuss selecting word parts to teach and procedures for teaching them.

Selecting Word Parts to Teach

Because many prefixes and suffixes are very common, most secondary students already know a lot of them, and you certainly do not have time to "teach" students things they already know. For this reason, before you do any instruction with prefixes and suffixes, find out what your students already know about them. Doing so is an easy task. To get an idea of students' knowledge of prefixes, just give students some prefixed words, have them remove the prefixes, and have them define the prefixes. To get an idea of their knowledge of suffixes, give them some words with suffixes, have them remove the suffixes, and have them alter the spelling of the remaining root, if necessary, so that the spelling is correct. Because suffixes generally have grammatical meanings that are very difficult to define and because students typically have tacit knowledge of these grammatical meanings even before they enter school, it is both unnecessary and inappropriate to ask students to define suffixes.

Most Latin and Greek roots are not very common, and most secondary students know very few of them. These include such elements as *audire* meaning "hear," and used in such words as *audience* and *audio*, and *potare* meaning "carry," used in such words as *import* and *portable*. Because most Latin and Greek roots are not very common and because there are many of these elements, the best place to identify those worth teaching is the material students read in your class. Those that appear fairly often are appropriate to teach; others are not. However, if you want to get an idea of the roots that may come up in your materials, Fry, Polk, and Fountoukidis (1993) provide lists of those that tend to be used in various content areas.

Teaching Word Parts

In typical content classes, where there is a limited amount of time and a good deal of material to cover, the following procedure suggested by Moore, Moore, Cunningham, and Cunningham (1994) is quite appropriate. It requires relatively little time and uses words out of your content area. The procedure has four steps.

A Procedure for Teaching Word Parts

1. **Write two familiar words containing the word part on the board or overhead, and have students define them.**
   Suppose you wanted to teach the word *subterranean* and emphasize the prefix *sub-*. Most students know what a *submarine* is and what *subzero* weather is, so these would be appropriate words to use here.

2. **Underline the word part and note its spelling. If the word part is a prefix or a root, point out its meaning to students, or have them give its meaning.**
   Sub-, of course, means below.

3. **Write the word you want to teach in a sentence on the board or overhead.**
   With the word *subterranean*, you might use the sentence, "Stories of *subterranean* creatures, monsters that come to the surface and terrorize entire cities, are fairly common in science fiction literature." Ask students to use their knowledge of *sub-*, the elements that remain when the prefix is removed (in this case, *terra*, a Latin root meaning earth, and *-ean*, a suffix), and the context of the sentence to arrive at a meaning for the word. *Subterranean* means beneath the earth's surface. At this point, it's a good idea to check the meaning in the dictionary, and to caution students that although both word parts and context are useful in identifying word meanings, neither is completely reliable. Thus if one wants to be absolutely certain of a word's meaning, it's necessary to check the dictionary.

4. **Give an example of a word students know in which the letter group just taught does not represent the meaning taught, and caution them that letter groups that look like prefixes, suffixes, or roots are sometimes just groups of letters.**
   The letter group *sub-* does not have the meaning "below" in *substantial*.

▼
PRACTICE ACTIVITY 2.6

This would also be a good point at which to stop and jot down some of the Latin and Greek roots that come up in your subject area. You will probably need to scan one of your textbooks to identify them. Also, you may want to look through a list of Latin and Greek roots such as that provided by Fry, Polk, and Fountoukidis (1993) to suggest some roots to look for. In any case, jot down those you identify and keep them with your notes on this chapter.

▼ ▼

Using the Dictionary and Thesaurus

Students routinely receive some instruction in using the dictionary in elementary school. Elementary schools provide instruction in alphabetizing, in using guide words, in using pronunciation keys, and, perhaps, in choosing meanings appropriate for the context in which one finds a word. However, such instruction does not adequately prepare students to effectively use the second most popular book in the English language (Scott & Nagy, 1997).

Quite possibly the most important thing students need to learn about dictionaries is which dictionaries are appropriate for them. Eighth graders, for example, will generally find that dictionaries intended for junior high students serve them better than college-level dictionaries. Students also need to know the characteristics and features of the particular dictionary they use: what the entries for individual words contain and how they are arranged, what aids to its use the dictionary provides, and what features beyond the basic word list the dictionary includes. Much of the important information appears in the front matter of the dictionary, but it is very seldom read, and simply asking students to read it is hardly sufficient instruction. Thus, direct instruction in how to use specific dictionaries is needed.

One other matter is particularly worth alerting students to because when looking up words they very frequently pick the first definition regardless of the context in which they have found the word. Since many words have more than one meaning, students need to pick a definition appropriate for the context in which the word occurs. If, for example, the word *latitude* is encountered in the sentence, "The judge agreed to give the prosecutor some *latitude* because the witness was being very uncooperative," then the appropriate dictionary definition is "freedom from limitations" and not "position in relation to the equator." Although this appears obvious, it is something that many students seem not to realize. Occasionally taking the time to mentally model the process you go through in choosing a definition appropriate to the context is definitely worthwhile.

Additionally, in today's world, students need to be made aware of computerized dictionaries, sold on their power and ease of use, and taught how to use them. For example, the *American Heritage Electronic Dictionary* (Houghton Mifflin, 1990) contains the complete word set of a pocket dictionary and can be very easily accessed by students as they are writing on a word processor. It provides definitions, pronunciations, parts of speech, and spelling information—in seconds and without leaving the computer. Many students that would all too rarely go to a bookshelf and look up a word will routinely access a computerized dictionary. Even more powerful dictionaries are available on CD-ROM. The *American Heritage Talking Dictionary* (Softkey International, 1994), for example, pronounces words with the click of a mouse, gives very complete information on each entry, and even includes a dictionary of cultural literacy.

Students also need instruction in using the thesaurus. Specific attention to the thesaurus is worthwhile because the thesaurus is used for a somewhat different purpose than is the dictionary. In general, the dictionary is used when a word has already been identified—when you have read it and want to be certain of its meaning or when you are considering using it in writing and want to check its meaning or its spelling. A thesaurus, on the other hand, is much more likely to be used when you are looking for a word to use. A thesaurus is useful when you have something to say but want a new way of saying it. Getting students in the habit of using a thesaurus is a step toward getting them to enlarge their active vocabularies, as well as a step toward getting them interested in words.

As is the case with the dictionary, in today's world, students need to be made aware of, sold on, and taught how to use computerized thesauruses. The *American Heritage Electronic Dictionary* and the *American Heritage Talking Dictionary*, for example, are also thesauruses. Students can identify synonyms for words with a simple keystroke or the click of a mouse. Most word processing programs also contain very useful thesauri. *Microsoft Word* (Microsoft, 1995), for example, comes with an integrated thesaurus that provides a list of synonyms and lets a student automatically replace a word in a text he or she is working on with a selected synonym. As is the case with computerized dictionaries, students who would rarely—possibly never—take a thesaurus off the bookshelf to find a more powerful or more appropriate word to use in their writing will readily use an electronic thesaurus.

PROMOTING WORD CONSCIOUSNESS

Up to this point, we have discussed three approaches to promoting vocabulary development—wide reading, which we discussed briefly but which is an extremely effective approach, and teaching individual words and preparing students to learn words independently, which we described at some length and which are also very effective approaches. Here we add one more approach—promoting word consciousness (Anderson & Nagy, 1992), the ability and proclivity to notice words, to think about them, to value them, and to consciously use them in precise and effective ways. This is another approach we will discuss briefly, but it is an approach that can be extremely effective. As Blackowicz and Fisher (1996, p. 180) point out in discussing the value of word play, "Things we enjoy and view as sources of pleasure stay with us throughout our lives." Promoting word consciousness increases the likelihood of students learning words while reading, makes them more receptive to learning the words you teach, and increases their interest in word-learning strategies such as using context and word parts.

Word consciousness is a disposition toward words that is both cognitive and affective. The student who is word conscious knows a lot of words, knows them well, and is interested in words, and gains enjoyment and satisfaction from using them well and from seeing or hearing them used well by others. The student who is word conscious is also cognizant of the power of words and realizes that they can be used to foster clarity and understanding or to obscure and obfuscate matters. In other words, the goal in promoting word consciousness is "to turn students on to words" (Scott et al., 1994, p. 5).

Promoting word consciousness takes time and is a goal to be striven for throughout the school years, but at the same time, it is an easy thing to do and something that does not take much preparation. Repeatedly demonstrate your interest in words, and give students opportunities to show their interest and to play with words. Each of the five suggestions shown below can arouse students' interest in words and enhance their inclination to build more powerful and precise vocabularies.

Ways of Promoting Word Consciousness

- Occasionally include colorful and perhaps novel words in talking with students.

- Point out particularly adept word choices in the material students are reading.

- Compliment students when they make adroit word choices in their speech or writing.

- Discuss connotations of words, particularly value-laden ones such as the difference between *firm* and *stubborn,* that can help students distinguish between biased and unbiased language.

- Consider bringing in games such as *Scrabble* (Selchow & Righter, 1976) or *Taboo* (Milton Bradley, 1989) and word-play books such as *Sniglets* (Hall, 1985).

Here, for example, are Mr. Tibbets' opening remarks as he hands back a set of short essays in which he asked his AP science students to reflect on why scientists often get so caught up in their work.

Mr. Tibbets: I certainly wasn't surprised, but you know I'm really impressed with the feel that many of you have for science and what it means to many scientists. I'm particularly impressed with some of your diction. Maria, when you wrote that during the *apogee* of his career, science so *invigorated* Einstein that he often needed no sleep for days, it seems to me that both *apogee* and *invigorated* were just the right choices. And, Frank, when you pointed out that the engineers we saw on the video of the first Apollo flight responded almost as one with the word *"beautiful!"* after the successful lift-off and noted that this showed that they actually had an *aesthetic* response to a *technological* achievement, I thought you demonstrated some real insight and chose just the right words to capture it.

CONCLUDING REMARKS

In all, we have listed nine areas in which you can assist students in gaining an increased control of their English vocabulary—promoting wide reading, four sorts of tasks students face in learning specific words, three generative skills that students need if they are to become independent word learners, and promoting word consciousness. In concluding the chapter, we emphasize several points common to all of these tasks.

First, most of the instruction you provide should involve active teaching that includes explicit teacher talk, modeling, giving students opportunities to actively manipulate the ideas and procedures introduced, listening to students' responses, and assisting students in reaching more accurate interpretations when their understanding seems to be wrong or slightly askew.

Second, effective vocabulary instruction requires teachers who themselves appreciate words and the English language more generally, who are knowledgeable about language, and who are precise in their diction and articulate in their speech and writing. Without such teachers, the plan outlined here would be of no value; with such teachers, students can master the English vocabulary and skillfully use their vocabulary knowledge to understand what they read as well as to communicate in speech and writing.

Finally, it needs to be recognized that instruction directed at any of these goals fosters achievement of the others as well. Thus, for example, instruction that teaches students individual words strengthens the likelihood that they will learn other words from context, and teaching students prefixes makes it easier for them to learn and remember individual words employing those prefixes.

REFLECTIONS
▼▼▼

This section provides you with opportunities to reflect on some of the major topics of the chapter, consider how they apply to your content area, and make some decisions about the vocabulary instruction you will include in your classes.

1. A point made early in the chapter was that students need to learn to read a tremendous number of words. Select a chapter, article, or short story typical of the reading students do in your content area, then go through it and identify the words you suspect some of your students won't know.

2. Your search for challenging words is likely to have yielded more words than you have time to teach or need to teach, that is, more than ten or so words. If so,

apply the three criteria we have suggested for selecting words to teach and identify the most important words to teach.

3. Once you have selected the most important words to teach, identify the word-learning task that each word probably represents for your students.

4. Now that you have identified the most important words to teach and the word-learning task or tasks they represent, select a teaching method to use. Note that we say *method* rather than *methods*. Typically you will only use one method in teaching the words for a particular selection. If the method is not appropriate for all of the words you selected to teach, you will need to decide whether to skip some of the words you originally selected or use the method with all of the words even though it is not a perfect match.

5. Consider the three approaches to preparing students to learn words independently; decide which one or two of them best fit with your content area, students, and teaching priorities; then make a commitment to work with your students on those one or two approaches.

REFERENCES
▼▼▼

Anderson, R. C. (1996). Research foundations to support wide reading. In V. Greaney (Ed.) *Promoting reading in developing countries*. Newark, DE: International Reading Association. A very powerful argument and marshaling of evidence for the value of wide reading.

Anderson, R. C., & Freebody, P. (1981). Vocabulary knowledge. In J. Guthrie (Ed.), *Comprehension and teaching: Research reviews*. Newark, DE: International Reading Association. Insightful discussion of the effects of word knowledge on reading comprehension.

Anderson, R. C., & Nagy, W. E. (1992). The vocabulary conundrum. *American Educator*, Winter, 14–18, 44–47. A forceful examination of the instructional implications of the fact that children's vocabularies are very large and grow very rapidly.

Anglin, J. M. (1993). Vocabulary development: A morphological analysis. *Monographs of the Society for Research in Child Development*, 58, (10 serial no. 238). An extremely well-done but technical report on the growth of children's vocabularies.

Baumann, J. F., & Kameenui, E. J. (1991). Research on vocabulary instruction: Ode to Voltaire. In J. Flood, J. M. Jensen, D. Lapp, & J. R. Squire (Eds.), *Handbook of research on teaching to English language arts*. New York: Macmillan. A comprehensive review of research.

Beck, I. L., & McKeown, M. G. (1983). Learning words well. A program to enhance vocabulary and comprehension. *The Reading Teacher*, 36, 622–625. A description of the authors' approach to intensive instruction.

———. (1991). Conditions of vocabulary acquisition. In R. Barr, M. Kamil, P. Mosenthal, & P. D. Pearson, (Eds.), *Handbook of reading research* (Vol. 2). New York: Longman. A definitive review of research.

Beck, I. L., Perfetti, C. A., & McKeown, M. G. (1982). The effects of long-term vocabulary instruction on lexical access and reading comprehension. *Journal of Educational Psychology*, 74, 506–521. Empirical study showing the effects of in-depth instruction.

Blackowicz, C., & Fisher, P. (1996). *Teaching vocabulary in all classrooms*. Columbus, OH: Merrill. A well-conceived and quite comprehensive description of vocabulary instruction.

Bradac, J. J., Bowers, J. W., & Courtright, J. A. (1982). Lexical variations in intensity, immediacy, and diversity: An axiomatic theory and causal model. In R. N. St. Clari & H. Giles (Eds.), *The social and psychological contexts of language*. Hillsdale, NJ: Erlbaum. Demonstrates the effects of vocabulary used on judgments of the author and his or her message.

Dole, J. A., Sloan, C., & Trathen, W. (1995). Teaching vocabulary within the context of literature. *Journal of Reading*, 38, 452–460. Describes and presents evidence for a program training students to identify and learn important words from their reading.

Duin, A. H., & Graves, M. F. (1987). The effects of intensive vocabulary instruction on expository writing. *Reading Research Quarterly*, 22, 311–330. Demonstrates positive effects of vocabulary instruction on students' writing.

Elley, W. B. (1991). Acquiring literacy in a second language: The effects of book-based programs. *Language Learning*, 41, 375–411. Evidence for the positive effects of book floods in various countries.

Frayer, D. A., Frederick, W. D., & Klausmeier, H. J. (1969). *A schema for testing the level of concept mastery*. Working paper no. 16. Madison: Wisconsin Research and Development Center for Cognitive Learning. The original description of the Frayer method for teaching concepts.

Freebody, P., & Anderson, R. C. (1983). Effects on text comprehension of differing proportions and locations of difficult vocabulary. *Journal of Reading Behavior*, 15, 19–40. Empirical study demonstrating the effects of difficult vocabulary in text.

Fry, E. B., Polk, J. K., & Fountoukidis, D. (1993). *The reading teacher's book of lists* (3rd ed.). Englewood Cliffs, NJ: Prentice-Hall. An extremely handy source of word lists and other lists helpful in the classroom.

Graves, M. F. (1992). The elementary vocabulary curriculum: What should it be? In M. J. Dreher & W. H. Slater (Eds.), *Elementary school literacy: Critical issues* (pp. 101–131). Norwood, MA: Christopher-Gordon. A detailed look at the elementary school curriculum.

———. (1994). Vocabulary knowledge. In A. Purves (Ed.), *Encyclopedia of English studies and language arts* (pp. 1246–1248). New York: Scholastic. A brief summary of what we know about word knowledge.

Graves, M. F., & Slater, W. H. (1996). Vocabulary instruction in content areas. In D. Lapp, J. Flood, & N. Farnan (Eds.), *Content area reading and learning: Instructional strategies* (2nd ed.). Needham Heights, MA: Allyn & Bacon. Source of the context-relationship procedure and other approaches to instruction for older students.

Hall, R. (1985). *Sniglets (snig'lit): Any word that doesn't appear in the dictionary, but should*. New York: Collier Books. Entertaining book on words that might have been.

Heimlich, J. E., & Pittelman, S. D. (1986). *Semantic mapping: Classroom applications*. Newark, DE: International Reading Association. Practical guide to this useful procedure.

Klare, G. R. (1984). Readability. In P. D. Pearson (Ed.), *Handbook of reading research*. New York: Longman. A comprehensive review of research.

Moore, D., Moore, S., Cunningham, P., & Cunningham, J. (1994). *Developing readers & writers in the content areas: K-12* (2nd ed.). New York: Longman. Source of our procedure for teaching word parts.

Nagy, W. E. (1988). *Teaching vocabulary to improve reading comprehension*. Urbana, IL: National Council of Teachers of English. Well-thought-out approaches to vocabulary instruction for this purpose.

Nagy, W. E., & Anderson, R. C. (1984). How many words are there in printed school English? *Reading Research Quarterly*, 19, 304–330. Definitive study on this topic.

Nagy, W. E., Anderson, R. C., & Herman, P. A. (1987). Learning word meanings from context during normal reading. *American Educational Research Journal*, 24, 237–270. Source of our estimate of how many words students learn from context.

Nagy, W. E., Herman, P. A., & Anderson, R. C. (1985). Learning words from context. *Reading Research Quarterly*, 20, 233–253. Empirical evidence of learning from context.

Neilsen, L., & Piché, G. L. (1981). The influence of headed nominal complexity and lexical choice on teachers' evaluation of writing. *Research in the Teaching of English*, 15, 65–73. Demonstrates how vocabulary affects teachers' judgments.

Pittelman, S. D., Heimlich, J. E., Berglund, R. L., & French, M. P. (1991). *Semantic feature analysis: Classroom applications*. Newark, DE: International Reading Association. Practical guidelines for this useful approach.

Ryder, R. J. (1985). Student activated vocabulary instruction. *Journal of Reading*, 29, 254–259. Practical guidelines for this useful approach.

Ryder, R. J., Graves, B. B., & Graves, M. F. (1989). *Easy reading: Book series and periodicals for less able readers* (2nd ed.). Newark, DE: International Reading Association. Annotated bibliography of materials for less-able readers.

Scott, J. A., Jones, A., Blackstone, T., Cross, S., Skobel, B., & Hayes, T. (1994). The gift of words: Creating a context for rich language use. Unpublished manuscript, Simon Frazer University, Burnaby, Canada. Description of an innovative program for fostering word consciousness.

Scott, J. A., & Nagy, W. E. (1994). Vocabulary development. In A. Purves (Ed.), *Encyclopedia of English studies and language arts* (pp. 1242–1244). New York: Scholastic. Brief overview of what we know on this topic.

Scott, J. A., & Nagy, W. E. (1997). Understanding the definitions of unfamiliar verbs. *Reading Research Quarterly*, 32, 184–200. Research report revealing some of the tasks involved in understanding definitions.

Stahl, S. A., & Fairbanks, M. M. (1986). The effects of vocabulary instruction: A model-based meta-analysis. *Review of Educational Research*, 56, 72–110. Important and convincing review of research.

Sternberg, R. J. (1987). Most vocabulary is learned from context. In M. G. McKeown & M. E. Curtis (Eds.), *The nature of vocabulary acquisition*. Hillsdale, NJ: Erlbaum. A powerful argument for the importance of context.

White, T. G., Graves, M. F., & Slater, W. H. (1990). Development of recognition and reading vocabularies in diverse sociolinguistic and educational settings. *Journal of Educational Psychology*, 82, 281–290. Empirical study of vocabulary size and growth.

White, T. G, Power, M. A., & White, S. (1989). Morphological analysis: Implications for teaching and understanding vocabulary growth. *Reading Research Quarterly*, 24, 283–304. In-depth study of the role of morphology in vocabulary growth.

White, T. G., Slater, W. H., & Graves, M. F. (1989). Yes/No method of vocabulary assessment: Valid for whom and useful for what? In J. E. Readence & R. S. Baldwin (Eds.) *Cognitive and social perspectives for literacy research and instruction*. Chicago: National Reading Conference. Demonstration of the effectiveness of the yes/no approach.

Comprehension: Preparing Students for Reading and Learning

CHAPTER OVERVIEW

In this chapter we present activities that prepare students for learning, as well as a comprehensive plan for guiding students through activities prior to, during, and following a reading assignment. The first section, "The Structured Reading Lesson," presents the comprehensive plan. The second section, "Planning Prereading Instruction," discusses the factors that need to be addressed as you engage in lesson planning. The third section, "Establishing a Purpose for Reading," discusses ways to have students generate objectives, and the use of teacher- or student-generated summaries. In the final and major section, "Activities to Enhance Background Knowledge," we present a number of instructional strategies that build students' background knowledge.

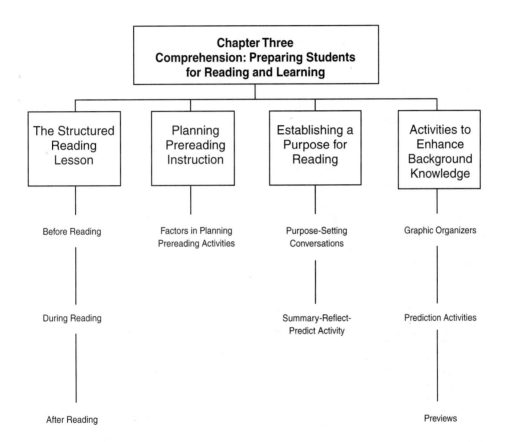

This chapter presents activities that prepare students to learn in the subject matter classroom, as well as a comprehensive plan for pre-, during-, and postreading activities. Chapter 4, "Comprehension: Engaging Students in Reading and Learning," deals with instructional activities and issues to facilitate students' comprehension as they are actively engaged in a reading or learning activity. Chapter 5, "Promoting Critical Thinking and Deep Understanding" addresses the process of promoting higher-level understanding. Consistent with the view of the reading process described in Chapter 1, most of the activities in this chapter stress the importance of allowing students to draw upon their existing knowledge, to engage in activities that allow for cooperative learning and the construction of knowledge, and to provide them the tools for gaining knowledge beyond the memorization of facts.

THE STRUCTURED READING LESSON

By now it should be apparent that learning from text requires much more than the ability to read, memorize information, and recite the details that were learned. As we noted in Chapter 1, proficient readers employ a number of strategies before, during, and after they have read a selection of text. Similarly, the process of assisting students in becoming more proficient readers—readers that gain both a deeper understanding of the process of learning and the content being studied—requires that teachers draw upon instructional activities prior to reading, during reading, and after reading. One useful approach to constructing these activities is application of the structured reading lesson (SRL), a modification of the scaffolded reading experience, which is described in detail elsewhere (Graves & Graves, 1994; Graves, Graves, & Braaten, 1996; Watts & Graves, in press). While most of this chapter deals with activities that prepare students to learn, it is important to note that instructional planning should consider all facets of a lesson. Activities that prepare students for learning should facilitate activities students engage in during and after reading. For example, questions (whether directed by the teacher or generated by the student) addressed during recitations and discussions during and after reading (see Chapter 4) become more relevant and purposeful when students engage in activities prior to reading that either build background knowledge or draw upon and relate to the students' existing knowledge. The SRL provides teachers with a mechanism to plan the scope and sequence of instructional activities to accomplish the stated lesson objectives. The components of the SRL are the following:

Components of SRLs		
Before Reading	**During Reading**	**After Reading**
-Establish a purpose	-Focus attention	-Reflection
-Draw or build upon students' knowledge	-Stimulate discussion	-Engage in higher levels of thinking
-Present vocabulary	-Relate prior knowledge to text information	-Facilitate written and oral summaries
-Build motivation		

Note that the before reading, during reading, and after reading stages of the SRL are mediated by the lesson objectives and by the ongoing assessment of students' learning. The lesson is structured to facilitate lesson objectives, then modified (when necessary) according to how well students perform during the three stages of instruction. This model acknowledges several of the guiding principles of content area reading addressed in Chapter 1. First, the model recognizes that students acquire meaning through the application of strategies, skills, and prior knowledge to the text material. The SRL allows planning based upon the students' need to acquire knowledge—instructional activities are tailored to meet the needs of the student, allowing them to interact with the content of the reading. Second, the SRL provides for the exchange and interpretation of information and knowledge among students who possess different intellects and cultural backgrounds through active learning. The sharing of background knowledge and construction of objectives prior to reading, and the active involvement in discussions during and after reading promotes the exchange of ideas and recognition of the contributions of all students in the class. Third, the SRL allows the teacher to plan activities that are adaptable to the time constraints of the classroom. The prereading activities presented in this chapter, the comprehension activities during and after reading presented in Chapter 4, and the critical thinking activities to promote higher levels of understanding during and after reading presented in Chapter 5 are viable instructional alternatives to directing the reading lesson. The nature of instruction during each of the three stages of the SRL include the following.

Before Reading

Prereading activities are structured to establish a purpose for learning, to instill curiosity and motivation, to draw upon or build background knowledge, and to present vocabulary which may be unfamiliar to students. A purpose for reading is established through activities shared by the teacher and students. Two of these types of activities—purpose-setting conversations and summary-reflect-predict—are presented in a later section in this chapter.

Curiosity and motivation are essential elements in keeping the students' attention and maintaining a positive classroom environment. Students are more likely to become curious and motivated when they become active participants in the learning process, when they are provided reasonable purposes to learn, and when the instruction is seen as relevant. Most of the activities presented in this chapter can increase the students' motivation and stimulate their curiosity. The success of these activities, however, is dependent upon the teacher's awareness of the students' needs and interests and the teacher's ability to display a sense of enthusiasm for the content and the shared learning process.

Building and drawing upon the students' backgrounds is a primary goal of prereading instruction, and its importance is noted throughout this book. Many of the activities discussed throughout this chapter were designed for this purpose. In preparation for these activities, it is important to consider the concepts and ideas required to meet stated objectives, whether this information is adequately addressed in the reading, and then to consider ways to draw upon the students' background knowledge that may contribute to an understanding of this information.

Finally, prereading activities can be designed to teach students vocabulary essential to acquiring an understanding of the reading selection. Specific procedures for selecting words to teach and strategies for vocabulary instruction are discussed in detail in Chapter 2.

During Reading

During-reading activities are structured to focus the students' attention on lesson objectives, to stimulate discussion centered around lesson objectives, and to relate prior knowledge to information in the text. Typically, students' attention is directed to lesson objectives through questioning. This can take the form of questioning by the teacher to the students, questioning by the students to the teacher, or by students questioning themselves. Questions focus on information, point out relationships in the information, and draw upon background knowledge and text information to engage students in critical thinking. Preparation for questioning activities requires an understanding of the goals and limitation of questions, and the types of questions that can be presented to students. Questions can also draw the students' attention to various types of text structures as they read. A thorough discussion of ways to construct, present, and engage students in questioning activities is presented in Chapter 5.

After Reading

After-reading information and ideas obtained during reading are used to reflect upon the meaning of the text, to engage students in higher levels of thinking that go beyond surface-level information, and to facilitate written and oral summaries of what was learned. Again, many of these activities involve questioning through recitation and discussion. These questions often tend to cover more content than during reading questions, to require the learner to understand relationships between ideas, to apply text information to other contexts, or to engage in critical thinking activities where they are allowed to construct their own meaning from a reading selection. After-reading questions can be used to assess the students' understanding. When gaps in the students' understanding are apparent, it may be necessary to restructure questions to redirect the students' attention to information that was not understood or to provide the students with supplemental sources of information in the form of readings, visuals, demonstrations, or teacher-led discussions. Activities to extend understanding through teacher-directed questions or self-questioning are presented in Chapter 4. Guidelines and activities to engage students in critical thinking are presented in Chapter 5.

Here is an example of an SRL for a social studies unit dealing with minority groups.

Lesson Objectives:

1. Students will understand the definitional characteristics of racial minorities.
2. Students will understand the definitional characteristics of ethnic minorities.
3. Students will understand how racial and ethnic minorities have difficulty assimilating into the dominant groups in a culture.

Prereading Activities:

1. The teacher determines that an anticipation guide (discussed in detail later in this chapter) will serve to motivate students, draw upon their background knowledge, and provide an informal assessment of the students' knowledge of the lesson objectives. Each student is asked to read

the following statements, then indicate whether they agree or disagree with each of them.

Anticipation Guide

Agree   Disagree

_____   _____   All students in this class have the same body structure.

_____   _____   All students in this class speak only one language.

_____   _____   All students in this class belong to the same religion and practice the same customs during holidays or other special occasions.

_____   _____   It is not uncommon to refrain from social contact with people who have different customs.

_____   _____   It is not uncommon for those in the majority to ostracize those that might hold views different than their own.

Once students have completed the anticipation guide, the teacher reads each statement, tallies the students' responses, then discusses with the students their justification for the responses for each item.

2. The teacher now presents a concept map (see Figure 3.1) that previews the major concepts in the lesson. As the concept map is presented, the teacher continually seeks to clarify information presented in the map and to add information to the map that is obtained from the students during the discussion.

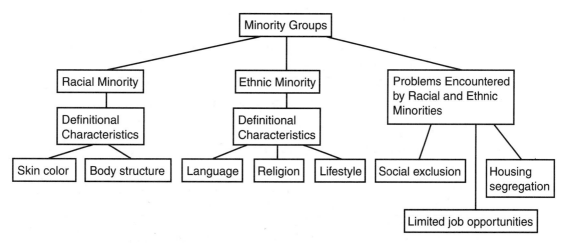

Figure 3.1
Sample Concept Map

During-Reading Activities:

1. **Prequestions**—The teacher asks students to read the text selection on ethnic and racial minorities in order to answer the following questions:
   - ▼ What are some of the characteristics of racial and ethnic minorities?
   - ▼ What are the differences between racial and ethnic minorities?
   - ▼ What is the dominant group? How is the dominant group different than the minority group?

   As students read the text selection, each of the above questions are answered. Once they have completed the reading, the whole class discusses each question.

2. **Relate prior knowledge**—Students are now asked to work in cooperative groups to answer the following questions:
   - ▼ What are some of the racial and ethnic minorities in our area?
   - ▼ Examine some of the neighborhoods in the city or town where you live to determine where ethnic and racial minorities live or go to school. Have these groups been assimilated?
   - ▼ Examine groups of students in this class that tend to socialize with one another. Define any characteristics of their physical appearance that are similar (they way they dress, how they style their hair, etc.).

After Reading Activities:

1. **Critical thinking**—Students are asked to use the information they acquired from the reading and class discussion to respond to the following question:
   - ▼ Obtain articles on civil rights legislation during the past twenty years from the library. Use this information to predict what sorts of legislation will be passed over the next five years that would lessen the economic and social consequences experienced by racial and ethnic minorities.

2. **Reflective writing**—The teacher asks students to reflect upon the information they have learned about ethnic and racial minorities, then write a summary of that information by addressing each of the following topics:
   - ▼ What are the characteristics of racial and ethnic minorities?
   - ▼ What are the effects of being a member of one of these minorities?
   - ▼ What is the dominant group, and how does this group influence the lives of those that belong to a racial or ethnic minority?

The SRL is a tool for planning experiences that prepare students for learning, engage them in the content of the lesson, and allow them to reflect upon or extend their understanding. By structuring each aspect of the lesson in a manner that integrates the students' knowledge, information contained in the text, and the teacher's instruction, students should acquire a better understanding of the content and the process to learn new information and construct meaning.

This section has presented some of the factors involved in planning prereading activities. No doubt dealing with these factors presents a rather formidable challenge. For teachers who may be unfamiliar with the content of a particular class or grade level, the students' background knowledge, or expectations of what the students should learn, planning will require some additional effort. However, attention to these factors should allow the teacher to become more familiar with instructional materials and the students' readiness to learn.

PLANNING PREREADING INSTRUCTION

Selection and application of prereading activities is an important element of an overall instructional approach for a body of content. Careful lesson planning will increase the likelihood that an activity is successful, that students have a positive learning experience, and that lesson objectives are accomplished. Attention should be directed to each of the following: (1) the nature of the content presented, (2) the students' prior knowledge, (3) the learning objectives, and (4) the available time and resources. Note from Figure 3.2 that these are not isolated factors. Attention to one factor impacts on others. Note, for example, that the number of lesson objectives depends on the time available for instruction and the extent that the structure of the text and the students'

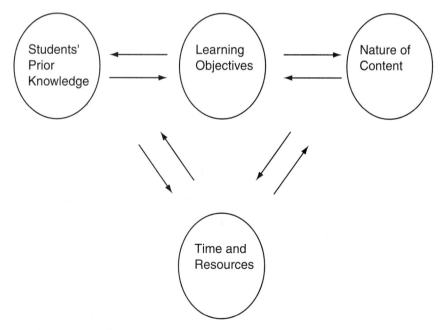

Figure 3.2
Planning Prereading Activities

prior knowledge facilitates those objectives. Following is a brief description of these factors and how they may be used in planning for prereading activities.

Factors in Planning Prereading Activities

Nature of Content Presented.   There are two considerations here. One deals with the structure and content of the text. The other deals with the match between the content of the text and your instructional goals. First, a number of factors related to text structure and lesson content can be examined. Examining new vocabulary, sentence length and structure, the coherence of information and concepts, and the length or depth of the presentation of information will provide a good estimate of the text's difficulty (these factors are discussed in greater detail in Chapter 9). Second, examining the content of the selection will help determine if the content is consistent with instructional goals. If, for example, an art teacher defines an instructional goal that includes the students' ability to understand and apply techniques for shaping a clay sculpture, but the selection examined primarily contains information on the properties of clay, then a mismatch exists between instructional goals and text content. When a mismatch exists, consider an alternate selection or teach the information absent from the selection to students directly.

Students' Prior Knowledge.   As noted throughout this book, the students' prior knowledge plays an integral role in learning. There are times when the students' lack of prior knowledge will interfere with their ability to learn. In this case the teacher may want to select prereading activities that teach this requisite information. At other times, students may possess adequate prior knowledge, but they may be unable to apply this knowledge to reach higher levels of understanding. Knowing the nature of the students' prior knowledge will help you determine which prereading activities are most suitable for lesson objectives.

There are several practical techniques to assess the students' background knowledge. One is to ask students if they know the concepts, facts, or vocabulary essential to understanding a given selection. Constructing this form of prior knowledge assessment is a straightforward task. First, the teacher lists the concepts, facts, or vocabulary he or she believes students should know. Next, this list is presented to students with the directions to examine each item, and respond if they know or don't know its meaning. An example of this form of assessment is depicted in Figure 3.3.

A second technique is to conduct an informal assessment through classroom discussion. One such approach, the prereading plan (PreP) (Langer, 1982), includes a procedure for assessing the students' understanding of text concepts, and steps to enhance prior knowledge. This approach begins with the teacher identifying three to five concepts in the text. Next, each concept is presented in the form of a word, phrase, or picture to determine the students' initial association with the concept:

▼   **In English:** What do you think of when you see the word *conflict*?

▼   **In Physical Education:** What do you think of when you hear the word *hyperventilation*?

▼   **In Vocal Music:** What comes to mind when you think about *harmony*?

Directions: *Examine each of the following words or phrases, then respond whether you know or don't know the meaning of the word or phrase.*

	Know	Don't Know
Presidential government	_____	_____
Party systems	_____	_____
Parliamentary government	_____	_____
Separation of powers	_____	_____
Plurality	_____	_____
Coalition	_____	_____

Figure 3.3
Example of Prior Knowledge Assessment: Social Studies Lesson on Forms of Government

Following the association activity, the teacher asks the students to reflect on their associations.

▼ **In English:** Why do you say that conflict is what happens when people get angry with one another, Marie?

Marie: Well, it seems that you can tell if something was a conflict after it happens. Usually, if people are very angry, then it's a conflict.

▼ **In Vocal Music:** Toni and Tyronne, you indicated that harmony is when people sing in a way that is pleasant, is on key, and is at the right pitch. Why is that important in vocal music? How do you feel when something is not in harmony?

Toni: It isn't that easy to be in harmony. Sometimes you really have to listen to the other person and then change your pitch based on their voice. Practice is really important if you want to be in harmony.

Tyronne: Bad harmony is bad music. Not that many people sing in harmony anymore. I'm not sure why. If you don't sing in harmony, people won't care to listen to you.

In the final step of the PreP, the teacher prepares students for the reading by developing the students' background knowledge.

▼ **In Vocal Music:** Today we are going to learn about what is called functional harmony. In this type of harmony all chords are related to one of the three basic chords of a key. This type of harmony was abandoned by many composers in the early 1900s in favor of different forms of harmony that we will examine later. Once I have provided you some examples of functional harmony, we will listen to some music written in the 1800s that makes use of functional harmony, then we will produce and sing our own lyrics that make use of functional harmony.

A PreP can be a practical and efficient way to assess the students' prior knowledge. Care must be exercised, however, in drawing generalizations solely from classroom dialogue. Frequently, students have a grasp of concepts, but experience difficulty expressing themselves in language that is readily understood by adults. This potential problem can be addressed by probing the students' understanding with questions requiring them to provide examples or elaborate and justify a response.

Learning Objectives   Learning objectives define the outcomes or products of instruction. Constructing objectives is central to successful prereading activities. Effective teachers have a firm grasp on what they want students to learn, and communicate these objectives to students before instruction is initiated (Rosenshine, Meister, & Chapman, 1996). However, for too many teachers, planning tends to be limited to identifying activities that will be presented to students. These teachers have failed to first define learning outcomes, then develop activities that will facilitate those outcomes (Clark & Yinger, 1980). Beginning teachers are likely to remove themselves from planning altogether, relying instead on published curriculum materials as their planning guide (Clark & Peterson, 1986). Instructional planning should begin with a clear definition of lesson objectives. Whether these objectives are selected from an external source (a textbook, a curriculum guide, etc.) or you select them, they should be tailored to meet the needs of your students and be presented in a form that is informative and purposeful.

One form of communicating objectives is the central question (Anderson & Roth, 1989). Figure 3.4 presents examples of central questions from a variety of

---

High School Biology

How are the circulatory systems of species that have a rapid rate of movement (such as a jaguar or hummingbird) different from species that have a low rate of movement (such as an armadillo or opossum)?

Middle School Home Economics

What are the long-term health benefits of following a balanced diet?

High School English

Why do writers of fiction often reflect the political and social events of their time in their writings?

Middle School Art

Why is clay a good medium for the beginning stages of learning to sculpt?

High School Physical Education

Which sports are good for lifelong activities? What are the advantages of playing these sports?

Figure 3.4
Examples of Central Question Objectives

subject matter areas. Central questions are intended to communicate what students will learn, arouse prior knowledge, and stimulate discussion. Additionally they establish a purpose for reading—directing student's attention to selected content as they read. Regardless of the form used to describe lesson objectives, recognize that it may be necessary to modify or abandon those objectives during the course of a lesson as students' progress is assessed and additional strengths and needs become apparent.

Available Time and Resources   A common refrain voiced by teachers is the lack of instructional time to cover the prescribed content over the course of a year. There is little doubt that subject matter curriculums have the tendency to expand over time; each year it seems there is more content to teach. Textbooks are more lengthy, and greater amounts of time are needed for curricular issues that are integrated within all subject matter areas. With less time available for instruction, priorities must be assigned to instructional objectives. There are numerous ways to reduce instructional time. An alternate text, use of supplemental resources (such as films, videotapes, trade books, periodicals), or demonstrations may take less instructional time than reliance upon a single textbook. In other instances, the amount of reading the students engage in can be reduced by directing them to read selectively. Or it may be advisable to assign specific topics to groups of students, who then summarize and present their information to the entire class. Finally, as noted, generating lesson objectives tailored to your students will reduce instructional time. Rather than reading an entire chapter, for example, students may read only those sections or pages related to your objectives.

▼ PRACTICE ACTIVITY 3.1

Consider the following scenario describing the experience of a first-year teacher. After you have read the scenario, respond to the question provided.

> Jake was in his third month of teaching a middle school science class and was becoming increasingly frustrated with the level of learning that was occurring in his classroom. He decided to seek the help of a more seasoned teacher in an effort to improve the quality of his instruction. Asked to describe how he went about planning and administering a lesson, Jake indicated that he would first consult the district's curriculum guide to determine what he should be teaching. Next, he would locate that content in one of the district's science textbooks. He would then read the material, construct study guides for the readings that were provided to the students, and construct a demonstration that he would present to the students in class that addressed the content studied. When the seasoned teacher inquired as to how he would prepare students for a session or how he would motivate them to learn the content, Jake responded that his preparation usually entailed reading key components of the text

aloud to the students. Motivation, according to Jake, came from his use of a study guide.

As you reflect on this scenario, refer to the factors for planning prereading instruction discussed in the section of this chapter you just finished reading. Using these factors, what could Jake do to improve his instruction?

▼▼

ESTABLISHING A PURPOSE FOR READING

Constructing a purpose for daily learning tasks is a routine activity in our lives. Knowing what we want to learn allows us to focus on what we need to know and what experiences and knowledge we can draw from our own experiences that will assist us in the task. For students, learning is not always so purposeful. Many students assume that all information in a reading selection is of equal importance and they attempt to commit everything to memory. Discussing with students what they will learn, and why they will learn it, will help them acquire an understanding that reading should be selective and purposeful. Defining objectives need not be directed exclusively by the teacher. Eventually students can actively engage in activities that define purposes for reading. This section contains two procedures for generating objectives in collaboration with your students. Both define objectives through a prereading activity that engages students in the lesson content.

Purpose-Setting Conversations

Purpose-setting conversations are designed to facilitate the students' ability to generate purpose-setting questions from global objectives established by the teacher. This process consists of the following four steps:

STEPS TO PURPOSE-SETTING CONVERSATIONS

1. Teacher presents central objective.

2. Students skim material to answer central objective.

3. Clarify purpose through class conversation.

4. Generate purpose-setting questions or tasks.

Purpose-setting conversations begin with the teacher defining lesson objectives in the form of questions. In the next step, students are asked to skim the selection to generate responses to the questions. As part of an interdisciplinary lesson dealing with basic economic concepts, for example, one of us observed a middle school mathematics teacher introduce the lesson with a central question objective,

"How can statistical measures be used in running a retail business?" Working in cooperative groups, students skimmed a chapter containing a description of the concepts of means and weighted averages, then generated a response to the central question. In the third step, the teacher engaged the class in the following conversation to clarify and refine objectives:

Teacher: Imagine for a moment that you own a small business such as a pizza place, or a small computer store, or maybe an audio CD store. What are some of the ways that you might need to use statistics?

Julius: We thought that means could be used to figure out which days are busy or slow. That is, you can look at the mean daily sales over a month, then look at which days are above or below that mean.

Teacher: That is an interesting idea. That procedure certainly would be a good use of the mean and would help the owner identify high-volume days. What are some other ways we can use statistics?

Anita: We thought that weighted averages could be used to determine peoples' wages.

Teacher: Can you tell me how you would use weighted averages to determine wages?

Anita: Well, we thought that you could take the wages of people that worked, say, five years, four years, three years, two years, and one year to figure out how people that worked longer were making more money.

Teacher: That is an interesting approach. It does require the use of statistics in running a retail business. What did your group come up with Kim?

Kim: We thought we could use the mean to find out how much money we made.

Teacher: How would you do that? Tell me how you could use the mean to calculate profits.

Kim: Well, we would add up all the money we took in, then subtract how much we paid for the products and that would give us the profit.

Teacher: That would give you a rough idea of profits. Are there other things that you must consider when determining profits?

Kim: No, I don't think so.

Teacher: How did you use the mean to figure out the profit? Just to refresh your memory, the mean is like a mathematical average. Why don't you and your group take a few moments to talk about how you might be able to use the mean in calculating profits.

Note that this step of purpose-setting conversation allows an informal assessment of the students' understanding of text concepts and their background knowledge. Kim's group, for example, displayed an apparent lack of understanding of the concept of a mean (the group was not able to clarify its meaning after a second effort) and limited background knowledge of the various costs of operating a business. At this point the teacher may clarify misconceptions, fill in gaps in the students' background knowledge, or consider modifying the initial objectives in light of the student feedback.

In the final step of purpose-setting conversation, the teacher and students engage in a dialogue to construct purposeful questions or activities that will direct their reading. These questions should acknowledge the stated central question objective, although they may not be limited to the information in the reading. Students may find, for example, the need to use supplemental readings or other information resources to answer their questions. The product of this step for the mathematics class discussed above was an activity centered around the creation and maintenance of a popcorn stand designed to allow students to work directly with the various elements of running a retail business, then applying the concepts of mean and weighted averages. As they engaged in this activity, students were asked to respond to the purpose-setting questions that were generated through the teacher-student dialogue.

Purpose-setting conversations have the advantage of allowing students to understand the gist of the lesson content before reading by directing their attention to global objectives presented by the teacher. The teacher, therefore, maintains some control of the lesson content, but students tailor that content by shaping questions that reflect their interest and background knowledge. The conversational dialogue provides an informal assessment of the students' background knowledge and their understanding of the text they examined. Information obtained from the conversational dialogue can then be used to structure additional prereading activities.

Summary-Reflect-Predict Activity

A second procedure to establish a purpose for learning is the summary-reflect-predict (SRP) activity. The first step of this three-stage process begins with the teacher presenting a brief summary of the reading assignment. This synopsis contains the main ideas or themes of the reading and, where possible, should attempt to relate that information to the students' background knowledge.

In the second step of the SRP activity, students reflect on the summary, then respond to the following questions:

---

1. What do I know about the concepts presented here?
2. Why is this information important?
3. What don't I understand?
4. What more do I need to know?

Finally, students are asked to generate questions they believe could be answered from reading the material that has been summarized. The students and teacher then discuss these questions with the goal of selecting those that might best serve the interests and needs of the students. An example of an SRP activity for an English lesson introducing science fiction is presented in Figure 3.5.

As with the purpose-setting conversations, the SRP activity provides an informal assessment of the students' background knowledge and allows for an interchange of ideas and the testing of predictions with the teacher. The structured ques-

Step 1. The teacher presents the following summary.

Science fiction is a type of imaginative literature. Themes of this genre address topics such as space exploration, travel in the third dimension, and futuristic or amazing inventions. In science fiction, most themes are not fantasy. Generally the themes can be supported from accepted theory or scientific practice. The beginnings of science fiction can be traced as far back as prehistoric myths, although modern science fiction began in the 1600s. Science fiction has been popularized in the last twenty years through such films as *Star Wars* and *E.T.* and through a wealth of paperbacks that fill the bookstores.

Step 2. Students are asked to answer the following questions.

1. What experience do you have reading or viewing science fiction?
   (an example of "What do I know about the concepts presented here?")

2. Why do you think science fiction might be an important type of literature?
   (an example of "Why is this information important?")

3. From what you know from the summary, what don't you understand about science fiction?
   (an example of "What don't I understand?")

4. What additional things do you think would be important to know about science fiction?
   (an example of "What more do I need to know?")

Step 3. Students are asked to respond to the following question.

From what we have learned about science fiction, what questions should we be able to answer when we finish reading this selection that addresses the nature and development of science fiction?

Figure 3.5
Example of an SRP Activity

tions set a purpose for reading and the summaries provide essential background information and a structure for examining the content as it relates to the students' interests and experiences. One dilemma with this activity is the students' tendency to generate purpose-setting questions removed from defined lesson objectives. Students will generate numerous creative and thought-provoking questions. And while it is tempting to recognize their efforts, the lack of instructional time will not permit questions that direct students away from essential concepts.

The purpose-setting activities presented in this section recognize the importance of actively involving students in establishing learning objectives. These activities provide insight into the students' understanding of the lesson content and their ability to formulate questions or activities that will direct their learning. Finally, the information students obtain from summaries, question generating, and conversations will enrich their background knowledge and increase their understanding of the lesson content.

ACTIVITIES TO ENHANCE BACKGROUND KNOWLEDGE

This section presents a variety of strategies designed to increase the students' background knowledge. These activities have been divided into three groups: graphic organizers, prediction activities, and previews. Each are forms of advance organizers, a general approach for the improvement of the students' understanding of subject matter material. Advance organizers were originally conceived as a means to link new information to that already known by the learner by providing a based on which more detailed information can be added (Ausubel, 1968). More recently it has been suggested that advance organizers can be used to activate relevant schemata for the material to be learned and to modify schemata on the basis of the new information presented (Mayer, 1984). It should be emphasized that the types of advance organizers we describe here are those that will teach students content and that they can be created by students as they engage in independent learning.

Graphic Organizers

Graphic organizers are pictorial representations of hierarchical relationships between facts and concepts (Barron, 1979). Generally they are presented prior to the presentation of new information. Three types of graphic organizers presented here are frames, concept maps, and the list, group, label activity.

Frames

A frame is a grid, matrix, or framework that represents knowledge (West, Farmer, & Wolff, 1991). Its purpose is to display the organization of information in the form of a matrix where main ideas are depicted in both rows and columns. An example of a two-dimensional frame is shown in Figure 3.6.

Frames show relationships between main ideas, identified in the columns and rows, and information, which is represented in the boxes or slots. In the circulatory frame (Figure 3.7), the columns identify components and the rows identify their function, location, and size. In the box displaying the function of the aorta, one might insert "the major conduit moving blood from the heart to the body" or "the main transporter of blood from the heart."

	DAIRY PRODUCTS	FRUITS AND VEGETABLES	MEATS
CALCIUM	Milk Yogurt	Dark leafy vegetables	Canned fish
IRON	None or little in dairy products	Leafy greens	Organ meats Fish

Figure 3.6
Two-Dimensional Frame for Sources of Nutrients

Figure 3.7
Matrix Frame of the Circulatory System

	Veins	Arteries	Capillaries
Function			
Location			
Size			

Frames can be constructed using the following steps, which we have adapted from those identified by West, Farmer, and Wolff (1991).

1. **Identify the major ideas, concepts, and principles in the selection.** Note and list topics, transition statements, introductions, and summaries.

2. **Once the text material has been identified, determine if it lends itself to the *matrix frame* (Figure 3.7), the *goal frame* (Figure 3.8), or the *problem-solution frame* (Figure 3.9).** Matrix frames are particularly suited for information that displays comparison/contrast, simple cause/effect relationships, form/function, or advantage/disadvantage. Goal frames are useful for displaying organizational structures of material that display linear relationships in the form of goal-plans-actions-outcomes (Armbruster & Anderson, 1984). These frames are useful for narrative and expository text that contains information presented in a temporal or sequential order. Finally, problem-solution frames are effective when a problem or issue is identified, an action is taken to address that issue, and there is a resolution or consequence of that action.

3. **The final step is to draw the frame by creating and labeling the rows and columns.** Most often characteristics or relationships are identified in the column; topics, main ideas, or concepts are identified in the rows.

How the frame is used depends upon your purpose and the level of background knowledge of your students. Initially the frame should contain labels for the columns and rows. Students actively involve themselves in examining and manipulating information to be placed in the boxes or slots. If students are not familiar with the concepts, information, or vocabulary that is placed in the slots, then you may consider providing a

	Problem	Action	Results
Cuban Missile Crisis (1962)			
Iraqi Invasion of Kuwait (1990)			

Figure 3.8
Goal Frame of Military Crises

	Development	Products of Storm	Season in Which They Occur
Hurricanes			
Blizzards			
Thunderstorms			

Figure 3.9
Frame Activity on Types of Storms

brief explanation of that information, listing it in random order, then asking students to place it in the appropriate slots. An example of this application of the frame is provided in Figure 3.9. Using the information from the list, fill in the slots of the frame to get a feel for this activity.

Another application of the frame is to structure information presented in previews or demonstrations. Here students are provided a frame displaying labels for the columns and rows. As information is presented in the form of an oral summary, demonstration, or discussion, students examine the labels, then note the information in the appropriate slot.

Finally, frames are an effective way of improving students' writing (Armbruster, Anderson, & Ostertag, 1987). As a writing strategy, the frame provides an excellent tool to organize and structure information. Written summaries generated from the content of the frame allow students to reflect upon the content of the frame, to elaborate on its application, and to note relationships or draw distinctions between concepts and information. Here is a paragraph summary composed by a ninth grader using the frame presented in Figure 3.9.

> Thunderstorms, blizzards, and hurricanes are all forms of severe weather. Thunderstorms, which develop from the rapid development of clouds during the hot, humid weather of summer, produce high winds, widespread lightning, and heavy rain. Blizzards are winter storms that develop from large low-pressure systems and the clash between very cold air and air that carries moisture. Blizzards produce strong winds, cold temperatures, and snow. Hurricanes, in the U.S., are large storms that develop out of the equator during the fall. These storms produce high winds and waves, and heavy rain.

Concept Maps

Concept maps are graphic displays of concepts and the relationship or links between those concepts (West, Farmer, & Wolff, 1991). Generally, information presented in concept maps proceeds in a hierarchical manner from the more general (superordinate) to the more specific (subordinate). Common types of concept maps include the structured overview (Barron, 1969), semantic webs (Heimlich & Pittleman, 1986), and information mapping (McAleese, 1986). An example of a concept map is given in Figure 3.10.

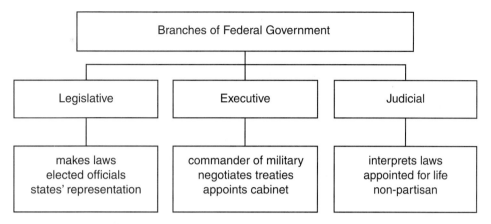

Figure 3.10
Concept Map on Branches of Government

There are several notable features to the concept map presented in this example. First, conceptual linkages are clearly established through the use of lines and arrows. Second, a variety of graphic forms are used to set off information at coordinate, superordinate, and subordinate levels. Finally, the overall organization of the map presents a structured (in this case proceeding in a hierarchical manner) pictorial presentation that can be accommodated both visually and conceptually. Here are the steps in the construction and presentation of the concept map.

1. **Identify the most important concepts in the material.** Constructing a concept map begins with a thorough reading of the material to be presented to the students. As you read, note concepts (a class label for objects or events that share certain characteristics) and words or phrases that show information that can be linked to the selected concepts. Concept maps are not outlines, *only concepts and information that are important to your lesson objectives should be noted*. Identifying concepts can be a difficult task when using a poorly written text that embeds concepts and related information, and contains excessive amounts of irrelevant information. It may be useful, therefore, for the teacher to draw upon his or her background knowledge to identify and include concepts that may not be clearly identified in the reading selection. If the content is not familiar, the teacher should consider examining several selections that address the selected topic.

2. **Organize concepts and identify linkages.** Begin by creating a title that is descriptive of the map's content. A well-written title can stimulate curiosity, focus attention, and generate associations and predictions from prior knowledge. Presume you are sitting in an auditorium about to hear a presentation from an entomologist. Take a moment to reflect on the title "Insects." What do you associate with this term? Does the title pique your curiosity? Does it inform you of the content you might learn? Now consider the title "Insects That are Dangerous to Your Health and How to Avoid Them." Most likely your associations are now narrowed, your curiosity is somewhat heightened, and you have a good sense of the content of the entomologist's presentation.

Once an appropriate title is constructed, the lesson's concepts can be organized according to whether they are superordinate, subordinate, or coordinate. Initially, place each concept on a slip of paper, place the slips of paper on a large flat surface, then, proceeding from the title, arrange the slips of paper to display a hierarchical arrangement. Finally, information that is linked to the concepts is identified and placed under the conceptual label.

3. Refinement and Elaboration. The final step in constructing concept maps involves attention to factors that will refine and enhance their structure and appearance. First, keep the amount of information presented in the map to a minimum. The effect of a map containing excessive information is shown in Figure 3.11. By reducing the amount of information presented (Example B), the map is more clearly organized and easier to understand. If the amount of information displayed in a map cannot be reduced, you may find it necessary to restructure concepts so that they are displayed in separate maps (Example C). Second, where possible, assign distinct graphic symbols to the coordinate, superordinate, and subordinate information. Shapes or forms are more likely to draw the students' attention to key conceptual categories and distinguish those categories from others representing different conceptual relationships. Finally, provide some additional space on your map to accommodate information presented by your students. Most teachers find that maps are most effective when both students and the teacher contribute to their construction.

Constructing concept maps at first can be relatively time consuming, and you may find that your final product requires some amount of modification after it is presented and discussed with your students. For those unacquainted with cognitive maps, the majority of preparation time is often directed at learning the material and identifying concepts related to lesson objectives. Over time, as teachers become more familiar with their reading selections and lesson objectives become more refined, concept maps can be constructed spontaneously during classroom instruction.

Presentation of the Concept Map   The following steps should be used when presenting a concept map to your students

1. Introduce the Map. Begin with a clear description of the title of the concept map, a description of the purpose of the map, and a brief explanation of how the map can be used as a learning tool. Next, describe each concept and related information as the map is presented on an overhead or on the chalkboard. If the map is displayed on a transparency, consider displaying the concepts one at a time by covering the transparency with a sheet of paper that is gradually moved down as you discuss each concept. This technique reduces the amount of visual information and focuses attention on the concepts as they are presented.

2. Student Elaboration. As we noted earlier, concept maps are more effective when students become actively involved in their construction. Sharing their knowledge adds to the relevance of the map and heightens the students' attention and motivation to learn. The products of the students' efforts also provide insight into their understanding of the lesson's content and provide you the opportunity to clarify any misconceptions and to evaluate the students' familiarity with the map's content.

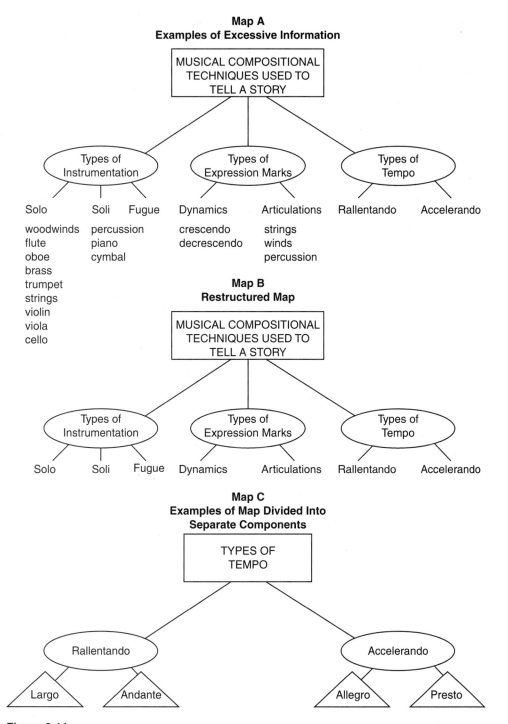

Figure 3.11
Examples of Organization of Concept Maps

Once the entire map has been displayed and discussed, encourage students to examine each concept and identify information from their background knowledge they can add to the conceptual linkages.

3. Follow-up. Instructional applications of maps extend beyond their use as tools to introduce important concepts and information. During reading, they can be used as study guides. As they encounter concepts in the text, students can refer to completed maps to seek clarification, or they may use the map as a note-taking device to highlight additional content or elaborate on concepts already presented.

Concept maps are powerful tools to help students locate, select, sequence, integrate, and restructure information (Jones, Palincsar, Ogle, & Carr, 1987). Their uses prior to reading include establishing lesson objectives, drawing upon students' prior knowledge, and acquainting students with essential concepts and information contained in the reading. Initially, concept maps may seem to be quite similar to traditional outlining. While both are structured representations of concepts that may be hierarchical and linear, there are important distinctions between the two. Maps allow for inclusion of information beyond that found in a reading because students and the teacher are encouraged to add information from their background knowledge. Furthermore, maps are more visual than traditional outlines. They display multiple and coordinating relationships, often through the use of graphic symbols.

Finally, the use of maps is not limited to prereading activities. Maps have also been found to be effective learning tools when constructed by students during or after the study of subject matter selections (Bean, Singer, Sorter, & Frazee, 1986; Boothby & Alvermann, 1984; Hawk, 1986; Holley & Dansereau, 1984). Following a reading, a discussion, a demonstration, or a visual presentation such as a film, the map is a useful tool to organize and review important information.

▼ PRACTICE ACTIVITY 3.2

Listed below are a number of concepts and pieces of information for a map entitled "The Effects of Oil Spills on Society." Take a moment to place the following concepts and information, which are arranged in random order here, on pieces of paper, then arrange them in a hierarchical manner. Answers are found at the end of the book.

Economic costs	Destruction of animals and plants	Environmental costs
Cleanup	Health costs	Reduction in tourism
Polluted water supply		

▼▼▼

List, Group, Label

The list, group, label activity (Taba, 1967) engages students in reflective learning where they construct conceptual arrangements from their prior knowledge. The activity requires little teacher preparation, promotes cooperative learning, and is well suited for students with diverse needs and backgrounds. The list, group, label activity begins as the teacher presents a word or phrase that describes the topic or theme of a lesson, asking students to suggest words they associate with the specified topic. As the students identify words, they are listed on an overhead or chalkboard. If students produce words seemingly unrelated to the topic, they are asked to provide a rationale for their response and, if necessary, they are encouraged to provide an alternate response. If students have difficulty generating words, it may be necessary for the teacher to provide additional clues or prompts. If these prompts fail to generate additional responses, the teacher may need to provide the relevant terms. Following are words dealing with a lesson on the Navajo Indians. The list has been generated by students and supplemented with words provided by the teacher (marked with an asterisk).

The Navajo Indians of the American Southwest

Arizona	sheep	farmers	craftwork
desert	blankets	sand painting*	Utah*
New Mexico*	tribal religion*	horses	pottery
hogans*	healing	medicine men	weaving
wool	hunting		

In the next step, students work in small groups to organize the terms into categories sharing common attributes or features. They then construct a label for the category. Here is one example of the groups and labels for the words listed above.

Location of Tribes	Spiritual Practices	Making a Living	
Arizona	medicine men	farmers	hunting
Utah	healing	craftwork	horses
New Mexico	sand painting	blankets	weaving
desert		wool	

In the final step, each group presents a rationale for its categories. This is followed by a large group discussion focused on reaching group consensus on the categories and their respective words. During this final step, it is likely that students will generate additional words for the various categories, or they may decide to restructure by deletion, consolidation, or division. The teacher should limit the students' attention to words and concepts that facilitate lesson objectives. Inclusion of words or concepts not addressed in the lesson may establish learning expectations that cannot be met. Coaching students to provide a rationale for their groupings is another important function of the teacher. As students discuss their rationale for their groupings, additional associations are likely to be triggered, producing a spiral-ing effect. The more students describe and elaborate on their constructed topics, the more associations are triggered by other students.

The list, group, label activity may also be used at the conclusion of a lesson to review and reinforce text concepts (Moore, Readence, & Rickelman, 1989). The proce-dure is the same as that outlined above, but the process now focuses on knowledge gained from the lesson in addition to the students' prior knowledge. This provides students the opportunity to reflect on the lesson content, to integrate information discussed prior to the lesson, and to deal with higher-level relationships. As a postreading activity, the list, group, label activity also serves as an authentic form of classroom assessment. Students' descriptions of the concepts they have learned and their ability to present a rationale for the relationships between these concepts pro-vide the teacher with rich and meaningful insights into the students' learning strate-gies and their knowledge of the lesson content.

Commentary: Graphic Organizers

Graphic organizers provide a flexible strategy to promote learning. Prior to reading they can be used to acquaint the reader with the information in a text and provide clues about how that information is structured. They can direct the reader's attention as he or she is studying a text, and they can be used to review and extend one's thinking at the conclusion of a reading, regardless of the age group, or content area (West, Farmer, & Wolff, 1991). As a prewriting tool, they can be used to help students organize infor-mation (Armbruster, Anderson, & Ostertag, 1987; Van Patten, Chao, & Reigeluth, 1986) and improve thinking, creativity, and decision making (West, Farmer, & Wolff, 1991).

Although graphic organizers are effective instructional devices for the subject matter classroom, they do have certain shortcomings. First, benefits of their use may not be evident immediately. Jones et al. (1987), for example, report that some studies of graphic organizers showed effects only after weeks or months of sustained instruc-tion. For that reason, you may consider initiating instruction with the most straight-forward of the strategies outlined here—the list, group, label activity. It is easy to use, is readily adaptable to most groups of students and subject matter areas, and results are attained quite readily. It also provides a good transitional step to the introduction and application of frames and concept maps.

The second shortcoming is that graphic organizers are sometimes difficult to apply to certain types of material or learning objectives. In circumstances where stu-dents have little or no background knowledge, the use of frames and the list, group, label activity will likely produce frustration and confusion. Similarly, when learning objectives address objectives that rely upon knowledge acquired through direct experience (demonstrations, discussions, experiments, visuals, etc.) the teacher may find the effect of graphic organizers prior to these experiences to be limited. In those circumstances, it may be necessary to first engage students in the activity, then use the graphic organizer as a form of review or reinforcement.

Finally, graphic organizers may produce disappointing results in those circum-stances where the teacher fails to identify objectives or where the teacher is not thor-oughly familiar with the content of the reading selection. As noted at the beginning of this section, graphic organizers are constructed to reflect teacher objectives and text information that will facilitate those objectives. If objectives are not defined, the use of graphic organizers usually leads to products that outline the entire content of a selection and that fail to engage students in learning activities beyond the memorization of surface-level information

Prediction Activities

Prediction refers to the prior reduction of unlikely alternatives (Smith, 1978). In the subject matter classroom, prediction serves to aid comprehension by activating schemata, thus making text more familiar. Its use, according to Anderson (1984), allows students to integrate what they know with what is presented in print. Prediction may also enhance the students' critical thinking by drawing their attention to key concepts in order to hypothesize logical relationships (Nessel, 1988) and by drawing their attention to known concepts that may conflict with those presented in the text (Frager & Thompson, 1985). Instructionally, students can generate predictions prior to reading by drawing upon their existing knowledge; when their background knowledge is limited, students may generate predictions from information they acquire from surveying titles, headings, subheadings, or short passages (Brozo & Simpson, 1991). Prediction can help students set a purpose for reading by drawing upon prior knowledge (Harris & Cooper, 1985), increase their attention to text objectives, increase their motivation to read (Nichols, 1983), instill curiosity (Shablak & Castallo, 1977), and heighten motivation (Lunstrum, 1981). In what follows, we discuss the use of anticipation guides, a prediction activity designed to actively engage students in the response to predictions made prior to reading.

Anticipation Guides

Anticipation guides consist of a series of statements that cause readers to draw upon their prior knowledge, then use that knowledge interactively with information in the reading. Prior to reading, students examine a series of statements, respond whether they agree or disagree with them, then discuss their responses to provide justification or add information. Following this discussion, students read the selection, then return to the statements to consider modifying their responses in light of the information presented in the reading. The statements in Figure 3.12 provide an example of an anticipation guide constructed for a high school English class.

Here are the procedures for constructing anticipation guides:

1. Identify major concepts. Examine the reading to identify the major concepts or information, then select those that are essential to your learning objectives. These concepts were identified from an interdisciplinary lesson in science and social studies.

- ▼ Governmental funding of AIDS research has increased as a result of public and political pressure.
- ▼ Inclusion of AIDS preventative measures in the curriculum is often based on the social norms of the community.
- ▼ As a wider segment of the population contracts AIDS, efforts to prevent its spread and find a cure have increased.

Directions: *Read and carefully consider the statements provided below. Determine whether you generally agree or disagree with each statement and mark the appropriate response. When you encounter a "Why?" in the item, please provide a brief explanation for your response.*

1. Strange noises are more frightening when one is alone.

   _____ Agree   _____ Disagree   Why?

2. Generally, events are more frightening if they occur at night in darkness rather than during the day in light.

   _____ Agree   _____ Disagree   Why?

3. Homes, at times, seem to take on human characteristics.

   _____ Agree   _____ Disagree   Why?

4. When a strange or unfamiliar event occurs, we try to explain it by relating it to something we know.

   _____ Agree   _____ Disagree   Why?

5. Trapdoors are usually associated with trickery or illusions.

   _____ Agree   _____ Disagree   Why?

6. Inanimate objects sometimes appear to have a soul.

   _____ Agree   _____ Disagree   Why?

Figure 3.12
Anticipation Guide for "Trapdoor," a Short Story by Ray Bradbury

2.   Translate lesson concepts into thought-provoking statements. Concepts now need to be translated into a form that is short, clear, interesting, and reflects the daily lives of students. Avoid narrow statements focusing on details or factual information. Statements should be general enough to elicit diverse points of view. Recognize that translating dry, abstract concepts into statements that attract students' attention and stimulate discussion can, at first, be a difficult process. The statement "Congress has the constitutional authority to impeach the President" is tedious, mechanical, and rather lifeless. Replacing it with "The people should always have the authority to remove individuals in positions of power and influence" would more likely gain attention and promote an interaction reflecting diverse opinions.

Here are some statements generated from the concepts identified in step 1.

Individuals in government are more likely to act if a lot of people call out for action.
                    _____ Agree   _____ Disagree
Its not easy to support something that goes against your beliefs.
                    _____ Agree   _____ Disagree

A tragedy would have a lot more impact upon me if it occurred to someone I knew as opposed to someone I read about in the newspaper.
_____ Agree   _____ Disagree

3. Present and discuss statements. Direct students to examine each statement, consider that statement based upon their experience and knowledge, and then select an appropriate response that they may be asked to defend during class discussion that will follow. Statements may be listed on a chalkboard, displayed on a transparency, read aloud, or placed on a handout. Responses to statements may follow several forms. First, responses may be elicited prior to reading, as shown in the statements listed under step 2. Instruct the students to examine the statement, then respond on the basis of their background knowledge. The teacher then tallies the students' responses and engages in a discussion focusing on the point of view and justification of their responses. Students are then asked to read the selection and reflect upon the statement after reading to determine if the text information would justify modification of their initial response:

A tragedy would have a lot more impact upon me if it occurred to someone I knew as opposed to someone I read about in the newspaper.
        Before Reading   After Reading
_____ Agree   _____ Disagree   _____ Agree   _____ Disagree

In the second method for responding to the statements presented in the anticipation guide, students answer the statement before reading based on their judgement, answer the statement following reading based on the information provided by the author, then provide a written justification for what they consider to be the best response. This method recognizes that there may be occasions when students construct a view that, while logical and informed, may not agree with that presented in the text. Allowing students to justify their responses should encourage class discussion, stimulate critical thinking, and encourage students to regulate their own thinking. Figure 3.13 is an example of this method of response.

Commentary: Anticipation Guides

Anticipation guides are an effective way to activate and relate prior knowledge to themes or constructs presented in a reading, film, videotape, filmstrip, or audio recording. Students' engagement in the statements is likely to focus attention on important concepts, arouse curiosity, and promote participation. And as class discussion centers on individuals' ability to defend or explain their positions, the teacher is afforded an opportunity to engage in a meaningful and authentic form of assessing students' prior knowledge. Results of this assessment can be used to identify students who could profit from further enrichment activities or alternate readings (Moore, Readence, & Rickelman, 1989).

Directions: *Based on what you know about the environmental movement, respond to the following statement.*

Environmentalists' main goal is to gain political and economic power on a worldwide basis.

<table>
<tr><td colspan="2">Your Response</td><td colspan="2">Author's Response</td></tr>
<tr><td>___ Agree</td><td>___ Disagree</td><td>___ Agree</td><td>___ Disagree</td></tr>
</table>

Now read the following excerpt of an editorial appearing in The Wall Street Journal, then determine how the author of this article would respond to the statement above.

There have been Western elites in the past who believed that the hordes of humanity in developing countries should be beaten back and controlled. Following in their footsteps today are the environmental elites who want to prevent the Third World's economies from ever using the industrial techniques that will make them First World countries. They'll do this by imposing an international tax on carbon dioxide emissions and a freeze on human procreation.

[Source: Editorial, *The Wall Street Journal,* June 1, 1992].

Consider the statement you responded to above. Now that you have read the selection, provide a justification for what you believe is the best response to the statement.

JUSTIFICATION: _____

_____

Figure 3.13
Example of Procedure for Justifying Response to Anticipation Guide

Since the anticipation guide relies on predictions constructed from prior knowledge, statements based on material containing new and difficult concepts is likely to arouse little more than frustration as the students respond to information that is seemingly dry and difficult. Similarly, material that is primarily factual or contains information unlikely to stir emotion, raise debate, or be open to interpretation may not be suitable for this prereading strategy.

While prediction activities are a powerful instructional tool, their use is conditional. Material containing concepts and information far removed from the students' background knowledge may not be well suited to prediction activities. Responding to statements or generating questions based on unfamiliar material can be a difficult and frustrating experience. Under these conditions, it may be useful to first preview the material using prereading strategies that will provide students with some acquaintance with the material, then involve them with prediction activities.

Recognize also that certain types of material may not be suited for prediction activities. Highly scientific or factual selections as well as those containing information unlikely to stimulate discussion, debate, or interpretation may be less conducive to prediction activities.

▼ PRACTICE ACTIVITY 3.3

Below is an anticipation guide designed to engage students in a discussion on the effects of violence on our culture. Examine each statement carefully to determine if it (1) is clearly written, (2) contains content that is general enough so that most students will be able to respond, and (3) addresses the lesson objective. Answers can be found at the end of the book.

Agree	Disagree	
____	____	The increased awareness of violence has changed how people live, where they go, and the level of concern they express about violence.
____	____	It would seem that watching violent acts on television and hearing about them constantly could make some people think that violence is acceptable in our culture.
____	____	There is some evidence that violent behaviors are inherited.
____	____	In 1989 there were 1,200 people on death row in state penal institutions.

▼▼▼

Previews

The final type of prereading activity presented in this chapter is the written preview. This is a script of moderate length that the teacher reads aloud before students read an expository or narrative selection. The preview is particularly useful for difficult material. Once presented, students gain background knowledge, a purpose for reading, and the opportunity to discuss or question information prior to reading. Graves, Prenn, and Cooke (1985) recommend the preview be constructed to reflect three components: an introduction linking the selection to students' lives and ending with discussion questions, a written summary, and purpose-setting questions.

Constructing previews requires attention to the content of the selection, knowledge of the students' background knowledge, and clearly defined objectives. Consider these steps. First, become familiar with the selection by reading it several times. As you read, note important concepts, characters, events, and the like, then define what you consider to be the major themes or ideas. Next, consider how you can make this information relevant and practical to your students. The purpose here is to construct an introductory statement that can link information in the selection to the background and interests of your students. This section ends with a question that draws upon the students' prior knowledge. The next section of the preview, the summary, is written to include the main ideas and supporting information, in the order in which it occurs in the text. The heaviest emphasis should go to information that appears earlier in the text, and with narratives, the preview should definitely not give away the resolution. In the final section of the preview, purpose-setting questions and brief notes about the structure of the selection are provided. You may, for example, tell the students to omit certain portions of the selection, or you may draw their attention to a particularly important section or to a poorly written section.

Presentation of the preview, generally requiring five to ten minutes, follows these steps described by Graves, Prenn, and Cooke (1985):

1. **Introduction.** Inform students that you are about to provide an introduction to a reading selection. For example:

> We are about to begin a unit on the study of water. Over the next two weeks, we have combined your science and geography class so we may learn about the distribution and use of water as well as some of its chemical properties. Today, we will learn about the need that living things have for water.
>
> There is water in all living things. What percent of the following living things do you suppose is composed of water? (Give the examples humans, corn, mice, and elephants.)
>
> You may be surprised to learn that all of these living things are composed of 60% to 70% water. Why is such a large percentage of our body composed of water?

2. **The summary.** Read the summary portion of the preview.

> The selection we will be reading is entitled "Body Functions: The Importance of Water." In it you will learn that all living things need water to stay alive, and you'll learn some of the reasons why living things need water to stay alive. Your body is about 65% water, about the same as a mouse, an ear of corn, or an elephant. Water is necessary to carry on the functions of taking in food, breaking down the food into its usable nutrients or food substances, and carrying away waste products. Solutions in your body that are composed of a great deal of water, like your blood, transport nutrients. Water also helps in the chemical reactions that break food into materials you need to grow and repair body tissues. While you could survive about two months without food, you could live only about a week without water.

3. **Purpose-setting questions and study aids.** Provide students a purpose for reading and provide suggestions that may facilitate their understanding of the selection.

> Now read the selection. As you read, determine how water is used to break down food and remove wastes from your body. You may skip

the second page of the reading because it addresses an issue we aren't concerned with. Also, before you begin reading, study the illustrations on page 41 and 42. Looking at those illustrations will make the reading easier to understand.

Commentary: Previews

The presentation of previews prior to reading has been shown to be an effective way to establish an organizational framework to stimulate the appropriate background knowledge and to provide new information about the selection that will be read (Graves & Palmer, 1981; Graves, Cooke, & LaBerge, 1983; Graves & Prenn, 1984). Moreover, previews stimulate curiosity, enhance the motivation to read, and provide a way to link text material to background knowledge. Additionally they have been shown to be an effective strategy for second-language learners (Chen & Graves, 1996). Intuitively, although it might seem that previews would reduce interest in reading a selection, students have repeatedly reported that previews help them to read and understand selections without ruining them. Note, however, that the use of previews should be limited to material that is challenging to students.

CONCLUDING REMARKS

This chapter began by addressing the importance of having a comprehensive plan for guiding students through activities prior to, during, and following a reading assignment, which we call a structured reading lesson. It addressed planning and implementing prereading activities, establishing a purpose for learning, and providing activities for enhancing background knowledge. In summarizing this chapter, four points integral for preparing students to learn from text should be emphasized.

First, in setting up a classroom situation in which all students can be successful in reading and understanding a text selection, it is essential to have an overall plan. Such a plan needs to be a coherent sequence of pre-, during-, and postreading activities that are coordinated and that reinforce each other. The structured reading lesson is one such plan.

Second, prereading activities are essential to sound classroom practice. Many students experience uncertainty or frustration as they attempt to define a purpose for independent reading. By activating and building upon the students' schemata, reading becomes more purposeful and focused. As the teacher models the process of relating prior knowledge to new or difficult content, students begin to acquire a greater awareness of the process for generating questions, sharing information, and the importance of obtaining information from sources outside of the textbook.

Third, students should increasingly assume responsibility for establishing objectives, relating background knowledge to these objectives, and enhancing background knowledge through cooperative efforts with their peers. The gradual release of instructional responsibility from the teacher to the student increases the likelihood that activities in this chapter can become part of the individual's repertoire of strategies applied independent of the teacher's assistance. Some students will be able to apply these strategies on their own, while others will require the continued assistance of their peers. But all students will have a better understanding of the process of establishing goals and the importance of drawing upon prior knowledge.

Finally, it should be noted that prereading activities are an important element in improving the students' attitudes toward learning. Many of the activities presented in this chapter rely upon group learning, an approach that we examine in detail in Chapter 7, "Cooperative Learning". This context fosters an appreciation of each student's contributions to the learning process and the diverse points of view evident in a classroom. Group activities also increase the likelihood that students will engage in risk taking and generate knowledge from information provided from teachers, peers, and the reading material.

REFLECTIONS
▼▼▼

Now that you have become more familiar with ways to prepare students for reading text, complete the following questions as a review of some of the topics addressed throughout this chapter.

1. Construct a purpose-setting conversations activity for a lesson that could be presented to a class of students. Script each step of the procedure, then administer the lesson to a class in your subject matter area.

2. Select content appropriate for a unit of study in your subject matter area. Construct and list instructional objectives, then construct a series of concept maps that could be used to preview the lesson content to a group of students. Present these maps to a group of students or peers and solicit their feedback on the usefulness of the maps in building prior knowledge.

3. Obtain a reading of approximately three to four pages in length. Construct a series of frames for the article, adhering to the guidelines discussed in this chapter. Present the frames to a group of your peers. Next, ask your peers to generate a written summary by referring to the frames you constructed. Finally, ask your peers to comment on the merit of using the frames for writing.

4. Construct an anticipation guide for a portion of a chapter in this text. Ask one of your peers to complete the anticipation guide prior to reading the chapter, then ask him or her to comment on the usefulness of this activity in establishing a purpose for reading.

5. Examine the teacher's edition of a subject matter textbook to determine the scope and nature of prereading activities recommended for instruction. Summarize these activities by noting (1) the types of activities suggested, (2) the frequency with which the activities are presented, and (3) the degree that the activities allow students to become actively involved. Finally, note any suggestions you may have for improving or modifying these activities.

6. Interview students to determine their awareness of the use of prereading activities and their views as to the usefulness of these activities.

7. Construct a prereading lesson that would consume approximately one hour of class time. In constructing this written lesson, define your learning objectives, the

rationale for selecting the prereading strategies used, and a description of how you will present these strategies. If possible, administer this lesson to a group of students. Ask a peer or a teacher to evaluate the effectiveness of this lesson by (1) examining how well the activities addressed your stated objectives, (2) evaluating the extent that your activities allow for students' active participation, and (3) evaluating if the lesson followed the procedures for administrating the activities as discussed in this chapter.

REFERENCES

▼▼

Anderson, C., & Roth, K. (1989). Teaching for meaningful and self-regulated learning in science. In J. Brophy (Ed.), *Advances in research on teaching* (Vol. I). Greenwich, CT: JAI Press. Describes strategies and instructional format for promoting students' ability to read independent of the teacher's direct instruction.

Anderson, R. C. (1984). Role of the reader's schema in comprehension, learning, and memory. In R. Anderson, J. Osborn, & R. Tierney (Eds.), *Learning to read in American schools: Basal readers and content texts.* Hillsdale, NJ: Erlbaum. Presents a detailed description of schema and its function in acquiring knowledge.

Armbruster, B. B., & Anderson, T. H. (1984). Mapping: Representing informative text diagrammatically. In C. D. Holley & D. F. Dansereau (Eds.), *Spatial learning strategies: Techniques, applications, and related issues.* New York: Academic Press. Details the application of concept maps as a means of promoting understanding during reading.

Armbruster, B. B., Anderson, T. H., & Ostertag, J. (1987). Does text structure/summarization instruction facilitate learning from expository text? *Reading Research Quarterly, 22,* 331–346. Presents a research study exploring how summaries and direct instruction of types of text structures influence readers' understanding of text.

Ausubel, D. P. (1968). *Educational psychology: A cognitive view.* New York: Holt, Rinehart & Winston. Highlights theories and processes of learning in the context of schools.

Barron, R. (1969). Research for the classroom teacher: Recent developments on the structured overview as an advance cognitive organizer. In

H. Herber & J. Riley (Eds.), *Research in reading in the content areas: The fourth report.* Syracuse, NY: Syracuse University Reading and Language Arts Center. Summarizes various studies dealing with the use of concept maps and their role as a prereading activity.

Bean, T. W., Singer, H., Sorter, J., & Frazee, C. (1986). The effect of metacognitive instruction in outlining and graphic organizer instruction on students' comprehension in a tenth-grade world history class. *Journal of Reading Behavior, 18,* 153–169. Describes the effect of teaching students to self-regulate their thinking as they construct outlines and concept maps as students are reading.

Boothby, P. R., & Alvermann, D. E. (1984). A classroom training study: The effects of graphic organizer instruction on fourth graders' comprehension. *Reading World, 26,* 325–339. Examines how teacher-prepared concept maps presented prior to reading affect students' comprehension.

Brozo, W. G., & Simpson, M. L. (1991). *Readers, teachers, learners: Expanding literacy in secondary schools.* Columbus: Merrill. Presents instructional strategies and issues related to the integration of reading, writing, and listening in the secondary subject matter classroom.

Chen, H. C., & Graves, M. F. (1996). Effects of previewing and providing background knowledge on Taiwanese college students' comprehension of American short stories. *TESOL Quarterly, 29,* 663–686. A report on college students' use of previews.

Clark, C., & Yinger, R. (1980). *The hidden world of teaching: Implications of research on teacher planning.* Research Series No. 77. East Lansing, MI: Institute for Research on Teaching. Reviews the research on teacher planning and its effect on instruction and student learning and presents a through discussion of the role of planning in teaching.

Clark, C. M., & Peterson, P. L. (1986). Teachers' thought processes. In M. C. Wittrock (Ed.), *Handbook of research on teaching* (3rd ed., pp. 255–296). New York: Macmillan. Focuses on teachers' perceptions of their classroom instruction and the significance of these perceptions on efforts to modify the nature of teaching.

Frager, A. M., & Thompson, L. C. (1985). Conflict: The key to critical reading instruction. *Journal of Reading*, 28, 676–683. Discusses the role of prediction and arousing curiosity in the form of conflict resolution as a means of directing students' attention as they read.

Graves, M. F., Cooke, C. L., & Laberge, M. J. (1983). Effects of previewing difficult short stories on low ability junior high school students' comprehension, recall and attitudes. *Reading Research Quarterly*, 18, 262–276. Presents findings of a research study examining how previews affect less-able readers' understanding and attitude when reading difficult text.

Graves, M. F., & Graves, B. B. (1994). *Scaffolding reading experiences: Designs for student success*. Norwood, MA: Christopher-Gordon. Offers a wide variety of activities to promote students' independent reading.

Graves, M. F., Graves, B. B., & Braaten, S. (1996). Scaffolding reading experiences for inclusive classrooms. *Educational Leadership*, 53 (5), 14–16. Overviews the importance of scaffolded instructional lessons.

Graves, M. F., & Palmer, R. J. (1981). Validating previewing as a method of improving fifth and sixth grade students' comprehension of short stories. *Michigan Reading Journal*, 15, 1–3. Reports on a study examining how previews affect middle schools students' comprehension of short stories.

Graves, M. F., Prenn, M., & Cooke, C. (1985). The coming attraction: Previewing short stories. *Journal of Reading*, 28, 594–599. Discusses the use of previews with short stories and details the processes of constructing and presenting previews in the classroom.

Graves, M. F., & Prenn, M. C. (1984). Effects of previewing expository passages on junior high students' comprehension and attitude. In J. Niles &

R. Lalik (Eds.), *Changing perspectives on research in reading/language processing and instruction*. Rochester, NY: National Reading Conference. Reports on a study examining how previews affect middle school students' comprehension of classroom readings and students' perceptions of previews as an instructional strategy.

Harris, T. L., & Cooper, E. J. (1985). *Reading, thinking and concept development: Strategies for the classroom*. New York: College Board Publications. Presents numerous classroom strategies for facilitating reading and thinking prior to, during, and following reading.

Hawk, P. P. (1986). Using graphic organizers to increase achievement in middle school life science. *Science Education*, 70, 81–87. Discusses the use, importance, and adaptations of concept maps in promoting students' understanding of readings and demonstrations in the science classroom.

Heimlich, J. E., & Pittleman, S. D. (1986). *Semantic mapping: Classroom applications*. Newark, DE: International Reading Association. Designed for the classroom teacher, details the use and application of semantic maps as a means to promote students' vocabulary and conceptual development.

Holley, C. D., & Dansereau, D. F. (1984). *Spatial learning strategies: Techniques, applications and issues*. Orlando, FL: Academic Press. Presents theoretical and instructional issues as well as classroom strategies that deal with the use of various forms of graphic organizers.

Jones, B. F., Palincsar, A. S., Ogle, D. S., & Carr, E. G. (Eds.). (1987). *Strategic teaching and learning: Cognitive instruction in the content areas*. Elmhurst, IL: North Central Regional Laboratory and the Association for Supervision and Curriculum Development. Presents numerous teacher- and student-directed strategies to enhance higher-level understanding of subject matter materials.

Langer, J. (1982). Facilitating text processing: The elaboration of prior knowledge. In J. Langer & T. Smith-Burke (Eds.), *Reader meets author/Bridging the gap*. Newark, DE: International Reading Association. Discusses the theory and step-by-step process of using the PreP activity to generate students' active involvement and build upon their background knowledge.

Lunstrum, J. P. (1981). Building motivation through the use of controversy. *Journal of Reading*, 24, 687–691. Discusses the importance of controversy and prediction as an instructional device prior to reading and their importance in motivating the student to engage in subject matter content.

Mayer, R. E. (1984). Twenty-five years of research on advance organizers. *Instructional Science*, 8, 133–169. Reviews the role of advance organizers in promoting students' understanding, with an emphasis on the use of advance organizers in the science classroom.

McAleese, R. (1986). Computer-based authoring and intelligent interactive video. In C. W. Osborne & A. J. Trott (Eds.), *International yearbook of educational and instructional technology*. New York: Kogan Page. Overviews several applications of concept maps in the construction and use of interactive video instruction.

Moore, D. W., Readence, J. E., & Rickelman, R. J. (1989). *Prereading activities for content area reading and learning*. Newark, DE: International Reading Association. Provides a description of the importance of and examples of numerous prereading activities for the subject matter classroom.

Nessel, D. (1988). Channeling knowledge for reading expository text. *Journal of Reading*, 32, 225–228. Discusses the importance of teaching secondary students strategies for reading expository text.

Nichols, J. N. (1983). Using prediction to increase content area interest and understanding. *Journal of Reading*, 27, 225–228. Overviews the importance of prediction in the classroom and describes several strategies designed to engage students in prediction.

Rosenshine, B., Meister, C., & Chapman, S. (1996). Teaching students to generate questions: A review of the intervention studies. *Review of Educational Research*, 66, 181–221. Details the knowledge base on the use of self-generated questions, how students are taught to generate questions, and suggestions for further research in this area.

Shablak, S., & Castallo, R. (1977). Curiosity arousal and motivation in the teaching/learning process. In H. L. Herber and R. T. Vacca (Eds.), *Research in reading in the content areas: The third report*. Syracuse, NY: Syracuse University Reading and Language Arts Center. Presents an overview of the importance of prediction and motivation prior to reading as a means to facilitate students' comprehension and instill a greater degree of involvement in reading assignments.

Smith, F. (1978). *Understanding reading* (2nd ed.). New York: Holt, Rinehart and Winston. Presents an overview of the nature of the reading process and instructional issues arising from the topics presented in the text.

Taba, H. (1967). *Teacher's handbook for elementary social studies*, Reading, MA: Addison-Wesley. A social studies method text for elementary classroom teachers detailing the nature of social studies curriculum and instructional activities.

Van Patten, J. R., Chao, C. I., & Reigeluth, C. M. (1986). A review of strategies for sequencing and synthesizing information. *Review of Educational Research*, 56, 437–472. A rather extensive review of research on the influence of various instructional strategies used to promote students' ability to organize, summarize, and synthesize information during and following reading.

Watts, S. M., & Graves, M. F. (in press). Fostering middle school students' understanding of challenging texts. *Middle School Journal*. Focuses on deeper understanding.

West, C. K., Farmer, J. A., & Wolff, P. M. (1991). *Instructional design: Implications from cognitive science*. Englewood Cliffs, NJ: Prentice-Hall. Provides a detailed explanation of how research in cognitive science can be applied to the design of instructional materials.

Comprehension: Engaging Students in Reading and Learning

OVERVIEW

This chapter presents activities that help students understand and learn from subject matter reading material. It is composed of two major sections. The first section, "Activities to Structure Subject Matter Content," begins with a discussion of questioning, then presents teaching activities that assist students' learning of particular content. The second section, "Activities to Promote Independent Reading," discusses activities that help students learn from texts on their own through strategic reading and studying. This chapter should be viewed as a continuation of the comprehension activities discussed in Chapter 3. Similarly, this chapter is closely connected with Chapter 5, "Critical Thinking," which addresses activities to enhance the students' ability to engage in higher-level thinking.

The authors wish to thank Judith Winn for her contributions to a previous version of this chapter.

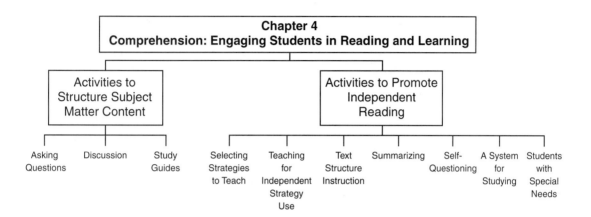

Chapter 4
Comprehension: Engaging Students in Reading and Learning

Activities to Structure Subject Matter Content

Activities to Promote Independent Reading

Asking Questions

Discussion

Study Guides

Selecting Strategies to Teach

Teaching for Independent Strategy Use

Text Structure Instruction

Summarizing

Self-Questioning

A System for Studying

Students with Special Needs

M any students find the reading material in their subject matter classes difficult to understand. As a result, it is not uncommon to find students who
don't read the text, relying instead on the information they acquire from
in-class lectures or from discussions or demonstrations, or students who "go through
the motions" of reading but are able to construct very little meaning. Comprehending
text is difficult when students lack background knowledge of or an interest in the material, when the texts are poorly written, or when the students do not have well-developed
reading comprehension behaviors. Here are two examples of comprehension difficulties
likely to be encountered in content area classes. Both revolve around a senior high
school history class located in the mid-Atlantic states which is about to begin reading
about the Anasasi culture that resided in southwestern Colorado from 750 to 1300 A.D.

Kim

Kim has been assigned to a group of students who have been
directed to engage in a problem-solving question. Their task is to read
about the topographical and climatological characteristics of the region
the Anasasi inhabited to determine how the culture survived for such a
lengthy period. Kim has never traveled beyond the mid-Atlantic states.
She has little understanding of the semiarid steppe climate of the
Colorado plateau, the effect of the intense solar radiation at an altitude
of 7,100 feet where the Anasasi lived, or the relationship between altitude, climate, and vegetation. Lacking background knowledge of these
concepts, she experiences considerable difficulty reading about them.

Paulo

Paulo is a member of Kim's group. He lived most of his life in Cortez, Colorado, just a few miles from the present-day ruins of the Anasasi culture. He has visited these ruins on numerous occasions. Paulo locates six sources of information dealing with the climate and topography of southeast Colorado. He reads these sources in the manner he is accustomed to—focusing on facts and figures which he then lists in his notes. Once these notes are completed, he turns them over to his group anticipating that they will somehow apply the information to their problem-solving task.

Kim typifies a student who has difficulty comprehending text because of limited background knowledge. For such students, the lack of background knowledge makes it very difficult to read to gain a higher level of understanding. Paulo, on the other hand, has considerable prior knowledge of the concepts contained in the reading selections, yet he fails to adapt his notetaking strategy to meet the demands of the problem-solving task presented by the teacher. Neither of these students is likely to be able to successfully comprehend and learn from their content area reading material on their own, albeit for different reasons. Instruction that concentrates on building and activating background knowledge, as discussed in the preceding chapter, helps students construct meaning from the text by organizing and making sense of new information in terms of what they already know. Instruction can also help students develop control of their understanding and learning from reading so they can use the information in the reading material to meet the varied demands of their content classes.

Two types of instructional activities are presented in this chapter. The first type of activities are those that help structure the content of the text to enable students to meet the learning objectives. The second type of activities are those that can be used to guide students toward becoming more proficient independent readers in subject matter areas. These activities address subject matter content as well as the processes of reading.

ACTIVITIES TO STRUCTURE SUBJECT MATTER CONTENT

This section begins with a discussion of the role and use of questioning. This is followed by a discussion of the use, limitations, and benefits of discussion as a means to facilitate learning. Finally, the section concludes with consideration of the construction of study guides to enhance learning.

Asking Questions

By far the most prominent classroom activity to enhance students' understanding is the presentation of questions either by the teacher or a textbook. While teachers initiate a lot of questions in the classroom—about 1.3 questions per minute (Daines, 1986)—most of these tend to focus on factual bits of information (Alverman & Hayes, 1989; Bloome, 1987; Smith & Feathers, 1983; Wiley, 1977). Unfortunately these lower-level questions are not the type likely to promote understanding or the development of conceptual learning (Prawat, 1989). A good set of questions can engage students in reasoning activities that help integrate the material being learned with background knowledge. One advantage of this use of questioning is its emphasis on application of knowledge rather than the assessment of the students' ability to recall facts (Wilen, 1986). Another advantage is that by sharing their approaches to these sorts of questions with the teacher and their peers, all students gain a better insight into the thinking process. Within the subject matter classroom, students should be encouraged to ask questions. Whether question generation is an individual or cooperative effort, it is likely to enhance the students' involvement in learning and increase their understanding of the processes involved in constructing questions. Ultimately, if students are proficient at generating knowledge and understanding through self-directed learning, then students and teachers need to be asking self-generated questions (Commeyras, 1995).

The Role of Questions in Comprehension Instruction: Facilitating Learning and Thinking

While questioning can serve a number of purposes (e.g., assessment, management, focusing attention), the one most relevant to this chapter is facilitating learning and thinking. The goals of these questions are to

1. **Highlight lesson content.** Questions can be used to direct students' attention to particular information, concepts, or ideas in the text that are relevant to the learning objectives.
   - ▼ **In Science:** Describe the process of homeostasis.
   - ▼ **In Physical Education:** Describe three types of defense in basketball.
   - ▼ **In Art:** Describe the difference between hue and saturation.
   - ▼ **In English:** From *Of Mice and Men*, describe Lennie's physical characteristics.

2. **Integrate lesson content with material learned previously.** Questions can assist students in applying previously learned material to the content of a particular reading.
   - ▼ **In Science:** What effects does the aging process have on homeostasis?
   - ▼ **In Physical Education:** What is the relationship between the weight, size, and speed of a basketball team and their ability to engage in a full-court press?
   - ▼ **In Art:** Why do the various levels of saturation evoke different types of emotional reactions from humans?
   - ▼ **In English:** Compare and contrast the problems faced by the main characters in *Of Mice and Men* with the main characters in *The Grapes of Wrath*.

3. Structure higher-level understanding. Questions can be sequenced in a manner that encourages students to apply that information to novel situations or contexts.

- ▼ **In Science:** How can our knowledge of homeostasis help us explain the functioning of the circulatory system?
- ▼ **In Physical Education:** How will the Minnesota Timberwolves need to adjust their defensive strategy when they play the Chicago Bulls?
- ▼ **In Art:** What colors would you select for painting a police station waiting area?
- ▼ **In English:** Presume that you were to rewrite *Of Mice and Men* to take place in a contemporary urban setting. How would the characters and setting change?

4. Promote the integration of students' knowledge, values, and cultural background with lesson objectives. Learning can become more relevant and meaningful when students are encouraged to draw upon their knowledge and background. Questions that encourage students to construct meaning using their values, knowledge, and cultural perspective can provide a rich and stimulating environment for all.

- ▼ **In Science:** Consider a number of world cultures. How do these cultures vary in the way they adjust their way of life to meet the demands of their environments?
- ▼ **In Physical Education:** Think about your own neighborhood. How many kids play basketball and how often do they play?
- ▼ **In Art:** Certain cultures use different levels of color saturation in the clothes they wear. What are some of the traditional colors worn by your family or your ancestors?

5. Generate learning within the classroom context with authentic learning tasks.

- ▼ **In Science:** In this unit on forms of human-produced pollution, consider the problems and solutions raised, then examine with the members of the class their position as to how different aspects of pollution should be addressed. You may want to consider some of the trade-offs in making these decisions, such as loss of jobs, higher taxes, more governmental control, or loss of personal freedoms.
- ▼ **In Physical Education:** As adults you may engage in different forms of physical exercise. Consider what forms of exercise would be selected for a specific lifestyle or vocation. What are some of the reasons that different people may select a specific form of exercise or any exercise at all? Discuss what some of the variables may be in making your decision.
- ▼ **In Art:** Consider the various motivations that students in this class have regarding the study or production of art. Given these views, should art be studied or practiced? That is, should most of your time be devoted to producing objects of art, studying techniques from others, or should other forms of instruction be used?

Developing questioning activities requires making decisions about what type of questions to ask, when to ask them, how students may be involved in question generating, and how you can assist students in answering various types of questions. Below, we address the task of generating various types or cognitive levels of questions. In the following sections, we address question placement, ways of supporting students as they respond to questions, and the process of helping students generate and respond to their own questions.

Cognitive Levels of Questions

Questions vary in the cognitive demands placed on the learner. Some questions can be answered readily on the basis of one's knowledge of surface structures of the language, while others require the reader to draw generalizations formulated from the integration of conceptual information being learned with concepts previously acquired. Consider the following example of a surface-level question and one requiring higher-level conceptual understanding. Note in the surface-level question that it is quite easy to respond simply on the basis of one's knowledge of grammatical structures.

Surface Level

Text: "The flofs bemped the four worgers."

Question: How many worgers did the flofs bemp?"

Higher Conceptual Understanding

Question: Recognizing the role of the Supreme Court in interpreting the Constitution on matters pertaining to civil rights, consider the outcome of the Court's rulings in the past twenty years if there had been no effort by the Justice Department in enforcing the Court's decisions.

Recognizing the significant variation in the amount of understanding and conscious effort required to respond to various types of questions, educators have developed a number of schemes for classifying questions. While these schemes are useful, some tend to be rather extensive in their description of levels of understanding. We have developed a straightforward, three-level classification scheme proceeding from the more readily answered surface-level question to complex questions requiring predictions and hypothesizing. Here is a brief description of the characteristics of these questions.

Level 1 questions require the learner to name, define, observe, match, select, and describe important information. Answers to these questions are found directly from the reading material and normally require no more than the ability to locate an answer.

Level 2 questions require students to form relationships between concepts presented; this is done through summarizing, identifying cause and effect, classifying, organizing, and forming analogies.

Level 3 questions require students to use the information they have gathered to predict, plan, hypothesize, and evaluate new situations. These questions tend to draw extensively on students' background knowledge.

Shown below is a short text followed by examples of questions from each of the three levels.

Marilyn had been having difficulty sleeping during the night as a result of her visit to the doctor the previous day. When the sun rose she felt like staying in bed, but knew that it was important to be at school to meet the new teacher. Once she was up she glanced out the window, carefully examined the sky, her outdoor thermometer, then turned on the radio for the weather forecast. She then got dressed, went to the kitchen where she consumed a small amount of food and six vitamins for breakfast, then went to the closet to take out her umbrella, raincoat, and a wide brimmed hat. She then proceeded to the protection of the porch to wait for the school bus.

Level 1: Surface Level
Why did Marilyn believe it was important to be at school on this particular day?
What did Marilyn use to listen to the weather forecast?

Level 2: Combining Information
How did the weather conditions affect the items of apparel and accessories that
    Marilyn selected from the closet?
Why did Marilyn wait on the porch for the bus?

Level 3: Constructing a Novel Response
What happened at the doctor's office that caused Marilyn to lose sleep?
What type of personality does Marilyn have?

Several characteristics of the three levels of questions in the taxonomy can be noted in the examples provided above. Level 1 questions normally have a single correct response, and this response can be obtained directly from the text. Level 2 questions require the combination of information in the text and background knowledge. Thus, depending upon the personal experience of the learner, various plausible answers can be provided for a given question. For example, there are a number of valid responses to the question regarding why Marilyn was waiting on the porch: the weather was bad and she wanted to keep out of the rain; she was sensitive to the sun and had to shield herself from its rays; she was afraid to wait on the corner. Finally, level 3 questions are based primarily on the learner's background knowledge and thus have a wide range of plausible answers reflecting the student's ability to make use of (1) appropriate background information, (2) reasoning skills, (3) logical connections between information contained in the text, and (4) information or views from other sources (text, individuals, etc.).

Use of questions in the classroom, whether generated by the teacher or by students, or obtained from a textbook or teacher's guide, should provide students the opportunity to engage in learning that involves various types of meaningful cognitive tasks. Unfortunately, in most classrooms students are engaging in few questions that go beyond surface-level understanding. Armbruster et al. (1991), for example, found that only 10% of questions asked by teachers require students to generate inferences.

Most teacher questions focus on trivial information and on defining vocabulary terms, and the questions themselves are poorly constructed (Shake & Allington, 1985; Armbruster et al., 1991). Constructing questions that are well written and engage students in meaningful conceptual learning requires a consistent effort on behalf of the teacher. The following section provides guidelines for generating classroom questions. This is followed by a section on the process of sequencing questions so that they engage students in conceptual learning.

Suggestions for Classroom Questioning

Classroom questions should be carefully constructed as well as sensitive to students' background knowledge and interest in the subject matter and the learning objectives. Here are some general guidelines for asking questions. Those that follow have been adapted from Wilen (1986) and Grossier (1964).

1. Ask questions that are clear and specific. Although questions should not be phrased so they direct students to an answer they should assist students in their thinking. Vague questions provide little structure for students, and are likely to either lead students away from desired information or discourage students altogether. Here are some examples of vague questions and a corresponding revision to present a more clearly worded question.

Vague:
"What is going on in the story with the landlord?"

Revision:
"Why did the landlord force the young couple out of the apartment when he thought the tenants had ruined the carpeting?"

Vague:
"What is the problem with destroying the rain forests?"

Revision:
"Consider how the rainforest helps in the production of oxygen and the reduction of pollutants as well as the numerous unique animals and plants that reside within the forest. What will be the consequences of destroying these rainforests?"

2. Ask questions in natural language. Try to avoid using "textbook" language. Rather, use phrasing that would be used if raising a question outside of a reading assignment. In asking students to justify their statements, a question like "What principles or theories do you embrace that would support your position?" may be too formal. "What evidence can you provide for your answer?" or "Why do you think that is so?" are more natural and thus are more likely to lead to natural dialogue.

3. Ensure that students have an opportunity to respond to questions of various levels of difficulty. Students need the opportunity to respond to a variety of types of questions. Lacking continual experiences with various questions, students are likely to become less engaged with the material and will likely process that material for the sole purpose of memorizing information. Encourage all students, even the more reticent ones, to become involved in thinking about responses to questions. Strategies to facilitate student involvement may include the assignment of distinct questions to cooperative learning groups. Within these groups, students compose a group response where they are asked to provide justifications for their contribution, relying on the text as well as their background knowledge. In providing the justifications, students are helped to pull together more information than they may do when responding directly to a question. The group may consider several alternatives, again something less likely to occur if the students are responding on their own.

4. Ask questions that encourage more than a "yes" or "no" answer. Yes/no questions encourage students to guess as well as promote impulsive thinking and "right answer" searching rather than conceptual thinking (Ornstein, 1988). They also provide little information to the teacher about mastery of information or understanding.

5. Provide adequate time for students to respond to questions. Rowe's (1986) research points to dramatic effects of extending the amount of time that teachers wait at two points: (1) after they ask a question and (2) after students respond. Rowe reports that the typical "wait time" for students to respond to a question or to ask a subsequent question is one second. When wait time is increased to three seconds, the following changes have been found:

1. Students' responses are longer (between 300% and 700%).
2. Students are more likely to support inferences with evidence and logical argument.
3. Students engage in more speculative thinking.
4. Students ask more questions.
5. Students talk more among themselves.
6. Students' failure to respond decreases.
7. Students are more attentive and cooperative.
8. More students participate.
9. Students appear more confident.
10. Teachers ask fewer questions, but those they do ask are more likely to invite the students to provide clarifications or elaborations.

As is true for all suggestions in this section, the use of wait time is flexible. If the goal is drill and practice, a rather quick pace may be appropriate. However, if the goal involves students reasoning about the material rather than mainly recalling it, longer wait times seem especially important (Good & Brophy, 1987).

Sequencing Questions

Well-designed questions "fit together" conceptually, with one question building upon or facilitating another. Generally, sequencing requires the presentation of level 1, level 2, and level 3 questions. However, on some occasions it may be best to focus solely on level 1 questions to establish a base from which to reason about the material. Even if only level 1 questions are asked, it is important to sequence them carefully, according to what concepts the students are to be focusing on. A well-planned sequence of level 1 questions can foster insight (Good & Brophy, 1987) as seen in the following example:

Unsequenced Questions
1. When did people in the United States begin moving out of the large cities into the suburbs?
2. How many people move themselves?
3. How many people living on farms during the 1950s left agriculture?
4. How many people lived in the central part of cities in 1950?
5. Where did the people who lived on farms move to?
6. Can you deduct a move on your federal income taxes?

Sequenced Questions
1. What was the rate of growth of population in the central cities and the suburbs from 1950 to 1960?
2. What factors drew people to the suburbs from the cities?
3. How was life in the suburbs different from that of city dwellers?
4. With all the people moving to the suburbs, what types of problems soon emerged for the suburbanites?

The unsequenced questions encourage the random collection of facts about moving. They do not build on each other nor do they lead to a point. In comparison, the sequenced questions encourage the students to use the facts they collect to think about reasons for moving to the suburbs and the problems that occurred once the suburbs became more populated.

In sequencing questions asked on one or multiple levels, think about the following:

1. The need for students to see connections among questions. The well-sequenced questions above have a logical connection; each question builds toward a final conclusion.

2. The supporting information students will need to answer each question and whether or not this information should be highlighted through other questions. For example, if students will ultimately be asked to make judgments about the value of two different meals, it may be necessary to first ask them how to determine the nutritional content of foods. Supporting information may come from the use of the text or reference sheets, but it may also come from questions the teacher asks.

3. The highest-level thinking students will use in answering the series of questions. The question requiring this level of thinking may be asked last or first. It is generally asked first if the teacher needs to highlight supporting information through questions. Asking the highest-level question first, however, can limit students' understanding to information related to the question. On the other hand, if the question is presented last students are afforded the opportunity to gain an understanding of the content, then reflect upon information or reread to seek clarification.

▼
PRACTICE ACTIVITY 4.1

Here is a short selection followed by a series of questions. Examine each question carefully and determine if it is a level 1, 2, or 3 question. Answers are found at the end of the book.

> Caloric needs vary by age and level of activity. Many older adults need less food relative to younger, more active individuals, in part due to decreased activity. People who are trying to lose weight and eating little food may need to select more nutrient-dense foods in order to meet their nutrient needs in a satisfying diet. Nearly all Americans need to be more active because a sedentary lifestyle is unhealthy. Increasing the calories spent in daily activities helps to maintain health and allows people to eat a nutritious and enjoyable diet.

1. Why do the amount of calories in one's diet vary by age?
2. Why do older adults need less food?
3. What will be the consequences if one engages in a diet high in calories and low in nutrients and one is also a sedentary individual?
4. Would an active older adult require more calories than an inactive older adult?

▼▼

Commentary: Asking Questions

Questions can be used to focus students' attention on critical information, direct them to reason with this information, and assist them in applying what they have learned to new situations. Questioning schemes such as those based on cognitive levels of thinking can help in designing questions that guide students to integrate their background knowledge with the text as they reason about the material. Care must be taken, however, in the wording of questions to avoid students misinterpreting them (Heath & McLaughlin, 1993).

There are several cautions to keep in mind when planning instructional questions. Both pertain to the students' level of involvement and participation. First, although questions can help students focus on relationships, the relationships they are likely to focus on are those suggested by the questions rather than those they identify on their own. At times, therefore, the questions may constrain the ways in which the students reason about the text. For example, after reading a text that describes a computer program, if students are asked to list cautions about buying the program, they may focus only on its disadvantages.

The second caution concerns the over reliance on teacher-generated questions. Proficient readers generate their own questions to keep track of their comprehension and whether or not they are meeting their purposes for reading. Besides answering questions, students need to learn to ask them, a difficult endeavor for many. Procedures for teaching question generation will be covered later in this chapter. Before that, teacher-directed activities that use questioning to help students understand and learn particular subject matter from reading material will be considered.

Discussion

Discussion is characterized by verbal interactions within the classroom whereby students communicate with one another and the teacher in a manner that allows discussants to present multiple points of view (Alvermann, Dillon, & O'Brien, 1987). Well-designed discussions promote the students' ability to consider the views and counterarguments voiced by others in the classroom community, and such discussions tend to sharpen students' conceptual understandings by allowing students to defend their views or statements and encourage students to focus on and address incomplete, inconsistent, or erroneous communications.

Use of Texts in Discussions

Alvermann, Dillon, O'Brien, and Smith (1985) have identified different ways that teachers use textbooks in discussions and the advantages and disadvantages of each. The first use identified by Alvermann et al. (1985) is for *verification*. Students can be guided in the use of the text to check the accuracy of what they say or to back up their points. Verification can help students tell the difference between directly stated and inferred information and thus help them identify instances in which they may be overrelying on background knowledge. If verification is overused, however, it can curtail students' independent thinking. The second use of the text is for *indirect reference*, or clues, which can lead to students comparing and contrasting present and past information. Use of indirect reference is useful when students can recall the correct information, but not when they are unsure of the material in the text. *Refocusing* discussions, the most frequent use of the text found by Alvermann et al., serves the purpose of keeping the discussion centered on the learning objectives. Care must be taken, however, to emphasize the students' ability to draw upon their own knowledge and problem-solving abilities, rather than placing too much importance on the text. The fourth use of the text is having the students *paraphrase*. Paraphrasing can give the students security as well as help their comprehension and memory of the material. Again, students should be encouraged, when possible, to draw on their own knowledge. Finally, students can be asked to recall the text rather than refer to it during discussion. *Closed book* discussions are used to encourage reading in preparation for discussion as well as assessment. A problem with closed book discussions is that they may deter students from critical thinking about the material as they focus on remembering the information.

Although it may seem that the disadvantages cancel out the advantages of each use of the text, this does not have to be the case. Taking into consideration all of the uses presented, there are several general guidelines for deciding how to use the text. First, try to establish a balance between asking students to justify and validate their responses using textbook information and using their background knowledge.

Second, encourage students to become more aware of different ways they can use the text in their contributions to discussions. They can be asked to identify the sources of their answers as well as whether using those sources is warranted, given the question asked.

Besides considering how to use the text for discussion, it is important to think about which sections of the text to use. Alvermann, Dillon, and O'Brien (1987) make several suggestions for using the textbook to support the discussion's purpose. For one, if the purpose of the discussion is to focus on ideas that are counterintuitive to what the students think, then it is important to use the portion of text containing these new ideas. For example, use of a text that explains the reason water droplets form on the outside of a glass holding a cool drink on a hot, humid summer day most likely will challenge students' conceptions that somehow the moisture is coming from the liquid inside the glass. If the purpose is issue oriented, the portion of the text selected for the discussion should stimulate thinking about that issue. If the discussion will focus on a problem (initiated by the teacher or by students), the part of the text that links with the problem should be used.

Use of Discussion Webs

The discussion web strategy promotes the use of discussion through the use of a graphic device containing students' responses to questions, tasks, or issues centered on a textbook (Alvermann, 1991). This strategy is particularly useful in directing students' attention and active involvement as they interact with a text selection or a nontext-based learning activity. The process of presenting the discussion web begins with the teacher's construction of a graphic display containing a statement followed by a column for responses to support the statement and a column to negate the statement. Finally, the graphic contains space for students to generate conclusions based on the discussion supporting and negating the statement presented. An example of a discussion web is presented in Figure 4.1. Once the web is constructed the teacher presents the discussion question to the students, assists in assigning students to groups who are directed to respond positively or negatively to the question, then circulates among the groups providing assistance, directing students to additional resources, or clarifying the question. Next, groups may present their position on the question to the entire class. Once these positions are presented, students are encouraged to debate, refine, or clarify their responses. Finally, students are asked to form a conclusion to the original question taking into account the various points of view and information presented in the discussion.

Commentary: Discussions

Initiating and maintaining discussions can be difficult. There is less teacher control, more ambiguity, and more on-the-spot decision making than in recitations. Generally, there are no "right" answers, and the teacher is frequently challenged to weave students' interpretations and opinions together to keep the discussion flowing. Successful discussions take place in an atmosphere of trust and encouragement of risk taking. It is important that students understand that the goal of participation is not always to identify the answer the teacher is looking for, but rather to share and

---

Directions: List reasons that support and do not support this statement.

The decline in communistic forms of government during the past decade is due primarily to economic failures of these governments rather than the political structure of these governments.

SUPPORT	DO NOT SUPPORT
_____	_____
_____	_____
_____	_____
_____	_____
_____	_____
_____	_____
_____	_____
_____	_____
_____	_____
_____	_____

Conclusion

Figure 4.1
Discussion Web for Social Studies

justify their thoughts on the topic. If they understand that their contributions are listened to and respected, they are more likely to participate. This atmosphere can take time to develop, but the time is well spent.

Discussions provide teachers an instructional activity to help students structure and organize the information in the text and the way in which they reason about it. The next instructional activity, the use of study guides, is another way in which the teacher can help students organize and reason about information in the text.

PRACTICE ACTIVITY 4.2

The graphic organizer, found in Figure 4.2, is designed to highlight important points in the past sections on discussion. Complete the outline, adding to or modifying it so that it will be most helpful to you in reviewing and consolidating these sections. A completed organizer is found at the end of the book.

▼ ▼

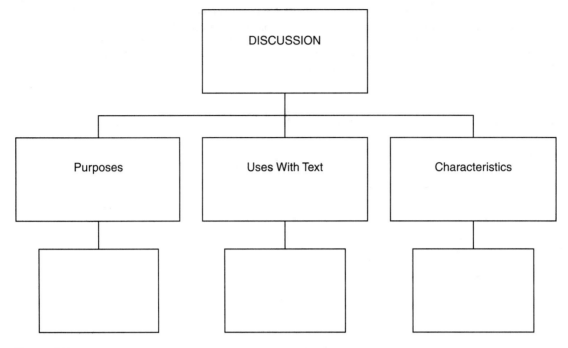

Figure 4.2
Discussion

Study Guides

Study guides highlight important concepts and information that students respond to while reading (Wood, Lapp, & Flood, 1992). Not only do these guides improve comprehension (Andre, 1987; Hamaker, 1986) but they also aid students in their metacognitive control of reading by signaling them to alter their reading rate, check for understanding, and think about what information is important (Wood, 1987).

To be successful, however, study guides should be constructed and administered using the following guidelines.

1. Provide students with supportive assistance and scaffolding. Begin with relatively simple content as you acquaint students with the process of reading with a study guide. Gradually increase the difficulty of the content and the tasks displayed in the study guide. Once familiar with the process of using the study guide, students should be challenged with higher-level thinking activities.

2. Use a variety of study guide formats that are suited to the needs of the students, the nature of the materials, and the level of difficulty of the objectives. To make study guides most beneficial, it is also important to explain their purpose and demonstrate how to use them (Wood, 1988).

3. Provide for discussion and cooperative efforts. Study guides need not be done individually. Allowing students to discuss their interpretation of activities on the guide will facilitate the process of using the guide and students' understanding of the content.

4. Refrain from presenting students study guides directing their attention to trivial or irrelevant information. The purpose of the study guide should be to both enhance students' learning and to facilitate their ability to engage in meaningful learning activities.

There are many kinds of study guides. Which to use depends on the learning objectives, the nature of the text, and the students' preparedness to learn the material. The next section describes several different types of study guides and general considerations for developing guides appropriate for particular lessons.

Three-Level Study Guide

The three-level study guide (Herber, 1978) consists of statements requiring level 1, level 2, and level 3 understanding. Construction of the three-level guide proceeds as follows:

1. Analyze content. Consider the content of the lesson and determine the main ideas. Determine which information is critical for grasping these ideas. Look for relationships among the information and between the material and students' background knowledge that will also aid in developing the principles. Finally, identify applications of the material.

2. Use declarative statements. Prepare the study guide, presenting statements students are to agree or disagree with. Level 1 statements can be supported by material found directly in the lesson. To support level 2 statements, the students need to put ideas together. To support level 3 statements, the students need to rely heavily on their background knowledge. The completed guide is then presented to the students who are instructed to respond to statements supported in a reading, demonstration, or class discussion. Finally, students are prompted to discuss the evidence for their selections. An example of a three-level study guide is shown in Figure 4.3

Textbook Activity Guides

Textbook activity guides, or TAGs (Davey, 1986) contain three components: questions and activities about the subject matter, cues about the processes to use to respond to these, and self-monitoring cues. Students work in pairs using strategy and self-monitoring codes to complete the guides. Each question or activity directs the student to the relevant pages in the text. Davey suggests the following strategy and self-monitoring codes be used.

Strategy Codes
P   Discuss with your partner
WR   Provide a written response on your own

Three-Level Study Guide For "A Jonquil For Mary Penn"

Directions: *Check the sentence or sentences that best answer each question.*

Gathering and Recalling Information: What are some of the qualities or attributes of Elton Penn?

_____ 1. Elton raised horses.

_____ 2. Elton was a rather independent individual—he started his own farm at the age of fourteen.

_____ 3. Elton had a good sense of humor.

_____ 4. Elton was sensitive to the needs of his wife, Mary.

_____ 5. Elton worked hard and played hard—he lived life to its fullest.

Making Sense of Gathered Information: What did the author mean to say about life in the farmland of America during the Great Depression?

_____ 1. People were much more sensitive to the needs of their community and family.

_____ 2. Most farmers were well off and had considerable time for leisure activities.

_____ 3. The spirit of community and dedication to the land gave people assets other than money.

_____ 4. Some of Mary's strongest and most pleasant emotions came from the simple things in her life.

Applying and Evaluating Actions in Novel Situations: The theme of this story applied to our daily lives today would suggest that

_____ 1. People are often distracted from their true inner emotions by the demands of their daily lives.

_____ 2. You can't earn respect for yourself if you are unable to be compassionate and sensitive to those around you.

_____ 3. We really don't have a need for community in today's fast-paced world.

_____ 4. Some of our most pleasant experiences are gained from relatively simple pleasures.

Figure 4.3
Three-Level Study Guide for "A Jonquil for Mary Penn"
Source: Berry, W. (1992) A jonquil for Mary Penn. *The Atlantic, 269*(2), 73–84.

Skim   Read quickly for the purpose stated; discuss with your partner

Map   Complete a semantic map of the information

PP   Predict with your partner

Self-Monitoring Codes

_____   I understand this information

_____   I'm not sure if I understand

_____   I do not understand and I need to restudy

Only parts of the text relevant to the learning objectives are focused on in the TAG, and only the strategy codes applicable to the tasks are suggested. A sample of a TAG is provided in Figure 4.4.

Bluegrass Music

Names _____   Date(s) _____

_____

Strategy Codes

P   **Discuss with your partner**

WR   **Provide a written response on your own**

Map   **Complete a semantic map of the information**

PP   **Predict with your partner**

Self-Monitoring Codes

___   **I understand this information**

___   **I'm not sure if I understand**

___   **I do not understand and I need to restudy**

1. ___PP   pp. 332–340 Look over the headings, pictures, and charts. What do you think you will learn about in this chapter?

2. ___P   pp. 332–335 Read the first two sections and discuss the most important information in each.

3. ___WR,P   pp. 337–338. Read the third section and jot down the differences between bluegrass and country music.

4. ___WR   pp. 338–340. Read the fourth section and answer the question at the end. Be prepared to discuss your answer.

5. ___Map   With your partner, make an outline of the development of bluegrass music.

6. ___P   pg. 340. With your partner, listen to the two songs on the tape. Which most clearly is an example of bluegrass music? What is your opinion of this song?

Figure 4.4
Texbook Activity Guide

The following procedure is recommended for developing a TAG (Davey, 1986):

1. Identify the learning objectives.
2. Identify sections of the text, headings, diagrams, etc., that are relevant to the learning objectives.
3. Select and sequence parts of the text that will be used in the TAG.
4. Select a study guide task that corresponds with each objective. Some objectives are best met through having the students discuss among themselves, others through drawing a diagram, others through listing.
5. Identify a strategy code that signals how to respond to each question and activity. Sometimes more than one strategy code is used for particular tasks. Write the tasks, strategy codes, and lines for the students to self-monitor on the guide.

Students complete the guides together and then can check their work with an answer key. They can also discuss their responses with the teacher, with other students, or with the whole class.

Collaborative Listening-Viewing Guide

The collaborative listening-viewing guide (reviewed in Wood, Lapp, & Flood, 1992) is designed to help students take notes and reason about information contained in a discussion, video- or audiotape, multimedia presentation, or lecture. This study guide is completed individually, in small groups, or as a class. There are five phases in completing the guide:

1. Preview/review. In this phase, background knowledge is accessed or constructed through brainstorming, teacher-directed vocabulary instruction, or any relevant prereading activities (adapted for listening or viewing). The students write the important previewed or reviewed information on their forms.

2. Record. As the students watch or listen to the presentation, they individually write down brief notes about important ideas or events.

3. Elaborate. The students work in small groups to organize the notes they have taken and to add details to them.

4. Synthesize. As a class, the students work together to identify and discuss the main concepts of the presentation. As in all phases, they record their conclusions on the form.

5. Extend. In pairs, the students apply the information learned. This may be done in a variety of ways including writing summary paragraphs, making semantic maps of the information, or identifying further research questions they would like to explore.

Graphic Organizers

Recall that graphic organizers, discussed in Chapter 3, are pictorial representations of relationships among facts and concepts. Used before reading, graphic organizers can provide students with clues about how the material is structured; used during reading, they can serve as a study guide to focus the students' attention on important information and relationships. Students can complete and modify graphic organizers as they read to focus on specific information, to note relationships, or to engage in higher-level thinking. The organizers can also be completed and modified in small groups in which students have to explain and justify the relationships they have identified.

Graphic organizers can be used in conjunction with questions to focus attention on relationships. For example, before reading, the students can be given a question that involves their reasoning about the material in the text. For example, they could be asked to think about the economic as well as political factors that led to a rise in taxes. To assist students in addressing the question, they can then be given a graphic organizer, partially filled in. As a class, or in small groups, they complete the organizer as they read.

Identification and presentation of text structures in graphic organizers are likely to enhance the students' understanding of content and the construction of the text. Figure 4.5 has sample representations of organizers based on two text structures— description and problem/solution. Figure 4.6 contains examples of two other forms for study guides: the questioning guide and the partially completed outline. Refer to Chapter 3 for suggested procedures for developing graphic organizers.

By now it should be clear that study guide formats can range from the presentation of statements to the use of graphic devices that promote discussion and facilitate students' monitoring of their own thinking. Several factors can guide decisions about whether to use a study guide and which format to use (Wood, Lapp, & Flood, 1992). These include

▼   the concepts, vocabulary, and information that are important to the lesson

▼   the difficulty of the material, or portions of it

▼   the skills and strategies students will need to understand and learn from the material

▼   whether individual, small, or whole group activities are preferred

▼   time constraints of the teacher for both preparation and instruction.

Types of Measurement			
Weight	**Distance**	**Temperature**	**Volume**
gram ounce	inch millimeter	Farenheit Celsius	pint liter
____ ____	____ ____		____
	____ ____		____

Figure 4.5
Example of Descriptive Text Structure with Concept Map Study Guide

---

Questioning Guide

As you read the article on the schooling of black Americans, answer the following questions. Some of the questions ask you to form a response before you read a section of the article, other questions are designed to be answered during or after the reading.

Before Reading

1. What are some of the obstacles you have encountered that you feel may have had an adverse effect upon your education?

2. What role do your family and friends have in your desire to obtain an education? How has your parents' and relatives' level of education affected your desire to go to college or finish high school?

During Reading

1. Read the first two pages of the article. As you are reading note the explanations provided by the author as to why blacks encounter so many obstacles in obtaining an education.

2. Read the final four pages of the article. Consider this question as you read, and write a response when you have finished reading the article.

   "The author addresses the need to improve the self-esteem of black students in schools. Note the suggestions she provides, then write a summary of the actions you believe would be effective in improving self-esteem.

After Reading

Interview your school principal or a district administrator to determine what steps have been taken by the district during the past ten years to address some of the issues raised in this article. Based on the information you obtain, draft a plan of action you believe would address the problems raised in this article.

Figure 4.6
Examples of Alternative Forms of Study Guides

Commentary: Study Guides

Study guides can assist students' learning of information and concepts deemed important by the teacher. However, if the use of study guides is limited to gathering information, students may be denied the opportunity to construct their own interpretation or questions about the material presented. Nonetheless, they do serve as a model for students of ways in which they can help themselves organize information.

Study guides can take considerable time and effort to prepare. An alternative to teacher-made study guides are those generated by students in cooperative groups. Initially the teacher shares his thinking in creating a guide, emphasizing the relationship of the text to the learning objective and the way in which he searches for important

Partially Completed Outline

As you read the information on nails and screws, fill in the information in the partially completed outline provided.

I. Nails

   A. Sizes of Nails
      1. length designated in inches
      2. diameter designated _____

   B. Driving Nails
      1. length of nail should be three times thickness of wood
      2. nail should be driven through the _____ part of the wood
      3. factors that increase holding power of nail
         a. _____
         b. _____
         c. _____

   C. Function of Nailheads
      1. spread load over surface
      2. _____
      3. _____

II. Screws

   A. Sizes of Screws
      1. length designated by _____
      2. size designated by _____

   B. Types of Screws
      1. Dome head
         a. function = decorative screw
      2. _____ screw
         b. function = fasten end-to-end joints
      3. Hanger bolt
         a. function = _____

   C. When to Use Screws
      1. Need to increase fastening power
      2. When things need to be _____.

Figure 4.6
Continued

concepts in the text. Next, the teacher and students create a guide together. Finally, the students, in groups, create guides for their peers. Each group can make a guide for a separate section of the text or they can all focus on the same section and compare the ways in which they reasoned about it. Besides reducing teacher preparation time, student-generated guides facilitate higher-level thinking as the students look for important concepts and discuss these in their groups. A final benefit is the assessment of the students' ability to identify the important points of the material. Study guides have been presented as instructional activities to be used in guiding students to learn from and reason about subject matter content. Through the use of these activities, teachers can help students organize information. The activities also suggest to students ways in which they can reason about the material by examining relationships between text information and prior knowledge.

The past sections have included suggestions for having students assume responsibility for their learning in such ways as generating questions for recitation and discussion as well as developing study guides. For the remainder of the chapter, the focus will be on instructional activities that prepare students to become independent learners who can reason about and learn from text in subject matter areas on their own.

ACTIVITIES TO PROMOTE INDEPENDENT READING

Over the past fifteen years, researchers have identified and validated a number of powerful strategies students can employ in learning from text (Pearson, 1996; Pressley & Woloshyn, 1995; Rosenshine, 1995; Wood, Woloshyn, & Willoughby, 1995). It is important that processes or strategies used to independently comprehend and learn from text occur in the context of everyday subject matter learning rather than be presented only in isolation. To be useful, students should be able to select an appropriate strategy, adapt it to the particular texts they read (Pressley, Johnson, Symons, McGoldrick, & Kurita, 1989), and evaluate their success in doing so. By learning strategies that are meaningful and authentic within the confines of subject matter texts, students are more likely to recognize those strategies that help them understand that particular content (Peters, 1990). Instruction for proficient reading can be framed by the following guidelines.

1. Focus on strategies that are truly helpful for meeting the goals of real tasks in content area learning.
2. Help the students learn the strategies while they are also learning the content so they will see the value of the strategies.
3. Incorporate discussion and sharing of strategies and their helpfulness into instruction.

Selecting Strategies to Teach

There are many strategies used by proficient readers. The type of strategy used for a given text depends on the purpose for reading, the characteristics of the reader, and the characteristics of the text. Some texts lead to one type of strategy while others do not. For example, the strategies used in reading a newspaper editorial differ from those used in reading a novel. The task of reading to study for a test differs from that of reading to get an idea for a term paper, as do the strategies used for completing these tasks. If a text has a clear structure, such as a fairy tale, strategies involving predictions based on text structure can be used. Yet if the text is disorganized and without clear structure, this strategy would not be as helpful.

Students with little background knowledge about particular subject matter will use different approaches to understanding the text than those who have the ability to connect information in the text with information previously learned. Strategy use is also a matter of personal preferences. Students should be encouraged to use strategies that "work for them," and research shows that students will modify strategies to fit their personal need (Garner & Gillingham, 1996).

Palincsar (1986) presents three useful guidelines for selecting strategies to teach. The first guideline is the ease of instruction. If teaching a strategy is too complicated, the students are not likely to be able to attend to the content they are using the strategy with and thus will not see its value. The second guideline is the flexibility of the strategy. Strategies that can be used across a wide variety of reading situations are those that should be taught rather than those with only limited use. The final guideline is the use of the strategy for comprehension monitoring, or helping students determine whether or not they are understanding and learning.

By considering the general guidelines along with the particular students, the particular text, and the purpose of reading it, appropriate and useful strategies can be identified. Sharing reasons for selecting particular strategies with the students can serve as a model for them to use in selecting strategies they will use in their independent reading and studying.

PRACTICE ACTIVITY 4.3

Consider the learning strategies you use in the following: Presume that you will make a twenty-minute presentation to a local community organization on the role of the school-to-work curriculum in the public schools. Now consider the strategies you will use to gather information, form generalizations, recognize new concepts, and draw conclusions.

▼▼▼

Teaching for Independent Strategy Use

Instruction for proficient independent reading can be seen as fitting the model of **gradual release of responsibility** (Pearson & Gallagher, 1983), shown in Figure 4.7. The teacher's role can be seen along a continuum of directiveness. When students are first learning strategies, the teacher provides *direct, explicit instruction*. As the students begin to use the strategies on their own to guide their reading, the teacher provides *supportive instruction*, giving them the help they need to use the strategies while reading particular texts. Through this process, the students move toward independent use of the strategies to direct their reading.

Following is a closer examination of direct, explicit instruction and supportive instruction of comprehension activities.

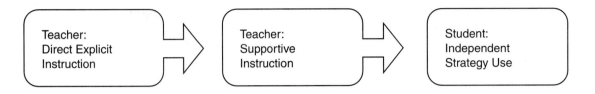

Student Dependence   **Student Independence**

Figure 4.7
Gradual Release of Responsibility

Explicit Instruction

Teachers provide explicit information to students about comprehension strategies through the use of explanations and mental modeling. They talk about and demonstrate the thinking processes that they use while working to understand the text. Following are descriptions and examples of each.

Explanations

Too often, students' and teachers' understanding of the point of lessons do not coincide. Perhaps one of the reasons for this is that the purpose for what they are learning has not been clearly explained to the students (Roehler & Duffy, 1986). Roehler and Duffy (1991) define explanations as explicit statements about what is being learned, why it is being learned, why it can be used, and how to use it. Students need to learn the **what, why, when,** and **how** of strategy use (Paris, Lipson, & Wixon, 1983) if the goal is for them to use these strategies on their own to control their reading and learning. Following is an explicit explanation about self-questioning using headings given to seventh graders in a science class.

> Today we are going to learn about a way to check our understanding of what we are reading (what is being learned). We will use the headings to form questions before we read each section and then see if we can answer those questions (when to use it). As you know, headings often give us clues about what the important information in the sections will be. By turning those headings into questions, we can focus our attention on the important upcoming information. Learning the important information will prepare us for understanding upcoming sections. Answering the questions will help us know whether we are understanding the important information. I have found this quite helpful to me in keeping track of my understanding (why it is being learned). This is a strategy that can be used in any books or articles that have headings (when it can be used). To use this strategy, we think about the information that the heading tells us is likely to be in the next section, and use one or two question words to begin questions about this information that we think will be answered from reading the section. When we have read the section, we will try to answer the questions (how to use it).

▼ Practice Activity 4.4

What kinds of information (what, why, when, how) does Mr. Smith include in the following explanation of the use of summarizing to his eighth-grade social studies class? What is missing? "Today we will be learning about summarizing chapters. There are three steps in summarizing that you can follow. First, identify important information. Second, put the information in categories. Third, write two to three sentences for each category."

Answers can be found at the end of the book.

▼▼▼

Students can be invited to expand upon the teacher's explanations. Generally, they will be at least somewhat familiar with the strategies introduced by the teacher. Just as it is important to help students activate their background knowledge about subject matter, it is also important to bring to the forefront what they know about strategic approaches to reading. Not only will this prepare them to learn more about strategies, it will also prompt them to think about ways in which strategies can and do benefit them.

Mental Modeling

Another means of providing information to students is through mental modeling, or thinking aloud. Mental modeling refers to the teacher talking about what he is doing while doing it, focusing on the reasoning involved while carrying out the task (Roehler & Duffy, 1991). The teacher thinks aloud about a strategy (or strategies) as he uses it (them) to understand the text, sharing with the students thoughts about selecting, using, and evaluating the strategy(ies). Mental modeling differs from explanation because it occurs while the teacher is actually using the strategy. Like explanations, mental modeling makes the reasoning involved in strategy use clear. In the following example, Mr. Lotsky models his reasoning while he uses text structure to identify important information while reading about mail fraud.

> (Before reading): I really hope I learn something from this text because I saw the tail end of a television show on this subject. The commentator was saying that millions of dollars are lost every year through mail fraud and that there are important steps we can take to prevent this from happening. I would like to know what we can do.
>
> (After reading the first paragraph): I now understand more about what mail fraud is and who can be affected by it. It sure is a problem. I am expecting, given the title of this article, *Saving Americans from Falling Victims to Mail Fraud,* that I am going to learn some solutions to this problem. I sure hope I do. I know in articles like this, once a problem is stated, a solution is often suggested. I sure hope I am right about this article. I am going to read to find solutions and jot them down as I find them to help me remember how I can prevent this from happening to me.

> (While reading): Here is something I think is a solution: call the Better Business Bureau if you do not receive something you ordered through the mail in eight weeks. I'll bet the people at the bureau could track down the problem. I wonder if we'll read about their "track record."

In the above example, Mr. Lopez was not only modeling his thinking about what strategy he would use and why he would do so. He was also modeling his use of background knowledge to make predictions and set a purpose for reading. Mental modeling provides a wonderful opportunity to share the reasoning about strategy use in a natural, realistic context.

Supportive Instruction

As students become more able to use reading strategies, instruction becomes less directive and more of a support. This support can take the form of guided questions that lead the students to become more aware of how, why, and when to use strategies. For example, the teacher may ask: "What do you know about section headings and, using that knowledge, what do you think we will learn in this chapter?" It can also involve on-the-spot modeling of the use of a strategy in a particular reading situation such as:

> The heading indicated we were going to learn how to distinguish impressionist and postimpressionist paintings. I am not sure I can do that, though. Sometimes it helps me to stop and review. Let's see: How are the two styles alike and how do they differ?

Another way to provide support is through feedback about the way in which understanding is affected by the use of a strategy, as seen in the following:

> Those questions you asked about drilling for oil make sense in light of what we learned about coal mining in yesterday's chapter. Oftentimes, chapters in books are structured similarly. The kinds of information we get from one chapter may give clues about the kinds of information we'll get in the next one.

Peer Support

Peers working together in cooperative or collaborative groups can also provide a means of support during strategy learning (Conley, 1990). Students working cooperatively on such tasks as creating graphic organizers, writing questions, constructing summaries, or even more generally sharing their reactions to texts have the opportunity to discuss, justify, and question their own approaches. It is important for students to "discuss their goals with others, help one another understand the tasks required, and help one another to work hard" (Conley, 1990, p. 121).

While reading and thinking about applying the particular instructional activities to teach independent proficient reading in the next section, consider ways in which cooperative groups could be used to help move the students toward independent strategic reading. The activities to be presented are text structure instruction, summarizing, self-questioning, reciprocal teaching, and content processing guides.

Text Structure Instruction

The organization or structure of the text itself can be used to guide students' understanding of the reading material. There are five common expository text structures (Richgels, McGee, and Slaton, 1989). The first is *description* or "a grouping of ideas by association" (Richgels, McGee, & Slaton, 1989, p. 168) as exemplified in this paragraph:

In the near future buildings will be heated by energy produced within a structure, or "free heat." This is heat that is produced by people, the lights in the building, and the equipment that uses energy in the building such as refrigeration, electrical appliances, computers, etc. While this source of heat isn't free—there is a cost to run the equipment generating the heat—it is existing heat than can be stored and used at times that heating equipment would need to be drawn upon to warm a building.

The second structure is *collection*. In this structure, ideas are groups with an organization, order, or sequence.

There are a number of ways of reducing the energy used for illuminating buildings. First, electrical lighting can be reduced by making use of sunlight as a source of illumination. Buildings in Japan now have fiber-optic cables that carry sunlight throughout a building. Second, a building can be equipped with photosensitive sensors that operate blinds, constantly adjusting them to maintain a certain level of light. Third, reflectors can be placed on windows to direct light to alternative locations within a building.

In *causation*, the third structure, students look for causal connections between ideas.

A rather cost-effective procedure and time-honored strategy for reducing the energy consumption of a building is to shade it with trees and shrubs and paint it a light color. At a temperature of 85 degrees Fahrenheit a light-colored building that is shaded by trees reflects the sun's rays to the point of reducing the energy needed for cooling by about 300%.

The fourth structure builds on the third, but has even more structure. This is the *problem/solution* structure.

The biggest problem faced in reducing home energy consumption is increasing the energy efficiency of motors, lights, and refrigeration used to cool foods. One low-cost solution is to replace incandescent lighting with fluorescent lighting, which consumes 75 to 85 percent less electricity than incandescent sources of lighting. Another solution is to purchase one of the new lines of highly efficient refrigerators which, on average, consume 80 to 90 percent less electricity than conventional models.

The fifth structure is *comparison/contrast*, in which similarities and differences between elements or ideas are noted.

> Conservation of energy can be achieved through more prudent use and through application of technology. While prudent use is an individual decision and may require changes in one's lifestyle, the application of technology normally involves the outlay of capital to obtain an immediate reduction in the consumption of energy. Long-term, radical reduction in energy consumption will require more widespread prudent use and the application of technology.

Figure 4.8 presents questions based on the different text structures.

Text structures can be used for developing questions when the text is well structured as well as when it is more loosely organized. Many students are unfamiliar with these structures and how these structures can be used to improve their understanding of text. Text structures can be used as strategies to help students comprehend, remember, and learn from text (Flood, Lapp, & Farnan, 1986; McGee & Richgels, 1985;

Figure 4.8
Text Structure Questions

Text Structure Questions

Description
- What is being described?
- What did we learn about it?

Collection
- What happened first, second, last, etc.?

Causation
- What happened?
- What were the reasons for ...?
- What caused ...?

Problem/Solution
- Was there a problem? What was it?
- What was the solution to the problem?

Comparison/Contrast
- What was being compared?
- What are the similarities?
- What are the differences?

Piccolo, 1987). Using the structure of texts, students can form predictions about what they will be reading and ask questions to organize the information as they read it.

Here are some suggestions, adapted from Piccolo (1987), for encouraging students to use text structure to guide their reading.

1. Write prereading questions for the students that correspond to text structures. Share with the students the ways in which you identified the text structure and used it to develop questions.

2. Model for students how to use headings and subheadings to predict the questions the text will answer or what the content will be. Have them make text structure-based predictions in cooperative groups and then justify these predictions to the class.

3. Instruct students to skim for clue words, or words that signify particular structures (see Figure 4.9). The students can use the signal words and the topic sentence to make predictions about the kinds of information they will learn and to formulate prereading questions. As the students read the text, they can jot down the answers to the text structure questions.

Summarizing

Summarizing has been shown to be related to an increased comprehension of the material being summarized, learning of new material, recall of the text, vocabulary

---

Signal or Clue Words for Text Structures

Description
- No specific clue words.

Collection
- First, second, third, next, last, finally

Causation
- So, so that, because, as a result of, since, in order to

Problem/Solution
- Problem is, solution, solved by, the issue here

Comparison/Contrast
- Alike, same as, similar to, resembles, compared to, unlike, different from

---

Figure 4.9
Signal or Clue Words for Text Structures

development, and the promotion of critical reading (Hill, 1991; Pearson & Fielding, 1991). It is also an excellent way of keeping track of comprehension during and following reading. Although summarizing is difficult for many students, especially when reading poorly structured or complicated texts (Hill, 1991), the benefits of summarizing make it an important strategy to teach.

Summarizing consists of the use, in some form, of the following rules identified by Brown and Day (1983):

1. Delete trivial or unimportant information.
2. Delete redundant information.
3. Provide a name for categories of information (e.g., recreation, influences on weather).
4. Identify and use the author's main ideas.
5. Create your own main ideas if they are not stated.

In teaching summarizing, there is much opportunity for both explicit instruction and mental modeling. Along with this, there is ample opportunity to demonstrate to students how writing can enhance reading.

GRASP, or the guided reading and summarizing procedure (Hayes, 1989), is an instructional activity designed to help students learn to independently write summaries for reports as well as to increase their ability to recall information, self-correct, and organize material. Following is a description of GRASP:

1. Getting ready. Hayes suggests using an article from an encyclopedia to teach summarizing, although any reading material may be used. The teacher tells the students that they are going to learn how to summarize the information and then talks about situations in which this may be valuable. The students are told that the procedure for writing a group summary is similar to the procedure they can use on their own.

2. Reading for information. The teacher directs the students to read the article and remember all they can. After reading, the class compiles a list of all information remembered. Next, the students are instructed to reread the material to see if there was any other information that should be on the list and to correct any misinformation.

3. Organizing remembered information. At this point, the students and teacher attempt to identify the major topics of the text. The topics are used as categories into which the students and teacher group the recalled information. Following this, they discuss and identify relationships among the categories.

4. Writing the summary. The teacher now explains that there are three things to do with the material: (a) put important information in the summary and leave out unnecessary details, (b) combine information if possible, and (c) add information to make the summary coherent. The teacher proceeds to model, turning the first category into one sentence, talking about the selection and combination of information. The students write individual summaries for the next category, as does the teacher. Volunteers read their sentences. The teacher and class discuss the strengths of the volunteers' summaries and compare them to the teacher's summary. The teacher's summary is revised based on the students' alternatives. Hayes suggests that a visible record of the revisions be made by crossing out rather than erasing. This makes the revision process more concrete for the students. The class proceeds through each category in the same fashion until a summary of the entire passage is written. In later lessons, the teacher can focus on revising the summaries even further so they are more clearly and conventionally written.

Hayes's procedure focuses on the reasoning involved in summarizing. The teacher's modeling, as well as the group discussion of students' ideas for summaries, makes the thinking processes explicit. Working with a real text, the students are exposed to the "real-world" difficulties involved in summarizing. Figure 4.10 presents an example of the use of GRASP.

Summaries can help students study for a test, prepare for a presentation, or more generally check their understanding. They should be encouraged to use this strategy informally, jotting an outline of a summary, making an organizer that represents categories and details, or identifying the main categories of information. It is an excellent strategy to work on in small groups; the questions raised as the group composes a summary will force the students to verbalize how they are organizing the material they are reading, an important precursor to doing this on their own.

Self-Questioning

When self-questioning, students ask themselves questions about the text rather than answering questions asked by the teacher. The students' questions can guide their reading of upcoming sections as well as check their understanding of what they have already read. Questioning gives them purposes for reading. Many instructional studies (Rosenshine, Meister, & Chapman, 1996) have found that students' increased their reading performance after instruction in self-questioning.

Like summarizing, question asking is difficult for many students. For much of their school lives, they have become accustomed to answering rather than asking questions. Students are not likely to become proficient at this if only told to practice (Davey & McBride, 1986). Rather, students need to be taught how to ask questions to guide and check their reading. There are a variety of ways to teach students to ask themselves questions as they read. However self-questioning is taught, it is important to focus on why and how questions are used (Wong, 1985), to model the reasoning involved in question generation, and to provide sufficient opportunities for the students to practice asking questions (Balajthy, 1984). Following are several procedures for helping students develop question asking.

Reciprocal Questioning

The reciprocal questioning, or ReQuest, procedure (Manzo, 1969) was designed to help students set purposes for reading through questioning, but can be extended to help them self-check their understanding throughout the reading process. Manzo and Manzo (1990) describe the steps in this procedure:

Example of the Guided Reading and Summarizing Procedure (GRASP)

Trade association is a nonprofit organization that represents a group of business firms. Businesses join their associations voluntarily and manage them cooperatively. The companies work together to accomplish goals that nosingle firm could reach by itself.

A trade association may have only a few members, as in the ironmaking and steelmaking industry. Or it may have thousands of members, as in an association of retail grocers. The size of the trade association's membership has little to do with the effectiveness of the organization. It is more important that the association include most of the companies in the industry. About 3,600 trade associations operate on the national level in the United States.

Trade association activities include promoting business for the industry, encouraging ethical practices in the industry, cooperating with other organizations, and holding conventions. Such associations also work to obtain good relations with the government, the industry's employees, and the general public.

Trade associations sponsor much of the industrial research work in the United States. This research helps improve the quality of goods and services sold by individual firms. Setting industry standards is another important trade association activity. By obtaining agreements among firms, the trade association sets standards of size and quality for articles and services.

A trade association acts as a source of information about its industry. It may issue bulletins on business trends and provide statistical information. Some publish magazines that are distributed to the public. Trade associations date back to the guilds formed in Europe during the Middle Ages.

From *The World Book Encyclopedia.* © 1993 World Book, Inc. Reprinted by permission of the publisher.

Details Remembered From the Encyclopedia Article

Students' First Recollections	Additions/Corrections
few or many members	Information source
do research	*sponsor* research
3,600 trade unions	work for good relations
have conventions	promote business
encourage ethics	cooperative management
voluntary	represents group of firms
nonprofit	
publish magazines	*some* publish magazines
important to have most companies set standards	

Figure 4.10
Example of the Guided Reading and Summarizing Procedure (GRASP)

1. The teacher tells the students that they will be learning to set purposes for reading.

2. The teacher and students look over the text and read the title and first sentence. The students ask the teacher questions about the first sentence which the teacher answers. The students are told to ask questions that a teacher might ask.

3. The teacher now asks the students questions that focus their attention on the purpose of the selection or the key ideas. If the students cannot answer the teacher's questions, they are asked to explain why.

4. The students and the teacher continue to ask each other questions about each sentence. The teacher begins to model questions that require integration of material across sentences. The process should continue until the students comprehend the first paragraph and have set a purpose for reading the rest of the selection. After reading the selection, the students discuss whether they set a good purpose and then proceed to answer their purpose question.

To concretely illustrate this procedure, here is an example of a seventh-grade interdisciplinary lesson focusing on the formation of hurricanes and the social and economic effects of their destruction.

Step 1: Defining the Purpose for ReQuest

Teacher: As we begin our study of hurricanes—how they are formed, their destructive power, and their effect on people—we will be learning how to set a purpose for reading.

Step 2: Student Questioning

Teacher: Read the title of the selection and the first sentence. When you have finished, create some questions like those you think a teacher would ask.

> Hurricanes develop from the growth of waves that may develop into a tropical depression with winds up to 31 miles per hour; then it may develop into a tropical storm with winds up to 74 miles per hour; and ultimately it may develop into a hurricane with winds over 74 miles per hour.

Student A: Why do the waves move from east to west?

Student B: Why do these storms produce such strong winds?

Student C: Do all hurricanes start out as tropical depressions or tropical storms?

Step 3: Teacher-Generated Purpose-Setting Questions

Teacher: What are some of the central ideas of this selection?

Student A: It's about hurricanes.

Student B: The selection describes how hurricanes are formed.

Student C: I think that the selection will eventually talk about the movement and destruction of hurricanes.

Teacher: Which has more destructive force—a tropical depression or a tropical storm?

Student A: It must be the tropical storm because the winds are greater.

Student B: I'm not certain either one can really destroy very much.

Student C: I don't know the answer. The sentence doesn't really talk about destruction.

Teacher: It might be useful to focus on the force of winds for a moment to determine how powerful they must be to be destructive. As you recall, last summer we had a powerful thunderstorm with winds of 50 miles per hour. Remember how many trees went down? How many of you were without power for several days because of the power lines that fell down in that storm?

Step 4: Integration of Material Across Sentences

Teacher: Read the following sentence.

Hurricanes move westward along the equator until they fully develop, turning northward and picking up speed until they reach temperate latitudes, where they turn east and lose their strength over cool water.

Teacher: Now consider this sentence and the first sentence we read. Remember that we learned that hurricanes are formed from the buildup of waves. As the hurricane is building, in what direction are the waves moving?

Student A: In the direction of the hurricane.

Student B: They are moving toward the west because the hurricane moves toward the west, and waves cause the hurricanes.

Reciprocal questioning can also be used when selections of the text are particularly difficult. The students and teacher can question each other about their understanding of what they have read. It is important for the teacher to model questions that require students to focus not only on details but on main ideas and connections among ideas.

Interactive Questioning Activity

The interactive questioning activity (Winn, Ryder, & Netzo, 1993) is a procedure to help students focus on the main points while reading a biography, but it can be used with other types of texts that have many details. To help students organize details, as well as to develop their ability to make inferences, the procedure involves the following strategic routine:

1. Read a segment of the text and write down the information learned. This can be presented to the students as similar to taking notes.

2. Categorize the information and explain why you grouped the information as you did. This can be done in small peer groups, sharing categories generated for the same text.

3. For each category, develop a question that the information can answer. The students can be guided to develop questions that involve putting the information together and making inferences from it. Students are more likely to self-generate questions when they are provided instruction using generic question stems (Rosenshine et al., 1996). These stems appear to provide students the opportunity to initiate the recall of background information resulting in more comprehensive questions focusing on deeper levels of understanding. Instruction on the use of the following generic questions should be particularly useful:

   ▼ How does _____ affect _____? Why is there such a relationship?

   ▼ What is the meaning of _____?

   ▼ What is an example of _____ and what else do I know that is similar?

   ▼ Describe _____ and why is this important?

   ▼ What events or factors lead up to _____ and what is the impact of this on the future?

This procedure is similar to Hayes's (1989) summarization instruction discussed earlier. In both, the students begin with details and then organize these into categories or main ideas. Also in both, the students are encouraged to share their thinking about how the information is organized.

It is important to note that students do not benefit equally from self-questioning instruction. Several studies (Andre & Anderson, 1978–1979; Wong & Jones, 1982) have shown that lower achieving or learning disabled students benefited more from instruction in self-questioning than did higher achieving students. Most likely the more proficient learners are already using this strategy; perhaps they could serve as peer tutors and guides for others in the class as this strategy is being presented.

A System for Studying

Many of the strategies discussed in the first half of this chapter assist the reader in comprehending text independent of the teacher's assistance. Self-questioning, graphic organizers, summarization, and the use of text structure are also useful and effective strategies to facilitate students' studying. Each of these activities can be used by the students to improve their understanding as they read, to review classroom notes, or to gather information in preparation for writing activities. This section contains a comprehensive system for studying.

Proficient readers engage in a number of behaviors to comprehend from text as they study. Decisions must be made as to where information can be located, which information is important, and how to organize and make some sort of record of that information in order that it may be retrieved and communicated at a later date (Anderson & Armbruster, 1984). While study strategies have been shown to be effective (Alvermann & Moore, 1991; Anderson & Armbruster, 1984; Nist, Simpson, & Hogrebe, 1985), it is evident that most teachers do not teach these strategies (Alvermann & Moore, 1991; Durkin, 1978–1979), and students who could benefit from them the most (those having difficulty comprehending text) don't generally use them (Simpson, 1983).

As with other types of instruction that focus on the acquisition of strategies, students will be more likely to acquire study strategies when the teacher explains their use, models the process of applying the strategy to subject matter material, and eventually assumes a supportive role as students use the strategy in the context of a group process or independent reading.

SQ3R: A System of Study

SQ3R (Robinson, 1961) is a time honored and systematic study strategy that involves prereading, reading, and postreading activities. SQ3R consists of the following steps:

1. Survey. The student examines text headings and titles to acquire a gist of the concepts presented in the reading selection.
2. Question. The student attends to each of the headings or titles located during step 1 and then generates a question from that heading or title.
3. Read. The student reads the text with the goal of answering the questions generated in step 2.
4. Recite. The student evaluates responses to the questions, then makes notes on important information or concepts that were learned.
5. Review. The student now closes the reading and covers up the notes and attempts to summarize the important information or concepts learned.

While SQ3R has been in use for over fifty years, relatively little is known about the effectiveness of this study system. In a review of six studies that examined the effectiveness of SQ3R with adolescents and adults, Adams, Carnine, and Gersten (1982) report mixed results. Because this is a time-consuming and rather complex study system, it has been suggested that its effectiveness may depend upon extensive training, especially for students who lack effective study strategies (West, Farmer, & Wolff, 1991). This training should consist of (1) modeling the strategy, (2) providing structured guidance with the strategy, and (3) engaging students in cooperative efforts to refine the application of the strategy.

Modeling the Strategy
The teacher models the steps of SQ3R with a short text passage. This process begins with the teacher defining the purpose of SQ3R, how it will benefit the students' ability

to learn from text, and finally presenting the students with a handout that lists the various steps of the strategy. Modeling begins as the teacher draws the students' attention to each heading or title, then thinks aloud to the students about how these headings are used to anticipate the content of the selection. Thus if the first heading reads "How the Media Affects the Presidential Campaign," the teacher may want to draw upon background knowledge to predict that this section may contain information about how the candidates use the media to their advantage, or how the media uses controversial issues in the campaign to market the sale of its own products (advertising time or viewer ratings). When a text lacks headings, a heading can be constructed by reading the first sentence of each paragraph and then, on the basis of this information, generating a heading that would seem to define the content of the paragraph or group of paragraphs. The teacher then thinks aloud to the class about how this heading was used to formulate a question, and the question is placed on a transparency or chalkboard. The section of text immediately following the heading is read aloud to the class, then the teacher again thinks aloud about how the question is answered, and the response is noted on the transparency or chalkboard. This question-read-review process is repeated for several headings. Finally, the teacher presents the responses to the various questions on a transparency or chalkboard and demonstrates to students how this information can be summarized, again thinking aloud about the process of reviewing information acquired from the selection.

Guidance with the Strategy

The students are now reading to learn the SQ3R strategy through a step-by-step process directed by the teacher. This should be viewed as a cooperative effort—teacher and students share equally in their effort to learn the strategy. The process begins with the students reviewing the steps of SQ3R, then examining the heading of the first section of text. Again, in the absence of headings, students may read the first sentence of each paragraph and generate headings based on the content of the sentence. Having acknowledged the heading, the teacher elicits questions from the students which are noted on a transparency or chalkboard. It is important to ask students to explain the process they used in generating their question, paying particular attention to the cues they draw from the headings. It is likely that this step will result in the identification of a wide variety of questions addressing both factual-level information and higher-level thinking. It is important to clarify to students that these questions reflect their personal goals for reading, that SQ3R is a personal study strategy, and that a range of questions is therefore anticipated. With the questions displayed to the students, the teacher can then ask them to select a question and read to answer that question. Once students have answered their question, they describe what they have learned as the teacher notes this information on the chalkboard or a transparency. Once all questions have been answered and the students' responses are displayed, the teacher directs a discussion by asking students to think aloud about the process they used to review and summarize. Finally, the teacher reviews the steps of SQ3R, asks students to comment on its effectiveness, and summarizes the insights gathered from class discussion. These insights may be recorded on a bulletin board, in students' learning journals, or on a handout to be distributed to the students.

Cooperative Efforts

The final step in training students how to use SQ3R involves their application of the strategy in cooperative groups. The goal here is to promote discussion among students on the process of applying SQ3R to the subject matter content, then to reflect upon and describe that process to the class. For each group, the teacher designates an individual to record the group's questions and responses, an individual to direct the group through the steps of SQ3R, and an individual who summarizes the group's insights and evaluates their strategy. Students are provided a two- to three-page reading selection and are directed to adhere to the following guidelines:

1. The group leader assumes the responsibility of leading the group through the various steps of SQ3R.
2. All group members are encouraged to generate questions.
3. As questions are answered, group members should describe the process used to answer questions. The recorder should record these comments.
4. Once all questions have been answered, the reading should be removed and the group should summarize what they have learned from the reading.
5. The group should discuss their views of the effectiveness of SQ3R. These comments should be noted by the recorder so they may be presented to the entire class.

Use of cooperative groups can be an effective way to begin the process of allowing students to apply the SQ3R strategy as they engage in independent studying. By sharing their views on the usefulness of the strategy, students should become more aware of their own thinking as they apply this strategy. They should also gain additional insights by listening to the comments of their peers.

As noted earlier, SQ3R is a comprehensive strategy. At first, students may find this approach to be tedious or distracting. It may be helpful, therefore, to begin teaching the strategy with short selections, or limiting its application to the first few pages of a reading assignment. Over time, as students receive more extended instruction in its use, they should gain a better appreciation of its effectiveness.

Commentary: Activities to Promote Independent Reading

The research (Pearson & Fielding, 1991; Pressley & Woloshyn, 1995; Rosenshine 1995; Wood et al., 1995) clearly points to the importance of teaching students about strategies they can use to guide their comprehension and studying of text. In this section, selected approaches for teaching strategies and strategic approaches to learning within the context of subject matter instruction have been presented. These are "starting points" for creating an atmosphere in your classroom in which both the subject matter content and process are intertwined, and are discussed and reflected upon. By sharing their approaches to reading tasks, students can become more aware of what they are doing to understand texts and the effects of the strategies, or processes, they use to meet their needs. In addition, they can try new approaches based on what their peers have found to be effective.

It is important not to present strategies as ends in themselves. Mastering summarizing is not the point; understanding and learning from the text to meet reading purposes is the goal. Interestingly, it has been reported that, over time, the dialogues in reciprocal teaching focus less explicitly on the use of the strategies and more on content. This indicates that the use of the strategies has become internalized to the point that the students can benefit from their use but pay little attention to them. It is also important to consider findings like those in the self-questioning literature (Wong, 1985) indicating that lower achieving students profited more from instruction. Perhaps the higher achieving students have developed strategic approaches to reading that are sufficient. Although they can benefit from explaining these to their peers and sharing in dialogues in which they reflect on strategy effectiveness, strategy instruction should not be overemphasized with them. The linking of subject matter content and process instruction, supported in this chapter as a necessary and ideal way to learn to be proficient readers, can serve to avoid an overemphasis on process.

Instruction that links content and process involves multiple considerations and needs to be carefully planned. In the following section, the major considerations that need to be taken into account in planning for subject matter comprehension instruction in today's classrooms are presented.

Students with Special Needs

Students with reading difficulties may have limited background knowledge or may have problems accessing and using the knowledge they have (Swanson, 1989). In addition, they have often been found to have less strategic awareness and control of their reading than do students who are not experiencing difficulties (August, Flavell, & Clift, 1984; Baker & Brown, 1984; Garner, 1987). Students with learning disabilities have often been viewed as students who do not possess certain strategies, who do not select ones appropriate for given tasks, and/or who do not monitor their reading (Swanson, 1989). Another characteristic is the students' poor self-concepts about their reading ability (Butkowsky & Willows, 1980; Johnson & Winnograd, 1985). Poor self-concept may appear to be low motivation, disinterest, or disruption. Although difficulties calling up and using relevant background knowledge, difficulties using strategies to control reading, and poor self-concept do not cause all reading problems, these characteristics are often implicated in reading difficulties.

Many of the instructional activities suggested in this chapter and the previous one are appropriate and helpful for all students, including those with special needs, because they directly address the characteristics noted above. Instructional activities focused on building and accessing background knowledge, as well as using strategies to guide reading, are particularly helpful. Students with learning difficulties may need the instructional activities to be more explicit, as well as more sustained, but they are not the only ones who can profit from extra instruction. Recently a special education team teacher, whose students with learning disabilities were included in general education classes throughout the day, talked about how she uses study guides: She prepares them for the students with learning disabilities but shares them with any other student who asks for them (and she does get requests).

Along with attending to the need to structure content as well as to teach strategic approaches to reading, it is important that students be exposed to rich subject matter content. There has been much attention in the literature about students with reading problems who lack exposure to instruction focused on developing the behaviors and attitudes associated with proficient reading, as well as the lack of opportunities for them to engage in sustained reading (e.g., Allington, 1994; Stanovich, 1986). Over the years, instruction for students with reading difficulties has emphasized isolated skills practice; without experience with "real" reading and writing, students not only miss the chance to develop the fluency that can come with practice, they also miss the opportunity to develop the rich background knowledge that will facilitate comprehension.

One way to provide opportunities for students with reading difficulties to read as well as gain experience with subject matter content is to make available alternative reading material about the topics being studied. The school or community librarian can be very helpful in suggesting and locating sources. Utilizing cooperative learning activities is another approach to providing exposure to subject matter content; proficient readers can be assigned roles involving explaining the material from the more difficult texts. The other students can profit from the explanations and share what they have learned from alternative sources.

If students with reading difficulties are working with a resource teacher, it is very important to coordinate this instruction with that of the general education classroom. It is critical that subject matter teachers and resource teachers keep in close contact and explore ways in which they can coordinate their instruction, guiding students to be aware of and benefit from the connections.

In summary, the following planning considerations should be addressed when planning for instruction:

1. The subject matter
2. The students' background knowledge of the concepts and processes to be studied
3. The learning objectives
4. The necessity of helping students structure and organize the information in the text
5. The strategies that could help students comprehend the material
6. The structures (whole group, cooperative groups, independent) that will best facilitate students' meeting the objective
7. The approaches that will maximize the opportunity for all students to comprehend the subject matter

These considerations are interactive—each influences the other. Attending to these considerations and their interactions is important in providing a learning environment that enhances the students' ability to learn subject matter content and to become independent thinkers capable of constructing knowledge of the world on their accord.

▼
PRACTICE ACTIVITY 4.5

To make planning for reading comprehension more concrete, contrast the planning of two seventh-grade math teachers. As you read about them, think about the problems that may arise if all of the planning considerations are not made. Comments are provided at the end of the book.

Example 1

Ms. Trujillo, a seventh-grade math teacher, is planning a lesson in which she wants the students to apply the concept of sets to real-world problems. Examining the text, she finds that the concepts of sets are poorly presented, with the examples far removed from the students' prior knowledge, and that there is much difficult vocabulary. Because the text does not clearly present the defined concepts, Ms. Trujillo obtains two supplemental readings on different levels, provides the students a set of study questions for these readings, and plans for a discussion of the questions once the students have the opportunity to read and respond to the questions independently. After the discussion, Ms. Trujillo plans a cooperative learning activity engaging the students to use the material in the text in interpreting and solving real-world problems. Following this activity, she plans to have the students share their approaches to these problems with the class. She plans the compositions of her groups carefully, ensuring that the students with reading difficulties are placed with more proficient readers and assigned roles in the groups that will capitalize on their strengths.

Example 2

Ms. Andres is also teaching seventh graders a lesson on applying the concept of sets to real-world problems. She examines the objectives listed in the teachers guide and the questions provided for the students at the end of the chapter. Although none of these questions address the concepts of sets, she constructs two questions requiring students to apply sets to the everyday world of microbiologists. She provides the students an example of sets, instructs them to read the text describing sets, then asks the students to individually complete the two questions she has constructed.

▼▼▼

CONCLUDING REMARKS

This chapter has presented instructional activities that can be used to help students comprehend and learn from their subject matter reading materials. Instructional activities were presented in two categories: activities to structure subject matter content and activities to promote independent reading. Throughout the chapter, the interconnectedness of subject matter content and process was emphasized. In summarizing this chapter, there are three points that are critical to comprehension and learning in subject matter areas.

The first point is the importance of engaging students in higher-order thinking about the material they are reading. Comprehension is much more than memorizing facts; it involves students' reasoning about the text as they look for relationships and integrate the material with their background knowledge.

Second is the importance of instruction that aims at making students capable of independent control of their reading. Although subject matter texts are not necessarily written to be read in total without teacher guidance, students are often asked to read and study them on their own and, in addition, to pursue other reading materials in subject matter areas. To foster the development of independence, it is important that instruction allow students to take responsibility for monitoring and regulating their own comprehension.

The final point concerns the importance of creating an atmosphere in the classroom in which there is genuine curiosity and excitement about the information the students are reading, as well as about how they are processing and reasoning about this information. In this kind of atmosphere, students are supported and made to feel secure about freely sharing their interpretations and emotional reactions to the material, as well as their struggles as they work to construct meaning from text.

REFLECTIONS
▼▼▼

Now that you have learned about ways to facilitate student comprehension of subject matter text, complete the following questions as a review of the various concepts and activities addressed throughout this chapter.

1. Obtain a copy of a textbook or supplementary instructional materials in your subject matter area that contains questions. Examine at least 10 to15 of these questions and label them according to one of the question strategies presented in this chapter.

2. Select a textbook, article, or other type of printed information for a 30- to 50-minute lesson you might teach in your classroom. Generate a list of questions that are sequenced to present the various question types defined in one of the questioning strategies in this chapter.

3. Select a reading selection from 3 to 10 pages in length that you might teach in your classroom. Examine this selection to identify your lesson objectives. Based on these objectives, construct a three-level study guide, or a study guide in the form of a graphic organizer.

4. Obtain three types of text material used in your subject matter classroom (textbooks, articles, supplementary curricular materials). Examine each of these

sources carefully to determine the various types of text structure (description, causation, collection, problem/solution, compare/contrast). Summarize how frequently these structures are found and the distribution of the various types.

5. Working with a group of your colleagues or by yourself, practice the SQ3R strategy as you engage in reading a subject matter selection. Note the strengths and limitations of this strategy and discuss your views with your colleagues or an individual who is knowledgeable about the use of this strategy.

6. Visit a subject matter classroom to observe and monitor questioning during discussion. As you observe classroom questioning, record the number of questions presented, the types of question presented, and the use of pivotal and emerging questions. Following your observation, write a critique of the questioning activity you observed to include suggestions to modify the lesson.

7. Select a short text selection from a subject matter lesson. Construct a lesson using the GRASP summarization activity to present to your colleagues. Following the presentation of this lesson, solicit your colleagues' comments on the lesson.

REFERENCES
▼▼

Adams, A., Carnine, D., & Gersten, R. (1982). Instructional strategies for studying content area texts in the intermediate grades. *Reading Research Quarterly*, 18, 27–55. Reviews studies examining the effectiveness of the SQ3R study strategy.

Allington, R. L. (1994). The schools we have. The schools we need. *Reading Teacher*, 48, 14–28. Thought-provoking essay considering some central characteristics of today's schools and how these must change if all students are to become accomplished readers and writers.

Alverman, D. E. (1991). The discussion web: A graphic aid for learning across the curriculum. *Reading Teacher*, 45, 92–99. A thorough presentation of the discussion web technique.

Alverman, D. E., Dillon, D. R., & O'Brien, D. G. (1987). *Using discussion to promote reading comprehension*. Newark, DE: International Reading Association. Addresses strategies and techniques for classroom discussion.

Alverman, D. E., Dillon, D. R., O'Brien, D. G., & Smith, L. C. (1985). The role of the textbook in discussion. *Journal of Reading*, 29, 50–57. Examines the role of discussion in the study of traditional textbooks.

Alverman, D. E., & Hayes, D. A. (1989). Classroom discussion of content area reading assignments: An intervention study. *Reading Research Quarterly*, 24, 305–335. Examines the nature of questioning in classroom discussion and textbook assignments.

Alverman, D. E., & Moore, D. W. (1991). Secondary school reading. In R. Barr, M. L. Kamil, P. Mosenthal, & P. D. Pearson (Eds.), *Handbook of reading research* (Vol. 2., pp. 951–983). New York: Longman. A rather comprehensive review of the current status of secondary reading instruction.

Anderson, T. H., & Armbruster, B. B. (1984). Studying. In P. D. Pearson, R. Barr, M. Kamil, & P. Mosenthal (Eds.), *Handbook of reading research*. New York: Longman. A comprehensive review of the current thought regarding the process of studying.

Andre, M., & Anderson, T. (1978–1979). The development and evaluation of a self-questioning study technique. *Reading Research Quarterly*, 14, 605–622. This study examines the effectiveness of a self-questioning strategy.

Andre, T. (1987). Questions and learning from reading. *Questioning Exchange*, 1, 47–86. Examines the role of questioning and study guides in promoting students learning from textbooks.

Armbruster, B. B., Anderson, T. H., Armstrong, J. O., Wise, M. A., Janisch, C., & Meyer, L. A. (1991). Reading and questioning in content area reading lessons. *Journal of Reading Behavior*, 23, 35–59. Describes the nature of questioning that occurs in content area reading classrooms.

August, D. L., Flavell, J. H., & Clift, R. (1984). Comparison of comprehension monitoring of skilled and less skilled readers. *Reading Research Quarterly*, 20, 93–115. Explores the differences in the way good and poor readers attend to their thinking and self-regulating process as they engage in reading.

Baker, L., & Brown, A. L. (1984). Metacognitive skills and reading. In P. D. Pearson, R. Barr, M. Kamil, & P Mosenthal (Eds.), *Handbook of reading research* (pp. 353–394). New York: Longman. A rather thorough description of the role of metacognition in the reading process.

Balajthy, E. (1984). Using student-constructed questions to encourage active reading. *Journal of Reading*, 27, 408–411. Explores the use of the process of having students generate questions as a means to improve comprehension and active involvement in reading.

Bloome, D. (1987). Reading as a social process in an eighth-grade classroom. In D. Bloome (Ed.), *Literacy and schooling*. Norwood, NJ: Ablex. A case study of the nature of learning in the social context of a middle school classroom.

Brown, A. L., & Day, J. D. (1983). Macrorules for summarizing texts: The development of expertise. *Journal of Verbal Learning and Verbal Behavior*, 22(1), 1–14. Discusses the steps in summarization from an experimental and instructional view.

Butkowsky, I. S., & Willows, D. M. (1980). Cognitive-motivational characteristics of children varying in reading ability: Evidence of learned helplessness in poor readers. *Journal of Educational Psychology*, 72, 408–422. Examines students of various reading abilities and differences in their perceptions of themselves as readers.

Commeyras, M. (1995). What can we learn from students' questions? *Theory Into Practice*, 34, 101–106. Describes the nature of classroom social dynamics during small group discussion and questioning.

Conley, M. W. (1990). Instructional planning and teaching in reading and writing. In G. G. Duffy (Ed.), *Reading in the middle school* (2nd ed., pp. 111–123). Newark, DE: International Reading Association. Examines, in part, the nature and

role of small group and cooperative efforts when engaging in content area reading strategies.

Daines, D. (1986). Are teachers asking higher level questions? *Education*, 106, 368–374. Discusses the lack of higher-order questions found in classroom discussion and recitation.

Davey, B. (1986). Using textbook activity guides to help students learn from textbooks. *Journal of Reading*, 29, 489–494. Describes in detail the use of the textbook activity guide.

Davey, B., & McBride, S. (1986). Effects of question-generation on reading comprehension. *Journal of Educational Psychology*, 78, 256–262. This research study examined students' ability to generate questions and how this promotes the understanding and retention of reading materials.

Durkin, D. (1978–1979). What classroom observations reveal about reading comprehension instruction. *Reading Research Quarterly*, 14, 481–533. A frequently cited study reporting observations of classroom comprehension instruction.

Flood, J., Lapp, D., & Farnan, N. (1986). A reading-writing procedure that teaches expository paragraph structure. *Reading Teacher*, 39, 556–562. Describes an activity to promote understanding of expository structures.

Garner, R. (1987). *Metacognition and reading comprehension*. Norwood, NJ: Ablex. Outlines the role and importance of metacognition.

Garner, R., & Gillingham, M. G. (1996). *Internet communication in six classrooms: Conversations across time, space, and culture*. Mahwah, NJ: Erlbaum. This book describes in detail a study examining the use of the Internet and its effects on students' communications and social interactions.

Good, T. L., & Brophy, J. E. (1987). *Looking in classrooms* (4th ed.). New York: Harper and Row. Frequently cited book describing the social context of classroom instruction.

Grossier, P. (1964). *How to use the fine art of questioning*. New York: Teachers Practical Press. Book on how to use questioning in the classroom.

Hamaker, C. (1986). The effects of adjunct questions on prose learning. *Review of Educational Research*, 56, 212–242. Examines the effect of adjunct questions on students' comprehension.

Hayes, D. A. (1989). Helping students GRASP the knack of writing summaries. *Journal of Reading*,

32, 96–101. Complete description of the GRASP technique.

Heath, S., & McLaughlin, M. (Eds.). (1993). *Identity and inner-city youth: Beyond ethnicity and gender*. New York: Teachers College Press. Describes some of the challenges facing educators in urban schools.

Herber, H. L. (1978). *Teaching reading in content areas* (2nd ed.). Englewood-Cliffs, NJ: Prentice-Hall. Focuses on practical instructional strategies.

Hill, M. (1991). Writing summaries promotes thinking and learning across the curriculum—but why are they so difficult to write? *Journal of Reading*, 34, 536–539. Interesting presentation of various issues on efforts to integrate writing across curricular areas.

Johnson, P. H., & Winograd, P. N. (1985). Passive failure in reading. *Journal of Reading Behavior*, 17, 279–310. This research article examines how passive forms of reading—reading that does not promote metacognitive awareness—affects students' understanding and strategic processing of text.

Manzo, A. V. (1969). The ReQuest procedure. *Journal of Reading*, 13, 123–126. Thorough description of the ReQuest activity.

Manzo, A., & Manzo, B. (1990). *Content area reading: A heuristic approach*. Columbus, OH: Merrill. Text devoted to a description of content area reading instruction.

McGee, L. M., & Richgels, D. J. (1985). Teaching expository text structure to elementary students. *Reading Teacher*, 38, 739–748. Describes ways to teach expository text structure to elementary students.

Nist, S. L., Simpson, M. L., & Hogrebe, M. C. (1985). The relationship between the use of study strategies and test performance. *Journal of Reading Behavior*, 17, 15–28. Examines the effect of study strategies on students' performance on examinations.

Ornstein, A. C. (1988). Questioning: The essence of good teaching—Part II. NAASP *Bulletin*, 72, 72–80. Rather thorough description of the importance of classroom questions.

Palincsar, A. S. (1986). Metacognitive strategy instruction. *Exceptional Children*, 53, 118–124. A good summary of the importance of metacognitive instruction.

Paris, S., Lipson, M. Y., & Wixon, K. K. (1983). Becoming a strategic reader. *Contemporary Educational Psychology*, 8, 293–316. A useful overview of the elements of becoming a strategic reader.

Pearson, P. D. (1996). Reclaiming the center. In M. F. Graves, P. van den Broek, & B. M. Taylor (Eds.), *The first r: Every child's right to read*. New York: Teachers College Press. Discusses current thought regarding the nature of comprehension instruction.

Pearson, P. D., & Fielding, L. (1991). Comprehension instruction. In R. Barr, M. L. Kamil, P. Mosenthal, & P. D. Pearson (Eds), *Handbook of reading research* (Vol. 2, pp. 815–860). New York: Longman. A comprehensive review of the current thinking regarding comprehension and its instruction.

Pearson, P. D., & Gallagher, M. (1983). Instruction of reading comprehension. *Contemporary Educational Psychology*, 8, 317–344. Discusses the importance of allowing students to learn a strategy from a point of being dependent on the teacher to applying the strategy independently.

Peters, C. W. (1990). Content knowledge in reading: Creating a new framework. In G. G. Duffy (Ed.), *Reading in the middle school* (2nd ed., pp. 63–80). Newark, DE: International Reading Association. Outlines the importance of authentic learning tasks in comprehension.

Piccolo, J. A. (1987). Expository text structure: Teaching and learning strategies. *Reading Teacher*, 40, 1987. Outlines practical approaches to teaching students how to use text structures.

Prawat, R. S. (1989). Promoting access to knowledge, strategy, and disposition to students: A research synthesis. *Review of Educational Research*, 59, 1–41. Outlines the nature of higher-order thinking and strategies to facilitate knowledge acquisition.

Pressley, M., Johnson, C. J., Symons, S., McGoldrick, J. A., & Kurita, J. A. (1989). Strategies that improve children's memory and comprehension of text. *Elementary School Journal*, 90, 3–32. Useful overview of the factors and techniques involved in comprehension instruction.

Pressley, M., & Woloshyn, V. (1995). Cognitive strategy instruction that really improves children's academic performance (2nd ed.). Cambridge,

MA: Brookline Books. Gives details of validated cognitive strategy instruction.

Richgels, D. J., McGee, L. M., & Slaton, E. A. (1989). Teaching expository text structure in reading and writing. In K. D. Muth (Ed.), *Children's comprehension of text* (pp. 167–184). Newark, DE: International Reading Association. Discusses expository text structures and their instruction.

Robinson. F. (1961). *Effective study*. New York: Harper & Row. Describes in detail the SQ3R strategy and other study techniques.

Roehler, L. R., & Duffy, G. G. (1986). Studying qualitative dimensions of instructional effectiveness. In J. V. Hoffman (Ed.), *Effective teaching of reading*. Newark, DE: International Reading Association. An interesting examination of factors inherent in instruction and the social context of the classroom that affect understanding.

———.(1991). Teachers' instructional actions. In R. Barr, M. L. Kamil, P. Mosenthal, & P. D. Pearson (Eds.), *Handbook of reading research* (Vol. 2) pp. 861–883). Examines teacher behaviors as they relate to reading.

Rosenshine, B. (1995). Advances in research on instruction. *Journal of Educational Research*, 88, 262–268. An interesting and informative article on instructional research.

Rosenshine, B., Meister, C., & Chapman, S. (1996). Teaching students to generate questions: A review of intervention studies. *Review of Educational Research*, 66, 181–221. A comprehensive review of the instruction of self-questioning.

Rowe, M. B. (1986). Wait time: Slowing down may be a way of speeding up! *Journal of Teacher Education*, 37(1), 43–50. Discusses the role and importance of wait time when asking questions.

Shake, M. C., & Allington, R. L. (1985). Where do students' questions come from? *Reading Teacher*, 38, 432–438. Discusses questions presented in the classroom and their level of difficulty.

Simpson, M. L. (1983). Recent research on independent learning strategies: Implications for developmental education (ERIC Document Reproduction Service No. ED 247 528). Reviews study strategies and their use by students.

Smith, K., & Feathers, K. M. (1983). The role of reading in content classrooms: Assumptions vs. reality. *Journal of Reading*, 27, 262–267. An interesting article describing the reality of classroom activities related to improving students' comprehension.

Stanovich, K. E. (1986). Matthew effects in reading: Some consequences of individual differences in the acquisition of reading. *Reading Research Quarterly*, 21, 360–407. An enlightening article on some of the inequalities of reading instruction.

Swanson, H. L. (1989). Strategy instruction: Overview of principles and procedures for effective use. *Learning Disability Quarterly*, 12, 3–14. Ways to address the instructional needs of students with special needs.

West, C. K., Farmer, J. A., & Wolff, P. M. (1991). *Instructional design: Implications from cognitive science*. Englewood Cliffs, NJ: Prentice-Hall. Discusses numerous adjunct learning aides for effective instruction.

Wilen, W. W. (1986). *Questioning skills, for teachers* (2nd ed.). Washington, DC: National Education Association. Addresses classroom questioning.

Wiley, K. B. (1977). The status of precollege science, mathematics, and social science educational practices in U.S. schools: An overview and summary of three studies. Washington, DC: U.S. Government Printing Office. Summarizes the status of instruction in these areas in the mid-1970s.

Winn, J. A., Ryder, R. J., & Netzo, B. (1993, February). *Using a biography to teach strategic reading*. Roundtable presentation at the annual meeting of the Learning Disabilities Association, San Francisco, CA. A strategy designed to promote self-questioning with students having special educational needs.

Wong, B. Y. (1985). Self-questioning instructional research: A review. *Review of Educational Research*, 55, 227–268. Review of the research on self-questioning.

Wong, B. Y., & Jones, W. (1982). Increasing meta-comprehension in learning-disabled and normally-achieving students through self-questioning training. *Learning Disability Quarterly*, 5, 228–240. A study examining the effect of metacognitive instruction with learning disabled students.

Wood, E., Woloshyn, V., & Willoughby, T. (1995). *Cognitive strategy instruction for middle and high school.* Cambridge, MA: Brookline Books. Provides a detailed description of validated approaches to cognitive strategy instruction for older students.

Wood, K. D. (1987). Helping readers comprehend their textbook. *Middle School Journal*, 18(2), 20–21. Defines effective ways of improving students' understanding of texts.

——(1988). Guiding students through informational text. *Reading Teacher*, 41, 912–920. Discusses strategies to promote understanding with expository textbooks.

Wood, K. D., Lapp, D., & Flood, J. (1992). *Guiding readers through text: A review of study guides.* Newark, DE: International Reading Association. An informative summary of study guide strategies.

5

Promoting Critical Thinking and Deep Understanding

CHAPTER OVERVIEW

In this chapter we examine ways to teach students strategies they can use to improve their thinking and way of fostering deep understanding in students. In our first section, "Characteristics of Critical Thinking," we discuss some of the important elements of higher-level cognition, then present a working definition of critical thinking. The next section, "Teaching Critical Thinking," focuses on the importance of solving practical problems in the context of your subject matter curriculum. The section after that, "Stategies for Teaching Critical Thinking," describes three powerful procedures for doing so. The last section, "Teaching for Understanding," describes what it means to teach for understanding and presents three specific procedures for doing so.

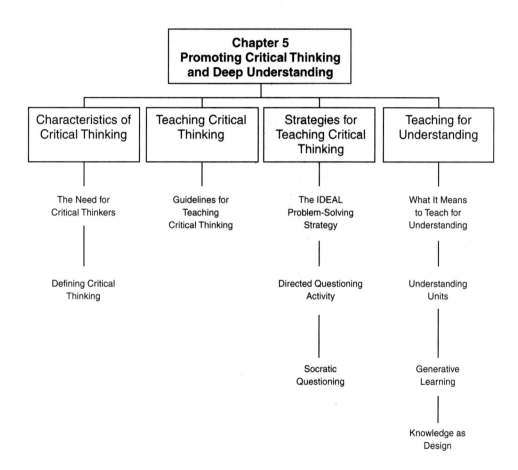

CHARACTERISTICS OF CRITICAL THINKING

This section presents the characteristics of critical thinking, a model to describe the critical thinking process, and concludes with a definition of that process. This chapter should be viewed as an extension of the comprehension strategies discussed in Chapter 4, in that both chapters focus on improving the students' ability to comprehend. This chapter, however, is restricted to higher-level literacy tasks such as those of level 2 and level 3 types of questions where students must use their background knowledge in concert with or as a supplement to the text information.

The Need for Critical Thinkers

In recent years there has been an ever-increasing recognition that critical thinking should be a fundamental outcome of a students' kindergarten through twelfth-grade schooling. Citing the need for workers and citizens who can generate solutions to problems and tasks encountered in the workplace and life in the modern world, it is apparent that all students must learn the high-level thinking skills required in our society (Resnick, 1995).

These calls for advancing the thinking curriculum come at a time when we acknowledge the disparity between societal expectations and students' performance. As the findings of the National Adult Literacy Survey (Kirsch, Jungeblut, & Kolstad, 1996) indicate:

> Growing numbers of individuals are expected to be able to attend to multiple features of information in lengthy and sometimes complex ways, to compare and contrast information, to integrate information from various parts of a text or document, to generate ideas and information based on what they read, and to apply arithmetic operations sequentially to solve a problem. The results of this and other surveys, however, indicate that many adults do not demonstrate these levels of proficiency.

There are a number of assumptions as to what is involved in critical thinking. At one extreme, critical thinking is thought to be directed by a set of skills removed from content, while at the other, it is thought to be directed by the generation of ideas and concepts richly embedded in content-specific materials. It is not surprising, therefore, to find significant variation in definitions of critical thinking. For some, it is thinking that is reasonable and focused on what an individual should believe or do (Ennis, 1987). For others, it is a step-by-step process that involves (1) identifying a problem, (2) generating a hypothesis, (3) gathering evidence, (4) testing the hypothesis, and (5) drawing conclusions (Haggard, 1988). And for still others it is the product of an element of intelligence that comprises the mental processes, strategies, and representations that people use either to solve problems, learn novel concepts, or make deductions (Sternberg, 1986).

Although there is lack of agreement on the definition of critical thinking or how it should be taught, two general conclusions about the nature of thinking critically can be drawn. First, critical thinking is much more than the ability to recall details and facts at the concrete, surface level of meaning. It involves the use of formal logical procedures, problem solving, and accessing one's cognitive and metacognitive processes. Second, responses or solutions to critical thinking tasks depend on an individual's knowledge of concepts and ideas in a given subject matter domain. Responses to these tasks, therefore, will vary between students as a result of the unique knowledge a given student may decide to draw upon.

Defining Critical Thinking

In shaping a definition of critical thinking for this text, consideration is given to three characteristics that could be likened to a "cognitive engine" that propels the critical thinking process. These three elements, shown in Figure 5.1, include (1) the ability of the learner to draw upon background knowledge, (2) the ability of the learner to obtain or derive meaning from diverse sources of information, and (3) the ability of the learner to recognize or generate objectives that direct attention and regulate thinking. These elements are used interactively, with constant adjustments being made in order to reach a solution to the problem. Possessing background knowledge for a critical thinking task, for example, a student might decide to acquire additional information. Yet lacking the ability to direct their thinking in a manner that would allow them to actually "use" that information, it would be unlikely that the student would engage in critical thinking.

With these elements of critical thinking in mind, here is the definition of critical thinking used throughout this chapter.

> **Critical thinking is the active use of formal logical procedures involving cognitive and metacognitive processes to understand the world beyond its literal meaning.**

This is a rather broad definition. Note that it embodies problem solving—an element of cognition in which the learner has a goal in mind, and a set of mental operations or steps required to reach that goal (van Dijk & Kintsch, 1983). And it involves creative thinking—the ability to form new combinations of ideas to fulfill a need (Halpern, 1984). The definition also emphasizes the learner's ability to actively engage in and monitor thinking strategies. Less emphasis is placed on labeling the

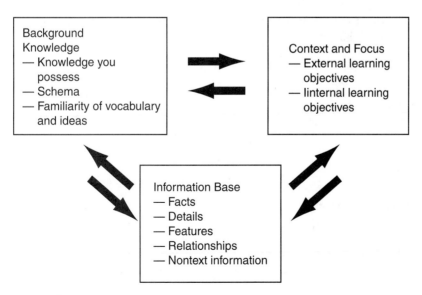

Figure 5.1
Critical Thinking Elements

outcomes of a critical thinking task in favor of defining ways to teach students how they can successfully engage in higher-level cognitive tasks.

This section has presented characteristics and a definition of critical thinking. In closing, it is important to emphasize that critical thinking requires background knowledge, the ability to draw upon and recognize the information presented or obtained from various sources, and the ability to define an objective or goal that directs and regulates the critical thinking process. As such, critical thinking is intentional learning. Students who are proficient at higher-level thinking know what they want to learn, and they know how to redirect their thinking when their goals are not immediately realized. Students who have difficulty with higher-level thinking lack many of these same characteristics. Yet with the teacher's assistance, all students can succeed with critical thinking tasks.

▼ PRACTICE ACTIVITY 5.1

Read the following paragraph, then answer the two critical thinking questions that follow. Answers can be found at the end of the book.

> Acid rain occurs when the rain reacts with a variety of gases in the atmosphere. Some of these gases or particles are naturally occurring. Forest fires, lightning, and the decomposition of organic matter are all sources of acid-producing substances. As factories add chemicals to the air by burning fossil fuels, acid rain has increased. Acid rain often falls in areas far away from the source of pollutants. Generally, factors that influence where acid rain will fall include the temperature, wind direction and speed, humidity, and the intensity of sunlight.

1. Would acid rain continue if we no longer burned oil, coal, natural gas, or gasoline?
2. Why are the effects of acid rain in the United States much more visible in the eastern part of the country than in the west?

▼▼

TEACHING CRITICAL THINKING

All students, regardless of their ability, should be provided the opportunity to engage in critical thinking. Unfortunately, many students rarely have the opportunity to do so. Even when students are presented with higher-level questions, their responses are often muted by a reluctance to engage in tasks they perceive as having a high level of failure or ambiguity (Doyle, 1984), and the perception that this engagement lacks any immediate payoff (Perkins & Simmons, 1988). As Resnick (1987, p. 7) has noted:

> Although it is not new to include thinking, problem solving, and reasoning in *someone's* school curriculum, it is new to include it in *everyone's* curriculum. It is new to take seriously the aspiration of making thinking and problem solving a regular part of a school program for all of the population, even minorities, even non-English speakers, even the poor. It is a new challenge to develop educational programs that assume that all individuals, not just an elite, can become competent thinkers.

Teaching critical thinking is not easy. It will require you to fill in gaps in students' background knowledge, present reasonable and effective strategies, and scaffold instruction so that students eventually will be able to engage in critical thinking independent of your assistance. Clearly, critical thinking instruction is not limited to reading. Critical thinking tasks frequently occur during class discussions, recitations, demonstrations, class projects, physical activities, and activities involving the arts. For example, Figure 5.2 presents a question involving the ability to examine and apply visual information to mathematical concepts. The answers appear at the end of the book.

A response to this question requires knowledge of how to compute volumes and areas of a surface and the ability to visualize the arrangement of objects in a specified area (the inside of the container). It also requires prior knowledge (the fact that the top of a one-half pint milk container is an empty space). The question is typical of the everyday critical thinking problems that require the application of mathematics in that students must do far more than engage in computation skills.

We now turn to three guidelines for teaching critical thinking in the subject matter classroom.

Guidelines for Teaching Critical Thinking

1. Critical thinking strategies should be taught in conjunction with subject matter content. The transfer of critical thinking skills to everyday problem solving

Presume that you own a dairy farm and that you are initiating efforts to reduce shipping and packaging costs. You decide to begin reducing costs associated with the half-pint size containers of milk you sell. Presume that the following two containers are made of the same mateial and that they both contain the same amount of milk. If each of these containers is packed in a 2 foot by 3 foot by 1 foot shipping box, which of the two containers would provide the largest savings in shipping and packaging costs?

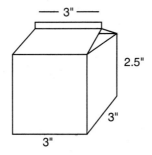
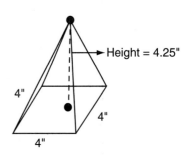

Figure 5.2
Critical Thinking Involving Geometric Figures

rarely occurs unless students are shown when and why specific critical thinking strate-gies are useful (Brown, Campione, & Day, 1981). Whether students can learn critical thinking strategies apart from the content of a specific area of study is a matter of con-siderable debate. Resnick (1987), for example, argues that if students lack subject mat-ter knowledge, teaching general critical thinking strategies is impossible. Critical think-ing is not likely to be based on an abstract set of rules that can be applied in any situation. Rather, it is purposeful thinking about information that is familiar (McPeck, 1981). Smith (1990) suggests that critical thinking does not require a set of learned skills, but knowledge of what one thinks about. An expert in a field of study is likely to be highly successful at critical thinking tasks related to that field. Unfortunately, mastering concepts and skills in a profession does not ensure transfer or understanding of its real-world applications (Bransford, Sherwood, Rieser, & Vye, 1986). And mastering a large amount of factual information is not likely to generate critical thinking by itself. This problem was addressed many years ago by Whitehead (1929), who noted the dangers of inert knowledge—knowledge used only in a very limited situation or context. White-head's concern that educational programs in the early part of this century produced knowledge that remained inert reflects a condition that still exists today. The challenge to the subject matter teacher is planning an instructional lesson that addresses both the acquisition of information and the application of critical thinking strategies. Meeting this challenge requires the application of the appropriate strategies by stu-dents, and initially it requires some additional planning and preparation on your part.

2. Critical thinking instruction should present students with real-life prob-lems. Presentation of instructional activities that reflect real-life problems increases the likelihood that students will transfer critical thinking strategies to problems encountered outside the classroom and that they will develop methods for identify-ing and solving these types of problems (Sternberg, 1988). Selection of real-life prob-lems should, however, be directed by their ability to motivate students and engage them in a cognitive process that will transfer to other learning situations (Anderson, Reder, & Simon, 1996; Carpenter, Fennema, & Franke, 1996).

3. Critical thinking instruction may be novel. Critical thinking instruction is likely to be different from the sorts of activities found in the traditional classroom. Critical thinking instruction is more than asking questions that require students to "think critically." It is an approach that often includes (1) cooperative learning, (2) the use of multiple sources of information, (3) the willingness to allow for a wide range of student responses, and (4) an emphasis on allowing students to become aware of their own cognition. While this may appear to be an excessively complicated effort, it is a natural part of many teachers' day-to-day instruction. On the other hand, if a teacher is accustomed to relying upon a single text, regularly requiring students to engage in individual seatwork activities, and stressing the memorization of details, then critical thinking instruction will require a concerted effort.

How is critical thinking instruction different from the more traditional forms of instruction? A comparison of two approaches to teaching mathematics that requires students to engage in critical thinking is presented here. The first example follows a very traditional approach whereby the teacher provides a lecture or discussion of a topic, then directs students to work independently on a series of problems. The second example exemplifies the four aspects of critical thinking instruction noted earlier. Each involves the presentation of the concept that *distance traveled* equals *rate* times *time traveled* (D = RT).

Traditional Instruction

1. Teacher introduces the formula Distance = Rate × Time by first discussing the meaning of each component of the formula, then providing students examples of calculating the formula.

2. Students receive the following three problems to complete independently.

   a. If John travels to Lake Elmo in 2½ hours and covers 102 miles in that time, what his average rate of speed?

   b. United Airlines Flight 601 travels 1200 miles at a speed of 425 miles per hour. How long did the flight last?

   c. Jose's car has enough gas to go 50 more miles. If he has been traveling for 4 hours at an average speed of 52 miles per hour and needs to travel a total distance of 490 miles, will he have enough gas to complete his trip?

Critical Thinking Instruction

1. The teacher provides students with the following critical thinking question: "You and a friend have decided to drive your automobile from your home in Kansas City to Denver, a distance of 400 miles. Consider that you and your friend will switch from driver to passenger every 2 hours. Unless you learn otherwise, presume that the entire distance will be driven on interstate highways where the posted speed limit is 65 miles per hour. You are driving a car that gets about 23 miles per gallon. You will leave at 7:00 A.M. Carefully consider the stops you will need to make to eat breakfast, lunch, and perhaps dinner, as well as the time needed to procure gasoline. Also consider construction projects along the way that may delay your travel or cause you to detour from your route. Given all these conditions, what time do you estimate you will arrive in Denver?

2. The students are now assigned to cooperative learning groups. The students are assigned specific tasks (such as checking on road conditions, calculating the amount of time required to stop for fuel and meals, etc.), then instructed that they will need to report back to the class on the information they obtained. The students will be directed to solve the entire problem once they have received information from each of the cooperative groups.

3. The teacher introduces students to the formula Distance = Rate × Time by first discussing each component of the formula, then providing several examples of calculating the formula. The students should receive a handout containing the formula and examples of its application. The students should be given the opportunity to reexamine the problem and their solutions, then modify their solutions based on the teacher's presentation.

4. Each group presents their response and rationale for solving the problem. Following the groups' presentation, the teacher leads a discussion to describe the students' process in solving the problem. The teacher attempts to summarize the process by defining the steps the students followed and, where applicable, generalizing these steps to other problem-solving situations.

The preceding example demonstrates the application of cooperative learning, the selection of information obtained from various sources, the attention to students' awareness of their own cognition, and the acceptance of a range of plausible responses. Although the problem could be solved by students individually, consider the consequences of using that approach. Students would be limited to their own resourcefulness, they would not share ideas with peers who may represent various cultural and intellectual backgrounds, and their opportunity to gain insight into the metacognitive strategies of their peers would be limited. Similarly, the problem could be simplified to reduce the amount and number of sources of information required to reach a solution and to limit the range of plausible responses. However, this would result in a problem unlike those encountered in everyday problem-solving tasks, thus reducing the likelihood that students would transfer problem-solving strategies beyond the context of the problem. And it could reduce the likelihood that students would generate answers based on creative approaches to solving the problem.

This section has presented some suggestions for the instruction of critical thinking in the subject matter classroom. By now it should be evident that critical thinking instruction is a process to construct knowledge within an area of study. It should not be viewed as a set of skills or strategies to be taught in isolation, but a component of the day-to-day instruction in the subject matter classroom.

PRACTICE ACTIVITY 5.2

Here is a problem identified by a seventh-grade student. Take a moment to determine which of the ten characteristics of everyday problems cited in this section are evident in this problem. The answer can be found at the end of the book.

You have been saving your money for some time to buy a compact stereo system. You are trying to determine if you want to purchase the various components of a system or a system sold only as an integrated unit. The component system sounds much better, and has all the features you want, but costs about $180 more than the integrated unit. You have exactly enough money for the integrated unit. Right now you own a portable cassette player with a good set of headphones. You have two criteria: you want a system now, and you want a great sounding system. What will you do?

▼▼

STRATEGIES FOR TEACHING CRITICAL THINKING

We turn now to the presentation of three critical thinking strategies. These strategies are flexible—they will apply to a variety of problem-solving tasks in a variety of subject matter areas. The first strategy presented here, IDEAL, is designed to encourage students to learn to solve problems on their own. The second strategy, the directed questioning activity, provides a sequential approach to teaching students a process for generating and answering higher-level questions. The third strategy, Socratic questioning, is a method of discussion to promote the students' ability to examine their own thinking and evaluate the thinking of their peers.

The IDEAL Problem-Solving Strategy

The IDEAL problem-solving strategy (Bransford & Stein, 1984) consists of five stages: (1) *identifying* the problem, (2) *defining* the problem, (3) *exploring* strategies to solve the problem, (4) *acting* on ideas to solve the problem, and (5) *looking* for the effects of one's thought processes. Here is a description of this five-stage process.

Identifying the Problem

The first step in the IDEAL model is identifying that a problem exists. For the student lacking background information or problem-solving strategies, recognizing the existence of a problem may be a difficult task. Accordingly, teachers may find it necessary to draw attention to problem identification strategies by encouraging students to discuss aloud the processes they use when identifying a problem. If students hesitate in their response, be prepared to provide them a description of this process.

Defining Problems

The second step of the IDEAL model involves a precise definition of the problem. Here the learner must go beyond the recognition that a problem exists. The problem itself must be defined and the factors or concepts related to the problem must be clearly identified. Consider the following scenario.

> One day while writing this text, one of us decided a bike ride would offer a much-needed reprieve from the word processor. Once on his bike, he noticed that he seemed to be exerting an unusually high amount of energy. Uncertain if the problem was the bike or the rider, he pulled alongside a rider of similar weight and asked that they coast in tandem down a lengthy hill. Within a few minutes, the second rider shot ahead of him. Pulling off the road, he picked up his bike and spun the wheels only to discover that the brake pads were rubbing against the rim of the wheel.

In this case the problem was recognized (excessive effort bicycling), then defined by isolated factors that were related to the problem (the problem was a mechanical problem with the bike involving the brake pads and the resistance the rubbing pads placed against the wheel).

Exploring Alternative Approaches

The third step of the IDEAL model is to explore the various approaches to solving a problem. Here the student must draw upon acquired problem-solving strategies to determine if these strategies are appropriate for the problem at hand. At times the student may find it necessary to adapt or modify a strategy to meet the requirements of a particular problem. Some students find it difficult to solve problems, either because they do not possess the appropriate strategies or because they don't know when to activate and apply an acquired strategy. In their effort to define approaches to solve problems, Bransford and Stein (1984) note that experienced problem solvers adhere to a conscious and systematic approach that includes the following steps:

1. Breaking down a complex problem into its various parts.
2. Working a problem backward.
3. Reworking the problem to solve a simpler, specific situation first.

While these appear to be steps most of us follow in problem solving, they may not always lead to a solution to the problem. For example, these steps are of little use if we don't understand the information necessary to solve the problem. Furthermore, these steps may not be strategies to direct thinking, but artifacts of the thinking process. Recognizing these limitations, Bransford and Stein (1984) recommend that problem-solving activities be preceded by the instruction of subject matter concepts required to solve the problem. In a science class, for example, presentation of the concepts of refraction, reflection, and absorption would aid students in solving a problem requiring them to determine how a thermos keeps liquids hot, or how we might construct windows that would better insulate buildings.

While assisting students in identifying relevant concepts will enhance their problem-solving abilities, eventually students will need to perform this task on their own. To accomplish this goal, consider the following steps once a problem has been defined:

1. Discuss with the students concepts they believe will assist in solving the problem. Have the students explain to the class why they selected these concepts.
2. Ask the students to identify procedures for locating concepts that may be of assistance in solving the problem. Emphasize to the students that identifying the concepts that apply to a problem is an important step in solving the problem.
3. Model to the students the steps you follow in trying to identify concepts that would aid in the solution of a problem.

Acting on the Plan and Looking at the Effects

The final two steps of the IDEAL model consist of acting on identified problem-solving strategies or solutions and looking carefully to see the effects of these strategies or solutions. Because these two steps are so closely related, they are combined in the discussion that follows.

Students should realize that generating alternate solutions can actually make problem solving more efficient. Many students, who may fail to act then evaluate each step in the problem, either generate an incorrect response or fail to recognize the existence of an error. Without alternative solutions, they may give up on the task altogether.

Although Bransford and Stein (1984) do not specify how to teach students the final two steps in the IDEAL strategy, you may find the following suggestions useful.

1. Provide students with a handout listing the steps to solving a problem. Direct students, now assigned to cooperative learning groups, to engage in the first step, then reflect upon and evaluate its effectiveness. Once each group has written their evaluation, share and discuss these evaluations and acknowledge any alternate strategies they may have identified.

2. Present a problem to students, then identify the number of steps involved in obtaining an answer. For each step, ask each group to generate a process for solving that component of the problem. These processes can then be shared and discussed with the entire class.

3. Work through the problem-solving process backwards. Provide students the problem and the answer to the problem. Then ask students to determine the various steps they would follow to construct an answer.

Commentary: The IDEAL Strategy

This strategy presents some general steps to aid students in their understanding of the process of problem solving. It has two notable strengths. First, it is a practical approach for increasing students' metacognitive awareness of the problem-solving process. Each of the five steps of the IDEAL strategy encourages students to think about and define the cognitive processes involved in problem solving. Clearly, this model will encourage students to think about thinking. Second, the IDEAL strategy offers a practical place for the teacher to begin the process of integrating critical thinking within the subject matter classroom. The steps of this strategy can be adapted to almost any subject matter area with minimal preparation.

While this strategy increases awareness of the problem-solving process, many students will experience difficulty transferring this strategy to independent reading. Note that this strategy does not present a process for monitoring each step of the problem-solving process. As a result, students may not know when they make an error and therefore will be unable to activate some sort of fix-up strategy when they fail to solve the problem. Use of this model, therefore, may need to be limited to instances where problem solving is addressed as a whole-class or cooperative-group activity.

▼ PRACTICE ACTIVITY 5.3

Note the importance of the *act* and *look* components of the IDEAL model in the following problem presented by Bransford and Stein (1984, p. 21). Read the problem, complete the first step of your solution, then refer to the following paragraph for further directions.

> There are 12 cannonballs. All look alike, but one is the "oddball."
> The oddball is either heavier or lighter than the other balls. You are pro-
> vided a balance scale that can hold as many cannonballs as you would
> like on each side of the scale. The problem is, in 4 weighings (4 uses of
> the scale), find the oddball.

For most people, the first step in solving this problem is to place six cannonballs on each side of the scale. However, this procedure does not lead toward a correct response to the problem. Since the oddball can be either heavier or lighter than
the other cannonballs, grouping the cannonballs does not advance the problem-
solving process. Only by acting on a solution, then looking at the outcome of an initial attempt at the problem-solving process does it become evident that an alternate
solution is necessary. A solution to this problem can be found at the end of the book.

▼▼▼

Directed Questioning Activity

All students can learn to improve their ability to monitor their own comprehension
through steps that show how a process will improve their comprehension and by
encouraging students to verbalize this process (Paris & Winograd, 1990). Moreover,
students can learn higher-level thinking strategies when provided signal words (who,
when, why) and question stems ("How does ... affect...?," " What are examples of ...?")
that direct their effort to engage in higher-level cognitive tasks (Rosenshine, Meister,
& Chapman, 1996). The directed questioning activity (DQA; Ryder, 1991) is an instructional process designed to increase the students' self-regulation of critical thinking
through active involvement requiring the integration of prior knowledge and text
information. The DQA is a form of scaffolded instruction—instruction that leads students from a point where they are dependent upon the teacher's guidance to a point
where they function independently. At the beginning of this activity, the teacher constructs questions that lead students toward higher-level thinking. Over time, the
teacher's role shifts from generating questioning to coaching students in their efforts
to generate and respond to critical thinking questions.

The DQA consists of two instructional components: text explicit instruction
and text implicit instruction. Text explicit instruction, conducted prior to reading,
builds the students' background knowledge and establishes a purpose for critical
thinking. Text implicit instruction occurs during reading to focus the students' attention on essential concepts and to provide direct instruction in the process of
responding to critical thinking questions. A description of the process of teaching
these two components follows.

Text Explicit Instruction

This component of the DQA contains activities that build background knowledge and
clarify objectives. These activities are limited to a portion of the reading assignment.
Preparation for text explicit instruction involves three steps. First, determine what
you want students to learn. Clearly, some of your objectives will involve objectives

requiring critical thinking. These objectives may be those you construct or those you select from a curriculum or teacher's guide. Second, group content into teachable chunks. The purpose here is to regulate the amount of information students read, to provide a purpose for reading that chunk, and to monitor the students' understanding and discuss their interpretation of information contained in the chunk of text read. Third, construct a structured overview, frame, or other form of graphic organizer that presents information contained in each chunk of the reading. A detailed discussion of the construction and use of these forms of graphic organizers is presented in Chapter 3. Figure 5.3 presents the overall objectives, the chunked objectives, and the accompanying graphic organizer for a lesson dealing with the Chernobyl disaster.

Text Implicit Instruction

In this stage of the DQA, the teacher directs questions to students either prior to or immediately after reading a chunk of text. Questions presented to students prior to reading have been shown to promote active involvement with text and increase comprehension, particularly for those readers who normally do not monitor their understanding as they read (Anderson & Biddle, 1975; Graves & Clark, 1981). Reading with a question in mind also tends to draw the reader's attention to your instructional objectives and promotes the categorization and evaluation of text information (Levin & Pressley, 1981). Students can gain insight into thinking when provided with questions

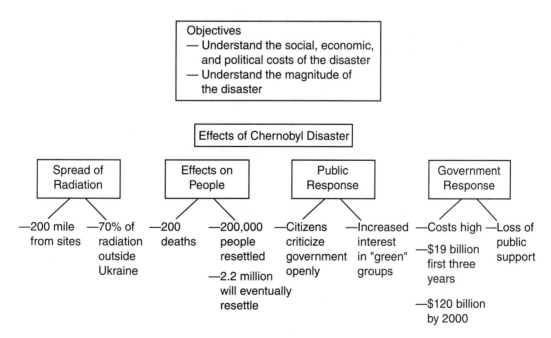

Figure 5.3
Graphic Organizer of Chernobyl Disaster

that guide their comprehension by making them aware of what they know and what they don't know (Roehler & Duffy, 1984). Commonly, students read a chapter or section of text, then answer questions included in the text or provided by the teacher. Generally these questions require the reader to identify details or construct a response by linking a number of concepts presented in the reading. If the reader does not understand a concept presented in the text, or if that concept is not actively recognized during the reading, linking concepts to form generalizations, inferences, conclusions, or hypotheses will be a difficult task.

The DQA limits the amount of text information students attend to at a given time. Students read a small portion of the text rather than an entire chapter or section of a text. Questions are presented prior to and during a reading rather than at its conclusion.

Prequestions.   Prequestions are presented to students immediately before they read. Generally one or two of these questions is adequate for each portion of a reading. Additional questions may be distracting. Once they have answered prequestions, have the class discuss them prior to presenting an additional set of questions. In responding to a prequestion, students attend to a small portion of a selection. This may be a paragraph or several pages, depending on the density of concepts in the reading, students' familiarity with these concepts, and the difficulty of the prequestions.

Adjunct Questions.   Adjunct questions are presented to students immediately after an assigned portion of a selection has been read. These are reflective questions. They require the reader to look back and think about an objective different than that presented in prequestions. Often this objective is to respond to a higher-level or critical thinking question. Adjunct questions are also cuing questions. The reader is redirected to important concepts or information, and often requested to create some sort of conceptual link.

Both prequestions and adjunct questions are more effective in enhancing comprehension than the traditional questions presented at the conclusion of a reading (Anderson & Biddle, 1975). The conditions for their use are dictated by certain characteristics of the text and the student. Prequestions can be presented when (1) the reading has numerous new or difficult concepts, (2) the reading is poorly written, or (3) specific text information is required in constructing a response to a critical thinking question. Adjunct questions can be presented when (1) concepts are not particularly difficult for the students or (2) it is desirable for students to reflect upon the reading with the purpose of linking information to respond to a critical thinking question. Critical thinking can be facilitated by presenting a series of prequestions that isolate important text information, then presenting an adjunct critical thinking question requiring the application of information acquired from the prequestions. Consider the following example demonstrating the use of prequestions and adjunct questions dealing with our lesson on Chernobyl (Figure 5.3).

Objective
On the basis of the graphic organizer and information addressed in the prequestions, students will determine the long-term social and economic consequences of the Chernobyl disaster on Russia.

Prequestions

How many people will eventually need to be resettled as a result of the disaster?

What is the cost of cleaning up the effects of the Chernobyl disaster?

In 1986 one of the three nuclear reactors in Chernobyl, a city located in the republic of the Ukraine in the Commonwealth of Independent States (CIS), overheated and exploded. The disaster resulted in widespread effects on the people, the land, and the economy of the CIS. Recent maps displaying the fallout remaining from the disaster indicate pockets of severe radiation more than 200 miles from the original 19-mile evacuation zone. It is now known that 70% of the fallout actually occurred in the republic of Byelorussia, which borders the Ukraine. In response to this information, the government now plans to permanently resettle 200,000 people over the next several years—effectively doubling the number originally evacuated from the immediate area around Chernobyl. Government officials in Byelorussia now estimate that 2.2 million people will eventually need to be resettled.

The economic costs of the Chernobyl disaster will be enormous: more than 600 people have participated in the clean up, which as of 1991 had cost $19 billion. The total cost by the year 2000 is estimated at $120 billion. The cost in human lives thus far has been estimated to be 300. American doctors estimate the eventual toll to be somewhere between 50,000 and 250,000 lives. The public response to the government's handling of the Chernobyl disaster was widespread. Grassroots movements have been influential in forcing local officials to take nuclear regulation into their own hands, and thousands of protesters have marched throughout the Ukraine and Byelorussia. In response to the public outrage, Boris Yeltsin signed a decree in 1990 prohibiting the construction of nuclear power plants.

Adjunct Question

Using information that you learned from reading the paragraphs above, what will be the long-term effects of the Chernobyl disaster on the economy and welfare of the people in Russia?

This example demonstrates some of the advantages and disadvantages of prequestions. One advantage is their ability to establish a purpose for reading, thus limiting the amount of text information students must learn. This is an important characteristic with text that contains many concepts, or text that is poorly organized. Once a prequestion has been examined, students are likely to ignore extraneous information, attending to concepts addressed in the question. Prequestions also have the advantage of demonstrating to students the importance of self-regulation. Unfortunately many students read without knowing what information in the text is important (Dole, Duffy, Roehler, & Pearson, 1991). Prequestions can assist the reader in setting goals and generating questions that direct attention and regulate thinking.

One drawback to the use of these questions, however, is that by restricting the students' attention to specific information, other information may not be attended to.

Adjunct questions such as the one presented in the Chernobyl selection engage the reader in the critical thinking process. The adjunct question directs the student to reread the selection, to restructure the information acquired in the prequestions, then to link that information to derive a response reflecting a higher-level of thinking. This process of redirecting the reader to higher-level thinking by applying information from prequestions is referred to here as staging. Answering a staged adjunct question requires inductive reasoning. The reader applies concepts and information acquired from the prequestions and prior knowledge to answer the adjunct question.

In introducing students to the process of responding to staged adjunct questions, these guidelines should be useful:

1. Model the process of answering a staged adjunct question using content familiar to the students. Describing strategies to use in responding to the critical thinking question will enhance the students' metacognitive awareness of how information obtained from prequestions can be linked to allow for higher-level thinking. Continue modeling this strategy over a period of time.

2. Coach students in responding to staged adjunct questions. Present and respond to prequestions with the entire class. Work cooperatively with students in formulating an answer to a staged adjunct question. Encourage students to describe how they use strategies when responding to these sorts of questions.

Moving Toward Independent Critical Thinking

Up to this point, the DQA is largely directed by the teacher. Ultimately the goal is to allow students to independently answer critical thinking questions. It is unlikely that the continued presentation of questions alone will aid students in their response to critical thinking required during independent reading. With the teacher's guidance, students can create and apply graphic organizers and generate questions to direct critical thinking. This process occurs through scaffolding (Wood, Bruner, & Ross, 1976), a process where teacher assistance is reduced gradually, eventually leading to the student's independent application of the strategy. Scaffolding the DQA begins with teacher modeling and concludes with student collaborative modeling. Here are some suggestions for beginning the process of teacher modeling.

Graphic Organizers

1. Present students with an oral summary of a portion of a reading assignment. As the summary is being presented, display terms and concepts on the chalkboard or overhead. Describe the process for organizing this information in the form of a graphic organizer and create the organizer. Once the graphic organizer displays the key concepts contained in the summary, describe to students the process of drawing upon prior knowledge, then adding that information to the organizer.

2. Have students skim a portion of a reading to identify key concepts and vocabulary. List these terms on the overhead or chalkboard. Next, describe the process of constructing the superordinate categories from these terms, then direct students to describe the process of generating subordinate categories.

Constructing Prequestions

1. Referring to the graphic organizer, model the process of generating questions that require information beyond that provided in the organizer. These sorts of questions generally will require elaboration or require the definitions of causal or temporal relationships.

2. Skim the first several sentences in each paragraph from a brief selection. Describe the process of using this information to generate predictions of the passage's content, and questions to clarify content or answer the predictions generated from skimming the passage. Explain to the students the importance of self-generated questions in regulating comprehension.

3. Modify step 2 by engaging in question generation as a group process. Skim a short passage. Encourage the students to generate questions from the group's skimming of the passage. Then read to respond to the student-generated prequestions.

Staged Critical Thinking Questions

1. Summarize the information obtained from the prequestions. Make a list depicting the concepts the questions address. Demonstrate to the students how your conclusions can be drawn from conceptual relationships in this information. Model critical thinking questions by asking and thinking aloud, "What isn't directly stated in that reading that I would like to know?" Emphasize that answers to these questions may not be found in the text. Discuss the importance of seeking information from additional sources to respond to these critical thinking questions.

Once the teacher has modeled these steps with the students, the students repeat the process in cooperative groups. The students now coach one another in the construction of graphic organizers, prequestions, and staged critical thinking questions. This step requires the teacher to carefully monitor the groups' progress and provide additional modeling when groups require assistance.

Commentary: Directed Questioning Activity

The DQA is an efficient and practical approach for teaching critical thinking strategies in content areas. Like the IDEAL strategy, the DQA involves elements of cooperative learning and group problem solving. The strategy also includes steps to acquaint students with the structure of text, the importance of relating background knowledge to text content, the importance of monitoring the process of higher-level thinking, and the process of linking text information and background knowledge to generate inferences. A distinctive element of this form of critical thinking instruction is the chunking of text information. By focusing on smaller portions of a text, students can concentrate on the process of responding to a higher-level question and not be distracted by the demands of finding information in the text. This process is a form of regulated inductive thinking: Concepts needed for critical thinking are defined through questions, then students are asked to apply that information in answering a higher-level question. At first this process is teacher directed. Gradually, however, more responsibility is placed on the student to self-direct the process of generating these types of questions.

Initially, elements of this approach, such as preparing graphic organizers and sequencing questions, may require considerable preparation time. However, with time and continued practice these instructional devices can be generated spontaneously.

Socratic Questioning

Socratic questioning (Paul, 1991) is a strategy to promote critical thinking through classroom discussion. According to Paul, this form of questioning helps students evaluate their own thinking, allows students to compare their own thinking to that of their peers, and promotes consideration of multiple ideas and the interrelationships between those ideas. In this form of discussion, the teacher promotes critical thinking by presenting questions in the following four directions, as identified by Paul.

Their Origin

Here the teacher asks the students to focus on the source of information used in the response to a question by asking, "Where did you come up with the information that helped you answer this question?" "Can you describe what you were thinking when you originally made this conclusion or learned this information?" "Do you remember if this is something you learned by yourself?" "Is this something you learned in school, from a friend, or from source of information such as a book, videotape, etc.?"

Their Support

Here the teacher asks the students to focus on their supporting facts by asking, "How do you substantiate this response, do you have proof?" "Where could you locate evidence to support your response?" "Do you think your response is based on fact, or is your response your personal belief?" "Is your response one that would be accepted by a good number of your peers?" "Would someone who is an expert in the area of the question provide a response similar to yours?"

Their Conflicts with Other Thoughts

Here the teacher helps the students anticipate other responses by asking, "What are some counterarguments that people might present to your response?" "Why would some people have a different point of view than that evident in your response?" "Under what conditions would you consider changing your response to this question?" "What additional information would you need to modify your response?" "How would you counter an opposing response?"

Their Implications and Consequences

Here the teacher helps the students consider the implications of their response by asking, "What are the consequences of this response?" "Is their any evidence for your response in the real world?" "What additional events or information would be necessary for your response to actually be put into effect?"

An example of questions reflecting these four directions is shown in Figure 5.4.

The procedures for planning and administering a Socratic discussion, adapted from Paul (1991), are as follows:

1. **Define the underlying concepts and information.** First, the teacher must consider the concepts, information, values, and the interrelationships between these elements that underlie the questions presented to the students. Additionally the teacher should attempt to predict the sorts of insights or values that may be

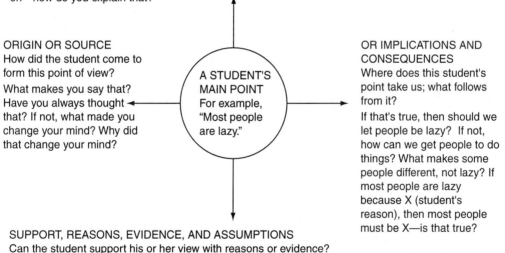

CONFLICTING VIEWS
How does this student's thinking conflict with other points of view?

What would you say to someone who said that people basically *want* to accomplish things and learn about things, that people *need* to work and keep busy and feel that they contribute? Could there be other reasons why people seem lazy, like maybe people are afraid of messing up, and that is why they don't go out there and do stuff? Your history book is full of people who did things, worked hard, fought, and so on—how do you explain that?

ORIGIN OR SOURCE
How did the student come to form this point of view?

What makes you say that? Have you always thought that? If not, what made you change your mind? Why did that change your mind?

A STUDENT'S MAIN POINT
For example, "Most people are lazy."

OR IMPLICATIONS AND CONSEQUENCES
Where does this student's point take us; what follows from it?

If that's true, then should we let people be lazy? If not, how can we get people to do things? What makes some people different, not lazy? If most people are lazy because X (student's reason), then most people must be X—is that true?

SUPPORT, REASONS, EVIDENCE, AND ASSUMPTIONS
Can the student support his or her view with reasons or evidence?

Why do you think so? Are there certain kinds or groups of people that aren't lazy? Why are most people lazy? How do you know? How could we find out if that might be so? Do people chooses to be lazy, or decide that it doesn't matter if they are lazy, or are they just that way naturally? Do you think most people think of themselves as lazy? Why?

Source: Paul, R. W. (1992). "Critical Thinking: What Every Person Needs to Survive in a Rapidly Changing World." Published by Foundation for Critical Thinking, CA. Second edition (p. 366).

Figure 5.4
An Example of Socratic Questioning

presented by the students. Attention to the underlying concepts and information will enhance opportunities during the discussion to assist the students in seeing the relationships between their own thinking, the views of others, and the information obtained from various print and nonprint sources.

2. Generate a few kernel questions for each of the four question directions. Constructing a few kernel questions for each of the four question directions will increase the likelihood that discussion will proceed smoothly, that questions will cover the various directions represented in the Socratic questioning technique, and that structure and organization will be applied to the questioning format. These kernel sentences may be presented to students in advance to allow them ample opportunity to fully consider their responses. Additionally a handout displaying these questions can serve as a listening guide for students—as questions are discussed, students note various responses presented by their peers.

3. Facilitate interdimensional thinking. Questioning proceeds in a manner that allows students to move back and forth between their own ideas and those of their peers, between their own ideas and those expressed in print and nonprint sources, and between various perspectives advanced by the teacher, other students, or a source external of the participants in the discussion. The teacher should attempt to draw attention to various points of view, note consistencies and inconsistencies in the responses provided by students, and bring closure on students' points of view.

4. Draw upon cooperative learning and attend to multicultural variation. Questioning can be enhanced by having students respond to questions in cooperative groups. According to Paul (1991), engaging in Socratic questioning in cooperative groups promotes the students' ability to probe each other's ideas for their support and implication, and it helps develop a sensitivity to what various participants are assuming. Note that cooperative grouping may also provide the opportunity to draw upon the array of cultural or social perspectives present in the classroom. As discussion proceeds through the four directions of questions, the teacher should attempt to draw attention to these perspectives, provide students with positive feedback for voicing these perspectives, and encourage all students to seek an understanding and appreciation of these cultural and social perspectives.

Commentary: Socratic Questioning

Socratic questioning is a time-honored strategy to promote critical thinking through classroom discussion. The teacher's presentation of the four directions of questioning in a discussion format should serve to advance students' metacognitive awareness of processes involved in responding to higher-level questions. Moreover, the ability of the teacher to direct students to the relationships between responses to the four directions of questioning should further the students' ability to conduct similar strategies independent of instruction. Clearly this is a strategy that promotes active learning—rather than relying upon information in a textbook, the teacher continually draws upon students' knowledge, directs them to reflect on the process they followed to generate a response, and encourages them to carefully consider and judge the views and information provided by their peers.

To ensure the success of this strategy, it is important that the teacher provide students with the necessary activities prior to and during reading so that they will learn the basic information and concepts necessary to engage in the Socratic questioning activity. While this strategy can stimulate a great deal of discussion, teacher-to-student questioning may limit the involvement of the entire class. Therefore, consideration may be given to posing questions to cooperative groups, allowing the groups to reach a consensus on the response to a question, then engaging in a class discussion of the question. This procedure is likely to directly involve a greater number of students and is more likely to allow students the opportunity to share their views with their peers.

TEACHING FOR UNDERSTANDING

In this section, we deal with fostering students' deep understanding of the material they read in various content areas. This section is divided into four parts: what it means to teach for understanding, understanding units, generative learning, and knowledge as design.

What It Means to Teach for Understanding

According to Perkins (1993, p. 13), one of the principal proponents of teaching for understanding, understanding enables a person "to perform in a variety of thought-demanding ways...[to] explain, muster evidence, find examples, generalize, apply concepts, analogize, represent in a new way, and so on." To teach for understanding, we must go beyond simply presenting students with information and ensure that students retain important information, understand topics deeply, and actively use the knowledge they gain. The reader who has attained an understanding perspective consciously seeks understanding and uses for the knowledge she gains through reading. Of course, everything we have discussed in this book thus far, and particularly the approaches we suggested earlier in this chapter and in Chapters 3 and 4, has understanding as an ultimate goal. But here, recognizing the importance of understanding, we treat it as a specific goal.

As we have stressed throughout this book, and authorities such as Prawat (1991), Perkins (1992), and Beck, McKeown, Hamilton, and Kucan (1997) point out, expectations of schooling and the level of knowledge and skills that our society requires have risen dramatically in recent years and will continue to rise, perhaps even more dramatically in the future. Yet as these same authorities indicate, and as empirical studies such as those conducted by the National Assessment of Education Progress (e.g., Beatty, 1996; Campbell, Donahue, Reese, & Phillips, 1996) have found, few American students are performing at the levels full participation in our society demands. Teaching for understanding can change this.

Thus far we have defined understanding, emphasized the importance of having understanding as a goal of instruction, and explained that all too few children are reaching the level of understanding they need. We turn now to explaining what teaching for understanding looks like. The basic principle underlying teaching for understanding is that our goal ought to be that students understand whatever topic we are considering. Despite the press of time, despite the need to "cover" the curriculum, despite the well-planned lesson you're anxious to get on with, when students do not understand you need to stop what you are doing and do your very best to help them understand. This suggests the most basic attribute underlying this approach—teaching for understanding takes time.

Prawat (1991) has suggested three other attributes:

▼   It requires focus and coherence.
▼   It involves negotiation.
▼   It is highly analytic and diagnostic in nature.

Because teaching for understanding requires a significant amount of time, it also demands focus. If you are going to spend a good deal of time on a topic, you had better be sure just what it is you are spending time on. Similarly, if you are going to spend a good deal of time on a topic, it needs to be coherent to you and to students. Thus, for example, if you are dealing with forms of government and focusing on monarchies, it is important that both you and the students understand that you are focusing on monarchies, that you understand what monarchies are, and that you understand why you are focusing on monarchies.

In order to ensure coherence, you will frequently need to negotiate meaning with students. As discussed in Chapter 1, the process of making meaning is a constructive one. Meaning does not simply spring from a text to the reader's head. Readers must grapple with a text, manipulate ideas, shape them, and interpret them if they are to derive significant learning from what they read. What readers get from reading depends heavily on the sum total of their experiences and intellectual makeup. No two readers or listeners will construct exactly the same meaning from a particular text or discussion. Thus, in situations in which you want students to construct the same meaning or very similar meanings, you will often need to engage in a give-and-take discussion in which you and your students talk through a topic, often rereading a text and listening to what the other is saying about it, attempting to understand what each other is saying, and attempting to come to some agreement on the meaning.

Finally, teaching for understanding is both analytic and diagnostic. That is, the teacher needs to continually analyze students' responses in an effort to determine what they are thinking, decide whether or not there is a problem of understanding, and if there is a problem, to diagnose its nature and come up with a solution.

There are a number of ways of teaching for understanding. Here we will focus on three approaches—approaches that we believe are particularly powerful. These are the use of understanding units, generative learning, and knowledge as design.

Understanding Units

Understanding units are a particular type of thematic unit. Thematic units last two to six weeks or longer and therefore give students the time to investigate topics in depth (Walmsley, 1996). Understanding units, however, go beyond typical thematic units to help students reach true understanding and give them opportunities to establish links among the many concepts necessary to really understand something. Perkins and Blythe (1992) have developed a useful framework for understanding units. This framework has four parts:

▼   Generative topics
▼   Understanding goals
▼   Understanding performances
▼   Ongoing assessment

Here we define each of these parts, briefly elaborate on each, and give an example or two of each.

Generative Topics

Generative topics are topics that are central to the subject area students are studying, accessible to students, and connectable to many other topics, both in the subject matter being studied and in other areas. Generative topics can be concepts, themes, procedures, historical periods, theories, ideas, and the like. For example, in the field of literature, plot is a generative topic. Plot is central to the study of literature, plot is an important element in many types of literature and in many individual pieces of literature, and plot exists outside of literature. Historical episodes, such as the Civil War period, basically follow a plot, as do our lives. As another example, consider the field of history. Cause and effect is a concept central to much of history, and like the generative concept of plot, cause and effect also exists in areas outside of history. In fact, most fields of study, such as science, humanities, and art, include some consideration of cause and effect. As still another example, consider the idea of beauty. Beauty is a central concept in art and literature, but beauty also plays an important role in our lives and even in science. Frank Press (1984), former president of the National Academy of Sciences, once spoke of the discovery of the double helix that broke the genetic code as not only rational, but beautiful. Finally, consider the topic of health. Health can be considered a part of science, but it is also a part of social science; there is psychological health as well as physical health. Of course, health can also be related to government—as when a powerful world leader becomes ill—and it can be related to a myriad of other areas, including our daily lives.

Working with highly generative topics whenever possible is important because, as we have already noted, teaching for understanding takes time. If you are going to spend a good deal of time on a topic, you need to carefully choose topics that are important themselves, that connect to many other topics, and that students can access and appreciate.

Understanding Goals

One problem with generative topics is that they are often too broad. Beauty, for example, could be studied in any age, in any medium, and in almost any field. Even though understanding units may last two to six weeks or longer, the time available is obviously not infinite, and you almost always need to select one or several parts of broad generative topics to focus on and some specific goals to be achieved. For example, one possible understanding goal for tenth graders studying the idea of beauty might be for students to understand that people's idea of physical beauty has changed over time, that, for example, the ancient Roman's idea of beauty differed from that held by Italians during the Renaissance and from that held by Italians today. Another possible understanding goal for these tenth graders might be that the idea of physical beauty also differs from culture to culture and even from individual to individual.

Or consider the generative topic of the election process in the United States, and assume that the students we are concerned with are ninth graders. Of course, ninth graders will be able to deal with only some aspects of this complex topic. In this case, one understanding appropriate for ninth graders might be that students gain a general understanding of the election process. Another might be that they understand the major issues in a particular campaign.

These goals are in fact those developed by two social studies teachers as they designed an understanding unit titled *"The Election Process and Campaigns of 1996"* (Briggs & Perkins, 1996), and here we will use a slightly modified version of their unit as an example as we discuss the remainder of Perkins's four-part format. Briggs and Perkins's understanding unit was developed for typical classes of ninth graders and involved students in a variety of interesting, involving, and creative instructional activities over a period of about four weeks. An outline of the unit is shown in Figure 5.5. As the titles of the lessons suggest, the unit dealt with a variety of topics—suffrage, voting requirements, campaigns, the role of the media, and others. It also involved students in a variety of activities including reading, writing, making a commercial, planning and participating in a debate, and casting their votes in a CNN student poll. This is indeed a significant set of topics and issues, and we would expect some significant learning and understanding from the unit.

Lesson	Topic
One	The Power of Voting
Two	The Significance of Suffrage
Three	Voting Requirements and Trends
Four	The Nomination Process
Five	Campaigns
Six	General Elections
Seven	Introduction to Issues
Eight	Issues in the Presidential Election
Nine	The Role of Media in Politics
Ten	Locating Relevant Information

Figure 5.5
Lessons from an Understanding Unit on "The Election Process and Campaign of 1996"

Understanding Performances

In Perkins and Blythe's (1992) four-part framework, students demonstrate their learning and understanding in what they call understanding performances. When students complete an understanding performance, they demonstrate that they have in fact understood. During the election unit we have outlined, students took part in a number of understanding performances. Fairly early in the unit, they demonstrated their understanding of voting requirements by creating concept maps showing voting requirements. Later in the unit, they demonstrated their understanding of referendums by actually developing referendums that they would like to propose for their school. And still later, they demonstrated their ability to locate information on political questions by using several Internet search engines to get a sample of media responses to major campaign issues. As we indicated, students engaged in these understanding performances throughout the unit; they did not go through the entire unit without doing much to demonstrate their understanding and produce a product only at the end of the unit. This is important; students should be engaged in understanding performances throughout a unit of study.

Ongoing Assessment

The last part of Perkins and Blythe's (1992) four-part framework, ongoing assessment, is very closely related to understanding performances. Just as students should be engaged in understanding performances throughout the unit, students and teachers should be engaged in ongoing assessment throughout the unit. One of the things that teachers assess is students' understanding performances. For example, if some of the referendums developed by students were not good examples, then the students who created them need feedback and some reteaching, and they need feedback and reteaching early on so that they do not continue through the unit with their misconceptions about referendums causing confusion and thwarting learning of other concepts. Each of the other understanding performances students undertake offer additional opportunities for ongoing assessment, and for feedback and reteaching if needed. However, ongoing assessment is not limited to understanding performances. At all points in the unit and with various techniques, such as individual conferences, small group discussions, writing assignments, or other events, it is important to constantly assess whether or not students are understanding. Also it is important to be ready to assist students in reaching understanding if they are experiencing problems. As Perkins and Blythe (1993, p. 7) put it, "To learn for understanding, students need criteria, feedback, and opportunities for reflection from the beginning of and throughout any sequence of instruction."

Certainly all of us want to teach for understanding. We obviously would not want to teach for misunderstanding or teach with the goal of students' forgetting whatever we were teaching. Yet we know that in all too many cases misunderstanding and forgetting take place. Teaching for understanding is hard, but by keeping the attributes of teaching for understanding—time, focus and coherence, negotiation, and frequent analysis and diagnosis—clearly in mind and by employing the four-part framework—generative topics, understanding goals, understanding performances,

- Draw themes from a variety of areas—for example, concepts such as survival or justice, content areas such as science or social studies, and contemporary concerns such as the environment and pollution.

- Balance teacher-generated and student-centered themes.

- Make sure that themes are the right size and complexity for the time you have available. We suggested a range of two to six weeks, but shorter and longer units are certainly possible.

- Use themes and activities that give students opportunities to exercise their "multiple intelligences"—linguistic, logical-mathematical, spatial, bodily-kinesthetic, musical, interpersonal, and intrapersonal (see Armstrong, 1994; Campbell, Campbell, & Dickinson, 1996; Gardner, 1991).

- Teach a theme at least twice to recoup your investment in it.

Figure 5.6
Some Suggestions on Theme Teaching

and ongoing assessment—in situations where it is appropriate, understanding is a goal we can reach.

Some Suggestions on Themes for Understanding Units

Walmsley (1996) has outlined several guidelines for improving theme teaching. In Figure 5.6, we include some of his suggestions particularly relevant to working with themes in understanding units, as well as several of our own suggestions.

PRACTICE ACTIVITY 5.4

Outline a teaching for understanding unit for a particular grade level. Choose a generative topic, state one or more understanding goals that fall under that topic, describe at least two understanding performances that students could engage in as they were engaged in the unit, and explain how you could provide ongoing assessment very early in the unit and periodically throughout the remainder of it. Do this in writing and make it just as specific and concrete as you can.

▼▼

Generative Learning

The concept of generative learning is a simple yet very powerful notion developed by Wittrock (1974, 1991). It applies primarily, although not exclusively, to informational reading. According to generative learning theory, meaningful learning, or what we have termed understanding in this chapter, occurs when learners themselves generate meaningful relationships involving the ideas that they want to learn about. These meaningful relationships include both links among the ideas in a text and links between the ideas in a text and ideas the reader already knows, believes, or has experienced.

For example, in reading a *National Geographic* article about alpine forests and discovering that alpine forests occur at high elevations and that alpine trees are often dwarfed, a student might generate a relationship between those two ideas by assuming that it is something about their high elevation that dwarfs alpine trees. Then, he or she might generate a relationship between the text and his or her experiences by recalling seeing forests of small trees while hiking in Rocky Mountain National Park. The processes of creating a causal link between high elevations and dwarf trees and linking the reading about small trees to actual experiences with them assist the student in understanding what he or she has read, in remembering it, and in being able to use that information in the real world.

As another example, consider a group of seventh graders reading about nutrition and eating a healthy diet. Their studies include the food pyramid, showing the proportions of fats, dairy products, meats, vegetables, fruits, and cereals that make up a well-balanced diet. In this situation, the teacher could prompt students to generate one relationship among ideas in their reading by asking them to compare the amount of vegetables to the amount of fruits in a good diet. Then, after students had discussed this relationship, the teacher could prompt them to consider another relationship among the ideas in the text by asking them to compare the recommended amount of fruits to the amount of meat. Next, the teacher might ask students to consider some of the things they ate at home and classify these foods according to their place in the food pyramid. This would involve students in generating relationships between ideas in the text (the food pyramid categories) and ideas from outside the text (their knowledge about what they eat at home).

In promoting generative learning, much of the teacher's role is to arrange situations in which such generation takes place. Thus, after students read and discuss the article on the food pyramid, the teacher's role is to set up materials and situations in which students have additional opportunities to work with relationships. As a relatively short activity, the teacher might bring in pictures of various food items and have students place them in the appropriate food category. As a longer activity, the class might keep a log of the cafeteria lunches for a week or so, classifying the foods served in the appropriate categories, and then developing a general statement about how good a job the cafeteria does in providing a balanced diet.

In addition to its main concern with generating relationships, the generative model suggests three other concerns that teachers should consider: motivating students, directing students' attention, and taking into account their schemata. These are matters that we have considered repeatedly throughout this book, but they deserve particular attention as they relate to generative learning. Motivation is particularly important because generating relationships requires a good deal of mental effort; and students need to be motivated to expend this effort. In part, this motivation consists of convincing students that whatever they are studying is worthwhile, that, for example, learning about the food pyramid is worthwhile because a balanced diet will help keep them from getting colds and the flu and give them more energy for school and for play. Another part of this motivation consists of showing students that the generative activities you are asking them to undertake will aid them in understanding and remembering what they read and will help them learn the material in less time than if they just relied on rote memory.

Directing attention is important because it is not sufficient for students to generate relationships among any ideas in a text. They need to generate relationships among just those ideas in the text that are important to understanding the concepts presented. For example, in reading the selection on alpine forests, students might learn that spruce trees can be found in alpine forests and falsely assume that it is something unique to spruce trees that creates alpine forests. In this case, the teacher would need to prompt students to consider the relationships among elevation, temperature, precipitation, and other factors crucial to developing alpine forests.

Finally, students' prior knowledge about the topic being studied influences their ability to identify crucial elements in the text and their ability to relate ideas in the text to their existing knowledge. Thus, for example, a student who has never seen an alpine forest, who has never seen or even thought about miniature plants such as bonsai, and who lives in the Midwest where flat land and fields extend for hundreds of miles in all directions will have a difficult time understanding and appreciating alpine environments. Conversely, a student from a town located in the mountains of Colorado may already understand and appreciate alpine environments, and your goal may simply be to formalize some of the knowledge he or she already has.

In further describing generative learning, Wittrock (1991) has identified a number of activities that can be used to generate relationships among ideas. In Figure 5.7 we present some of the activities he has listed and some of our own. If you are engaged in generating relationships among the ideas in this text, you will recognize that many of

Activities Involving Ideas in the Text	Activities Relating Ideas in the Text to Prior Knowledge
Composing titles	Giving personal examples
Composing headings	Creating new examples
Writing questions	Drawing pictures and other artwork
Paraphrasing	Giving demonstrations
Writing summaries	Making comparisons
Making charts and graphs	Drawing inferences
Articulating main ideas	Making predictions
	Reflecting on ideas
	Solving problems
	Creating stories, plays, essays, and other sorts of writing

Figure 5.7
Generative Learning Activities

the activities we listed in the Practice Activities and Reflections sections of the chapters of this book are generative activities. We present you with such activities in order to prompt you to understand thoroughly and remember the ideas in each chapter.

The following scenario will give you another glimpse of a teacher's attempts to engage a student in generative learning and a sample of the thinking a student might do as he generates the meaningful relationships being taught. In this case, the student is reading an autobiographical narrative, but his teacher is interested in him understanding it quite well and remembering from it some of what the class learns about the experiences of black men and women in our country. The student, a twelfth grader we will call Alex, has selected a book titled I *Know Why the Caged Bird Sings* by Maya Angelou from several the class has selected for their civil rights unit. The book is the story of the rural community in which Maya Angelou spent most of her early years in the 1930s. In the first pages of the book, Angelou relates the circumstances under which she and her brother, Bailey, went to live in Stamps, Arkansas. Then, the second chapter begins as follows:

> When Bailey was six and I a year younger, we used to rattle off the times tables with the speed I was later to see Chinese children in San Francisco employ on their abacuses. Our summer-gray pot-bellied stove bloomed rosy red during winter, and became a severe disciplinarian threat if we were so foolish as to indulge in making mistakes.

The passage is straightforward and not difficult to understand, and a student like Alex might very well read through it and gain a surface understanding of it without teacher suggestions that prompt generative learning. But a few brief questions or suggestions by the teacher could lead Alex to generate some relationships and both better understand and better remember what he has read. For example, after Alex read the passage, his teacher might ask him to reflect on what clues in the paragraph suggest that learning was important in Maya and Bailey's home.

The first clue, Alex realizes, is simply the statement that Maya Angelou and her brother used to rattle off the times tables. Alex could imagine two young children reciting the tables and compare their speed in doing so with the speed of students working on an abacus. Of course, if Alex doesn't know what an abacus is, he could look up the word or ask someone to explain it. The second clue, he notices, is that the pot-bellied stove "became a severe disciplinarian threat." Alex would probably think of a parent or an adult as being a disciplinarian and wonder how a stove could be described as one. This, then, would be a question to prompt further reading.

Of course, all of this reflecting is more mental work than Alex would need to do to gain a surface understanding of the passage. But as a consequence of engaging in this generative learning, Alex should achieve a deeper understanding of the passage and he will remember much of what he has read.

Now consider the next sentences of the passage and what the teacher does to lead Alex to generate relationships involving them. This time, the teacher asks him to *compare* the situation being described to his own learning of the "times tables."

> Uncle Willie used to sit, like a giant black Z (he had been crippled as a child), and hear us testify to the Lafayette County Training Schools' abilities. His face pulled down on the left side, as if a pulley had been attached to his lower teeth, and his left hand was only a mite bigger than Bailey's, but on the second mistake or on the third hesitation his

big overgrown right hand would catch one of us behind the collar, and in the same moment would thrust the culprit toward the dull red heater, which throbbed like a devil's toothache. We were never burned, although once I might have been when I was so terrified I tried to jump onto the stove to remove the possibility of its remaining a threat.

"Well," thinks Alex, "Angelou writes of being threatened by Uncle Willie to learn her math. She must not have realized he really wouldn't follow through with the threat. I can't imagine that he would have burned her. I certainly didn't learn my times tables like that. I'll have to keep reading to see if more of Angelou's life is very different from mine."

This time, the teacher's suggestion that Alex compare the scene he was reading about to his own learning resulted in even more generative learning than the teacher had in mind. Not only did Alex make some comparisons, he also generated a *problem to solve* to check as he read on and question how Angelou's schooling and life as a child compared with his. Because he actively grappled with the ideas in the text, he is likely to recognize and appreciate the many differences that exist between Maya Angelou's early life and his own.

All in all, in this brief bit of reading, the teacher has prompted Alex to establish a number of relationships among the ideas in the text and between the ideas in the text and his prior knowledge. With this amount of generating relationships, it is not surprising that Alex will understand and remember what he has read quite well. Similar results can be achieved with other students reading other texts.

Practice Activity 5.5

Consider this section on generative learning as the text that you are attempting to learn from and understand, and list several generative learning activities that you might use in doing so. Then choose one of these, use it with the section, and describe how you use it. If possible, discuss your use of the activity with a classmate.

▼▼

Knowledge as Design

Knowledge as design is a simple and straightforward yet very powerful discussion framework developed by Perkins (1986, 1994). Teachers and students can use this powerful technique to fruitfully investigate almost any topic.

Two basic principles underlie knowledge as design. One is that considering the design of a topic—the relationship between its structure and its purpose—allows us to talk meaningfully and insightfully about almost any topic. The other is that learning is a consequence of thinking. If we can get students actively thinking about a topic, then they will be learning about that topic. Knowledge as design suggests that students can productively answer the questions about a topic or object, as shown. Answering these questions as a group gives students the opportunity to share what they know about the topic and come up with a rich set of information about it.

Knowledge as Design Questions

What are the purposes of the topic?

What is the structure of the topic?

What are some examples of the topic?

What are some arguments for and against the topic?

As we said, the procedure is simple and straightforward. Consider as an example a ninth-grade civics class taking up the topic of advertising. As shown in the example, the class takes up the four design questions one by one, engaging in what Perkins calls a *design conversation*.

Purposes

Teacher: What are some of the purposes of advertising? Why do we see so much of it? Why do you look at television commercials or read ads in magazines?

Students: They're interesting sometimes, especially some of the ones on TV. Sometimes they really catch your eye and grab your attention. And sometimes I am persuaded to buy a particular brand of something because of what I see advertised.

Structure

Teacher: How are ads organized? What are they like? What are the parts of them?

Students: They're different. Some are very short, but some are longer, like when companies show new commercials during the Superbowl. Sometimes you can watch infomercials. Companies want you to think they are giving you information, but they are really trying to convince you about something. Sometimes they're humorous and get your attention that way.

Examples

Teacher: What are some examples? What are some commercials that you know?

Students: Companies like Pepsi and Coke are always advertising. Then there are a lot of jeans commercials. Car salesmen advertise a lot too, sometimes for a special holiday weekend sale, like on Labor Day.

Arguments

Teacher: What are some good things about advertising, some things you like?

Students: They're entertaining. Sometimes they're funny. They help you be aware of new stuff you can buy. And, when they announce sales, you can save money.

Teacher: What are some arguments against advertising, maybe some things you think or maybe some things your parents think?

Students: Sometimes there are just too many of them. Sometimes they're repeated too many times, and that really gets annoying. Sometimes the stuff's not for kids. And sometimes the things they say aren't really true.

Quite obviously, these students know a lot about advertising. Using the design conversation has enabled them to get what they know out on the table where the whole class can think about it and see what it means.

At this point, we will consider each of the three parts of a design conversation—choosing a topic, the conversation itself, and closure—in slightly more depth.

Choosing a Topic

The first step in using knowledge as design is to choose a topic. Although knowledge as design can be used with virtually any topic, it is most appropriately used with topics that are worthwhile and justify students spending time delving into them. Additionally, in order to ensure students' success with the procedure, it is a good idea to initially choose topics that are concrete, that students know a lot about, and that students are likely to be interested in. The *advertising* topic obviously meets the criteria of being concrete, something students know about, and something they care about. And when you consider that American students watch an average of about four hours of television a day and may see over 100,000 commercials over a lifetime, then it clearly also meets the criterion of importance.

Once you choose a topic, it's a good idea to see if it will work as a design conversation before giving it to students. To do so, simply jot down one or two purposes, the structure of the topic, one or two examples, and some arguments for and against it. With *advertising*, you could list persuading people and informing people as two purposes, half hour infomercials and short, 30-second spots as two of the structures, and Coke commercials and exercise machine infomercials as two examples. Finally, you could note that advertising sometimes gives people something to think about but is often pretty mindless. If the topic seems to work for you, try to think how it will work for students. Think about some of your students, what they know, and how they are likely to respond to each of the design questions. If it seems as if your students will be able to answer the design questions, then you have probably chosen a good topic.

Leading a Design Conversation

Once you have chosen the topic and are confident it will be a useful one for your students, the next step is to lead students through the four design questions. Frequently, the question "What are the purposes of the topic?" is the one asked first. Sometimes, however, you might begin by asking about the structure of a topic or asking students to give some examples of it. Wherever you begin, the procedure usually works best if you get as many responses as you can on one of the design questions before going on to another one. You will want to keep a record of the students' responses, and that can be done on the board or on an overhead with a template that provides convenient spaces for the students' responses to each of the questions. Such a template, which Perkins (1994) calls a design conversation worksheet, is shown in Figure 5.8.

As you are asking the questions, it is very important to do everything possible to promote an open discussion and encourage students to volunteer answers. This means treating all students' answers with respect by acknowledging partially correct responses and avoiding criticism. It also means being sure all students have opportunities to respond and seeing that students treat each other with respect.

Something else to consider as you conduct the design conversation is that the four categories of questions should be thought of in broad terms, not narrow or limiting ones. The purpose question, for example, can be thought of as a question about

Design Conversation Worksheet

Purposes

Pro Arguments

Specific Examples

Con Arguments

Structure

Conclusions

Figure 5.8
Blank Design Conversation Worksheet

goals, objectives, functions, or aims. In asking about purposes, you are asking, "What is it for?" "What does it do?" or "What can we accomplish with it?" Similarly, the structure questions can be thought of as questions about organization, features, materials, or parts. In asking about organization, you are asking, "How is it organized?" "What does it look like?","What is it made of?" "What are its parts?" and "How is it put together?" Interpreting each of the design questions broadly allows you to use the procedure with a very broad range of topics.

Closure

The third step of knowledge as design—closure—gives students the opportunity to synthesize the information they have produced, connect it to their existing knowledge, search for insights, and draw conclusions. With most topics, there are a variety of directions that closure can take. With the topic of advertising, for example, students might compare television advertising to other forms of advertising—radio, magazine, and newspaper. Given that so many American students watch so much television and see so many ads, we would be inclined to work toward closure that critically evaluated the huge influence that advertising has in our culture.

Continued Work with Knowledge as Design

As we suggested, in working with knowledge as design it is essential to choose topics that are relevant to students—things going on in their lives, things they're reading about, things they're interested in. As students become increasingly competent with the procedure, you can introduce topics from subject areas that will further challenge students' imaginations and thinking abilities. Shown in Figure 5.9 is a design conversation worksheet illustrating the responses twelfth graders might give on the topic of monarchies in a class studying types of governments.

The responses in Figure 5.9 show some real understanding of the nature of a monarchy, the sort of understanding that can help students as they delve into a new unit. The discussion helps them think about what they already know from information they have read or studied before, from what they have heard from the news, and perhaps from traveling to a country ruled by a monarchy. Also, the fact that students arrived at their understanding in a give-and-take class conversation strengthens the likelihood that they will internalize what they will learn in the upcoming unit and incorporate it into their own schema of knowledge about types of governments.

As students become increasingly competent with the procedure, you will want to include more abstract topics and ones students are not as familiar with. Also, as students become increasingly familiar with knowledge as design, they become able to work with the procedure without the teacher's leadership. Once they understand the procedure well, students can work in small groups, perhaps with several groups each working on part of a general topic and then sharing their knowledge. When students work with knowledge as design in groups, it continues to be important that they record their responses so that they can review the knowledge they have produced and share it with others. Reproducing the design conversation worksheet (Figure 5.8) as a handout gives students an excellent place to record their conversations and helps guide them in asking the design questions.

Design Conversation Worksheet

Purposes
Kings and/or queens rule the
    country, not the citizens
Royalty makes decisions
Way of keeping order in a
    nation

Pro Arguments
Clear pattern of authority
People in the country
    like all the royal ceremonies
    and traditions
Visitors can tour the palaces
The royalty can be a symbol for
    the country

Specific Examples
England
Norway
Denmark
Sweden
Monaco

Con Arguments
Can create a problem with
    human rights
The people can't decide for
    themselves
What happens if the royal
    family breaks the rules—like
    the Prince and Princess get
    divorced?

Structure
Positions are usually inherited
The royal family keeps control
    for possibly generations
The royalty live in palaces
Usually the royalty are wealthy

Conclusions
Maybe this type of
    government doesn't fit today's
    world as well as it did in the
    olden days
Maybe monarchies aren't as
    powerful as they used to be

Figure 5.9
Design Conversation Worksheet on Monarchies

In concluding consideration of knowledge as design, we want to say a word about how frequently you might use the procedure in your classroom. We believe that you and your students may choose to use it quite frequently, often including a design conversation as one of your weekly activities and particularly using them in conjunction with the reading students are doing. These discussions might occur either before students read about a topic or after. If you hold design conversations before students read a selection, it will need to be with topics students know something about, and in many cases it will be appropriate to complete the conversation after students have read the selection and gained additional information and insights. Of course, just how often you use the procedure depends on your students, the topics you deal with, and your purposes. How frequently you use knowledge as design also depends on what other discussion and thinking procedures you use in your classroom. Still, because knowledge as design is broadly applicable, because it is easy to use, and because it can lead to powerful learning, it is certainly a candidate for frequent use.

▼ PRACTICE ACTIVITY 5.6

Choose a design conversation topic appropriate for the class in which you are using this text, and hold the conversation with the class as a whole or with a small group. Once you have held the conversation, discuss with your classmates how useful knowledge as design was in helping you hold a purposeful discussion.

▼▼

CONCLUDING REMARKS

In this chapter, we have presented the characteristics of critical thinking and included a definition of critical thinking, three critical thinking strategies, and a discussion of teaching for understanding. In summarizing the chapter, we would make four points we believe are essential to promoting higher-level thinking in subject matter classrooms.

First, we believe critical thinking should involve the teacher as a facilitator to promote (1) active learning involving a great deal of teacher talk and modeling, and (2) cooperative learning whereby students talk a great deal to one another while the teacher monitors and assists in their collective efforts. Requesting students to independently complete questions or activities without first observing the teacher model a strategy and then having the opportunity to apply and refine that strategy with their peers seems to ignore the dynamic process of engaging in higher-level cognitive tasks.

Second, as we contemplate subject matter instruction, we picture teachers who themselves engage in critical thinking and deep understanding, who see the value of teaching their content by engaging students in practical and challenging problem-solving tasks, and who recognize the importance of educating all students to be more than consumers of surface-level information. This requires conscious and consistent integration of critical thinking strategies within day-to-day instruction. It also requires the perception that teaching should enhance the learner's ability to make sense of the world and to acquire knowledge that can be applied to self-directed learning.

Third, the strategies in this chapter should provide students with a more thorough understanding of the subject matter content. For example, problem-solving activities that require students to form ideas, experiment, and observe the application of these ideas will likely increase an understanding of factual information as well as more general concepts or themes.

Finally, like everyday problems themselves, teaching students to solve problems or engage in other forms of critical thinking and deep understanding are sometimes messy —answers may not come readily, students may be hard pressed to formulate any sort of acceptable answer, and the independent application of strategies may be agonizingly slow to develop. These sorts of results can be rather disquieting and the risks may appear too great. At this point, resorting to traditional activities may appear to be an attractive way to restore order and to obtain outcomes that are more "measurable." We would encourage all teachers to be persistent in their efforts, to continue to stress the importance of critical thinking strategies and deep understanding to their students, and to share their efforts with individuals outside the classroom. Ideally, teaching critical thinking and promoting understanding will require the cooperation of students, fellow teachers, administrators, and parents. All personnel should recognize the importance and goals of this form of instruction and the process required to develop students' lifelong ability to engage in higher-level thinking.

REFLECTIONS
▼▼▼

Now that you have become more fully acquainted with critical thinking instruction and teaching for understanding in the subject matter classroom, complete the following questions as a review of the various topics addressed throughout this chapter.

1. Prepare a critical thinking activity that could be used in your subject matter area. In constructing this activity, consider (a) how you may draw upon students' background knowledge, (b) make use of multiple sources of information, and (c) how you may engage students in cooperative learning as they engage in the critical thinking activity.

2. Examine each of the following to determine which of the following activities would display characteristics of real-life critical-thinking tasks..

(a) In an English class the teacher is about to deal with a novel that has an overriding theme addressing peoples' inhumanity toward one another. To prepare students for the novel, the students are directed to identify four historical events during the past 100 years that depict peoples' inhumanity toward one another. At least two of these events must have occurred outside the United States. Students are asked to read at least three different sources for each event, then compare and contrast the causes and outcomes of each event and draw generalities across these events.

(b) In a math class the teacher wants the students to understand how the calculation of areas of various surfaces can be used in real life. Students are provided tape measures, then are asked to calculate the surface area inside the classroom.

(c) In a science class students have been learning about the problems associated with the disposal of low-level radiation from nuclear power plants. As a culminating activity the teacher invites a group of individuals to serve as a consulting panel to the students. This panel consists of a scientist from the regional power company, an environmental activist, a scientist with the state environmental agency, and an oncologist specializing in cancers caused by radiation. Students are told that they must determine how to dispose of approximately 120,000 pounds of nuclear waste over the next ten years in a manner that is cost effective and that considers the public's health.

3. Construct an inductive tower by identifying information regarding the effect of television on students' acquisition of knowledge that would be useful in their schooling. You may also want to identify impediments to this learning (what students like to watch, their reason for watching, etc.).

4. Use the IDEAL model to solve the following. Jan, who lives in Minnesota, has stored her car on her brother's farm during the winter because she is afraid of the damage that may occur to the body from salt on the roadways. The car is placed in an old barn that protects it from the weather. She covers the car with a tarp, removes the battery, places a fuel stabilizer in the gas tank and departs waiting for spring. When she arrives in spring, she replaces the battery, fills the gas tank with high octane fuel, and cleans the car inside and out. On her way home there is a terrible shudder as she drives down the highway. The shudder becomes worse as she accelerates. What is the problem ? What caused it? What can she do now?

5. Arrange a meeting with a teacher in your content area and discuss the notion of teaching for understanding. Ask if he or she is familiar with the term "teaching for understanding" and the general point of view it represents. If the term and the concept are familiar, ask how he or she interprets teaching for understanding, what sort of job he or she thinks schools are doing in assisting students to develop deep and useful understanding, and what he or she is doing to teach for understanding. Also ask about what he or she sees as the barriers to teaching for understanding and about how these barriers might be overcome. If the teacher is not familiar with the term or the concept, explain it as fully as you can. Then, discuss the other matters we have listed here as much as possible.

6. In a separate meeting with the same teacher or in a meeting with another teacher, describe one of the three teaching for understanding procedures we have discussed—understanding units, generative learning, and knowledge as design—ask if he or she uses it or a similar procedure, and if so ask about how useful and effective they have found it to be. If the teacher you talk with hasn't used the first procedure, describe the other two and find out if he or she uses either of them. Finally, if the teacher does use one of the procedures, ask if you can observe his or her class using it, observe the class, and make some evaluative notes about how the procedure works in an actual class.

REFERENCES

Anderson, J. R., Reder, L. M., & Simon, H. A. (1996). Situated learning and education. *Educational Researcher, 25,* 5–11. A critical look at situated learning.

Anderson, R. C., & Biddle, W. B. (1975). On asking people what they are reading. In G. H. Bower

(Ed.), *The psychology of learning and motivation.* New York: Academic Press. Probes the nature of students' metacognitive awareness.

Angelou, M. (1969). *I know why the caged bird sings.* New York: Random House. Angelou's well-known biography of her childhood and early adulthood.

Armstrong, T. (1994). *Multiple intelligences in the classroom*. Alexandria, VA: Association for Supervision and Curriculum Development. A very practical book on multiple intelligences, written by a person who has studied the topic extensively and directed toward practicing teachers.

Beatty, A. S. (1996). NAEP 1994 U.S. *history report card*. Washington, DC: National Center for Educational Statistics. Full report on the 1994 NAEP history findings.

Beck, I. L., McKeown, M. G., Hamilton, R., & Kucan, L. (1997). *Questioning the author: An approach for enhancing student engagement with text*. Newark, DE: International Reading Association. The most detailed description of questioning the author.

Bransford, J., Sherwood, R., Rieser, J., & Vye, N. (1986). Teaching thinking and problem solving: research foundations. *American Psychologist*, 41, 1078–1089. Examines the nature of critical thinking from a theoretical perspective.

Bransford, J. D., & Stein, B. S. (1984). *The ideal problem solver: A guide for improving thinking, learning, and creativity*. New York: W. H. Freeman. Provides a thorough discussion of the process of implementing the IDEAL model to promote learning.

Briggs, M., & Perkins, D. (1996). *Teaching for understanding: The election process and campaigns of 1996*. Unpublished manuscript. An excellent understanding unit for high school students.

Brown, A. L., Campione, J. C., & Day, J. (1981). Learning to learn: On training students to learn from texts. *Educational Research*, 10, 14–21. Examines the notion of how well students can transfer strategies they are taught in the classroom.

Campbell, J. R., Donahue, P. L., Reese, C. M., & Phillips, G. W. (1996). NAEP 1994 *reading report card for the nation and the states*. Washington, DC: Department of Education. Full report on the 1994 NAEP reading findings.

Campbell, L., Campbell, B., & Dickinson, D. (1996). *Teaching and learning through multiple intelligences*. Needham Heights, MA: Allyn & Bacon. An explanation of multiple intelligences along with a wide array of practical classroom applications.

Carpenter, T. P., Fennema, E., & Franke, M. L. (1996). Cognitively guided instruction: A knowledge base for reform in primary mathematics instruction. 97, 3–20. A useful artical for those interested in examining the issue of whether cognitive tasks taught in the classroom can transfer to everyday learning tasks.

Dole, J. A., Duffy, G. G., Roehler, L. R., & Pearson, P. D. (1991). Moving from the old to the new: Research on reading comprehension instruction. *Review of Educational Research*, 61, 239–264. A comprehensive discussion of changes in the nature of reading instruction to promote comprehension.

Doyle, W. (1984). Academic tasks in classrooms. *Curriculum Inquiry*, 14, 129–149. Discusses, in part, the classroom environment in which critical thinking occurs and students' hesitation to engage in higher forms of learning.

Ennis, R. H. (1987). A taxonomy of critical thinking dispositions and abilities. In J. Baron & R. Sternberg (Eds.), *Teaching thinking skills: Theory and practice*. New York: W. H. Freeman. A rather precise description of various levels of critical thinking.

Gardner, H. (1991). *To open minds*. New York: Basic Books. Gardner's most recent general treatment of the topic. It describes the origins of the theory and developments since that time.

Graves, M. F., & Clark, D. L. (1981). Effects of adjunct questions on high school low achievers. *Reading Improvement*, 18, 8–13. Explores the effect of using adjunct questions on low ability readers' comprehension of textbook selections.

Haggard, M. R. (1988). Developing critical thinking with the Directed Reading Activity. *Reading Teacher*, 41, 532–.... Describes an instructional activity to facilitate higher-level learning through the use of prereading and reading activities.

Halpern, D. F. (1984). *Thought and knowledge: An introduction to critical thinking*. Hillsdale, NJ: Erlbaum. A useful text for an overview of the various types of higher-level thinking.

Kirsch, I. J., Jungeblut, A., & Kolstad, A. (1996). Executive summary from adult literacy in America. *Adult Education and Development*, 47, 261–270. Current findings on adult literacy.

Levin, J. R., & Pressley, M. (1981). Improving children's prose comprehension: Selected strategies that seem to succeed. In C. M. Santa & B. L. Hayes (Eds.), *Children's prose comprehension: research and practice*. Newark, DE: International Reading Association. Sound advice on improving comprehension of prose.

McPeck, J. (1981). *Critical thinking and education*. New York: St. Martin's Press. A rather complete text addressing the importance of critical thinking in schools and ways students may acquire higher-level thinking strategies.

Paul, R. W. (1991). Dialogical and dialectical thinking. In A. L. Costa (Ed.), *Developing minds*: A *resource book for teaching thinking*. Alexandria, VA: Association for Supervision and Curriculum Development. A thorough description of the Socratic questioning strategy.

Paris, S. G., & Winograd, P. (1990). Metacognition in academic learning and instruction. In B. F. Jones and L. Idol (Eds.), *Dimensions of thinking and cognitive instruction*. Hillsdale, NJ: Erlbaum. Thorough discussion of the role and importance of metacognition in higher-level thinking.

Perkins, D. (1992). *Smart schools: From training memories to education minds*. New York: Free Press. A well-written, engaging, and comprehensive plan for teaching for understanding.

———.(1993). Making education relevant: Teaching and learning for understanding. *New Jersey Educational Association Review*, October, 10–18. A good, journal-length description of Perkins's perspective on teaching for understanding.

Perkins, D., & Blythe, T. (1993). Putting understanding up front. *Educational Leadership*, 51(5), 4–7. A concise description of Perkins's approach to teaching for understanding.

Perkins, D., & Simmons, R. (1988). Patterns of misunderstanding: An integrative model of science, math, and programming. *Review of Educational Research*, 58, 303–326. A thoughtful article addressing thinking in the classroom.

Perkins, D. N. (1986). *Knowledge as design*. Hillsdale, NJ: Erlbaum. An in-depth look at the procedure and the thinking behind it.

Perkins, D. N. (1994). *Knowledge as design: A handbook for critical and creative discussion across the curriculum*. Pacific Grove, CA: Critical Thinking Press and Software. Detailed description and examples of knowledge as design that comes with an excellent videotape showing students engaging in the procedure.

Prawat, R. S. (1991). The value of ideas: The immersion approach to the development of thinking. *Educational Researcher*, 20, 3–10. A thoughtful discussion of the immersion approach to the teaching of critical thinking.

Press, F. (1984, May 30). Address given at the Annual Commencement Convocation, School of Graduate Studies, Case Western Reserve University, Cleveland, OH. The source of the statement about the beauty in science.

Resnick, L. B. (1987). *Education and learning to think*. Washington, DC: National Academy Press. Complete discussion of the role of thinking in the school context.

———. (1995). From aptitude to effort: A new foundation for our schools. *Daedalus*, 124, 55–62. An enlightening view of the role of higher-order thinking in our society and in our schools.

Roehler, L. R., & Duffy, G. G. (1984). Direct explanation of comprehension processes. In G. Duffy, L. Roehler, & J. Mason (Eds.), *Comprehension instruction*. White Plains, NY: Longman. An informative source to learn more about the effect of questions on comprehension.

Rosenshine, B. R., Meister, C., & Chapman, S. (1996). Teaching students to generate questions: A review of the intervention studies. *Review of Educational Research*, 66, 181–221. A thorough review of the state of knowledge regarding student-generated questions.

Ryder, R. J. (1991). The directed questioning activity for subject matter text. *Journal of Reading*, 34, 606–612. A thorough description of the DQA strategy.

Smith, F. (1990). *To think*. New York: Teachers College Press. A complete text on the instruction of thinking and its importance in students' education.

Sternberg, R. J. (1986). *Critical thinking: Its nature, measurement, and improvement*. Paper presented at National Institute of Education, Washington, DC. An informative presentation on the importance of critical thinking and its instruction.

————. (1988). When teaching thinking does not work, what goes wrong? *Harvard Educational Review*, 89, 555–579. A useful source for understanding the importance of teaching students real-life problems.

van Dijk, T. A., & Kintsch, W. (1983). *Strategies of discourse comprehension*. Hillsdale, NJ: Erlbaum. Examines the nature of comprehension and the role of the learner in constructing knowledge.

Walmsley, S. (1996). 10 ways to improve your theme teaching. *Instructor*, August, 54–60. Ten practical, powerful, and on-target suggestions for theme teaching.

Wittrock, M. C. (1974). Learning as a generative process. *Educational Psychologist*, 11, 87–95. The original statement of Wittrock's concept of generative learning.

————. (1991). Generative teaching of comprehension. *Elementary School Journal*, 92, 169–184. A recent update on generative learning.

Whitehead, A. N. (1929). *The aims of education*. New York: Macmillan. Even today this is an interesting perspective on the role of education.

Wood, D. J., Bruner, J. S., & Ross, G. (1976). The role of tutoring in problem solving. *Journal of Child Psychology and Psychiatry*, 17, 89–100. One of the initial articles on the process of scaffolding.

C H A P T E R

6

Writing

CHAPTER OVERVIEW

In this chapter we deal with ways in which writing can enhance students' reading and learning in content classes. We begin by discussing the importance of writing. Next, we consider some of what we know about writing—students' writing skills, the sorts of writing done in schools, and the components of the writing process. After that, we discuss the importance of motivation and providing a positive classroom atmosphere, present some general guidelines for writing in content areas, and consider the use of computers in writing. Then we describe five types of writing that students can profitably employ in content classes. These are answering questions, summarizing, writing to encourage critical thinking, expressive writing, and extended and formal writing. In the last section of the chapter, we take up the matter of responding to students' writing, stressing approaches that minimize the time teachers need to spend at this task, and the matter of assessing students' writing.

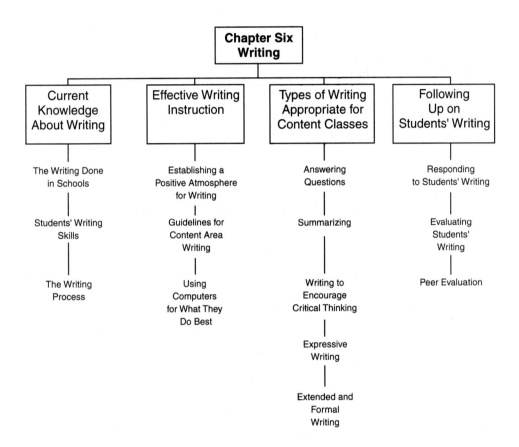

Chapter Six
Writing

| Current Knowledge About Writing | Effective Writing Instruction | Types of Writing Appropriate for Content Classes | Following Up on Students' Writing |

The Writing Done in Schools

Students' Writing Skills

The Writing Process

Establishing a Positive Atmosphere for Writing

Guidelines for Content Area Writing

Using Computers for What They Do Best

Answering Questions

Summarizing

Writing to Encourage Critical Thinking

Expressive Writing

Extended and Formal Writing

Responding to Students' Writing

Evaluating Students' Writing

Peer Evaluation

O ver the past 30 years, educators have learned a good deal about the relationships among reading, writing, speaking, and listening; and the importance of recognizing and building on the interrelationship among the language arts has become an increasingly frequent and significant theme (Carroll, 1966; Olson, 1996; Tierney & Pearson, 1983). However, today's scholars are certainly not the first to recognize the importance of this interrelationship. It was nearly 300 years ago that Francis Bacon coined his now famous aphorism—"Reading maketh a full man, conference a ready man, and writing an exact man." Contemporary scholars would hardly agree with Bacon's observation.

Contemporary scholars would also agree with the view of writing expressed by William Zinsser (1988, p. 11), the widely published writing teacher, novelist, essayist, and editor. "Writing," says Zinsser, "is not just a special language that belongs to English teachers and a few other sensitive souls who have a 'gift for words.' Writing is the logical arrangement of thought. Anyone who thinks clearly should be able to write clearly, about any subject at all." Moreover, Zinsser explains, writing, thinking, and learning are very closely related. By writing, students often find out what they know about a topic or what they want to say about it. And by teaching writing across the curriculum—by engaging students in writing in social studies, art, music, science, mathematics, and other subjects—teachers can do much more than encourage students to write; teachers can encourage students to think and to learn.

Writing also serves students in other ways. As Bacon's statement suggests, it can help students be precise about what they know and what they do not know. Additionally, as Vacca and Linek (1992) point out, writing offers students several worthwhile benefits. The benefits they suggest and one we have added are shown below.

Some Particular Benefits of Writing in Content Areas

- The opportunity to interact with the material they are learning

- The opportunity to become personally involved with a text

- The opportunity to use their background knowledge and experiences to make sense of the ideas and information they encounter in classes

- The opportunity to engage in meaningful communication about the ideas and information they encounter in classes

---

Importantly, all content areas offer students such opportunities. In mathematics, for example, students might write about a real-life situation in which they could use trigonometry to determine a distance they need to know. In physical education, students might write about some specific rule changes that they believe would improve high school basketball. Or in French class, American students might correspond with French students by email or surface mail, perhaps describing some of the slang used by American teenagers and asking about the use of slang by French teens.

Moreover, writing is not something that is useful just in school. Writing is useful throughout life. Not everyone, of course, writes a lot; but most people write something each day. Teachers write lesson plans, memos to principals or department chairs, letters to parents, reports of various sorts, and essays about teaching and learning. Those in business and industry write memos, reports, documentation for goods or services, descriptions of upcoming events, and newsletters. Those in politics and various other public positions write reports, position papers, news releases, and speeches. And almost everyone will have occasion to write for personal reasons—notes to family members, letters to friends, directions for doing something or getting someplace, and the like.

Thus, writing serves multiple functions. Not only does it help students learn about what they know and what they do not know and help them to get involved in their work and their studies, it also enables both students and the adults they become to communicate with friends, colleagues, business associates, and constituencies. In the remainder of this chapter, we first consider how much students write, how well they write, and the writing process. Next, we discuss the importance of establishing an atmosphere that encourages writing, present some guidelines for writing in content areas, and consider some of the most powerful uses of computers for writing. After that, we discuss the various types of writing you might use in your content area classes. Finally, we consider some matters involved in responding to and evaluating students' writing.

CURRENT KNOWLEDGE ABOUT WRITING

The topic of students' writing proficiency has recently received a good deal of national attention. National assessments of students' writing skills, recent surveys, and research and theorizing about the writing process have provided a great deal of useful information on the topic. Each of these matters is considered below.

The Writing Done in Schools

Current orientations to teaching writing generally endorse process approaches, approaches which focus on specific components of writing—topic selection, prewriting, drafting, revising, and editing. Such approaches emphasize writing as a thinking and communication process, and stress the importance of writers considering the purposes and audiences of their writing. Such approaches also underscore the importance of students engaging in these various practices and suggest that less attention should be given to the finished written products of writing. The most recent national survey of writing instruction available was conducted by the National Assessment of Educational Progress (NAEP) in 1992. Reports of that assessment (Applebee, Langer, Mullis, Latham, & Gentile, 1994; National Center for Educational Statistics, 1996) indicate that the majority of junior and senior high school English teachers believe in and generally follow a process approach and that students were writing more in 1992 than in 1988. This NAEP report also indicates that the three most frequent types of writing for junior high students are reports or summaries, narratives, and essays of themes, and that the most frequent types of writing for senior high students are essays or themes, reports or summaries, and narratives. In addition, a 1996 study by Landrum indicated that senior high school English teachers overwhelmingly endorsed the process approach and provided instruction in keeping with most of its tenets.

However, these same reports indicate some shortcomings of the writing done in schools. Applebee et al. (1994), for example, found that students spent an average of only about two hours a week on writing as compared to five hours a week on mathematics, that persuasive writing and writings of three or more pages were relatively rare even in junior and senior high school, and that about 25 percent of junior and senior high school students neither did planning before writing nor wrote multiple drafts. Somewhat similarly, Landrum found that none of the English teachers she observed dealt with the concepts of audience or purpose, and that all of the teachers put the majority of their comments on student's completed drafts, where they are likely to have very little effect. Additionally, it appears that the vast majority of writing is done in English classes and very little is done in other content areas.

Students' Writing Skills

The most comprehensive data on American students' writing skills comes from the NAEP survey. Applebee et al. (1994, pp. 2–3) sum up those results this way:

> Taken as a whole, the results show that given time and familiarity with the topic, the best students can write relatively effective informational and narrative pieces. Even the best students continue, however, to have difficulty with writing tasks that require them to muster arguments and evidence in persuasive writing. According to teachers and students, persuasive writing . . . received less emphasis in their classes than did informative and narrative writing.
>
> More importantly, the performance of the best students remains far ahead of the performance of most of their classmates. Whatever successes schools may claim in writing instruction, many students at each grade level continue to have serious difficulties in producing effective informative, persuasive, or narrative writing.

Clearly, American students need assistance in becoming more effective writers, and a good deal of that assistance can be delivered in content classes.

▼ PRACTICE ACTIVITY 6.1

Pause at this point and answer two series of questions—in writing. First, consider the information presented in the chapter, then answer these questions: How much writing do students typically do? What sorts of writing do students typically do? How well do students write? Next, consider your experiences as a student in the intermediate and secondary grades, then answer these questions: How much writing did you do in school? What sorts of writing did you do in school? How well did your experiences in school prepare you for the writing you do now?

▼▼

The Writing Process

Until fairly recently, teaching writing often consisted primarily of teaching grammar, and learning to write was largely defined as gaining control over linguistic conventions, many of which were mechanical. The concern was almost exclusively with the writer's finished product, and writing instruction was largely divorced from considerations about the context of the writing, the writer's purpose, or the audience to whom the writing was addressed. This was unfortunate because, as Hillocks's (1986) extensive review of the literature has clearly demonstrated, teaching grammar and emphasizing mechanics does not improve students' composing skills.

A good deal of current thinking about writing represents a very different view, and much of this thinking has contributed to a major shift in teachers' understanding of the writing process and the objectives of writing instruction. This view has led to wide acceptance of cognitive process models of writing, the realization that writing is a social process, and concern with what the writer can learn about a particular subject from writing about it. The view has also led to the realization that a writer can learn much during the writing process. Each of these matters is considered next.

Cognitive Process Models of Writing

Cognitive process models of writing deal with the thought processes that writers engage in as they write. Flower and Hays (1981) developed the most influential of these models, and Figure 6.1 shows some components of their model. As can be seen, the model includes the mental operations of *planning*, *translating*, and *reviewing* as well as several subprocesses. As indicated by the arrows, the model is recursive;

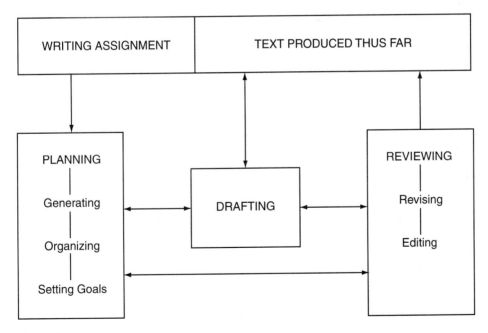

Figure 6.1
Some Components of the Writing Process

that is, the various subprocesses occur and reoccur in a variety of orders. A writer may begin with planning, translate some of his or her thoughts into a preliminary draft, pause and do some additional planning, do some additional drafting, and pause again, perhaps this time to set some different goals. Alternatively, the writer may begin drafting immediately without planning, finish a draft and review it, and only in the process of reviewing the draft really begin to think about setting goals. These, of course, are only two of the myriad of possible paths a writer may take with a particular piece of writing. Thus, the model emphasizes that writing is a complex and multifaceted process.

Not surprisingly, there are major differences between the writing processes of mature writers and novices. Skilled writers are knowledgeable about a variety of discourse types, purposes of writing, and audiences for writing; and they make conscious use of this knowledge as they write. They also do a lot of deliberate planning and goal setting. Many school-age writers, on the other hand, lack such knowledge and do little conscious planning and goal setting. They often begin writing without much thought or a plan, simply treating a writing assignment as a request to tell everything they know about the topic without giving much attention to the purpose of their writing, or its audience, or how they might accomplish their purpose. Attention to writing as a cognitive process has shifted the concern of writing teachers from matters of mechanics and correctness to providing instruction that deliberately engages students in the various subprocesses that mature writers employ.

▼ PRACTICE ACTIVITY 6.2

One important tenet of the process model of writing is that there is no single writing process but a variety of processes that writers use at different times and for different purposes. Outline some of the processes that you go through when doing different sorts of writing, and then write a comment on the extent to which your writing process differs from one situation to another. Our response is shown at the end of the book.

▼ ▼

Writing as a Social Process

In addition to the concern with writing as a cognitive process, there has been an increased interest in writing as a social process. This view of writing as a social process focuses on the role of the context in which writing takes place and the audience for whom something is written in shaping both the requirements of writing and the composing strategies students use. Students are most aided in becoming competent writers when they write material that has real communicative purposes and that requires them to plan and make choices as they shape their writing so that it is appropriate for their purposes, their readers, and the social circumstances in which it will be read. Content area classes offer students many legitimate and authentic opportunities to write for various purposes, for a variety of audiences, from different perspectives, and about diverse topics.

Writing to Learn and Feel

A third concern is that students need to realize that not all writing is directed to some outside person. One very important audience for the writer is the writer himself, and frequently the writing one does for oneself does not result in a polished product. Students can write to find out what they know about a topic. Students can also write to engage with a topic—to gain some feeling for, appreciation of, or interest in it. Both are very legitimate uses of school writing.

This latter type of writing has been called *expressive writing* (Britton, Burgess, Martin, McLeod, & Rosen, 1975), and it has been contrasted with the more typical type of school writing, which has been called *transactional writing*. Transactional writing is the objective, informational writing that people use in transacting business with each other. Virtually all the writing typically done in content classes is transactional, and most of this writing is relatively formal. Expressive writing, on the other hand, is closely tied to talk. Expressive writing employs the everyday language often used to discuss thoughts, feelings, and opinions with friends or family. In school, students can use expressive writing to consider what they are learning and to make some sort of commitment to it. They can use their background knowledge, their experiences, and their personal feelings to express the ideas they are exploring (Vacca & Linek, 1992). Through expressive writing, students can understand these ideas better, assess for themselves how well they understand the ideas, and generate some sort of personal involvement with the ideas. At least some of the writing students do in school—and quite possibly a good deal of it—should be expressive.

▼ PRACTICE ACTIVITY 6.3

These last two sections have been short ones, but in fact they can be made even briefer. Try writing a summary of the two sections. As much as possible, do this in your own words because that will help you better understand and remember the ideas.

▼▼

EFFECTIVE WRITING INSTRUCTION

Here we consider three facets of effective writing instruction: Establishing a positive classroom atmosphere, following guidelines appropriate for content area writing, and using computers for what they do best.

Establishing a Positive Atmosphere for Writing

Because writing is hard work and many students find writing a challenge, it becomes doubly important for teachers to motivate students to write and to create a classroom atmosphere in which they feel free to write. There are a number of things you can do that contribute to such an atmosphere.

The starting point in establishing a positive atmosphere for writing is to have students do a substantial amount of writing in which they do not attempt to produce a polished product to be handed in, judged, and graded. This means giving students opportunities to write to discover what they already know about a topic, to jot down notes as they read, or to write to engage themselves with the topic.

A closely related approach is to allow students to submit only a selected portion of the writing they produce to you for your comments. This gives students some sense of power, and it gives them valuable practice in evaluating their writing. After all, they will want to hand in their best work.

Also, before students hand in papers for your comments, and perhaps a grade, the papers should usually go through several rounds of peer review. As is the case with students selecting which work to hand in, peer review offers valuable practice in evaluating writing. It also give students practice in listening to each other closely and communicating with each other precisely.

Finally, when you do get papers, use a coaching and positive tone rather than a judgmental and critical tone in your responses. This will go a long way toward convincing students that writing is a risk they can afford to take.

Guidelines for Content Area Writing

The following guidelines include suggestions that both we and others (Tchudi & Huerta, 1983; Vacca & Linek, 1992) have found useful in dealing with writing in content areas. They are consistent with a number of points that have already been made about writing and teaching writing and constitute a review and extension of many of those points.

Guidelines for Content Area Writing

1. Keep the content of students' writing—what they are saying—as the central focus. Treat the form of their writing—how they say it—after dealing with the content.

2. Design writing activities to help students structure and synthesize their knowledge. Also, provide opportunities for students to write in order to record and recall ideas from their reading.

3. Give students varied audiences to write for. Their audiences should include themselves, their classmates, other students in your school and perhaps other schools, the community outside of school, and yourself. Be doubly sure that you are not the only audience for their writing.

4. When students are doing formal writing assignments, provide them with the time to engage in the full writing process—prewriting, drafting, and revising. Importantly, avoid situations in which students do not get much assistance and feedback until they hand in their final paper for a grade. One teacher's realization of the frequent fate of comments on final drafts is illustrated on page 197.

Continued

5. Make peer response a frequent activity. Remember, though, that students need to be instructed in how to give peer responses.

6. Differentiate between revising and editing, and make revising your students' first concern. Revising consists of modifying a piece of writing to make it clearer, more powerful, more gripping, more interesting, and the like. Editing consists of making sure that such matters as spelling, punctuation, and usage are correct.

7. Whenever possible, publish, display, or otherwise publicly acknowledge students' formal writing.

As Joseph Trahano handed back his eleventh-grade history students' essays on the causes of the Civil War, he felt a sense of accomplishment. He considered writing important and included a good deal of writing in all of his courses, and he believed that the assignment he was returning had really stretched his students' thinking and writing skills. Of course, evaluating the papers and giving his students some substantive feedback had taken a good deal of time—virtually the entire weekend. But he considered this time well spent; the extensive feedback he had provided students would be extremely useful for their next writing assignment.

But then as students received their papers, Mr. Trahano watched with increasing awareness as nearly every student took a quick look at the grade, folded the paper, and put it in his or her notebook. Why in his six years of teaching hadn't he seen this before, Mr. Trahano wondered dejectedly. Students pay very little attention to comments on a final draft, he realized. In the future, he resolved, that's not where he would spend his time on students' writing.

PRACTICE ACTIVITY 6.4

Select one of the guidelines for content area writing and list the advantages and the disadvantages of the idea. Then, consider both the advantages and disadvantages you have listed, and state your position on the matter succinctly in a paragraph or so. Our response to one of them is given at the end of the book.

▼ ▼

Using Computers for What They Do Best

Over the past decade, computers have become increasingly commonplace in schools, and access to the Internet is growing daily. Here we consider stand-alone computer applications that are particularly useful for writing. In Chapter 9 we deal with ways in which students can use the Internet in conjunction with their writing.

Both common sense and research suggest that computers can be very useful for writing. For example, as is shown in the figure below, the 1992 NAEP assessment (Applebee et al., 1994) indicated that in the top-performing schools only about one-fourth of the students did not have computers available for writing, while in the bottom-performing schools nearly half of the students did not have computers available.

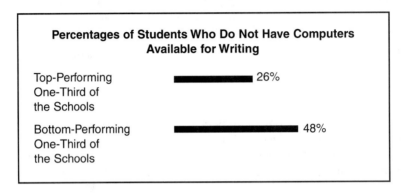

Percentages of Students Who Do Not Have Computers Available for Writing

Top-Performing One-Third of the Schools — 26%

Bottom-Performing One-Third of the Schools — 48%

Of course, not every use of the computer aids students in becoming better writers. For fostering students' writing skills in content classes and for making content area writing as productive as possible, a small number of applications are particularly useful. The most useful of these applications is word processing. Word processors make the planning, generating, drafting, revising, and editing processes so necessary to learning to write effectively and to producing accomplished pieces of writing feasible and acceptable to students. Everyone seems to have their favorite word processors. *Microsoft Word* is probably the most popular package for Macintosh computers, and *WordPerfect* is probably the most popular package for IBM and IBM-compatible computers. However, any computer and any word processor represent an immeasurable advantage over writing by hand or typing. Thus, the first step in using computers effectively is finding out what equipment and word processing programs are available in your school and arranging for students to spend significant amounts of time with them.

The next step is to become thoroughly familiar with the word processor yourself and then to instruct your students in its use. Many students will already be adept at word processing, but others will not; without specific instruction many students will not get the maximum benefits that word processing can give them. Basic functions such as keying in text and saving and retrieving files should be taught first, saving more advanced functions such as replacing words and larger units of text and formatting for later lessons. Of course, newer and more-powerful word processing programs include grammar checkers and drawing tools, and students are likely to profit from these and find them motivating. In addition, students' writing will certainly profit if they learn to use the spell check and thesaurus features that are included in many word processing programs. Many students who would almost never stop to look up words in a dictionary or consult a traditional thesaurus will quite readily run their writing through spell checkers and click a mouse to search for a more colorful or appropriate word.

Another extremely motivating feature of many of the more powerful word processors is their desktop publishing capability. Using a word processing program's resources of different fonts, different type sizes, and different styles such as bold or shadowed print makes it possible for students to produce work they can be truly proud of. Using other word processing features such as printing multiple columns, printing horizontally rather than vertically on a page, and importing graphics offers students additional opportunities to produce creative and compelling final versions of their writing. And the opportunity to produce something really professional looking will often provide students with the motivation to do the sort of drafting and revising that mature writers do.

PRACTICE ACTIVITY 6.5

Get together with two or three of your classmates, make a list of the ways you have used computers in your own writing, and brainstorm a set of additional ways that computers could be used in content classes.

▼▼

TYPES OF WRITING APPROPRIATE FOR CONTENT CLASSES

As you have probably noticed, up to this point in the chapter you have been asked to do quite a bit of writing. In fact, you have been asked to engage in five sorts of writing; four of five sorts of writing that are particularly useful in content classes. Here we discuss these five sorts of writing—answering questions, summarizing, writing to encourage critical thinking, expressive writing, and extended and formal writing. The first two of these are frequent activities in content courses, while the last three are less frequent. In addition, notetaking, another frequent activity, is discussed in Chapter 4. Although not all of these activities need to be part of every content course, you should consider the potential of each of them, and choose at least several of them to include in your repertoire.

Answering Questions

Answering questions is an extremely frequent activity that students undertake in conjunction with reading. As long as the questions are not objective ones such as true-false or multiple-choice items, they require at least some writing. Writing out answers is generally more beneficial to students than simply selecting from among choices because writing forces students to grapple with the meaning of the answers they are constructing. Thus, writing out answers to questions is a valid and useful activity. Attention to several guidelines can make the questions students write about more effective learning tools.

As Beck and McKeown (1981) have suggested, the most basic guideline for asking questions is to first ask those questions which lead students to the most important information in a text. Beck and McKeown further suggest that teachers should ask questions in the order in which they are answered in the text so that in answering the questions students build a model of the text in their minds. Finally, Beck and McKeown point out that sets of questions that get at the essence of a selection will typically include factual questions, inferential questions, and various sorts of questions that require the reader to relate the information in the text to other information, make judgments, or synthesize information.

This leads to a second guideline for asking questions. Make it a practice to ask students various sorts of questions. Try to include a balance of factual questions that are explicitly answered in the text, inferential questions that require students to synthesize information from the text, extension questions that require students to combine information in the text with knowledge they already have, and attitudinal questions that require some sort of personal response to the text. For example, questions for students to answer after reading a history chapter on the Civil War might include factual questions on the major battles of the war, inferential questions on the causes of the war, extension questions comparing the tactics used in the Civil War to those used in the Revolutionary War, and attitudinal questions about what it must have felt like to be a soldier on the night before a major battle.

A third guideline regarding writing to answer questions is to sometimes have the students write out their answers in complete sentences in relatively polished prose and at other times ask them to simply jot down phrases capturing the gist of the answer. Writing out answers fully gives students practice in writing and often prompts them to more fully consider and formulate their responses, quite possibly producing deeper learning. Jotting down brief responses, on the other hand, gives students an opportunity to appreciate the value of such informal writing and allows them to answer more questions in less time.

A fourth guideline regarding writing answers to questions is that doing so provides an excellent opportunity for cooperative learning like that described in Chapter 7. Each of several groups can be responsible for a set of questions, then the groups come together as a class to share their knowledge.

Summarizing

Summarizing is typically not as frequent a content area writing activity as answering questions. This is unfortunate because summarizing is an extremely valuable study strategy, and it should be a very frequent activity because it prompts active processing and synthesizing. By definition, a summary is a shorter yet generally inclusive version of what the author wrote; transforming a longer text into a shorter one requires students to actively engage with the text and synthesize ideas.

One approach to teaching summarizing was presented in Chapter 4. Here a second approach is described, one that follows the general model of explicit instruction explained in Chapter 4. Begin by motivating students: First, tell them that summarizing is an important skill. Next, explain that it is important because it forces them to pick out significant information and recast it in their own words; this means that the information is likely to be understood and remembered. Finally, demonstrate how effective summarizing can be. Have the students summarize some texts and simply read others, take a quiz on the texts they did and did not summarize, and compare their results on the two quizzes.

After these motivational activities, move to specific instruction in summarizing. Brown and Day (1983) have developed and tested some practical rules for summarizing, and these rules have been found to be very effective. In fact, summarizing is one of the best understood and most effective learning strategies (Pressley, Johnson, Symons, McGoldrick, & Kurita, 1989). Here are the rules for summarizing.

Brown and Day's Rules for Summarizing

1. Read the whole of a selection before you attempt to summarize it. Then, summarize first smaller and then larger units as noted below.

2. Summarize paragraphs by following these rules:

   • Delete trivial and redundant information.

   • Use superordinates, categories, and terms that are more general. For example, if the author mentions *perch, trout,* and *salmon,* you might write down *fish.*

   • Identify a topic sentence for the paragraph.

3. Summarize complete passages by first summarizing the individual paragraphs. Then, construct an overall summary of the complete passage.

Present these ideas on an overhead or the board, discuss them and take questions, and remind students of the value of active processing. Finally, tell students that with summarizing, as with other techniques they are likely to use in studying text, they get out of it what they put into it. That is, hard work and time spent studying is apt to pay off in what they learn. This message is likely to be most effective with students if you are candid and admit that hard work and time are costs, and summarizing is a relatively costly procedure. Thus, it is appropriate to suggest that students select writing summaries as a learning activity when the material they are reading is challenging and important and when they want to know it well.

An Eighth Grader's Summary of the Fitness Guidelines She Read About in Health Class

The author's major thing is balance and keeping fit in many different ways. You have to eat well, and you have to get enough sleep, and you should get some exercise. But you don't have to go nuts on any of these. A candy bar once in a while is fine. Also, you don't have to be on a team. You just have to be sensible!

Writing to Encourage Critical Thinking

There are many ways in which students can practice critical thinking. One of the writing activities already discussed, answering questions, gives students an opportunity to both gain knowledge from what they read and manipulate and react to that knowledge in various ways, including thinking critically about what they have learned. However, as explained in Chapter 5, critical thinking is extremely important and something that students can profit from doing more of. Writing offers excellent opportunities for critical thinking, and for this reason we have included this separate section on writing to encourage critical thinking.

As noted in Chapter 5, critical thinking requires students to actively use cognitive and metacognitive processes to go beyond what is explicitly stated in any single text. Critical thinking requires students to draw upon their background knowledge, derive meaning from several different sources of information, and recognize or generate objectives that will direct their thinking and completion of a task. Writing, particularly extended writing, gives students the time and the space to think critically and to record both the process of their thinking and the results of their thinking.

As Resnick (1987), Calfee and Patrick (1995), and a number of other authorities have pointed out and as we have repeatedly stressed, critical thinking is something that all students need to do and can do. Writing that encourages critical thinking is also something that all students need to do and can do. Writing that encourages critical thinking becomes doable for all students if you vary the topics you give students and the resources you give them to investigate the topics. That is, all students can think critically if they are given appropriate topics and appropriate assistance in dealing with those topics. Topics, for example, can vary from practical and concrete problems, such as deciding what sorts of plants are likely to grow well on the north side of a house in the Pacific Northwest, to philosophical problems, such as to what extent the public school system ought to teach youngsters to critically examine the political system in our nation. The resources you give students can vary from simply presenting students with the critical thinking task and telling them they can use libraries and any other sources of information they find useful to complete the task to actually giving them all the materials they need to complete the task.

In leading students to become critical thinkers, there is a place for relatively easy tasks and a place for more difficult ones, as well as a place for providing students with a lot of resources and a place for leaving them on their own. Give students topics and the amount of support they need to succeed and then gradually challenge them by presenting them with more complex tasks and less support; that is, follow the gradual release of responsibility model (Pearson & Gallagher, 1983). In the remainder of this section, we present examples of a fairly simple task with a lot of support and a fairly difficult task with which students are left largely on their own.

As the simpler task, consider that of students in a consumer education class making a decision about what sort of VCR to buy. The writing task is for students to document the process they went through in making the decision, to state the decision, and to explain why they made the decision they did. As resources, give students a profile showing the income and expenditures of the family they are to represent, a half dozen or so ads for VCRs, and an issue of *Consumer Reports* that evaluates VCRs.

Then ask them, individually or in groups, to analyze the situation and come up with a report in which they (1) define the problem, (2) describe the resources they have used to make their decision, (3) describe the process they used to reach their decision, and (4) state their decision. Also, as a further exercise in critical thinking, ask them to discuss how principled or arbitrary their decision was.

An Eleventh Grader's Preliminary Notes on the VCR Decision

1. Need to find out how to get the best VCR for the money. I wonder what makes a VCR best? Have to think about that.

2. I'll need the stuff Mr. Henkins gave us, but I could use some other stuff too. Maybe I'll talk to some people who recently bought VCRs.

3 and 4. I'll have to do these after I have my information. Also, I better talk to Mr. Henkins or someone about principled and arbitrary. I really don't know what he means.

Of course, this task could be made more challenging and require more critical thinking if you provide students with fewer resources. For example, it would become a great deal more challenging if you simply presented students with the problem of choosing a VCR and asked them to both determine what information they needed to make a reasonable decision and to find that information themselves.

As a more difficult task, consider some particularly talented senior high students in a social policy class that is dealing with the issue of public health care. The particular matter to be considered in this critical thinking and writing activity is the advisability of mandatory large-scale testing for various communicable diseases. The issue has come up in some of the class readings and has elicited a good deal of debate among the students, but this debate has produced a lot of heat without a great deal of light. In introducing the activity, you note this and tell them you think the issue is one worth their time and effort. You also provide the students with a single resource, a chapter on risk-benefit analysis out of Robin's *Matters of Life and Death: Risks and Benefits of Medical Care* (1984). The chapter presents a fascinating scenario of the risks and benefits of large-scale diagnosis.

After you have given this very brief introduction to the activity and distributed the chapter, tell students that they can work alone or in groups, but that beyond that they are on their own for a while. For this activity, they will need to start from the beginning and identify the specific problem they want to address. Then they will need to engage in at least some of the following steps and prepare a report in which they record some of these steps. The steps include (1) defining the problem, (2) explaining how they decided what resources they would need to solve it, (3) describing the resources they used to make their decision, (4) describing the process they used to reach the decision, (5) stating the decision, (6) justifying the decision, and (7) assessing how certain they are of their decision. As suggested in the previous exercise, as a further exercise in critical thinking you can ask them to discuss how principled or arbitrary their decision was. The decision as to which of these steps to record in their reports is one the students will need to make as part of the critical thinking they are engaging in.

It is important to recognize that these two assignments represent a wide range of difficulty and that the latter assignment is one that will really challenge many students. It may be too difficult for many students, and students who do work with it may need a good deal of support from you. At the same time, the problem is representative of the large, complex, and unbounded decisions that life presents; learning to deal with such problems is the essence of critical thinking.

▼ PRACTICE ACTIVITY 6.6

Brainstorm a list of half a dozen topics in your subject matter that invite critical thinking. Include both easier topics and more challenging ones, but definitely choose topics that require the complex sorts of thinking illustrated in the VCR and testing for communicable disease examples just given. If possible, get a colleague to join you in this.

▼▼

Expressive Writing

As noted earlier in this chapter, although there is not very much writing done in content classes, the vast majority of the writing that is done is addressed to the teacher and is transactional, meant to convey information. Students need more opportunities for expressive writing, writing that gives them opportunities to articulate their thoughts, feelings, and opinions about the topics they are studying.

Sometimes the expressive writing students produce will be directed to you as their teacher, to other students in the class, or to some wider audience beyond the classroom. Often, however, students will do their expressive writing for themselves and it will not be passed on to others. Partly for this reason and partly because students need the opportunity to make these personal responses without having to give a lot of attention to such matters as mechanics and usage, most of the expressive writing students do should be informal, not subject to a lot of rules and not subject to criticism and revisions. This makes your task in promoting and fostering expressive writing an easy one; there is not a lot of teaching or a lot of correcting that needs to be done here. However, your task is also likely to be a challenging one because students are unlikely to have done much expressive writing in the past, particularly in content classes.

Students' lack of experience with expressive writing means that several practices will be useful when you introduce expressive writing in your classes. First, explain to students what expressive writing is and why you are having them do it. This type of writing gives them the opportunity to express their personal feelings about topics that come up in their readings and in class, and expressing their personal feelings about topics will help students become involved with them and understand them.

Second, model expressive writing in response to class topics yourself, and share both the composing process you used and what you wrote with your students. For example, after reading a chapter about the Great Depression, you might write something like this: "I've read about the Great Depression before, and every time I read about it and see the pictures of the men and women doing nothing, just sitting, and looking tired and without hope. I wonder how they survived. I also wonder how I would survive in their situation." Although this writing is neither profound nor vivid, it is an honest personal response to the topic, and that is what you want students to give in their expressive writing.

Third, let students know that you are asking for their feelings and responses, that recording them as they occur is really OK, and that (unless you occasionally let them know differently) they do not need to share what they have written with you or with anyone. Because writing for themselves is a new experience for many students, you may need to repeat this a number of times, and of course you will need to demonstrate your sincerity by giving students time for expressive writing and by letting them keep such writing to themselves.

One sort of expressive writing that has recently been widely discussed and advocated is journal writing (Anson & Beach, 1995; Atwell, 1987). As described by Fulwiler (1982), journal writing occupies a place midway between diaries and class notebooks. The subject of a diary is the writer, while the subject of a class notebook is the course content. Journals deal with the relationships between the student and the course content. In the sort of journal writing considered here, students—and in some cases teachers—record relatively informal comments responding to class topics. Every class offers students numerous opportunities for journal responses to important topics. Students in a geometry class might speculate about the practical uses of the formulas they are learning. Students in a music class might write about the awe certain composers or certain music inspires in them. And students in a computer class might consider parallels between the incredibly rapid growth of the computer industry and the growth that has occurred in other industries during this century.

Three matters are particularly worth considering when designing journal activities. One is whether anyone other than the writer should read them. Opinions differ here, but if students spend fairly substantial amounts of time on journals, then teachers should read at least some of their entries. Of course, you may want to guarantee to students that certain journal entries will remain private.

Another matter is that of who should read them. Teachers and other students are both viable audiences. At some times you will probably want to read students' journals, and at other times students should be allowed to read each others' entries.

The third matter is that of choosing between individual journals and dialogue journals. Individual journals are simply journals kept by individual students. Dialogue journals, on the other hand, are extended conversations in which pairs of students respond at length to each others' entries. In such journals, students deal with both the course topic they are reading about and each others' responses to the course topic. For example, two students reading the same novel might dialogue back and forth about the theme of the novel and at the same time discuss each others' interpretation of the theme.

As already noted, the sort of expressive writing done in content class does not require much instruction. However, once you have introduced the notion of expressive writing, you will need to occasionally point out opportunities for its use. Here are just a handful of the myriad of topics students might want to expressively write about:

▼   the geological age of the earth, which one recent estimate put at 3.8 billion years

▼   abstract art, photography as art, or the right to freedom of expression

▼   big band music, the music of the Beatles, or any other sort of music

▼   the assassination of John Kennedy, Robert Kennedy, or Martin Luther King, Jr.

▼   the impact of Darwin on the modern world

▼   lowering the speed limit to 55 mph and then raising it again to 75 on some interstates

▼   woman's suffrage

▼   experiencing an earthquake, tornado, hurricane, or major thunderstorm

▼   genetic engineering

▼   cars, toasters, or other products designed to become obsolete or break.

▼ PRACTICE ACTIVITY 6.7

The above list of topics for expressive writing is a short one. It is also one that is not specifically tailored to your content area or students. Before you go on to the next section, jot down half a dozen or so topics in your content area that are likely candidates for students' expressive writing. Then, write a sentence or two of your own expressive responses to each of these topics.

▼▼

Extended and Formal Writing

Although most of you reading this book are content teachers rather than writing teachers and will therefore be using writing primarily as a vehicle to further students' success with your subject rather than as an end in itself, there are still occasions when you want students to engage in extended and relatively formal writing. For this sort of writing, the process approach is highly recommended and has been found to be particularly effective (National Center for Educational Statistics, 1996.)

The process approach was briefly discussed in the section on cognitive process models of writing. This approach (see, e.g., Graves, 1983) is currently the most widely discussed and advocated method of teaching writing. The approach gets its name from its emphasis on the process of writing, on the activities that a writer pursues as he or she plans a writing task, drafts the writing, and then reviews, revises, and edits the writing. The approach stresses that students need time and a good deal of freedom to appropriately engage in these tasks.

In using the process approach, students often engage in a series of activities:

Typical Components of the Process Approach

1. Freewriting or prewriting, brainstorming which involves students in choosing and exploring a topic of interest and searching for what they want to say about it

2. Initial drafting, the emphasis here being on the content of what students are saying rather than the form (there may be several drafts or parts of drafts done along with some peer discussion)

3. Sharing their writing with classmates and getting some response from their peers

4. Rewriting the draft into something closer to a final product (in many cases, students then meet individually with their teacher to conference on the writing)

5. Completing a final draft of a project

6. Sharing their completed writing with other students in the class or with an outside audience

---

Often in classrooms in which the process approach is used, students do not hand in all their final drafts but pick some of their best work to be read and evaluated by the teacher. As noted before, this is an excellent practice, since it gives students a sense of control, provides them with an opportunity to evaluate their own writing, and leaves the teacher with fewer papers to deal with. Finally, whenever possible, students in process writing classrooms should write for audiences other than the teacher.

In employing the process approach, a music teacher might ask students to describe a particular type of music and a particular selection exemplifying that type of music, and then explain why they liked it. Initially, students might meet in small groups to share their thoughts about types of music. Then, they might prewrite— quickly jotting down a number of alternative types of music and their likes and dislikes. Next, they might select one type of music and write a rough draft. They could then share these drafts with their group members, getting feedback and revising as needed. In their next draft, they would probably pay more attention to form, producing writing that looked more like a final product. After completing this second draft, they might again share their writing with others, probably looking for comments on form and mechanics as well as further comments on content. Next would come the third, and quite possibly the final, draft. As a concluding activity, each student might read his or her paper and play a tape of the musical selection they used as an example. After this, students might hand in their papers for the teacher's response (or they might not). The major purposes of the assignment—thinking about types of music, engaging with the topic, planning and drafting a piece, revising and editing it, and sharing their writing with an audience—have already been accomplished.

Of course, as a content teacher you will not always have time to engage in lengthy writing activities. Note, however, that you do not need to engage in a full-blown assignment such as this one to take advantage of the insights provided by the process approach. Any of the individual activities students engage in while completing this assignment—discussion, writing about something interesting, prewriting, drafting, peer reviewing, revising, editing, and sharing finished products with an audience—can be of value by themselves.

▼ PRACTICE ACTIVITY 6.8

Consider some extended writing that you might employ in your content area using the process approach. First, decide on some topics. Next, decide on how long you might devote to the writing. After that, determine an audience for the writing. Then, list the prewriting, writing, revising, editing, and sharing activities that students will engage in. Finally, decide on what sort of culminating activity you could have.

▼▼

FOLLOWING UP STUDENTS' WRITING

Once students write, teachers are faced with a stack of papers that cry out for attention. Here we discuss a number of matters to consider in responding to students' writing and two approaches to evaluating the writing students do.

Responding to Students' Writing

At the beginning of the chapter, we noted that during the past 30 years scholars have been reassessing the concept of writing and approaches to teaching writing. During this same period, a number of writing teachers began to consider response to student writing. It appears that one of the reasons students do not write well and one of the reasons teachers do not assign a lot of writing can be found in the ways teachers have typically responded to students' writing. Briefly, in the past teachers have almost always responded to students' writing with criticism, nearly filling their papers with red marks and angry symbols such as *awk* (awkward) and *frag* (sentence fragment). Most of the criticism has been of mechanical features—grammar, punctuation, spelling, and the like—with very little attention given to content. Often, students have received papers without a single positive comment. In addition, usually the only person to respond to students' papers has been their teachers.

Today, those who deal with students' writing have adopted a very different perspective on responding to it. Based on a variety of considerations of appropriate modes of response (see, e.g., Anson, 1989), a very telling article on the importance of praising students' writing by Daiker (1989), and the experiences we have had on projects in which college students respond to high school students' writing via telecommunications (Duin, Lammers, Mason, & Graves, 1994; Graves & Duin, 1997; Ryder, 1991), we offer the following guidelines for response. Following these guidelines not only makes good sense as a method of improving students' writing, but they also make response a lot less work for you; this of course increases the feasibility of having students write in your classes.

Realize first that you do not have to respond to everything students write. Much of the writing students do in content classes is done for the sake of their learning the material, or finding out what they already know about the material, or engaging with the material, and much of this sort of writing simply does not require a response. Moreover, as we have noted, even when students write formal papers, you do not need to respond to every paper they write. Many teachers have found that letting students select what they think is their best work from a set of three or four papers, handing in only that paper for teacher response, works very well. You'll have fewer papers to grade, so you can afford to spend more time on each paper. Students get better feedback on their writing, they get an opportunity to evaluate their own writing and decide which paper they want to hand in for a grade, and they are put in a much less taxing situation than when everything they write is graded.

Moreover, you do not need to be the only respondent to students' writing. Students can and should respond to each other's writing. Since there are about 30 students in most classes and just one teacher, students can respond to each others' writing in much more detail than teachers can. Also, the process of responding to each others' writing offers some valuable lessons. Finding out what sorts of responses other students want on their writing and what sorts of responses students give to each others' writing will teach students a great deal about writing.

Whether it is students responding to each other or you responding to students, a central concern in any response should be to give students positive feedback. As noted above, in the past the vast majority of teachers' responses to students has been criticism. In fact, Daiker (1989) reports that in most studies of how teachers respond to students' writing the ratio of criticism to praise is about 9 to 1, and in one study 15 of 25 teachers responding to a student essay found nothing to compliment. This simply is not the way to get students to do their best. Students need compliments on their writing. In fact, both teachers and peer respondents should generally try to provide at least one compliment for each critical comment made. Moreover, it is important to be specific with praise and to include praise throughout the comments, not simply at the beginning or the end of them.

In addition to being specific with praise, it is important to include both explicit comments and examples and general comments and prompts in your responses. In some cases, students need to be shown just what to do; they may even need to be given models, a sentence or two showing how you or a peer reviewer might make a point. In other cases, they just need to be pointed in a direction and should be given the freedom to find their own solutions to the challenges writing presents.

It is usually a good idea to limit the number of comments you make on students' papers, and to limit the length and complexity of your comments. No matter how many comments you make, students will only respond to a limited number of them. Making more comments than students will respond to is a waste of your time, and it does not help students. Selecting a few really important matters to comment on saves time, focuses students' attention, and does not present them with a paper discouragingly filled with suggestions for revision. This same suggestion applies to peer reviewers.

Finally, the most effective tone to adopt in responding to students' work is very often that of a coach, a coworker, or even a cheerleader. Think of a coach talking to a young man or woman during a time out. The youngster is playing fairly well, almost as well as he or she can, but might be able to do a little better with some encouragement and a few hints. This is a position students often find themselves in when writing. It is up to you to provide the encouragement and a few hints. Again, this suggestion is for peer reviewers as well as teachers.

Evaluating Students' Writing

Writing assessment in content classes should provide information on students' understanding and internalization of what they have read, their ability to reason from what they have read, and their proficiency in articulating their thoughts. Consideration of mechanics is important but secondary to consideration of content. In planning how to evaluate students' writing, content teachers face two major challenges. First, they must identify or create an appropriate method of assessment, one that deals primarily with content and secondarily with mechanics. Second, they must find a method that does not require an unrealistic amount of time, but one that provides students with meaningful feedback. If, for example, ten minutes are required to read and comment on each paper of 150 students, the teacher is faced with twenty-five hours of grading. Here we recommend two procedures that teachers can use in meeting these challenges—the use of a simple scale and some simple guidelines for evaluating students' writing and the use of students in evaluating each other's writing.

A *Simple Scale and Guidelines for Evaluating Students' Writing*

Noted writing instructor Peter Elbow (1996) recommends a set of guidelines and a scale for evaluating students' writing efficiently while at the same time providing them with the feedback they need. Below is a slightly modified set of those guidelines and the scale.

Elbow's Guidelines for Efficiently Evaluating Students' Writing

- Give fewer levels of grades, using three at most. Separate papers into strong, weak, and typical; use checks, check pluses, and check minuses.
- Announce the grading criteria to students before papers are handed in so that you don't have to explain your criteria in individually written comments to students.
- Give fewer graded assignments. Remember, you do not need to evaluate and grade everything students write.
- Use a grid like the one page 211 for your final comments. Reduce the "coldness" of the approach by writing an end comment.

Assessment Form for Final Drafts

Strong	Typical	Weak	
			Ideas, insights, thinking
			Genuine revision, substantive changes beyond editing
			Organization, structure, guidance for reader
			Language, sentences, wording
			Mechanics: spelling, grammar, punctuation, proofreading
			Overall

Comments:

That is all there is to it. We believe that this method is quite sufficient to provide students with meaningful feedback as well as feedback they are likely to attend to after completing the paper. Remember, as we stressed earlier, if you want to give students extensive feedback, do it as they are revising their papers, not after the final draft.

▼ PRACTICE ACTIVITY 6.9

Shown below is a portion of an eighth grader's writing on the agriculture of the Midwest. Take a few moments to read this writing sample and mark the scale below. We have left out the row dealing with revision because we are showing you the students' final draft only. Our evaluation is at the end of the book.

The farmers in the Midwest grow most of the corn and wheat produced in the United States. Increasingly over the past several decades, soybeans have also become an important crop. These crops grow well in this part of the country because the summers are hot and humid. Other parts of the country grow wheat and corn, but the temperature in those areas is not as warm as the Midwest. The stability of the small family farm has been threatened during the 1980s as worldwide demand for corn and wheat has declined. The lack of demand was also accompanied by many years of high production. As a result, prices of these crops declined significantly. Individual farmers were also hurt because they borrowed a lot of money from banks so they could buy more land. This added land produced crops that brought little profit and farmers were unable to make their payments. As a result, many of them lost their farms.

Strong	Typical	Weak	
			Ideas, insights, thinking
			Organization, structure, guidance for reader
			Language, sentences, wording
			Mechanics: spelling, grammar, punctuation, proofreading
			Overall

Comments:

▼▼▼

Peer Evaluation

As noted earlier in the chapter, the responsibility for evaluating writing can often be shifted from the teacher to students. Like the cooperative learning experiences described in Chapter 7, peer assessment allows students to learn from each other. Peer evaluation can reduce the time teachers devote to grading, thus making it feasible for students to write more frequently. Peer evaluation provides a social context that makes the evaluation more meaningful to individual students, and students may pay more attention to what their peers tell them than what the teacher tells them. Finally, peer review gives students an excellent context in which to improve their critical thinking and organizational skills and increase their appreciation of writing (Nystrand, 1986).

Ms. Tibbits had been an English teacher for ten years. But she had been grading student papers for even longer than that; in her junior and senior years in college, she worked as a composition reader in a high school near her apartment. After two years of that and another ten as a teacher, she just needed to do something to change her routine, and she did. What she did was to begin a systematic and long-term attempt to teach her students to respond to each others' papers. Teaching students to provide helpful responses to each others' papers wasn't at all easy she found. They really didn't know how to provide helpful responses, and they didn't want to criticize each other.

Teaching students how to respond and how to provide constructive criticism took a lot of time and effort—explanations, modeling on her part, responding to their responses, and periodically reviewing the techniques they had learned. But in the end she found that the time was incredibly well spent. Students knew more about writing, they cared more about writing, and they even learned some things about getting along with each other. At the same time, she of course ended up spending less time on student papers.

Peer review is typically conducted by small groups of students who examine the content, organization, style, and mechanics of a written piece. The scale suggested by Elbow (1996) and shown on pages 211 and 212 provides the sort of focus students need.

To begin peer evaluation, walk students through a writing assessment. First, put the scale on the overhead and describe it. Then, present the rationale for the scale and a brief description of its use. Next, model use of the scale with a writing sample. As the scale is being marked, it is important to provide a thorough rationale to students so they understand the evaluation criteria you are using and suggesting they use. Equally important, students need an opportunity to discuss the elements being evaluated.

In addition to using such a scale, or as an alternative to it, Gould (1996, p. 97) describes procedures that promote small group dialogue and direct students' attention to important elements of writing.

Gould's Guidelines for Peer Evaluation

- The writer reads aloud.
- The listeners respond, or if the piece is confusing, the listeners ask questions, then respond.
- The listeners focus on the content, perhaps asking questions about it. The writer teaches them about the subject.
- The focus shifts to the text. What will the writer do next and how will he or she do it?

Following these guidelines will prompt students to focus on the content of the writing as they provide feedback for each other. Following the guidelines also initiates a process through which students can better understand the components of good writing and good thinking. Finally, following them will ensure that students get some constructive feedback from each other. Listed below are some other suggestions for assisting students in becoming effective peer evaluators.

Additional Guidelines for Effective Peer Evaluation

1. Certain individuals within a group may "specialize" in the elements of writing they evaluate. A division of labor may speed up the evaluation process, provide more reliable feedback, and increase the evaluators' learning from the experience.

2. Students may sometimes wish to make use of colored highlighters to mark particularly well-written sentences or paragraphs. Limit highlighting to identifying strengths.

3. Attempt to set time limits for an evaluation and enforce these time limits to ensure that students stay on task.

4. Hold evaluators accountable for completing their evaluations, perhaps requesting oral presentations or written summaries.

5. Set length limits on writing assignments, at least initially, so that evaluators will have manageable pieces to respond to.

6. Maintain portfolios of students' written work containing samples of their writing from throughout the year along with evaluations of it.

7. Periodically direct all groups to conduct a holistic evaluation on the same writing sample to build consensus in scoring.

One excellent way to use peer evaluation is to use it along with your own sampling of students' writing. Each time students use peer evaluation, evaluate one or two papers yourself and compare your evaluation to those the peer groups have done. Over time, such sampling will provide you with a good sense of students' writing ability, their ability to communicate the content of the subject matter through writing, and their skill at evaluating each other's writing.

CONCLUDING REMARKS

We began this chapter by noting the importance of writing and then discussed how much writing secondary students do and how well they write. The central theme is that writing is important, not just in English classes or special writing classes but in all classes. It is also important to realize that many students do not write much and do not write well and that changing this situation is an important goal for all teachers.

The next section of the chapter considered current concepts of writing as a complex psychological process, a social process, and a means of students conversing with themselves. Each of these ideas—the view of the writing process as a recursive set of planning, drafting, and revising episodes; the view that one learns to write well by trying to communicate real messages to real audiences; and the view that the writer is sometimes the primary and sole audience for his or her writing—should influence the way content teachers work with writing in their classrooms.

Another section dealt with the vital importance of providing students with a positive classroom atmosphere, some of the most effective uses of computers in writing, and some general guidelines for content area writing. These included focusing on content, designing activities that require structuring and synthesizing, including varied audiences, providing adequate time for writing, using peer feedback, differentiating between revising and editing, and publishing students' writing.

The longest section of the chapter described five sorts of writing that are appropriate in content classes: answering questions, summarizing, writing to encourage critical thinking, expressive writing, and extended and formal writing. Consider all of them as you plan your classes and use those that seem to fit best with your classes and students. Remember, these activities do more than increase students' writing skills, they also increase students' knowledge and understanding of your subject matter.

The final section presented some guidelines for responding to students' writing and two methods of evaluating their writing. Following these guidelines will create an atmosphere in which students are willing to face the challenges of writing and work to improve their writing and their understanding of the content you teach. Using a simple scale and peer evaluation will result in evaluation that is fair, practical, and sensitive to what is important in students' writing. Moreover, using a simple scale and peer evaluation allows teachers to spend less time on evaluation, thereby making it feasible to assign more writing.

REFLECTIONS
▼▼

Now that you have considered students' writing and ways that writing can be used as an aid to reading and learning, complete the following activities in order to review and strengthen what you have learned in the chapter.

1. Summarize the information given about how much students write and what sort of writing they do. Then consider the subject matter you teach and compose statements describing how much writing and what sorts of writing students should be doing in your subject area.

2. Generate a list of 20 or so topics typically dealt with in your content area. Select six of these that you think would be good topics for expressive writing and create writing prompts for each of these topics.

3. One of the central points made about effective writing instruction is that students need the experience of writing for various audiences. Describe some of the audiences that students might write for when dealing with topics in your content

area. In some cases, it may be useful to have students assume a persona, for example, a particular historical figure, and write to an audience that person might address.

4. Select a short section from a text in your content area and write a set of questions that tap students' understanding of the most important content in the section. Go through your questions and see if they include factual, inferential, application, and attitudinal questions. If any of these types are missing, see if you can add some questions representing them. However, do not add questions unless they deal with important matters.

5. The chapter repeatedly stressed the importance of giving students positive responses to their writing as well as providing critical comments. Select several of your students' papers or obtain some papers from students in the grade level you plan to teach and generate a list of positive comments for each paper.

REFERENCES

Anson, C. M. (Ed.). (1989). *Writing and response: Theory, practice, and research*. Urbana, IL: National Council of Teachers of English. A representative collection of recent thinking about responding to students' writing.

Anson, C. M., & Beach, R. W. (1995). *Journals in the classroom: Writing to learn*. Norwood, NJ: Christopher-Gordon. The most comprehensive treatment of this topic.

Applebee, A. N., Langer, J. A., Mullis, I. V. S., Latham, A. S., & Gentile, C. A. (1994). NAEP 1992 *Writing Report Card*. Washington, DC: National Center for Educational Statistics. NAEP report on American students' writing proficiency and the instruction they receive.

Atwell, N. (1987). *In the middle: Writing, reading and learning with adolescents*. Portsmouth, NH: Boynton/Cook. A chronicle of the author's experiences in developing the writing and reading workshop approaches.

Beck, I. L., & McKeown, M. G. (1981). Developing questions that promote comprehension: The story map. *Language Arts*, 58, 913–918. Guidelines for writing questions on texts students read.

Britton, J. N., Burgess, T., Martin, N., McLeod, A., & Rosen, H. (1975). *The development of writing abilities*. New York: Macmillan. Report on a large-scale British study of writing and writing instruction.

Brown, A. H., & Day, J. D. (1983). Macrorules for summarizing text: The development of expertise. *Journal of Verbal Learning and Verbal Behavior*, 22, 1–14. Empirical study demonstrating how students can be taught to become better summarizers.

Calfee, R. C., & Patrick, C. L. (1995). *Teach our children well: Bringing K–12 education into the 21st century*. Stanford, CA: Stanford Alumni Association. Very readable book suggesting ways in which schools and teachers can foster critical literacy.

Carroll, J. B. (1966). Some neglected relationships in reading and language. *Elementary English*, 43, 577–582. One of the earliest considerations of the relationship between reading and the other language arts.

Daiker, D. A. (1989). Learning to praise. In C. M. Anson (Ed.), *Writing and response: Theory, practice, and research* (pp. 103–113). Urbana, IL: National Council of Teachers of English. Essay dramatically illustrating the need for respondents to student writing to praise more and criticize less.

Duin, A. H., Lammers, E., Mason, L., & Graves, M. F. (1994). Responding to ninth-grade students via telecommunications: College mentor strategies and development over time. *Research in the Teaching of English*, 28, 117–153. Study examining the strategies mentors employed, the responses they provided for students, and their perceptions of the mentoring process.

Elbow, P. (1996). Putting assessment and grading in their place. Summarized in *The Center for Interdisciplinary Studies of Writing Newsletter*. (Available from 227 Lind Hall, University of Minnesota, Minneapolis, MN 55455.) Source of the evaluation guidelines we give.

Flower, L. S., & Hayes, J. R. (1981). A cognitive process model of writing. *College Composition and Communication, 35*, 365–387. The most influential model of the cognitive process of writing.

Fulwiler, T. (1982). The personal connection: Journal writing across the curriculum. In T. Fulwiler & A. Young (Eds.), *Language connections: Writing and reading across the curriculum*. Urbana, IL: National Council of Teachers of English. Examines ways of using journals in various content areas.

Gould, J. S. (1996). A constructivist perspective on teaching and learning in the language arts. In C. T. Fosnot (Ed.), *Constructivism: Theory, perspectives, and practice* (pp. 92–102). New York: Teachers College Press. A contemporary perspective on several aspects of literacy instruction.

Graves, D. H. (1983). *Writing: Teachers and children at work*. Portsmouth, NH: Heinemann. Very influential book on young children's writing and writing instruction.

Graves, M. F., & Duin, A. H. (1997). *Writing via telecommunications* (Technical Report 18). Minneapolis: University of Minnesota, Center for Interdisciplinary Studies of Writing. Report centering on the sorts of responses college students gave when they tutored high school students via telecommunications.

Hillocks, G., Jr. (1986). *Research on written composition: New directions for teaching*. Urbana, IL: ERIC Clearinghouse on Reading and Communication Skills. A comprehensive and well-respected review of research.

Landrum, J. (1996). *The teaching of writing in Minnesota high schools. Suburban, private, and urban*. Unpublished doctoral dissertation, University of Minnesota, Minneapolis. Study of the writing instruction provided by nine high school English teachers.

National Center for Educational Statistics. (1996). Can students benefit from process writing? *NAEP Facts, 13* (3), 1–6. One in a series of short, interpretative reports about NAEP results put out by the U.S. Department of Education.

Nystrand, M. (1986). *The structure of written communication: Studies in reciprocity between writers and readers*. Orlando, FL: Academic Press. Discusses the interactivity of language and the reciprocity principle as they relate to writing.

Olson, C. B. (1996). Strategies for interacting with text. In *Practical ideas for teaching writing as a process at the elementary and middle school levels* (rev. ed., pp. 231–235). Sacramento: California Department of Education. Describes a variety of ways of responding to text, many of which involve writing.

Pearson, P. D., & Gallagher, M. (1983). The instruction of reading comprehension. *Contemporary Educational Psychology, 8*, 317–344. Reviews research on reading comprehension and presents the gradual release of responsibility model.

Pressley, M., Johnson, C. J., Symons, S., McGoldrick, J. A., & Kurita, J. (1989). Strategies that improve children's memory and comprehension of text. *Elementary School Journal, 90*, 3–32. Excellent description and discussion of key comprehension strategies.

Resnick, L. (1987). *Education and learning to think*. Washington, DC: National Academy Press. A short, very readable, and influential book examining how schools can more effectively teach higher-order skills.

Robin, E. (1984). *Matters of life and death: Risks and benefits of medical care*. Stanford, CA: Stanford University Press. A cost-benefit analysis of medical care. The book is discussed here simply as a prompt for student writing.

Ryder, R. J. (1991, June). *Application of analytical writing strategies to computer-based tutorial writing instruction*. Paper presented at the meeting of the National Educational Computing Conference, Phoenix, AZ. Report of research on a computer-based writing project.

Tchudi, S. N., & Huerta, M. C. (1983). *Teaching writing in content areas: Middle school/junior high*. Washington, DC: National Education

Association. One source for our guidelines for teaching writing.

Tierney, R. J., & Pearson, P. D. (1983). Toward a composing model of reading. *Language Arts, 60,* 568–580. One of the earliest discussions of the idea that reading is much like composing.

Vacca, R. T., & Linek, W. M. (1992). Writing to learn. In J. W. Irwin & M. A. Doyle (Eds.), *Reading/writing connections: Learning from research* (pp. 145–159). Newark, DE: International Reading Association. A selective review of the research on writing to learn along with the authors' views on educational implications of the research.

Zinsser, W. (1988). *Writing to learn.* New York: Harper and Row. An excellent book on the topic by an author who is both an excellent writer himself and one of the most articulate writers on writing.

C H A P T E R

7

Cooperative Learning

CHAPTER OVERVIEW

In this chapter we examine cooperative learning and ways in which cooperative learning can be incorporated in subject area reading activities. We begin with a brief definition of cooperative learning, contrasting it to competitive learning and independent learning. Next, we define cooperative learning in more detail, highlighting five necessary components of effective cooperative learning situations. Following this, we build a case for using cooperative learning, a case based on both theoretical considerations and research findings. Next, we describe five different types of cooperative learning, different ways of putting students together and arranging activities to promote successful learning. We then present principles for teaching procedural skills, a list of cooperative skills that students need to learn, guidelines for establishing cooperative groups, and specific methods of teaching cooperative skills. Next, we give specific examples of cooperative tasks that are appropriate in subject matter classes. Finally, we describe procedures for assessing cooperative learning.

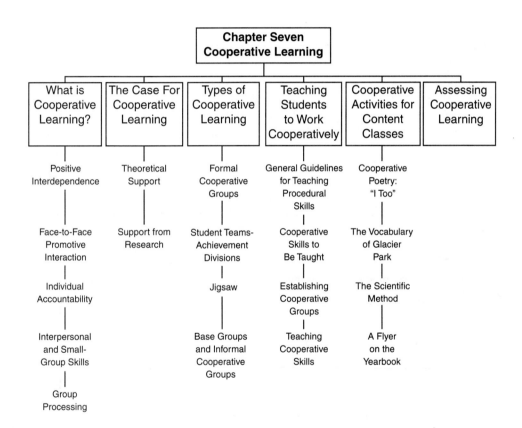

In describing cooperative learning, Johnson, Johnson, and Holubec (1994, p. 1) compare it to two other sorts of learning that are often used in classrooms—competitive learning and independent learning. In competitive lessons, students "engage in a win-lose struggle to see who is best." In independent lessons, students "work independently at their own goals at their own pace and in their own space to achieve a present criterion of excellence." In contrast, in cooperative lessons, students "work collaboratively in small groups, ensuring that all members master the assigned material."

Many classrooms employ all three approaches. Including a combination of these and other approaches in providing subject matter instruction is definitely appropriate. However, cooperative learning merits special attention because it is a very powerful approach. As Radencich, McKay, and Paratore (1995, p. 33) point out, "of all grouping options, cooperative grouping may represent the best opportunity for every student to contribute to the group." In this chapter we describe cooperative learning in detail and explain how to include cooperative learning activities as one important part of subject matter instruction.

WHAT IS COOPERATIVE LEARNING?

Cooperative learning is easy to define. Johnson et al. (1994, p. 3) define it as "the instructional use of small groups that allow students to work together to maximize their own and each other's learning." Slavin (1987, p. 8) notes that the term refers to "instructional methods in which students of all performance levels work together toward a group goal."

However, although these definitions are clear and concise, they by no means fully explain cooperative learning. Not every small group is a cooperative group. Even more to the point, not every small group is an *effective* cooperative group. Johnson et al. (1994) have identified five necessary components of effective cooperative learning situations.

Five Necessary Components of Effective Cooperative Learning

- Positive interdependence

- Face-to-face promotive interaction

- Individual accountability

- Interpersonal and small-group skills

- Group processing

Positive Interdependence

Positive interdependence refers to a situation in which each member of a group is dependent on each other member for his or her success. As one example of positive interdependence in the world of sports, Johnson et al. (1994) give the example of a quarterback and a receiver: It takes the best efforts of both the quarterback and the receiver to get a completed pass; neither a quarterback nor a receiver can complete a pass alone. In positively interdependent groups, each student has two responsibilities. Each student must learn the assigned material or procedure himself or herself, and each student must ensure that every other student in the group also learns the assigned material or procedure. Moreover, students must be aware of this positive interdependence and consciously coordinate their efforts with those of others in the group.

Face-to-Face Promotive Interaction

Face-to-face promotive interaction consists of direct interchanges in which students promote each other's successful completion of cooperative tasks. For example, in a group cooperatively writing an essay on wetlands preservation, one student might say to another, "That's a great introduction that will really wake up people to our cause. Now we need some sort of transition to our first example of what we can do to preserve our wetlands." It is vital to have such direct interactions because the interpersonal and verbal interchange that occurs in them is the driving force that prompts students to assist, support, encourage, praise, and challenge each other on their way to achieving the assigned goals of the group.

Individual Accountability

Those unfamiliar with cooperative learning may believe that it is based on a naiveté that assumes that all students in a group will naturally contribute their parts and work toward common goals. This is not at all the case. In effective cooperative learning groups, each individual is evaluated, and the results of his or her evaluation are given back to the individual and to the other members of the group. This is done for two reasons. First, if group members are to help each other, they must know who needs help and what they need help on. Second, each individual needs to understand that cooperative learning groups are not a place in which everybody gets a "free lunch"; that is, students need to know that each student is held responsible for his or her learning and for his or her contribution to others' learning. Students who do not contribute are not given credit for contributing.

Interpersonal and Small-Group Skills

Having or gaining appropriate interpersonal and small-group skills is a prerequisite for effective participation in cooperative learning groups. Simply putting students together and telling them to cooperate is not likely to accomplish much; in fact, simply putting students together and telling them to cooperate is likely to have a negative outcome and thus spell the death of efforts at cooperative learning. The skills students need in order to work successfully in small groups include getting to know and trust each other, communicating accurately, accepting and supporting each other, and resolving conflicts constructively.

Group Processing

As used here, group processing refers to the members of cooperative groups discussing how they functioned as a group—how effective they were in achieving their goals and how effective they were in working together to do so. In group processing, students reflect back on their working session and consider things they did that worked, things they did that did not work or may not have worked, and things they can do to improve their group's work together in the future. This sort of group processing should be a frequent part of every cooperative group's work because it is only by consciously striving to improve their functioning that groups will improve.

The following table, which Johnson et al. (1994) use to clarify the differences between cooperative learning groups and traditional learning groups, summarizes this section of the chapter and highlights some additional characteristics of cooperative learning.

Differences Between Cooperative Groups and Traditional Learning Groups

Cooperative Groups	Traditional Groups
Positive interdependence	No interdependence
Individual accountability	No individual accountability
Heterogeneous membership	Homogeneous membership
Shared leadership	One appointed leader
Responsible for each other	Responsible only for self
Task and maintenance emphasized	Only task emphasized
Social skills directly taught	Social skills assumed and ignored
Teacher observes and intervenes	Teacher ignores group
Group processing occurs	No group processing

▼ PRACTICE ACTIVITY 7.1

1. **Positive interdependence.** Try to fix the concept of positive interdependence in your mind by coming up with an example of your own. An example we developed is included at the end of the chapter. As emphasized in Chapter 6, whenever possible write down your responses in order to better remember the material.

2. **Interpersonal skills.** One of many arguments supporting cooperative learning is that people need to use the same sort of interpersonal and small-group skills practiced in cooperative learning in the world outside of school. Do you find this to be true? Name half a dozen jobs in which interpersonal skills are crucial to success. Our response is at the end of the book.

3. Group processing. Discuss with your classmates how often groups in which you have participated have processed their group work. Our response and some brief thoughts on the matter are included at the end of the book.

▼▼

THE CASE FOR COOPERATIVE LEARNING

A very strong case for using cooperative learning can be made by considering several theoretical notions and the results of a huge body of research on cooperative learning.

Theoretical Support

Theoretical support for cooperative learning can be found in a number of constructs, including Vygotsky's notion of the zone of proximal development and the concept of metacognition, as well as by considering some ways in which cooperative group work affects cognition. According to Vegotsky (1978, p. 86), a major part of children's learning occurs within what he calls the "zone of proximal development," which he defines as "the distance between the actual developmental level as determined by independent problem solving and the level of potential development as determined through problem solving under adult guidance or in collaboration with more capable peers." Students who are more capable in a particular area can improve the learning of those less capable in that area. One assumption motivating cooperative learning is that the members of a group differ in their skills and knowledge, with some members having advanced skills and knowledge in one area and others in another. In a group, a student's zone of proximal development is extended by the others in the group, and he or she is led to accomplish tasks he or she could not accomplish without the aid of others in the group.

Further theoretical support for cooperative learning comes from the construct of metacognition. As defined by Flavel (1976, p. 232), "metacognition refers to one's knowledge concerning one's own cognitive processes and products or anything related to them." Accomplished learners have metacognitive knowledge about themselves, the learning tasks they face, and the strategies they can employ in completing these tasks. The discussion, questioning, summarizing, and puzzling over problems that are parts of cooperative learning put students in the position of repeatedly having to be metacognitive. And being metacognitive—being actively aware of what one does and does not understand about a learning task and being able to use some sort of fix-up strategies when learning breaks down—are absolutely crucial to students becoming effective learners.

Additional theoretical support for cooperative learning can be found by considering how cooperative work affects cognition. Listed below are three of the cognitive effects Johnson and Johnson (1991) discuss. First, students in cooperative groups recognize that they will have to summarize what they have learned, explain it to others in their group, and teach others in their group. Second, being in a cooperative group means that students will frequently need to ask questions of others, rephrase the responses others give, and elaborate on what they know. Third, the fact that there are several students in a group and that groups are generally heterogeneous means that students who do not know something can turn to others for assistance. Moreover, students can assist each other in a number of ways. Different students know different facts; different students offer different perspectives on the same facts; and different students have different strategies that they can use and can assist each other in using. Thus, as suggested in the scenario below, cooperative groups offer students a myriad of opportunities to engage in the sorts of problem solving they will need to use in the world outside of school.

> **Coquita:** There's just no way around it. If Ted's not here to champion his position that citizens have the right not to vote, we just need to find someone else to take that position.
>
> **Jayme:** Well, I suppose I could fake it and take his place.
>
> **Manda:** No Jayme, you really can't. Remember most kids in the class know just where you stand, and if you fake a different position they'll see through you.
>
> **Coquita:** Manda's right, Jayme. We need someone else to do it, someone who can honestly take the position and be convincing with it.

Support from Research

Over the past several decades, the value of various sorts of learning by teaching—participating in cooperative learning and in various other sorts of tutoring—has become increasingly clear (Bargh & Schul, 1980). Not surprisingly, studies of tutoring demonstrate that both the students tutored and those who serve as tutors gain a better understanding of the subject matter covered and more positive attitudes toward the subject matter (Cohen, Kulik, & Kulik, 1982; Rekrut, 1994). As one group of educators (McKeachie et al., 1986) put it, "students teaching other students" is one of the most powerful methods of instruction available. "There is," McKeachie and his colleagues continue, "a wealth of evidence that students teaching other students is extremely effective over a wide range of content, goals, students, and personalities."

Much of that evidence comes from research on cooperative learning. In fact, according to Johnson and Johnson (1989) cooperative learning is one of the most thoroughly researched areas of instruction, with over 600 studies having been conducted in the past 90 years. Slavin (1987, p. 18) echoes these sentiments, noting that cooperative learning approaches are "among the most extensively evaluated alternatives to traditional instruction in use in schools today."

In the majority of these studies, cooperative methods are compared to more traditional methods, the majority of which would be classified as competitive and a lesser number of which would be classified as individualized. The evidence from these studies is extremely compelling. In one comparison, Slavin (1987) found that 57% of the studies favored cooperative learning, 41% of the studies found no differences, and a single study favored the group that did not engage in cooperative learning. In another comparison, this one including only studies in which the cooperative learning groups were working to achieve some goal and the success of the group depended on the individual learning of each group member, Slavin found that 83% of the studies favored cooperative learning.

Importantly, the advantages of cooperative learning occurred in a variety of domains. Students in cooperative groups showed superior performance in academic achievement, displayed more self-esteem, accommodated better to mainstreamed students, showed more positive attitudes toward school, and generally displayed better overall psychological health. In addition, students in cooperative groups displayed better interpersonal relationships, and these improved interpersonal relationships held regardless of differences in ability, sex, ethnicity, or social class (Johnson & Johnson, 1989).

Moreover, certain sorts of cooperative learning offer some particular advantages for teaching critical thinking. As tasks become more conceptual in nature, as increasing amounts of problem solving are required, as more creative answers are needed, as long-term retention is required, and as higher-level thinking and critical reasoning are increasingly demanded, the superiority of cooperative learning over competitive and individualized learning becomes even greater (Johnson & Johnson, 1991).

Given the theory and research supporting cooperative learning, it is important to include at least some cooperative learning experiences in subject matter classrooms.

PRACTICE ACTIVITY 7.2

List three theoretical arguments supporting cooperative learning; then list several domains in which students in cooperative groups have outperformed those not in cooperative groups. Our responses are at the end of the book.

▼ ▼

TYPES OF COOPERATIVE LEARNING

With the large number of investigations that have been done on cooperative learning and the many teachers interested in the approach, it should come as no surprise that there are many types of cooperative learning groups. Here we describe five types of groups. While you may not want to use all of these types of groups in your classroom, you will probably find uses for several of them.

Five Types of Cooperative Groups

- Formal Cooperative Groups
- Student Teams-Achievement Divisions
- Jigsaw
- Base Groups
- Informal Cooperative Groups

Formal Cooperative Groups

Formal cooperative learning groups are the basic group used in Johnson and Johnson's approach. Formal cooperative groups are heterogeneous groups of three or four students. Students in these groups typically differ in ability, ethnicity, social class, and gender. Such groups incorporate the five defining characteristics of cooperative learning—positive interdependence, face-to-face promotive interaction, individual accountability, the use of interpersonal and small-group skills, and processing of the group's work. These groups generally last for several class sessions. Tasks for such groups include problem solving and decision making, reviewing homework, solving specifically assigned problems, performing and writing up lab experiments, studying for exams, writing and editing assignments, and making class presentations. Importantly, this type of cooperative learning group is particularly effective in promoting problem solving, creativity, and critical thinking.

Student Teams-Achievement Divisions

Student teams-achievement divisions (abbreviated STAD) is the most frequently used of Slavin's approaches. STAD is a stylized approach in which groups of four students differing in ability, ethnicity, social class, and gender work together. STAD groups work as follows:

Framework for STAD Groups

1. The teacher initially presents the lesson.

2. Students in the group work together to ensure that each student in the group masters the material. For example, group members encourage each other, compare answers, work out discrepancies, suggest approaches to solving problems encountered, and quiz each other.

3. After preparing as a group, students are quizzed individually and receive points based on the extent to which each exceeds his or her previous performance.

4. Individual points are then totaled to form a team score, and students are rewarded for both their individual score and their team score.

The whole process generally takes three to five class periods. STAD has been used in a variety of subject matters including English, social studies, and mathematics. According to Slavin (1987), the approach is best suited to learning well-defined objectives with single right answers. Thus, it is particularly well suited for mathematical computations, first-language mechanics and vocabulary, second-language vocabulary, geography and map skills, science concepts, and facts out of various subject areas. It is particularly important to recognize that formal cooperative groups and STAD serve two different functions; the former is most appropriate for higher-level tasks, while the latter is more appropriate for more basic tasks.

Jigsaw

Jigsaw is an approach developed by Aronson (Aronson & Patnoe, 1997). Jigsaw, like STAD, is a stylized approach, but it is quite different from STAD. In the Jigsaw approach, a class of 30 or so students work in five heterogeneous groups of six or so students each on material that the teacher has broken into subsections for each student to work on. The major steps of the approach are listed below.

Steps in Using Jigsaw

1. Each student in a group learns one part of the material being studied. For example, in studying a particular state, one student in each group might investigate cities in the state, another in each group the state's agriculture, another its industries, and so on.

2. After studying his or her section individually, the member of each group who has studied a particular subpart of the topic gets together with the members from the other teams who have studied the same subpart.

3. The students in each of these "expert" groups discuss their subtopic, refining their knowledge about it.

4. The experts return to their own groups and teach their classmates about their sections. Because classmates afford the only opportunity for students to learn about sections other than their own, students are necessarily interested and motivated to attend to each other's presentations.

5. Students take individual exams on all of the material, both the material they taught to others and that they learned from others.

Jigsaw must be used in a situation where a subject can be broken into subparts for students to teach. With that single exception, the procedure is widely applicable.

Base Groups and Informal Cooperative Groups

Base groups and informal cooperative groups are special function groups recommended by Johnson and Johnson. Base groups are heterogeneous, long-term groups of four or so students who are likely to remain together for a semester or a year. The primary purposes of base groups are to provide support, encouragement, assistance in completing assignments, and general assistance for members of the group. Base groups typically meet weekly at the beginning of the class session and go through several routines. These are likely to include checking how each group member is keeping up with the demands of the class and their feelings about the course, reviewing the reading assignments for the past week, planning study topics and a study schedule for the upcoming week, reviewing for upcoming quizzes, and bringing any group members absent the previous week up to date on the class. Several of these functions are shown in the following scenario:

Curtis: Doris, you weren't here when Ms. Alveriz talked about it, but it turns out that Friday's quiz is going to be extra important. Ms. Alveriz says she isn't sure just what we have and haven't really understood about the suffrage movement, and she's going to use the quiz to find that out and decide whether or not we need to spend some more time on it. So we're going to meet both Wednesday night and Thursday afternoon over at Carmen's. Can you be there?

Doris: Well, I was supposed to work, but if it's that important I'll just have to ask for some time off.

In summing up the value of base groups, Holubec, Johnson, and Johnson (1995, p. 239) say this: "Base groups are a school family. Such groups help students learn how to be part of caring friendships built around important work. Students learn how to be helpful to others on a long-term basis and how to accept help from others."

Informal cooperative groups (Johnson, Johnson, & Smith, 1990) are pairs of students who work together for a single class session to better learn from a lecture, which for example might be given as an introduction to an upcoming reading selection. The general plan is for the teacher to build a lecture around a set of focusing questions and several brief lecture segments. The approach gives students an opportunity to prepare for the lecture, actively consider the content of the lecture as it is progressing, and formulate some sort of closure to the lecture. Here are the steps for using informal cooperative groups:

Steps for Using Informal Cooperative Groups

1. Prepare half a dozen or so guiding questions. Give these questions to the pairs before the lecture and give students about five minutes to discuss what they know about the topic, thereby creating a sort of advance organizer for the lecture.

2. Deliver the first segment of the lecture, taking no more than ten to fifteen minutes for the segment. Have the pairs conduct two to three minute "turn-to-your-partner" discussions on the lecture segment, perhaps answering the guiding questions the segment answered.

3. Deliver the other part or parts of the lecture, again limiting each segment to ten to fifteen minutes and again having the student pairs conduct brief discussions on each segment.

4. Give the pairs a concluding discussion task of perhaps five to six minutes that allows them to summarize the lecture and identify the essential learnings it conveyed.

While using informal cooperative groups will shorten the lecture time available, this loss of time will be more than offset by the students' increased involvement and interest in the lecture. Indeed, using such groups forces students to prepare for the lecture, to attend to it because they will need to discuss it, to review it several times as they discuss it with their partner, and to review and synthesize it a final time immediately after its completion. Moreover, the procedure is extremely easy to implement, fosters active learning, and is widely applicable.

▼ PRACTICE ACTIVITY 7.3

This section of the chapter described five types of cooperative groups. Name and very briefly describe each of these. Also, if you are presently teaching, take one of your class lists and divide the class into groups for any of the cooperative methods except informal cooperative groups. Then, jot down the general guidelines you followed in choosing students for the groups.

▼▼

TEACHING STUDENTS TO WORK COOPERATIVELY

Regardless of which particular types of cooperative learning you plan to use in your classroom, one thing remains constant: Students need to be taught how to effectively engage in cooperative learning. Here we present guidelines for teaching procedural skills, list the cooperative skills to be taught, provide guidelines for establishing cooperative groups, and make specific recommendations for teaching cooperative learning skills. Following these guidelines will enable you to introduce and use cooperative learning while maintaining a smoothly running classroom. The section draws heavily on the work of Johnson et al. (1994).

General Guidelines for Teaching Procedural Skills

To begin, recognize that the task of learning cooperative skills is a procedural one rather than a declarative one; that is, students need to learn how to actually do something, not merely learn about something. Procedural tasks are typically more difficult to learn and more time consuming than declarative learning tasks, and learning to engage in cooperative learning is no exception. This means, first of all, that both you and the students need to spend time and energy preparing for cooperative learning. It also means that your time and energy will be best spent if you follow some well-established techniques for teaching procedural skills. The following four steps have proven useful.

Teaching Procedural Skills

1. Teach students exactly what the skill is. If, for example, the skill is expressing support and acceptance for others' ideas, students need to know just how to do this. One way of expressing support is to do it verbally, saying something such as "Nice idea. I really think that will work." Another is to do it nonverbally, perhaps with eye contact, a pleasant look, or a nod.

Continued

---

2. Have students actually engage in the skill; have them get in a group that has a task to accomplish and overtly try to show support for each others' ideas.

3. Give students feedback on their successes and their failures at showing support so that they know when they are and are not engaging in supportive behavior. Initially you as the teacher are the one who will need to give this feedback; later students will become increasingly able to give feedback to each other.

4. Have students practice the correct procedures a lot so that they become nearly automatic in using them. Students need to be able to use the procedures without conscious attention. Getting to this automatic stage takes a good deal of practice; in addition, since you want to be sure students are practicing correct behaviors, you need to continue to give feedback during these periods of practice and consolidation.

Cooperative Skills To Be Taught

Johnson et al.'s (1994) list of cooperative skills to be taught includes three sorts of skills: forming skills, functioning skills, and formulating skills.

Forming Skills

Forming skills are beginning skills, competencies which are prerequisite to effective group functioning. They include (1) moving into cooperative groups without bothering others in the room, (2) staying with the group, (3) talking in quiet voices, and (4) encouraging everyone to participate in the group's activities.

Functioning Skills

Functioning skills are skills that students use as they participate in group work. They include (1) giving directions, (2) expressing support and acceptance of others' ideas, (3) asking for help or clarification when needed, (4) offering to explain or clarify a matter when another student needs assistance, (5) paraphrasing others' responses, (6) energizing the group if it begins to bog down, and (7) describing one's feelings, particularly when there is a problem that needs to be solved.

Formulating Skills

Formulating skills are the skills needed to perform the various roles of group members. These roles include those of (1) the summarizer, who summarizes the groups' learning—typically from memory, (2) the corrector, who checks the correctness and completeness of the summary, (3) the elaboration seeker, who elicits further information and explanation from group members, (4) the memory helper, who prompts group members to use memory aids to remember the material they are learning, and (5) the checker, who demands that group members make explicit the implicit reasoning behind their thinking.

PRACTICE ACTIVITY 7.4

Form a group that includes a summarizer, a checker, and an elaboration seeker; then define forming skills, functioning skills, and formulating skills, giving a specific example of each of these. After each member of the group has performed his or her role, compare your answers to those we give at the end of the book.

▼ ▼

Establishing Cooperative Groups

As you prepare to actually use cooperative groups in your classroom, several very practical questions undoubtedly come to mind. Among them might be how large groups ought to be, which students ought to be grouped together, and what characterizes good learning objectives. Each of these topics is considered here.

Deciding on Group Size

One of the first questions that comes to mind in setting up groups is how large to make them. There is no single answer to this question, for two reasons. First, as indicated earlier, there are several different types of cooperative groups and not all of these require the same number of students. Informal cooperative groups, for example, consist of pairs of students that prepare for and then actively process lectures. On the other hand, base groups—groups of students who meet over time to provide mutual support and encouragement to each other—are likely to be composed of five or six students. The other reason there is no single answer to the question of group size is that the optimal size of groups varies with the specific task to be completed, your experience and expertise with group work, and your students' experience and expertise with group work.

Although there are no absolute guidelines regarding group size, there are several general guidelines.

Guidelines on Group Size

- With the exception of a few special-purpose groups such as informal cooperative groups, groups seldom contain fewer than three students.

- Six students is often considered about the largest group one would typically work with. Having more than six students in a group often gets unwieldy.

- Start out using small groups and then gradually move to larger groups as you and your students gain experience with groups. This probably means starting with groups of three. Moreover, there is no hurry in moving to larger groups.

- Give careful consideration to the task the groups are going to complete. How many subtasks are there? Is there enough work for four or five students? Is there too much work for three or four students? Do students need to meet outside of class time? Will having larger groups make it difficult for students to find meeting times?

Recognizing that most groups contain between three and six students, that smaller groups are easier to handle when you are just beginning cooperative work, and that the specific task of the groups needs to be considered will usually provide you with the information you need to make effective decisions on group size.

Assigning Students to Groups

Other questions to consider when establishing cooperative groups include which students should comprise groups and who should decide which students to include in particular groups. There are several factors that should be considered in answering these.

The first thing to recognize is that one major purpose of using cooperative groups is to assist students in meeting, understanding, working with, and having empathy for the diverse people and cultures that make up our society. In any society, it is crucial that people learn to work with each other. However, in our multicultural society, just learning to work with others is not enough. Students need to learn to work with, understand, appreciate, and respect others who may be quite different from them in a variety of ways. Thus, one recommendation for grouping students for cooperative work is to deliberately group together students representing diverse cultures, races, ages, genders, abilities, interests, and levels of motivation.

Are there any limits to the amount of heterogeneity you should seek for groups? Of course there are! The groups have to function, and the individual students in the groups have to feel comfortable and believe that the group can function and that they can contribute to its success. This means giving particular attention to which students will work well together as you first begin group work. As you and your students get more accomplished with group work, you can move toward more heterogeneous groups.

Closely related to the matter of what sorts of students make up groups is that of how groups are assigned. For the most part, since you know what sort of mix you want in groups, you should assign them. Occasionally you might use random assignment, which will generally result in heterogeneous groups. Sometimes you will want to let students choose their own groups, although this will often result in fairly homogeneous groups and in groups that may have a larger social agenda than work agenda.

Also related to the matter of assigning groups is that of how long to keep groups together. Both common sense and compromise are required in making decisions here. On the one hand, groups should stay together and work together long enough that they learn to function well together. On the other hand, ideally, over the course of a semester or year, each student should have the opportunity to work with and get to know every other student in the class. Obviously, achieving both goals will require compromises.

To summarize, groups should generally be heterogeneous (but not so heterogeneous that they do not function well), you should generally be the one to assign students to groups, and groups should stay together long enough that they become effective but not so long that students get to work with only a few of their classmates.

Specifying Learning Objectives

Specifying learning objectives is always important, but with cooperative group work, specifying objectives becomes doubly important. Since students are working in various groups and you are not directly supervising them as you might be with whole-class instruction, students need to have a very clear idea of what they are trying to accomplish. Moreover, since mutual interdependence and individual accountability are central to cooperative learning, every student needs to understand clearly both what he or she is expected to accomplish and what his or her group is expected to accomplish.

Good objectives for cooperative learning groups generally have several definable characteristics. Learning objectives should be precise, concise, and limited in number. In addition, most assignments ought to allow students to set and pursue some objectives of their own. Also, keep in mind that cooperative learning groups have two sorts of objectives—academic objectives and group-processing objectives. Most considerations here are relevant to both sorts of objectives, but at the end of the section are a few comments specifically dealing with group-processing objectives.

Precise objectives are ones that students can clearly understand and recognize as being met or not met. For example, in teaching vocabulary, simply telling students to learn five words is not very precise. To more fully communicate what it is that you want students to do, you could tell them to learn the two most common meanings of each of the five words and be able to produce a sentence employing each meaning. Concise objectives are objectives that are deliberately stated in relatively few words. This does not mean that they should be too brief, but it does mean that most of the time it is a good idea to check your initial phrasing of objectives and see if there is a briefer and perhaps clearer way to state them. First attempts to phrase objectives are often rather wordy and sometimes fail to fully capture the intended meaning.

The advice to limit the number of objectives means just that. A long list of objectives is often inappropriate. How many is enough? That varies with the situation, particularly with the length of the assignment: a two-week assignment would usually have more objectives than a two-day assignment. However, having two to four objectives is often appropriate.

Multidimensional objectives are objectives that tap various levels on a continuum leading from immediate and specific objectives to more distant and general ones. For example, you would certainly have some specific objectives when dealing with a history chapter on the Great Depression. You would want students to know who Franklin Delano Roosevelt was, and you would want them to know some of the major features of the New Deal. Moving toward somewhat broader objectives, you might want students to be able to draw some comparisons between conditions in the United States at the beginning of the Depression and conditions just before the 1990 recession. Another objective for your study of the Depression—one much further toward the distant and general end of the continuum—would be for students to appreciate the hardships that their grandparents and others who lived through the Depression experienced and perhaps speculate about how today's Americans would react to such hardships. Finally, you might suggest some optional objectives. Students interested in art might choose to investigate what sorts of paintings were produced during the Depression; students interested in sports might try to find out what sort of attention sports received during this difficult time; and students interested in movies might research the contents and themes of movies of the period.

With respect to group-processing objectives, special note should be given to choosing those that will best contribute to students' success in their group work.

Johnson et al. (1994, p. 42) give the following set of seven group-processing objectives. These should be introduced to students one at a time. Explain and model each strategy, then give students ample opportunity to practice it and receive some feedback before moving on to another one.

Group Processing Objectives

1. Having each member explain how to get the answer

2. Asking each member to relate what is being learned to previous learnings

3. Checking to make sure everyone in the group understands the material and agrees with the answers

4. Encouraging everyone to participate

5. Listening accurately to what other group members are saying

6. Not changing your mind unless you are logically persuaded

7. Criticizing ideas, not people

Teaching Cooperative Skills

As noted earlier, teaching cooperative skills is a procedural teaching task rather than a declarative one, and consequently it is demanding and will definitely take time. Including cooperative learning in your repertoire of instructional approaches may be particularly challenging because doing so means handing over some of the responsibility for learning and for classroom control to students. The challenge, however, is well worth the effort because engaging in cooperative learning can result in students learning more, in their developing better attitudes toward learning, and in their becoming better prepared to deal with today's increasingly interdependent world. Moreover, although teaching cooperative skills takes considerable resources in terms of time and energy, it is a task that every teacher can complete successfully. It is simply something that needs to be done carefully and thoroughly. Johnson et al. (1994) provide the following step-by-step guidelines for successfully teaching students to work cooperatively.

   1. Show students the need for cooperative learning. Create a bulletin board—an ad—for cooperative learning. Tell students that cooperation is an important skill to learn and that cooperative learning is a very effective approach to learning. Cite the fact that much of their adult life will be spent working with others. Cite research showing the effectiveness of cooperative learning. Tell students that no one of them is as smart as all of them, then validate what you say. Show that you think cooperative learning skills are important by giving credit for students working cooperatively as well as for the learning that the cooperative groups produce.

2. Make certain that students really know what each skill you are teaching is. If you are teaching students to encourage each other in their groups, give them some specific examples of encouraging language—"That's right." "I think you really have something there." "Exactly!" "All right!" Model the behavior for them. Get in a group that is working on a task and demonstrate encouragement—verbally, through eye contact, nodding assent, or even rapping on the desk to show approval. Let students model the behavior, possibly initially through role playing—"Assume that Jake here has just come up with a solution to a problem your group has been working on for 20 minutes without success. What do you say to him, Tim? How can you show your appreciation?"

3. Have students repeatedly practice the skill. Remember, the goal here is automatic performance of the skill, doing it without having to think about doing it. The literature on fostering automatic behavior is clear and straight forward (LaBerge & Samuels, 1974). Behavior becomes automatic when it is repeatedly practiced in nontaxing situations. Having thoroughly explained a skill, modeled it, and had students role play its use, tell them you are going to be looking for the skill as they work in their groups. Or tell them that you want each member of the group to practice that particular skill during the day's group work—"Today, in your groups, I want each of you to give verbal encouragement to other members of your group at least twice, and I'm going to assign a recorder to each group to record each instance of verbal encouragement and then report back to you on what he or she found when you process your group work at the end of the hour."

4. Ensure that students process their group work and attend to their use of the various skills as part of this processing. In the above example, the teacher ensured group processing of the skill being stressed by specifically telling students to use a certain skill and then assigning a student to record the use of the skill and report to the group on it. This sort of teacher-directed processing of skills should be a frequent feature of group work when you are initially teaching students to work cooperatively. Moreover, even after students have become very adept at cooperative skills, you will still need to highlight certain skills from time to time and tell them to focus on using these skills as they process their work as a group. Ultimately, however, the goal is for the group to routinely process their work and give attention to their group skills without your having to remind them. Tell them this; then check from time to time to be sure they are continuing to check their skills.

5. Make certain that students continue to practice their skills over the long run. Group work can be demanding and it will not immediately or always pay dividends. Students need to be told that group work can be demanding. They need to be told that group work, like anything else, does not always work. And they need to be given the time, practice, and encouragement to repeatedly practice their cooperative skills and to learn that cooperative learning very frequently does produce large learning dividends.

Once students are actively and successfully working in groups, there is still important work to be done. Groups need to be monitored and when something goes awry or groups simply get stalled, you need to step in to get things back on track.

Eventually students need to monitor their own groups, but when you begin group work, you will probably need to take the bulk of the responsibility for monitoring them. Regardless of whether it is you doing the monitoring or your students, there are certain things to look for and certain questions to ask. Here is a beginning set of questions.

Questions to Ask When Monitoring Groups

- Are students physically in their groups?

- Are students courteously attending to each other?

- Are they talking quietly and otherwise behaving so that they are not bothering other groups?

- Do any students seem to be left out and ignored by their groupmates?

- Do students appear to understand the task?

- Are they making progress? Are parts of the assigned work completed or at least visibly in progress?

If students are just learning to work cooperatively and your answer to any of these questions is "no," then your assistance is definitely called for. Here, for example, Mr. Mallard realizes that Becky's group is pursuing a dead end and briefly interrupts to get the discussion back on track.

> **Mr. Mallard:** Becky, excuse me for interrupting, but I just happened to hear what you said to Deandre about the role of hydrogen in the reaction and I want to warn you that pursuing that isn't going to get you anyplace. Look at the list of elements that you began with again, and I think you can get started on a more productive line of thought.

Later as students become more experienced with group work, you may want to let groups struggle a bit so that they learn to solve their own problems. Later still when students are doing the monitoring, they should be the ones to intervene to get groups on track.

When you do intervene to facilitate students' success, two strategies are particularly useful. First, explain what you perceive is going wrong and how the problem can be corrected, being as direct and explicit as possible. Second, whenever the behaviors you are attempting to elicit are likely to be difficult, model them. Thus, for example, if you notice that in debating an issue students are tending to criticize each other, sit in on the group for a time and make it a point to respond to issues rather than people. After you have modeled several instances of responding to issues and after some students in the group have given responses that are directed to issues rather than people, stop and discuss what you have been attempting to do and why it is important to criticize issues rather than individuals.

▼ PRACTICE ACTIVITY 7.5

As a way of reviewing this section of the chapter, list the five steps for teaching cooperative skills. We have listed them at the end of the book. Once you have the five steps clearly in mind, discuss the answer to the following question with your classmates: To what extent are these same guidelines applicable in areas other than cooperative learning? As you will see if you check our response at the end of the book, we have some definite thoughts on the matter.

▼▼

COOPERATIVE ACTIVITIES FOR CONTENT CLASSES

In this section we present specific examples of cooperative learning activities for content classes. The activities were selected to represent a range of cooperative learning opportunities and therefore vary in a number of ways. They exemplify four sorts of cooperative learning: formal cooperative learning groups, student teams-achievement divisions, informal cooperative learning groups, and jigsaw. They are targeted toward middle school students, junior high students, and senior high students. They involve four content areas: English, geography, science, and journalism. Finally, three of them were constructed by us specifically for this book, while the other was constructed by Edythe Johnson Holubec as part of her work with the Johnsons' cooperative learning network. For additional information on cooperative learning in specific content areas, three collections edited by Stahl (1994, 1995, 1996) may be useful.

Although each of these activities deals with a specific topic that would be taken up in specific classes, each also serves as an example of an activity that could be modified for your classroom. As you study each activity, think of how it could be modified to be appropriate in your subject area.

Cooperative Poetry: "I Too" (a formal cooperative learning group lesson for a middle school or junior high class)

This activity, a formal cooperative learning group lesson, was created by Edythe Johnson Holubec (1987), an English teacher in Taylor, Texas. Note that suggested teacher dialogue is set in quotation marks.

Cooperative Poetry: "I, Too"

Subject Area: English

Grade Level: Junior and senior high

Lesson Summary: Students read a poem and answer questions about it.

Instructional Objectives: Students gain practice in reading and understanding poetry, in sharing their interpretations of a poem, and in listening to and considering other interpretations and other points of view.

Materials:

Item	Number Needed
Copy of Langston Hughes's "I, Too"	One per student
Discussion questions and agreement form	One per student
Observation sheet	One per group

Time Required: One class period

Group Size: Four (five if an observer is used)

Assignment to Groups: Teacher assigned, with a high-, two medium-, and a low-achieving student in each group. Also, each group should contain males and females and a mix of racial and cultural backgrounds.

Roles: **Encourager:** Watches to make certain all group members are contributing and invites silent members in by asking them for their opinions or help.

Reader: Reads the poems to the group. Also serves as the *Praiser,* who praises good ideas or helpful suggestions of group members.

Recorder: Records the group's answers and summarizes each until the group is satisfied with it.

Checker: Checks to make certain group members can explain each answer and the group's rationale for it.

Observer: (Optional) Does not take part in the discussion of the poem but observes the group's interactions, records the behaviors on the observations sheet, and reports to the group during the processing time.

From *Structuring Cooperative Learning: The 1987 Lesson-Plan Handbook* by D. W. Johnson, R. T. Johnson, and Edythe Johnson Holubec. Edina, MN: Interaction Book Company, 1987.

Continued

Discussion Questions and Agreement Form

1. What are the emotions expressed by the poem?

2. What do you think/feel about what the poem says?

3. What are the three key words in the poem? (Be able to defend your choice.)

4. What is the poem saying?

To group members: When you sign your name for the answers to these questions, it means that you have participated in the assignment and understand the questions and the answers. You also must agree with the answers and be able to explain them.

_____

Signatures

The Lesson

Instructional Task
"Your task will be to read a poem and answer the questions. I want you to come up with three possible answers for each question, then circle your favorite."

Positive Interdependence
"I want one set of answers from the group that you all agree upon."

Individual Accountability
"I will ask each of you sometime during the class period to give me the rationale for your group's answers."

Criteria for Success
"Your group will start with a grade of 100 on this assignment. I will pick someone at random to explain one of your group's answers to me. If he or she can do that, you will keep your score. If not, you will lose 10 points. I will check at least three of you on at least three of the questions."

Expected Behaviors
"I want to see each of you contributing and helping your group, listening to your group members with care, and pushing the group to look for all the possibilities before deciding on an answer. Also, your group will get a set of role cards. Pass them out randomly, read your role, and make cretain you know how to do it before

Continued

the Reader starts reading the poem. The Observer will report on how well he or she saw you performing your roles during the processing time." (If necessary, go over the roles to make certain the students understand them.)

Monitoring and Processing

Monitoring
Circulate among and listen to the groups. Check to make certain the groups are doing the task right (coming up with at least three possible answers, then agreeing on their favorite) and that group members are performing their roles.

Intervening
Feel free to interrupt while the groups are working. Push groups to explore interesting answers and elaborate on superficial ones. Praise examples of good group skills. If you see an interaction problem, encourage the group to stop and solve it before continuing.

Observation Sheet				
	Group Members			
Contributes ideas				
Encourages others				
Praises good ideas				
Summarizes				
Pushes deeper				
Other helpful behaviors noticed:				

Closing
After the groups have finished answering the questions, have a class discussion about the answers. Pick group members at random to explain answers, keeping track of contributors and groups and grading groups accordingly. List the groups' answers on the board, then see if the class can decide on answers all members agree on.

Processing
After the class discussion, have the groups get back together to process. Have the Observer report on what he or she saw and show each group their marks on the

Continued

observation sheet. Then have the groups write down their answers to the following questions:

1. What behaviors did we do well?
2. What behaviors do we need to improve upon?
3. How well did we perform our roles?
4. What would help us perform our roles better?

If there is time, have the groups share some of their answers with the whole class.

The Vocabulary of Glacier Park (a student teams-achievement division lesson for a middle school or junior high class)

In Chapter 2 we describe a number of approaches to vocabulary instruction. One of those approaches is the concept/relationship procedure. Here the approach is used with the student teams-achievement divisions version of cooperative learning to help students learn vocabulary from the selection they are studying. The class considered is a U.S. geography class, which, although not formally tracked, includes a number of students for whom reading is often a challenge. The text for this unit, *Glacier* (Root, 1988), is a very short book on Glacier National Park, a book specifically designed for middle school and junior high students who experience some difficulties with reading. Although this text is bound as a book, it is a very short book and could be read by most students in less than two hours. A class might spend five class periods working with the text and related activities. Here only the vocabulary aspect of the lesson is considered. We first describe the concept/relationship procedure itself and then we explain how it can be used with STAD.

The concept/relationship procedure is a fairly robust approach for teaching new words that do not present difficult conceptual challenges. It is frequently appropriate for teaching a set of ten or so words from a chapter-length text students are studying, which is what this short book on glaciers is. The heart of the procedure is a brief paragraph that uses the word to be taught three or four times. The paragraph is followed by a multiple-choice item that checks the students' understanding of the word. A sample paragraph and multiple-choice item for *glacier* and the steps for presenting each word are shown below.

Glacier

> A *glacier* is a huge mass of ice and snow that builds up gradually in extremely cold weather. At one time, *glaciers* covered much of what is now the United States. Although they move slowly, *glaciers* actually do move, and when they move they carve up the land that they pass over. The rugged peaks and valleys of Glacier National Park were formed millions of years ago by *glaciers*.

Glaciers are

_____ A. types of rugged mountain peaks.

_____ B. huge masses of ice and snow.

_____ C. violent winds that blow from north to south.

In presenting the concept/relationship procedure, the following steps are used:

1. Explain the purpose of the procedure—to learn words important to understanding the upcoming selection.
2. Pronounce the word to be taught.
3. Read the paragraph in which the word appears.
4. Read the possible definitions, and ask students to choose the best one.
5. Pause to give students time to check a definition, give them the correct answer, and answer any questions students have.
6. Read the word and its definition a final time.

For the sake of this example, assume that the instruction begins on a Monday. Preteach these eight words before students begin reading *Glacier—avalanche, Chinook, continental divide, crevasse, glacier, hibernate, moraine,* and *tundra.* Teaching all eight of them should take about ten minutes.

Following this initial presentation, students should be told that they will be working in STAD groups and the STAD procedures should be explained. The task for each group is to ensure that all members of the group have mastered these words. Students will be quizzed individually at the end of week, and points will be awarded based on the extent to which they meet or exceed their average score on previous vocabulary quizzes. Also, the total points they receive will be based on the points they receive individually *and* the average points received by other students in their group. Thus, to do well, each student must do well individually and he or she must do everything possible to see that other students in the group do well. It is vital that students understand this fully.

After the STAD procedure has been explained, students should be assigned to heterogeneous groups of four. For this first group session, students simply match vocabulary words and their definitions, and the session ends when all members of the group can successfully match all eight words and their definitions.

Later in the week, probably on Thursday, a second group session is held. This time students should first ensure that all in their group can still match words and definitions—something they can probably do with little additional work. Then students should ensure that all students in their groups can write appropriate definitions for the words. This production task is more difficult than the recognition task of matching, but actually producing definitions serves to better fix the definitions in the students' memory.

Finally, on Friday students are given a vocabulary quiz to complete individually. Following the quiz, points are calculated and awarded as soon as possible, probably on Monday of the following week.

The Scientific Method (an informal cooperative group lesson for a high school class)

This activity is intended for a senior high science class and would be used near the beginning of the course in preparation for their reading a selection on the scientific method.

The first step is to plan the lecture, focusing it around half a dozen or so questions students will be asked to deal with. Here are some focusing questions.

1. About when did the scientific method originate? Who is generally credited with originating it?

2. What sort of approaches preceded the use of the scientific method?

3. What is the scientific method? Define theories, hypotheses, data, observations, experiments, and scientific laws, and note how each of these is a part of the scientific method.

4. Who used the scientific method today? How widespread is its use? What are some opposing methods of inquiry?

This lesson can be given in a single period, with a little class time allowed on the following day for students to prepare for and take a short quiz. At the beginning of the lesson, allow students about five minutes for a focused discussion before the lecture, divide the lecture into two segments of about five minutes each, give students two to three minutes for turn-to-your-partner sessions following each of the two lecture segments, and give them about fifteen minutes for a classification task following the lecture. On the following day, give students about five minutes to prepare for the quiz and five minutes to take it individually.

Once the lecture is planned and the questions set, it is time to establish groups. Having each student pair up with a partner in an adjoining desk is fine for this sort of work. After students have partners, tell them that the scientific method and related concepts are central to the course and that they will have a quiz on this material the following day. Note also that each student will take the quiz individually but will receive a grade based on the average score obtained by both students in each group. Give students the focusing questions, probably on an overhead, and tell them that they have five minutes to write out the answers to as many of the questions as they can. Also, tell them that if they have any ideas at all about the answers, they should write them down. (Note that the scientific method is an appropriate topic for this sort of prelecture brainstorming because senior high students will have been exposed to the scientific method in the past and will know something about it. There are a number of other science topics about which students are apt to know very little and which do not lend themselves well to brainstorming.)

Once the five minutes are up, tell students that the first segment of the lecture will provide answers to the first two questions and that they will want to check their answers against those given in the lecture. Then give the first segment of the lecture. At the end of the lecture, tell students that each group will have two to three minutes to write one final answer to each of the first two questions. When this time is up, randomly call on one group to read their answer to one of the questions and another group to read their answer to the other question.

Next, tell students that this second segment of the lecture will provide answers to the third and fourth questions and that they should again check their answers against information given in the lecture. Give the second segment of the lecture and again have each group write out a single answer to each of the two questions. Again, after students have had time to write out their answers, randomly call on one group to read their answer to one of the questions and another group to read their answer to the other question.

As the last prompt for the day, give the groups four situations and ask them to classify each situation as a theory, a law, an experiment, or an observation. Tell students that each group can pick only one classification for each situation and that they should be prepared to give their reasons for each classification as well as the classification itself.

Here are the situations, which are adapted from Wilbraham, Staley, Simpson, and Matta (1987).

1. The ashes of a campfire weigh less than the wood that was burned. Therefore, it appears that mass is destroyed (lost) when wood is burned.

2. A body at rest tends to remain at rest.

3. Using a portable burner, you find that it takes ten minutes for a pint of water to boil in the lab at school, which is located close to sea level. However, when you use the same burner to heat water at your cabin in the mountains, you find that it takes twelve minutes to boil.

4. All matter is composed of atoms. Atoms, in turn, are composed of protons, electrons, and neurons.

Classifying these is not an easy task, and groups will need a good ten minutes to agree on their classifications and jot down their reasoning. Once they have finished this task, randomly call on groups for their answers and their reasoning, and provide enough feedback so that you are convinced that students understand the concepts and are free of misconceptions.

Toward the end of the period, give the reading assignment on the scientific method as homework—Wilbraham et al. (1987, pp. 3–5)—noting that the assignment is brief and essentially reviews the material dealt with during the period. Remind students that there will be a quiz the next day and that they will take the quiz individually but receive a grade based on the average score of their group.

At the beginning of the next class period, give the groups about five minutes to review the material, and then give the quiz.

A Flyer on the Yearbook (a jigsaw lesson for a high school class)

This activity is intended for a high school yearbook or journalism class. Specifically, the activity entails the writing, editing, and production of a two-page flyer or set of flyers advertising the upcoming yearbook. The activity would occupy about a week's class time, although during some of this time only one group member will be actively working on the project. Thus, other activities need to be available for the other group members.

The first step is to select the groups. For this activity, heterogeneous groups of four will work well, and thus there will probably be six or seven groups in all, each of which will construct a flyer. There are two phases to the activity, and each student in a group has a specific but different role during each phase.

In phase one, each student writes the initial draft of one section of the flyer. One student writes the introductory section—a general statement about the year-book and why students should buy it. A second student writes a feature section—a preview of an article that will actually be in the yearbook, perhaps a focus on volley-ball, or the prom, or school dress. The author should decide what to preview, and the criteria he or she uses should be that the topic previewed is representative of the articles in the yearbook and that it is likely to be interesting and exciting to a lot of students. A third student in the group writes a second feature section—another pre-view of an article that will be in the yearbook. This should complement the other fea-ture section, showing another side of the yearbook and perhaps appealing to differ-ent students than did the first feature. The fourth student writes the concluding section of the flyer. This should sum up the information that has been covered so far, plug the yearbook again, and tell students exactly how to place their orders.

During the second phase of the activity, students actually construct the flyer. In this phase, three students in the group each use a different computer software pro-gram to prepare the text for printing; the fourth student in the group monitors and coordinates the work and has the completed flyers printed.

First, one student enters the drafts of the group members on a word processor. This student is also responsible for using the spelling checker that is a part of the program, checking the length of the complete draft to see that it will fit in a two-page flyer, and correcting any obvious errors.

Second, another student takes the word-processed draft and runs it through a grammar and style checker, which checks a myriad of text features and even yields a readability level for the document. Among other things, it checks for double nega-tives, jargon, subject-verb agreement, pronoun errors, punctuation errors, and level of usage (formal, business, or casual).

Third, another student takes the draft that has now been word processed, checked for spelling, checked for length, and checked for various aspects of grammar and style, and uses desktop publishing software to produce the actual layout of the flyer. Here, the student might use *Pagemaker*, a popular desktop publishing program that performs a number of functions. The student can use it, for example, to create a banner headline for the flyer, to employ different type styles and sizes for various parts of the flyer, to set the number of columns to be used, and even to import graph-ics into the flyer and arrange the print so that it wraps around the graphics. Whatever the student chooses, he or she is responsible for the initial layout of the flyer.

Finally, the fourth student is the manager, who is responsible for keeping a record of how well the group worked together and leading the discussion when the group processes their work at the conclusion of the activity. The manager's tasks include setting up a schedule for completing each part of the work, sharing and if necessary negotiating the schedule with you, getting each group member's output to the member who is handling the next part of the production, calling the group together once the initial layout is completed so that each member of the group can check the draft before it is printed, getting the flyer printed or photo-copied, and calling the group together at the conclusion of the activity to process their work.

Once the groups are selected, explain both phases one and two to all students and assign group members to specific roles for each phase. This is a fairly complex set of activities, so written instructions would be useful. At this time, you will also need to give students the evaluation criteria. Give a single grade for each completed flyer, and base that grade on the quality of the writing and mechanical correctness of each of the four sections of the flyer, the audience appeal of each of the four sections of the flyer, and the layout of the flyer as a whole.

You also have a decision to make here—whether to print and distribute the fly-ers of all the groups or to have a contest to see which group's flyer is printed and dis-tributed. In either case, you need only one flyer for each student in school, so the total number of flyers printed would be the same. The question is whether or not you want to introduce some competition into the activity. As Aronson and Patnoe (1997) point out, a little competition can sometimes be useful to build cohesion within groups. However, as Aronson and Patnow also point out, a little competition can go a long way when your ultimate goal is to teach cooperation.

Once you have made a decision on this—you can make this decision on your own or share the decision making with students—the next step is to set a due date for the completed flyers. At this time, you should also schedule a total class meeting to share, discuss, and perhaps vote on the flyers. This meeting will also give you an opportunity to have the class as a whole process the groups' work.

The concluding steps are to hold a final meeting, grade the flyers and return them to students with plenty of feedback (they have spent a whole week on this), and distribute the flyer or flyers to all students in the school.

▼ PRACTICE ACTIVITY 7.6

At the beginning of this section, we asked you to think about how each of the coop-erative lessons described could be modified to make it appropriate for your subject area. At this point, we have a more demanding assignment. Identify one of the four types of cooperative learning described here—formal cooperative groups, student teams-achievement divisions, jigsaw, or informal cooperative groups—and make up a cooperative lesson of your own, one appropriate for a class you have now or the sort of class you are likely to have in the future. You can complete this assignment by (1) writing a one or two paragraph description of the activity or by (2) creating a detailed description of the activity similar to those given here.

▼ ▼

ASSESSING COOPERATIVE LEARNING

In this section we describe two procedures for assessing cooperative learning. Both teachers and students can profit from such assessments. Teachers can use the results to adjust the composition or structure of groups, provide students with additional assistance in specific cooperative procedures, or assist individual students who may have difficulty functioning within a group. Students can use the results to gain a better understanding of cooperative learning, acquire a better understanding of the strengths and weaknesses of their group's performance, and learn how to assist other students in better understanding their contributions to the group's learning.

One excellent form of assessment is a simple observation sheet such as the following one suggested by Johnson and Johnson (1994).

Simple Checklist of Observed Cooperative Behaviors

	YES	NO
1. Do students understand the task?	_____	_____
2. Have students accepted the positive interdependence and individual accountability?	_____	_____
3. Are students working toward appropriate criteria?	_____	_____
4. Are students demonstrating the specified behaviors?	_____	_____

This checklist is particularly useful for teachers who are just becoming acquainted with cooperative learning in their classroom. It will provide a reasonable indication of how well students exhibit the desired behaviors and demonstrate the importance of deliberate and systematic monitoring of students' behaviors during cooperative learning.

The other form of cooperative learning assessment we recommend is student self-assessment. Groups must be given opportunities to conduct discussions of their performance. One common error of collaborative learning arrangements is to provide too brief a period of time for students to process and discuss the qualitative aspects of their cooperation. Teachers need to remind students that assessment of their effort is an important part of their task. Emphasizing the importance of assessing their efforts may require that an assessment form be turned in along with the assignment. If students see tasks and assessment as a continuous process, they are more likely to hold each other accountable for fulfilling their roles as group members.

The following assessment form is intended to serve as a basis for group evaluation at the conclusion of a lesson.

Student Assessment of Cooperative Learning

Directions: For each of the following questions, circle the number that best describes how you feel. If you feel that your group *never* does what the question is asking, then circle 1. If you think your group *occasionally* does what the question is asking, circle 2. If you think your group *sometimes* does what the question is asking, circle 3. If you think your group *usually* does what the question is asking, circle 4. And if you think your group *always* does what the question is asking, then circle 5. Finally, if you don't know or *can't answer* the question, then circle 6.

1. In our group we openly share ideas and information.

    1   2   3   4   5   6

2. In our group we help each other by praising each member's work.

    1   2   3   4   5   6

3. In our group we all contribute to the task.

    1   2   3   4   5   6

4. In our group we are honest, but we also support each other.

    1   2   3   4   5   6

5. In our group we can learn more than if we work independently.

    1   2   3   4   5   6

6. In our group we all know what to do when we are given an assignment.

    1   2   3   4   5   6

7. In our group we conclude our work by summarizing what we learned and by evaluating how well we worked together.

    1   2   3   4   5   6

This form may be used for discussion purposes only, or it may be completed and turned in with the group's assignment. When the form is first introduced, it may be useful for you to use it to evaluate the entire class's performance. This approach allows you to discuss the use of the assessment form, to clarify the intent of the questions, and to provide students the opportunity to actively share and discuss procedures for examining their performance. As soon as possible, however, students should begin using the form themselves.

In this section we have provided two procedures for teachers and students to use in assessing cooperative learning. Both students and teachers can benefit from conducting these types of assessments. Sometimes, a teacher may be misled by concluding that, since students "are really busy in their groups," the groups are functioning

effectively. Like any new approach, cooperative learning requires the teacher to continually modify, refine, and perhaps reteach the procedures. Thorough monitoring of students as they are engaged in their groups will increase the likelihood that problems
can be addressed before they become obstacles and that students' successes can be
capitalized on to instill greater interest and participation. Similarly, students will gain a
more thorough understanding of roles and responsibilities of group members when
they directly attend to what they did that was successful and what they need to work
harder on.

CONCLUDING REMARKS

We began this chapter by defining cooperative learning and discussing its most
important characteristics. Next, we made a case for cooperative learning, citing both
theory and research, and then we described five different types of cooperative learning. Following this, we discussed procedures for instruction in cooperative skills:
First, we presented some general principles for teaching procedural skills; then we
gave a list of cooperative learning skills students need, and finally we described specific teaching methods. Next, we described four examples of cooperative learning
lessons. Finally, we presented two methods of assessing cooperative learning.

Three points are worth stressing here. One is that cooperative learning skills are
not easily or quickly taught, nor are they easily or quickly learned. Simply putting students together in groups does not constitute effective cooperative learning. Effective
cooperative learning demands that students internalize certain attitudes and employ
certain skills, with the prerequisite attitude being students' acceptance of their positive interdependence with other members of their group. Like most worthwhile learning, learning cooperative skills takes a substantial amount of time and energy—time
and energy on students' parts and time and energy on teachers' parts.

The second point is that teaching students to use cooperative skills is well
worth this effort. Remember, cooperative learning can produce gains in academic
achievement, better acceptance of students of diverse backgrounds and personalities, improved attitudes toward school, more positive self-concepts, and enhanced
interpersonal skills. The potential payoff from using cooperative learning in your
classroom is definitely worth the cost.

The third point is that while cooperative learning is an excellent approach to
use in many situations, it is only one instructional approach (Anderson, Reder, &
Simon, 1996) and should be used along with other approaches (Johnson et al., 1994).

REFLECTIONS
▼▼

This section of the chapter gives you an opportunity to reflect on cooperative learning, to consider what sorts of cooperative learning you want to implement in your
class, to consider how you will implement cooperative learning, and to think about
some topics in your subject area that lend themselves particularly well to cooperative learning.

1. As noted early in the chapter, competitive learning is frequently used in classrooms. Think back to your experiences in high school or experiences you have had in college and identify the class that you remember as the most competitive. Explain what made it competitive and assess the contribution that the competitiveness made to your enjoying the class.

2. Again think back to your experiences in high school or experiences you have had in college, but this time identify a class in which independent learning was emphasized. List two or three simple ways in which some of that independent work could have been done cooperatively.

3. Look back at the five necessary components of effective cooperative learning discussed in this chapter and identify the component you plan to emphasize first when introducing students to cooperative learning. Explain why you would emphasize this component first, then explain how you would begin working with this component in a classroom.

4. Consider the five types of cooperative learning described and identify the type you would introduce first to a group of students. Explain why you would introduce this type first. Now consider the five types again and identify the type you are likely to use most often with students. Explain why this is the type you would use most often. Finally, consider the five types once again and list any other types you will probably use at least occasionally.

5. As noted, the task of learning cooperative skills is a procedural one; learning to work cooperatively requires students to learn to do something, not just to learn about something. Think about some procedural skill you have learned to do well. Explain how you learned it and consider which of the guidelines for teaching procedural skills you followed in learning it.

6. List half a dozen topics in your subject area that lend themselves well to cooperative learning. From this list, select the topic that best lends itself to cooperative learning and explain why it is particularly well suited to cooperative learning.

7. The chapter described two procedures for assessing cooperative learning. Identify the procedure that you are likely to use most frequently and explain why you are likely to use it most frequently.

REFERENCES
▼▼

Anderson, J. R., Reder, L. M., & Simon, H. A. (1996). Situated learning and education. *Educational Researcher*, 25(4), 5–11. In this thought-provoking essay, three cognitive psychologists, one a Nobel Prize winner, argue against the educational fads that sometimes plague education.

Aronson, E., & Patnoe, S. (1997). *The jigsaw classroom* (2nd ed.). New York: HarperCollins. A recently released update of Aronson's work on the jigsaw approach.

Bargh, J., & Schul, Y. (1980). On the cognitive benefits of teaching. *Journal of Educational Psychology*, 72, 593–604. Empirical study demonstrating that teaching a topic is a powerful way of learning about it.

Cohen, P. A., Kulik, J. A., & Kulik, C. C. (1982). Educational outcomes of tutoring: A meta-analysis of findings. *American Educational Research Journal*, 19, 237–248. Although it needs updating, this is a thorough and thoughtful review of the research on tutoring.

Flavel, J. H. (1976). Metacognitive aspects of problem solving. In L. B. Resnick (Ed.), *The nature of intelligence* (pp. 231–235). Hillsdale, NJ: Erlbaum. One of the original discussions of metacognition.

Holubec, E. J. (1987). Cooperative poetry: "I Too." In D.W. Johnson, R.T. Johnson, & E. J. Holubec, *Structuring cooperative learning: Lesson plans for teachers*. Edina, MN: Interaction Book Company. Lesson plans created by teachers who have attended the Johnsons' workshops.

Holubec, E. J., Johnson, D. W., & Johnson, R. T. (1995). Cooperative learning in reading and language arts. In C. N. Hedley, P. Antonacci, & M. Rabinoqitz (Eds.), *Thinking and literacy: The mind at work* (pp. 229–240). Hillsdale, NJ: Erlbaum. Chapter focusing on the use of cooperative learning in these two areas.

Johnson, D. W., & Johnson, R. T. (1989). *Cooperation and competition: Theory and research*. Edina, MN: Interaction Book Company. A fairly technical and research-based treatment of the topic

——(1991). Collaboration and cognition. In A. Costa (Ed.), *Developing minds: A resource book for teaching thinking*. Alexandria, VA: Association for Supervision and Curriculum Development. Cooperative learning chapter focusing on student thinking.

——(1994). *Learning together and alone* (4th ed.). Englewood Cliffs, NJ: Prentice-Hall. An in-depth treatment of the Johnsons' approach to cooperative learning.

Johnson, D. W., Johnson, R. T., & Holubec, E. J. (1994). *The new circles of learning: Cooperation in the classroom*. Alexandria, VA: Association for Supervision and Curriculum Development. A brief, informative, and extremely readable description of the Johnsons' approach. Highly recommended.

Johnson, R. T., Johnson, D. W., & Smith, K. A. (1990). Cooperative learning: An active learning strategy for the college classroom. *Baylor Educator*, 15(2), 11–16. Focuses on cooperative learning at the college level.

LaBerge D., & Samuels, S. J. (1974). Toward a theory of automatic information processing in reading. *Cognitive Psychology*, 6, 293–323. The initial description of the theory of automaticity.

McKeachie, W. J., et al. (1986). *Teaching and learning in the college classroom*. Ann Arbor, MI: NCRIPTL. Consideration of college-level teaching by a research team that studied the topic extensively.

Radencich, M. C., McKay, L. J., & Paratore, J. R. (1995). Keeping flexible groups flexible: Grouping options. In M. C. Radencich & L. J. McKay (Eds.), *Flexible grouping for literacy*. Boston: Allyn & Bacon. Describes and recommends uses for various types of groups.

Rekrut, M. D. (1994). Peer and cross-age tutoring: The lessons of research. *Journal of Reading*, 37, 356–62. Presents research-based guidelines for using peer and cross-age tutoring.

Root, P. (1988). *Glacier*. Mankato, MN: Crestwood House. High-interest/easy-reading book on glaciers.

Slavin, R. E. (1987). *Cooperative learning: Student teams* (2nd ed.). Washington, DC: National Education Association. Succinctly presents the several forms of cooperative learning Slavin recommends.

Stahl, R. J. (1994). *Cooperative learning in social studies: A handbook for teachers*. Menlo Park, CA: Addison-Wesley. A collection of essays on applications to science.

——(1995). *Cooperative learning in language arts: A handbook for teachers*. Menlo Park, CA: Innovative Learning Publications. A collection of essays on applications to language arts.

——(1996). *Cooperative learning in science: A handbook for teachers*. Menlo Park, CA: Innovative Learning Publications. A collection of essays on applications to science.

Vygotsky, L. (1978). *Mind in society: The development of higher psychological processes*. Cambridge, MA: Harvard University Press. Classic and much-respected text on psychological development.

Wilbraham, A. C., Staley, D. D., Simpson, C. J., & Matta, M. S. (1987). *Addison-Wesley chemistry*. Menlo Park, CA: Addison-Wesley. A high-school science text.

Cultural and Linguistic Diversity

by Susan Watts-Taffe

CHAPTER OVERVIEW

This chapter focuses on cultural and linguistic diversity in the classroom. The first section defines cultural diversity and explains why content area teachers need to be concerned with this topic. It also sets forth the goals of multicultural education. The next two sections describe two groups of culturally and linguistically diverse students: students who speak English as a second language and students who speak a nonstandard form of English. The fourth section presents the idea that the classroom itself is a culture and that students from cultures that differ from the classroom culture may encounter difficulties learning in this environment. The final section describes characteristics of a multicultural curriculum.

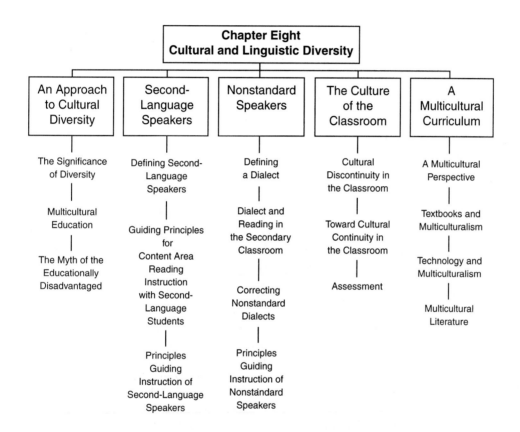

```
                    ┌─────────────────────────┐
                    │      Chapter Eight      │
                    │ Cultural and Linguistic │
                    │        Diversity        │
                    └─────────────────────────┘
```

An Approach to Cultural Diversity	Second-Language Speakers	Nonstandard Speakers	The Culture of the Classroom	A Multicultural Curriculum
The Significance of Diversity	Defining Second-Language Speakers	Defining a Dialect	Cultural Discontinuity in the Classroom	A Multicultural Perspective
Multicultural Education	Guiding Principles for Content Area Reading Instruction with Second-Language Students	Dialect and Reading in the Secondary Classroom	Toward Cultural Continuity in the Classroom	Textbooks and Multiculturalism
The Myth of the Educationally Disadvantaged		Correcting Nonstandard Dialects	Assessment	Technology and Multiculturalism
	Principles Guiding Instruction of Second-Language Speakers	Principles Guiding Instruction of Nonstandard Speakers		Multicultural Literature

AN APPROACH TO CULTURAL DIVERSITY

This first section explains the rationale for including a chapter on cultural diversity here and describes the philosophy underlying the teaching suggestions included in this chapter. A *culturally diverse* classroom is one in which the teacher and students represent a variety of languages, values, life experiences, and habits. In general, cultural diversity results from variations in racial and ethnic identity and/or socioeconomic class. The aim here is not to promote one culture over another. Nor is cultural diversity viewed as a problem for teachers to overcome.

Instead, the culturally diverse classroom presents an opportunity to enhance and enrich the learning of all students.

The Significance of Diversity

Cultural diversity in the United States is far from a new concept. What is new is the magnitude of the diversity. The 1980s saw the arrival of the largest and most diverse group of immigrants in the United States since the turn of the century, with most arriving from Mexico, the Philippines, China, Korea, and Vietnam.

Focusing on racial data, we find that during the 1980s people of color constituted 25% of the total population, up from 20% at the beginning of the decade (Lewis, 1991). The U.S. Census Bureau (1995) projects that one in three Americans will be a person of color by the year 2025. Among school-age youths, the demographic shift is occurring at an even faster rate. In 1990, 31% of school-age youths were minorities and by the year 2030 that figure will increase to 50% (Educational Research Service, 1995). In the early 1990s, students of color already comprised the majority in 23 of the 25 largest cities in the country. Thus, large-scale cultural diversity is quickly becoming the norm.

Of the students representing what used to be minority cultures, many speak a first language other than English. Nationwide, 7% of the school-age population participated in a bilingual or English-as-a-second-language (ESL) program during the mid-1990s, and that figure is likely to increase (U.S. Department of Education, 1995). And although there are certain parts of the country where second-language learners are more prevalent than others, most states in the nation reported gains in the number of ESL students in the early 1990s (Fitzgerald, 1995).

Current research suggests that students' native culture affects both their attitudes toward school and their learning. At the same time, research suggests that traditional classroom teaching—which is oriented to white, European-American, middle-class culture—is not meeting the needs of a sizable number of students who belong to a minority racial or ethnic group, live in a poverty household, and/or have a non-English-language background. For instance, results from the National Assessment of Educational Progress (NAEP) show that the reading and writing skills of black and Hispanic children are substantially lower than those for white children in grades 4, 8, and 12 (National Education Goals Panel, 1995). In addition, black, Hispanic, and Native American youths are less likely to complete high school than white youths (Cahape, 1993; National Education Goals Panel, 1995). More and more, educators are realizing that when students' cultural values and experiences conflict with the cultural values and experiences that dominate their classrooms, identification becomes more difficult, resulting in nonparticipation, misbehavior, poor achievement, and dropping out (Delpit, 1995; Schlosser, 1992). Interestingly, just as U.S. public school classrooms are growing more diverse, teachers have remained overwhelmingly white and female, and this trend is expected to continue (Delpit, 1995).

With growing heterogeneity in American classrooms, teachers are challenged to find appropriate ways to educate culturally diverse students. In a just society all teachers—including secondary content teachers—have a responsibility to help all students to be successful in school and the society at large. Even if you teach in a culturally homogeneous environment, you need to be concerned with cultural diversity. Your students will most certainly live in a global society, and they need the knowledge and the disposition to understand the world they live in and to live harmoniously with varied cultural groups.

Multicultural Education

Approaches to addressing cultural diversity in the classroom have varied significantly over the past century. The view that dominated America from the turn of the century to the 1960s was that of assimilation. This was the idea that America was to be a melting pot—a nation in which all cultural differences would combine to form a new and superior American culture. In actuality, however, the culture of the dominant immigrant group at the time rose to the top of the pot while the cultures of other groups stuck to the bottom (Banks, 1977). Thus, as agents of assimilation, schools weaned immigrant students, black students, and Native American students away from their own cultures and replaced them with the English language and Anglo customs.

Running counter to the idea of assimilation was that of cultural pluralism. Instead of being a melting pot, America was to be a salad bowl. Just as shredded lettuce, croutons, bacon bits, tomato wedges, and other ingredients retain their identity when tossed together in a salad, so too people would retain their cultural identity within the American society. Whereas assimilationists asserted that to be strong America needed a unified culture, cultural pluralists asserted that to be strong America needed cultural democracy, with every ethnic culture contributing to and enriching the total society. Although a few writers and philosophers espoused cultural pluralism at the beginning of the century, the concept did not take hold in America until the civil rights movement of the 1960s. Tired of assimilationist promises of blending in, black leaders demanded more control over institutions in their communities and fuller representation of their culture. For schools, this meant more African American teachers and administrators, and textbooks reflecting African American culture. Inspired by the civil rights movement, other ethnic groups—both nonwhite and white—began to reclaim cultural pride (Banks, 1993).

The concept of cultural pluralism led to the movement known as multicultural education. According to Banks (1993, p. 3), "multicultural education is at least three things: an idea or concept, an educational reform movement, and a process." Two of the overarching goals of multicultural education are (1) to help individuals better understand themselves by looking at their culture and behavior through the perspectives of other cultures and (2) to improve academic achievement.

Multicultural education stresses providing opportunities for all students—regardless of race, ethnicity, gender, socioeconomic status, or native language—to learn in school. It also stresses studying other cultures in school. However, it is not something that is added to the curriculum, instead it permeates the curriculum. It is not just for African American or Native American students, it is for all students. Multicultural education is an attitude, a philosophy, a way of being with others rather than a set of rules or a curriculum. It is an ongoing process rather than a product. As one teacher put it, "For me, multicultural awareness means to infuse this awareness and knowledge of others, their culture, and history into the instructional content and classroom climate rather than teach it" (Watts, 1992).

Nieto (1996) points out that multicultural education does not have as its ultimate goal to raise the self-esteem of minority students. Rather, this is a by-product of striving for a higher goal—providing learning environments in which all students can learn and in which students are able to learn about a variety of perspectives. Nieto (1996, p. 9) states:

> No educational philosophy or program is worthwhile unless it focuses on two primary concerns: (1) Raising the achievement of all students and thus providing them with an equitable and high-quality education, [and] (2) Giving students an apprenticeship in the opportunity to become critical and productive members of a democratic society . . . . Simply wanting our students to get along with, be sensitive to, and be respectful of one another makes little difference in the options they have as a result of their schooling.

In Banks's (1977) view the total environment of the ideal school would reflect the ethnic diversity of American society. Thus, the multicultural school would have a racially and ethnically mixed staff that respects and values ethnic diversity. Teachers and administrators would have positive attitudes toward and high academic expectations for all students. The curriculum in the multicultural school would help students view American society and history from a variety of perspectives and not just the perspective of European-American historians and writers. And not only humanities and history teachers would be concerned with cultural content, but science, music, home economics, physical education, and other teachers would be as well. Teaching strategies and methods would reflect the notion that the students' backgrounds and specific languages affect the way they learn. The school's testing and counseling program and expectations for student behavior would also reflect ethnic diversity.

To achieve the multicultural school, writes Banks (1995), system-wide reform is needed. Just using multiethnic materials, for example, is not enough. While ascribing to many of Banks's ideas, this chapter can only address a few of the issues and topics in multicultural education. To begin with, it will address the "at-risk" label as it relates to diversity.

The Myth of the Educationally Disadvantaged

For a number of years, students of color, students from poor homes, and students who speak limited English or nonstandard English have been labeled "educationally disadvantaged," "educationally deprived," or "at risk." Many teachers have been trained to believe that these students lack a viable culture, lack language skills and knowledge, and lack parental support for school success (Garcia, 1978). Their generally poor performance on standardized assessments (discussed later in this chapter) seems to affirm academic deficiency. As a result of these deficit views, an entire bureaucracy of compensatory education has evolved in which minority and low-income students are disproportionately separated into remedial and low-track classes to receive instruction in basic skills (Flores, Cousin, & Diaz, 1991; Sleeter, 1992; Walmsley & Allington, 1995).

Recent research suggests that labels such as "educationally disadvantaged" and "at risk" fail to recognize that so-called disadvantaged children have functional cultures, are proficient users of their native language, and bring a great deal of knowledge into the classroom (Flores et al., 1991). Labels such as "educationally disadvantaged" and "at risk" can be used to rationalize failure and can become a self-fulfilling prophecy (Nieto, 1996). If students are labeled "at risk" at the beginning of their school career, then no one is surprised when they later do fail. If students *are* at risk for failure, it may be because educators have disadvantaged them. It is, in fact, the educational system that is at risk of failing if it does not keep up with the movement of the nation toward increasing heterogeneity.

Practice Activity 8.1

Read the following descriptions of adolescents of various racial, ethnic, and socio-economic backgrounds. As a teacher, rank these adolescents from those you would most like to have in class to those you would least like to have in class (1 = most like). If you feel comfortable doing so, discuss your rankings with your classmates.

Song Vang came to the United States from Laos when she was a small child. She and her parents live in the local Hmong community. Since her parents have had difficulty learning English and adjusting to American ways, Song is the family interpreter and decision maker.

Laurie Dobson, a white teenager, lives with her mother and brother in a downtown shelter for the homeless. Although their living situation is difficult, Laurie's mother wants her children to get an education. She does the best she can to get Laurie to school every day.

Jose Sierra, his parents, and brothers and sisters have just moved into the local Hispanic community. His parents were able to find seasonal work in the pea-canning factory. Jose has attended schools in several states and speaks both Spanish and English fluently.

Marissa Sarawak is an exchange student from Malaysia. The daughter of a Kuala Lumpur businessman, Marissa speaks English quite well and is frequently asked to speak to civic and church groups about her native land.

Mustafa Hajrulahovic, a Muslim, is a recent refugee from ethnic violence in eastern Europe. He and his family arrived in this country with only the clothes on their backs. Mustafa speaks no English.

T. J. Thomas lives in the African American community on the city's north side. His father is an attorney and his mother is a schoolteacher. T. J. enjoys playing hockey and baseball in the city's recreation program.

▼▼

The following sections address the needs of two groups of culturally and linguistically diverse students in the classroom: students who speak English as a second language and students who speak a nonstandard form of English. The final section of the chapter discusses multiculturalism as it relates to the total curriculum. The hope is that you, as an individual teacher, will do what you can to create a multicultural environment in your classroom.

SECOND-LANGUAGE SPEAKERS

Imagine this scenario. You're a seventh-grade geography teacher. The school counselor has just informed you that beginning Monday you will have three new students in your second-hour class. These students, part of a large family of Vietnamese refugees being sponsored by a local church, speak only limited English. Specifically, their ability to read in English consists of recognizing words such as "Coca-Cola" and "Nike." On hearing this news, you begin to panic. How on earth can you teach geography to these students? After all, you don't speak their language, and you certainly don't have materials they can read. What are you supposed to do?

As emphasized in the previous section, such situations are becoming more and more common in American public schools. This section attempts to help subject matter teachers understand and teach the second-language speakers in their classrooms. It defines second-language speakers, describes general characteristics of second-language acquisition, and discusses the relation of reading to second-language learners.

Defining Second-Language Speakers

Second-language speakers have in common the fact that the first language they learned to speak was not English. Beyond that they are a diverse group. Some are fluent in both English and their native language (that is, they are bilingual), while others know little or no English. Some learn to speak English relatively quickly, while others learn more slowly.

In a school setting, students may take from four to eight years to become proficient users of English (Allen, 1991). Like first-language learning, second-language learning is creative and constructive (Allen, 1991). Rather than being passive receptacles of a second language, students are active interactors with that language. They constantly hypothesize about the rules of the language, test their rules, and revise them based on the feedback they receive. Figure 8.1 shows the typical stages of language development for ESL students.

School districts provide varying instructional programs for second-language students. One type of program, which is really no program, is submersion. Students must either "sink or swim" as they are thrown into the regular classroom with no special help. Another type of program is immersion. The language of the classroom is English, but the teacher knows the students' native language. In the bilingual classroom, instruction is carried on both in English and in the students' native language. A common type of program is the ESL classroom. In this program, students

Stages of Language Acquisition Among ESL Students
(adapted from Richard-Amato & Snow, 1992, p. 147)

Stage	Listening	Speaking	Writing	Reading
Low beginning	-Comprehends very few words and phrases -Depends on gestures, facial expressions, and pictures	-Speaks very little if at all	-Writes very little if at all	-Reads very little if at all
Middle to high beginning	-Comprehends words and short phrases when accompanied by gestures, facial expressions, and repetition	-Speaks haltingly, if at all -Gradually speaks more but with frequent errors in grammar, vocabulary, and pronunciation	-Writes short phrases with frequent errors in grammar and vocabulary	-Recognizes short written segments
Intermediate	-Recognizes more vocabulary -Continues to struggle with idioms	-Has more to say but still searches for acceptable form -Often misunderstood due to errors	-Writes with greater ease	-Reads more difficult text that is concrete
Low advanced	-Comprehends substantial segments of conversation when spoken at normal rates -Still requires some repetitions, especially with academic discourse	-Makes substantially fewer errors in speaking and speaks with more confidence	-Writes with much greater ease	-Reads with much greater comprehension
Middle to high advanced	-Comprehends most speech, both academic and social, without difficulty	-Speaks quite fluently but still makes some errors	-Writes fluently on both a concrete and abstract level with few errors -May experience some regression at times	-Reads concrete and abstract text at grade level with relative ease -May occasionally struggle with implicit meanings

Figure 8.1
Stages of Language Acquisition Among ESL Students

with limited English skills spend part of their day in a special classroom and part of their day in a regular classroom. The most common program options appear in Figure 8.2.

Even if second-language learners are receiving excellent instruction from well-qualified ESL teachers, they need the benefits of the regular classroom. For one thing, the goal of ESL programs is to help students master English, not to help them learn math, science, or history. While learning English, students still must advance

Common Program Options for ESL Students

(adapted from Tinajero, 1994)

Type of Program	Language of Instruction	Instructional Setting
Submersion (Note: This is really the *absence* of a program)	English	Students attend regular content area classes. Teachers have no special training and do not speak the students' native language.
Immersion	English	Language is taught through content area instruction. The teacher has training in ESL and receptive skills in the students' primary languages.
Bilingual	Dual language	A bilingual teacher uses the students' primary language to teach content until the student is ready to move to an English-only class.
ESL	English	An ESL teacher focuses on the development of the students' English language skills while students receive content-area instruction in the regular classroom.
Sheltered class	Modified English	ESL teacher and/or content area teacher use a modified form of English to teach content. Usually all students in the class are ESL.

Figure 8.2
Common Program Options for ESL Students

cognitively. Subject-matter teachers possess the content area knowledge these students need. For another thing, ESL students require much more practice in speaking, reading, and writing English than most ESL programs can provide. Although your goal is not to teach English, integrating the acquisition of English with learning content and establishing a language-rich classroom will significantly enhance language growth (Cummins, 1994). Finally, isolating students in ESL programs, as with any other kind of tracking, can lead second-language speakers to perceive themselves as poor learners and failures.

Too often limited English proficiency is equated with limited intelligence, the assumption being that because people do not speak English fluently they must be less intelligent. In considering the task students face in learning a second language, however, we can gain a new respect for their accomplishment. Already they have developed a vast knowledge of their own language. Now they are not only learning the forms and structures of a new language but are learning how to use that language with different persons, in different settings, and for different purposes (Peregoy & Boyle, 1993).

In summary, second-language learners are a diverse group, varying in their levels of English language proficiency and in the services they are provided in schools. Even so, there are several teaching principles with which you are already familiar that can guide your instruction.

Guiding Principles for Content Area Reading Instruction with Second-Language Students

In Chapter 1, five principles for content area reading instruction were presented. These principles, along with their application to second-language learners, are reviewed here.

Principle 1.   Content area reading instruction is based on the assumption that students acquire meaning through the application of strategies, skills, and prior knowledge to text material. As noted in Chapter 1, "to the student, content reading is a strategic process to acquire meaning; not a set of skills or exercises taught in isolation of content." Similarly, there is a difference between language acquisition (subconsciously acquiring a language in informal settings because there is a need to learn the language) and language learning (consciously learning the rules of a language in a formal setting). The former is more meaningful and useful to students, whereas the latter allows them chiefly to edit their own language output (Krashen, 1981). Your task as a content area teacher is to motivate second-language students to learn content—and in the process learn the language—by providing them with purposeful tasks. Moll and Diaz (1987) describe how a teacher in San Diego engaged Hispanic students in learning English language skills. Knowing the students were interested in finding out the community's opinions on bilingualism, the instructor had them develop and administer a questionnaire and then write a report on their findings.

Principle 2.   The classroom is a dynamic social and intellectual environment where students acquire knowledge. As stated in Chapter 1, "instruction within this environment draws upon students' knowledge collectively and individually . . .

teachers should acknowledge the cultural and social diversity of the classroom on an ongoing basis." It must be emphasized that the discussion here does not suggest extinguishing students' first language. In fact, bilingualism should be encouraged, and students' first language and culture should be used as a resource to widen the perspective and enrich the learning of mainstream students as well (Cummins, 1994). There are many ways to do this, such as by having students read a passage to the class in their native language or by having them translate vocabulary words into their native language. In the case of the Vietnamese students introduced earlier, you might have them describe similarities and differences between their native culture and the mainstream culture and teach common words and expressions in their native language.

Principle 3.   Content area reading instruction allows students to learn from numerous sources of information. The lack of sophisticated English reading skills among many second-language learners often means that using printed materials—especially the more complex texts of the secondary classroom—is not an option. In these instances, other approaches are needed to teach your subject matter content. Alternative approaches include visual teaching techniques such as conducting an experiment in science, acting out math problems, or showing films as part of social studies. Other visual approaches include using graphic organizers such as T-charts, Venn diagrams, semantic maps, and illustrated charts (Russell, 1995). Hands-on activities such as having students draw maps or make models also teach content. Alternative resources might also be people. Ask your second-language students who have a better mastery of English to explain assignments to students, or have students work in cross-language pairs. Another possibility is to invite English-speaking adults from the students' home or community to tutor students. This is an excellent way to build support between the school and home.

Principle 4.   Content area reading instruction is directed at the learner. According to this principle, learners do not passively absorb knowledge. Instead, they actively relate their existing knowledge to incoming information and organize and interpret that information in a manner that allows for constructing meaning. This principle has an important implication for second-language learners. In interpreting a text, they may use perfectly sound reasoning. However, if their background knowledge is different from that of the teacher, they may give an "incorrect" answer. Teachers need to be careful not to reject answers that on the surface seem wrong. They need to find out how students arrived at an answer and focus on their process of thinking. Here again, second-language learners can be a resource for other students, as well as the teacher, as they share their unique perspective and prior knowledge during group problem solving.

Principle 5.   Instructional strategies and activities in the content areas are adaptable to the constraints of the classroom. Having second-language learners in the classroom does not necessarily mean more demands on teacher time. In a review of the literature on teaching subject matter to second-language students at the secondary level, Reyes and Molner (1991) describe strategies that have proven successful with this linguistically diverse group. Furthermore, in each case the strategies were effective with mixed groups of language-majority and language-minority students enrolled in regular content area classrooms. This suggests that what benefits linguistically diverse students benefits mainstream students as well, proving the maxim, "Good teaching is good teaching is good teaching." Among the successful strategies they cite are Langer's PreReading Plan, or PReP (described in Chapter 5 of this text), semantic mapping (similar to the list, group, label strategy also described in Chapter 5), the experience-text-relationship method (similar to the directed questioning activity discussed in Chapter 7), and student teams-achievement divisions (STAD) and Jigsaw (both described in Chapter 3).

Text Topics

The preceding chapters have dealt with a variety of topics. Here are a few comments connecting some of these topics to second-language learners.

Cooperative Learning

Two theories of second-language acquisition are of interest here. Cummins (1980) distinguishes between school language—the language of textbooks and teachers—and social language—the language of hallways and cafeterias. According to Cummins, school language can be difficult for second-language speakers to learn because it tends to be abstract and distant. Social language, on the other hand, is easier to learn because it is often rich in context and immediate. In addition, the relative relaxation that students may feel in social situations facilitates their language learning (Tinajero, 1994).

Both these theories point to the value of linguistically heterogeneous cooperative learning groups for second-language learners. Not only do students learn language more quickly in informal peer groups, but also they are relieved of the pressure of having to perform independently. It has been noted that in cooperative classrooms minority students often make strong gains, are more involved in activities, receive more practice with learning concepts, spend more time on task, engage in higher-level thinking, and become motivated to learn (Garcia, 1992).

Vocabulary

Chapter 2 identified four word-learning tasks. Two of these—learning new labels for known concepts and learning words representing new and difficult concepts—are particularly important to keep in mind when teaching vocabulary to ESL students. Language expresses the ideas, values, experiences, and environment of a culture. Often, once a concept is presented, students can identify the word or words in their first language that describe the concept. At other times, this is not possible because the concepts, and thus the words, do not exist in the students' native culture. For example, an art instructor might be explaining the terms *azure* and *aquamarine* to a linguistically diverse class. If there are Navaho Indian students in the class, they will have no idea what the teacher is talking about because blue and green do not exist in their color spectrum. Only by knowing about students' culture can a teacher be sensitive to these differences.

Comprehension Instruction

For many years it has been assumed that students need to master a hierarchy of basic skills before being exposed to more advanced skills in comprehension. Language-minority students, in particular, were thought to need drill in phonics, vocabulary, and word decoding. Often these skills were taught as discrete skills with no relation to a meaningful whole. As a result, students became bored and frustrated with instruction. In recent years, however, cognitive psychology has shown that students with limited English proficiency can benefit from comprehension instruction that develops problem-solving and reasoning abilities. The reciprocal teaching strategy discussed in Chapter 4 has been cited as particularly effective (Means & Knapp, 1991).

It is also important to note that second-language learners often employ a strategy known as code switching (Garcia & Padilla, 1985). This involves reading the text in English, then mentally translating it into their native language for comprehension. Obviously the implication for instruction is to allow students time for code switching as they read and respond to questions or participate in discussions based on reading (Bernhardt & Kamil, 1998).

Critical Thinking

The concept of instructional scaffolding discussed in Chapter 7 is particularly pertinent to ESL students. To accomplish more-complex tasks, second-language learners will at first need the assistance of special materials and the assistance of the teacher and other students. One difference is that scaffolding must be supplied for the decoding process as well as for developing critical thinking strategies. This is done, for example, when teachers read text aloud to students, allowing them to practice critical thinking skills before they have fully mastered word decoding.

Writing Instruction

Studies have shown that second-language learners can begin to write in English long before they become fluent speakers. In fact, writing activities aid the development of oral language (Hudelson, 1984; Rigg, 1981; Urzua, 1987). Thus, many of the writing-to-learn activities described in Chapter 6 are appropriate for your second-language students. However, a note of caution is in order here. As in reading, second-language learners will often employ code switching during writing activities. For example, native speakers of Spanish will interject Spanish vocabulary and spellings, especially if they are having difficulty communicating their meaning. As a subject matter teacher, you will want to focus more on the content of second-language learners' writing than on the form. Too much emphasis on mechanics can discourage the writing endeavors of ESL students with fragile English skills. Look on errors in writing as an indicator of how far along they are in language acquisition.

Technology

Technology holds great promise for second-language learners. Through word processing, second-language learners experiment with language and make changes quickly and easily. And with the application of the Internet, students can communicate directly with students in their first language, and all students can gain a better understanding of various cultures throughout the world. Technology combined with social interaction, by having students work at the computer in pairs or triads, allows oral and written language development to reinforce each other. Building meaning through social interaction that is nonthreatening helps second-language learners develop fluency in English more quickly and easily (Diamond & Moore, 1995).

Principles Guiding Instruction of Second-Language Speakers

The section below recaps some of the ideas presented in the previous section and presents other points to consider when teaching a diverse student body. Many of these recommendations are based on the work of Garcia (1992), Richard-Amato and Snow (1992), and Walker and Tedick (1996).

Ways to Facilitate the Academic Growth of Second-Language Learners

1. Make a strong commitment to the educational success of your students.
   -Reject the notion that your students are intellectually or academically disadvantaged.
   -Work cooperatively with other professionals in your building such as the ESL teacher and the school librarian.

2. Show respect and interest in your students' cultural backgrounds.
   -Be sensitive to the fact that they may be experiencing culture shock and/or their home situation may be a difficult one.

3. Emphasize functional communication in the classroom.
   -Use discussion and collaborative, small-group projects in your teaching.
   -Talk with students regularly about the clarity of assignments and their roles in these assignments.
   -Focus on the content of what students communicate rather than the grammatical form of their communication.

4. Modify the language you use during instruction.
   -Speak clearly and slightly more slowly.
   -Avoid using idioms (e.g., "You're right on target.") and define key words in meaningful contexts.

5. Make instructions as clear as possible.
   -Provide verbal support for written directions, support verbal explanations with nonverbal cues such as gestures, facial expressions, actions, and manipulatives, and make clear verbal transitions from one activity to another.

6. Use nonprint resources and human resources to scaffold, or mediate, instruction.

7. Establish consistent and explicit classroom patterns and routines.

Practice Activity 8.2

Imagine that you are a science teacher. You have a class of 25 students. Five of these students are Hispanic. They speak English with varying degrees of fluency and their English reading and writing skills are minimal. Today's lesson is on photosynthesis. Your textbook contains a good description of this process. Using instructional strategies and ideas suggested in the previous section, explain how you would teach photosynthesis to your class.

▼▼

NONSTANDARD SPEAKERS

You may have students who regularly speak a dialect of English other than standard English, such as black English. On hearing such speech, the general public may cringe at what it perceives to be poor English and wonder why the schools aren't doing a better job of educating students. This section defines dialect, describes the relation of nonstandard dialect to reading, and discusses the issue of correcting dialect speakers' use of language. Because of its prevalence in American classrooms, the focus will be on black English. Before proceeding, however, you should note that racial, ethnic, and socioeconomic identity does not necessarily dictate the dialect a person speaks; specifically, not all African Americans speak black English.

Defining a Dialect

A dialect is a variation of a language, sufficiently different from the original to be considered a separate entity, but not different enough to be classified as a separate language (Wolfram, 1991). Differences occur in phonology, intonation, grammar, syntax, and vocabulary. In effect, dialects are the languages of subcultures. They vary by geographical region, socioeconomic class, and age. There may even be many versions of a single dialect. We all speak a dialect of English, and many of us are bidialectal, that is, we speak more than one dialect. In addition to black English, some of the more well-known American English dialects are Appalachian English, Pennsylvania Dutch, and standard English.

Dialects are complete and functional language systems. The grammatical rules, or predictable patterns, of black English have been well documented since the 1960s. For example, the verb *be* is used to denote habitual or ongoing action ("We be working after school"); multiple negatives are used in one sentence for emphasis ("Don't nobody want no friends like that"); the plural marker *-s* is omitted when there are other words in the sentence that indicate plurality ("I got two book") (Alexander, 1980; Smitherman, 1994). In addition, in recent years researchers have called attention to the fact that black English is rich in figurative language. For example, "playing the dozens," a verbal game of one-upmanship by insult especially common among

African American male adolescents, involves hyperbole and other creative uses of language (DeLain, Pearson & Anderson, 1985, p. 155):

> **Jesse:** Man, you so ugly that when you walk down the streets the dogs die!
>
> **Duane:** Well, man, you so ugly that when you walk down the streets blind folks turn their heads!
>
> **Jesse:** Well, you so ugly that when you were born the doctor slapped your face!
>
> **Duane:** Well, you so ugly that when you were born the doctor slapped your momma!

A study by DeLain, Pearson, and Anderson (1985) suggests that the experiences of African American youth with figurative language outside of school enhances their understanding of figurative language in school texts.

While no dialect is inherently superior for the purposes of communication, one dialect must be chosen as the standard in a region so that everyone can understand each other. The dialect chosen is usually the one spoken by the people with political and economic power. Their dialect then becomes the most prestigious. In the United States, the most prestigious dialect is what has come to be known as standard English. This is the dialect used in business, in government, and in most public classrooms.

Dialect and Reading in the Secondary Classroom

A main concern here is whether or not speaking black English or another nonstandard dialect affects a student's ability to comprehend oral and written standard English in the classroom. For example, when nonstandard speakers read orally, they may substitute their dialect features for the standard English of the text. Or, after reading a portion of standard English text, they may summarize the information or respond to a question in nonstandard dialect. Does this mean they are having trouble reading and comprehending? If so, what should be done to help them?

All speakers have a range of comprehension that extends beyond the limits of their own dialect (Goodman, 1969b). Research has shown that speakers of black English are generally able to comprehend oral and written standard English, even though they may choose not to use it. They have "receptive control" (Goodman & Buck, 1973). This is a major difference between the nonstandard speakers and second-language speakers who are just beginning to learn English. Interestingly, exposure to television, often thought of as a negative influence, is a major factor in the nonstandard speakers' ability to comprehend standard English (Alexander, 1980).

Numerous researchers (Bean, 1978; Rigg, 1974; Sims, 1972) have shown that nonstandard speakers' dialect-involved "errors" do not interfere with comprehension. In fact, Goodman's (1969a) work on miscue analysis suggests that nonstandard speakers are actually performing at a high level as they translate standard English text into black English. Ironically, many teachers, especially at the primary level, spend a great deal of time correcting the oral reading pronunciations of children who speak black English and underestimate their potential for comprehension. In some instances, perceived mispronunciations have even been the basis for assigning students to remedial reading classes.

Mechanically students' dialect should not present problems with comprehending oral and written standard English. However, misunderstanding may develop out of differences in background and cultural knowledge. For example, Reynolds, Taylor, Steffenson, Shirey, and Anderson (1982) had a group of white eighth graders and a group of African American eighth graders read the same passage. The passage could be interpreted as describing "sounding" (another name for "playing the dozens") or as describing a physical fight. The African American students applied their knowledge of sounding to interpret the text, while the white students thought the text was about a fight. In a classroom setting, comprehending this text would present a problem to the African American readers if it were, indeed, about fighting and, conversely, to the white readers if it were actually about sounding. The difference in comprehension is a result of differences in the readers' schemata.

Correcting Nonstandard Dialects

In the well-known musical *My Fair Lady*, Professor Henry Higgins spends a great deal of time and effort attempting to change the dialect of Eliza Doolittle. As the story goes, if Professor Higgins can just get Eliza to stop using Cockney and adopt the more "cultured" speech of the British upper class, she will be acceptable in high society. Much the same issue occurs in teaching nonstandard speakers in the American classroom. Should you be a Henry Higgins and attempt to change the dialect of the students in your class?

The answer is yes and no. On the one hand, students should be taught the truth: Their dialect is a valuable, unique, and meaningful expression of their culture and should be retained. They should be taught that the way they speak makes them neither bad nor good. On the other hand, students should be taught the reality: They need to be able to use standard English to move into many areas of our society. Not teaching standard English conventions and not insisting that students practice them denies students access to what Delpit (1995) calls "the culture of power."

Issues of language diversity and power need to be discussed openly and honestly. All subject matter teachers should be ready to point out how standard English may be more appropriate in some situations and dialect more appropriate in others. They should allow students to use their dialect in reading and speaking in the classroom, but model the standard and encourage them to use it. In addition, social studies and English teachers might use the following boxed activities adapted from Alexander (1980) and Delpit (1995).

African American folklore, idioms, proverbs, and other language patterns might be used as the basis for reading and writing activities and for motivating students to learn about other language patterns. In other words, teachers can capitalize on the language resources that students bring to the classroom. For example, have students work in cooperative learning groups to compose rap lyrics, which are no different from a sonnet in terms of having a set structure (Griffin & Cole, 1987).

Activities for Helping Students Increase Their Understanding of Dialects

1. Discuss the major dialect areas in the United States.

2. Read passages in other English dialects to your students to help them appreciate the variability of English and the legitimacy of their own dialect. (Also have students read trade books that reflect their dialects.)

3. Have your students conduct a television survey and note which programs use noticeable dialects.

4. Play recordings of speeches by Dr. Martin Luther King, Jr., who was a bidialectal master. See if students can hear in his speeches the call-response style of the African American preacher as well as the standard English dialect style of the international man.

5. Discuss historical and cultural influences on various English dialects.

6. Discuss the historical, social, political, and economic reasons why black English and other dialects did not become the standard English of this country.

Activities for Helping Students Become Proficient in Standard English

1. Discuss and role play different situations in which vernacular black English dialect and standard English dialect would be used.

2. Use pattern practice drills to help students develop an understanding of both black English dialect and standard English dialect.
   I talked to Mary Ellen every day. I been talkin' to Mary Ellen.
   I talked to Mary Ellen a *long* time ago. I been done talked to Mary Ellen.

3. Examine your own speech patterns and read to your students regularly.

Principles Guiding Instruction of Nonstandard Speakers

In summary, the following principles should be useful in guiding instruction of nonstandard speakers of English:

1. Develop and transmit respect for your students' dialect as a language system that reflects a culture.

2. Allow students to use their own dialect in the classroom, but model standard English and encourage them to use it.

3. Teach students about the arbitrariness of the dialect selected as "standard."

4. Show students that you believe they are capable of bidialectism.

▼ **PRACTICE ACTIVITY 8.3**

Read the following interaction between a teacher and a student. What does it say about the environment that has been established in this classroom?

> **Scene:** Vanessa is looking for something in her desk.
>
> **Mr. Ross:** What are you doing?
>
> **Vanessa:** Nuttin'
>
> **Mr. Ross** (laughingly): What?!
>
> **Vanessa:** Oh, nuthin'
>
> **Mr. Ross:** What?!
>
> **Vanessa:** Oh, nothing.
>
> **Mr. Ross:** Now . . .
>
> **Vanessa:** (interrupting): I know, "nuthin" is nonstandard English, and that's all right when I'm outside playing with my friends. "Nothing" is standard English, and that's what I need to use in the classroom.

Now compare the following interaction to the one above. What is the difference? Why?

> **Scene:** Mr. Ross is conducting a health lesson.
>
> **Mr. Ross:** How many kinds of bones does your body have?
>
> **Theo:** They be three bone, man.
>
> **Mr. Ross:** What are they?
>
> **Theo:** Long bone, short bone, and flat bone.
>
> **Mr. Ross:** Have you ever broken a bone?
>
> **Theo:** I ain't never broke no bone.
>
> **Mr. Ross:** Well, that's good!

▼▼▼

THE CULTURE OF THE CLASSROOM

Consider the following interchange among teachers in a high school teachers' lounge.

> **Ms. Wilson:** (looking up from the paper she is grading): I swear I think Dwayne is *trying* to fail chemistry. His test paper is pathetic.
>
> **Ms. Amos:** Was it an essay exam?
>
> **Ms. Wilson:** No. It's a simple multiple choice. But what do I expect? He's always talking while I'm teaching. Instead of copying the periodic table, he's busy making up a rap song of the elements.

Mr. Lewis (laughing): Yeah, he can't sit still in my class either. By this age, I think kids should be able to listen to a 45-minute lecture on World War II, take some decent notes, and study on their own.

Ms. Blair: Well at least that kid talks. I've got two kids who won't say a word. When I put them into groups, they won't participate with the other kids and they barely make eye contact with me. They want to do everything on their own. I'll tell you Choua and Mai are not very good at working with their peers.

Ms. Wilson: I'm just amazed at how many kids don't respect us as teachers. When I lecture, I expect them to listen without being told, and I'm sure when you assign group work you expect them to do it in groups, not the way they want to.

Mr. Lewis: Yeah. And I don't think it's fair that we're held accountable for the fact that they don't do well in school when they obviously don't value learning.

Perhaps you can relate to this conversation. Perhaps you have had some of the same sentiments in your own work with students. This section explores some of the assumptions behind the teachers' comments and sheds light on reasons why the students they discuss may be experiencing difficulty in school.

The premise of this section is that the classroom itself is a culture (Villegas, 1991). The American classroom is a community with its own language (typically standard English or the teacher's version of standard English), its own values (do your own work, don't copy anyone else's paper), and its own habits (when the bell rings, take your seat and be quiet). Villegas describes the traditional classroom culture more fully as follows.

Villegas' Description of the Traditional Classroom Culture

The dominant form of interaction is the teacher-directed lesson in which the instructor is in control, determining the topics of discussion, allocating turns at speaking, and deciding what qualifies as a correct response. Verbal participation is required of students. Implicitly, teaching and learning are equated with talking, and silence is interpreted as the absence of knowledge. Students are questioned in public and bid for the floor by raising their hands. They are expected to wait until the teacher awards the floor to one of them before answering. Speaking in turn is the rule, unless the teacher specifically asks for choral responses. Display questions prevail. Individual competition is preferred to group cooperation. Topics are normally introduced in small and carefully sequenced steps, with the overall picture emerging only at the end of the teaching sequence. (Villegas, 1991, p. 20)

Although you may not think of your classroom as a culture, Villegas's description highlights the traditional values, habits, and attitudes that may be taken for granted in school. The public school classroom generally reflects the culture of the teacher, the school district, or the dominant cultural group in the community. For most classrooms the culture will be that of white, middle-class Americans of European descent. Students who come from this background generally adjust to classroom routines and practices with no problems. Students, however, who come from different cultural backgrounds—with different learning styles and different patterns of communication—may have more difficulty. Unless there is sensitivity and accommodation to their needs, they will not be engaged in learning. As a result they may become disruptive, or they may fall silent. Eventually they may drop out.

You may recall that one of the goals of multicultural education is to provide equal educational opportunities to all students. This is not to be confused with providing the *same* education to all students (Nieto, 1996). As was just explained, an African American student, a Latina student, and a Native American student may all be in the same classroom, experiencing the same instruction, but may have very different learning opportunities depending upon the degree to which their cultures match the predominant classroom culture. A mismatch between the culture of the student and the culture of the classroom creates cultural discontinuity. Thus, students from different cultures may profit from some different classroom experiences.

Cultural Discontinuity in the Classroom

As a teacher or prospective teacher, it may be difficult to imagine how students would have trouble with traditional ways of learning. Thinking of your own culture shock in going from the high school classroom to the college classroom may help. If you were like most freshmen, you probably had some difficulty adjusting to college classes. Things were quite different from high school. Instead of involving you in question-and-answer dialogue, the professors lectured for an hour. You were expected to take copious notes (on which you would later be tested). You had homework in high school, but nothing like the extensive reading lists in college. You were expected to keep up with the reading without anyone checking on your progress. Altogether, the instruction was much more impersonal. If you had a question or problem to discuss with a professor, you had to make an appointment to see him or her during office hours. Unable to adjust to this new classroom culture, many students drop out of college after the first semester.

Cultural differences in learning tend to be most apparent in three areas: learning styles, communication styles, and attitudes toward teacher authority.

Learning Styles

Learning in the typical American classroom, especially at the secondary level, is teacher directed. The teacher decides on the objectives of instruction, assigns chapters to read, asks students questions on their reading and controls discussion, and tests students' achievement of the objectives. This method of classroom organization may present difficulties to students who come from backgrounds where learning is more self-directed or more peer directed.

Philips (1983), for example, investigated the learning patterns of children from the Warm Springs Indian Reservation in central Oregon. In school these children were extremely quiet, a quality often attributed to shyness or linguistic deficiency. However, Philips found that at home these children were accustomed to a high degree of self-determination. If they needed assistance in learning a task, they turned to other children or to older siblings. On the few occasions when they did learn from adults, they did so through observation rather than through verbal instruction. On their own initiative, the children then practiced the skill privately and did self-testing. When faced with interacting directly with the teacher at school, the children were at a loss as to what to do and fell into a silent role.

Other researchers have found peer interaction to be similarly important in the learning of Hispanic and African American students (Shade, 1994). On the other hand, for Chinese children interactions with the teacher were more helpful. In addition, one study found that when the teacher's lessons were clear and well organized, the Hispanic children did well, but they became inattentive when the teacher was unclear, whereas the Chinese children in the study became even more attentive when the teacher was unclear (Fillmore, 1986).

Communication Styles

In addition to varying learning, the use of language differs from culture to culture, and this may affect communication in the classroom (Fitzgerald, 1995). As part of a well-known study on language use, Heath (1983) investigated the communication patterns of the home and the school in Trackton, an African American working-class community, and Roadville, a white working-class community. She found that the linguistic environment of the classroom was quite different from that of the children's homes. In Trackton, one major difference was in the use of questions. In the traditional classroom, teachers asked "display" questions, questions that require students to show off their academic knowledge (for example, "What color is this crayon?"). Teachers already knew the answers to the questions they asked. Trackton parents, however, asked their children more open-ended questions, with answers unknown to the adults (for example, "What are you going to do with this color?"). Unaccustomed to a test style of questioning, the Trackton children were frustrated by their teachers' questions and did not know how to respond. As a result, they appeared academically incompetent. Differences in the use of questions are particularly significant, since so much of instruction in the traditional classroom is carried on through interrogative dialogue.

Another difference Heath noted was in the use of commands. Compared with middle- and upper-class parents, parents in both Trackton and Roadville gave more direct commands to their children (for example, "Put the book on the shelf."). However, middle-class teachers tended to give indirect, or veiled, commands (for example, "Is this where the book belongs?"). Children from the same background as the teacher understood that they were really being told to put the book on the shelf. But the other children believed the teacher was offering them a real alternative; that is, they could put the book on the shelf or they could put it somewhere else. Misinterpreting the teacher, these children seemed to be disobeying when they didn't put the book on the shelf.

A well-known study by Au and Mason (1983) provides another example of cultural differences in language use. These researchers examined the difficulties some teachers encountered during reading lessons with Polynesian children in Hawaii. A common speech event in the culture of these children is the "talk story" in which two or more individuals jointly narrate a story. Accustomed to collective turn-taking, the children responded poorly when teachers attempted to enforce the one-speaker-at-a-time rule of mainstream classrooms.

Attitude Toward Teacher Authority

Students view the authority of the teacher differently from culture to culture. According to Erickson and Mohatt (1982), Odawa Indian students react more favorably to teachers who avoid exercising direct social control. This reflects the Odawa value that one person should not openly try to control the behavior of another person. Thus, rather than ordering students around or waiting for everyone to do the same thing at the same time, teachers were more effective if they gave orders less directly and allowed students to shift from one activity to another gradually. The opposite may be true for African American students, many of whom expect teachers to act authoritatively. Teachers who are soft-spoken or chummy appear to be weak and ineffectual and not worthy of respect. Whereas white, middle-class children are often taught to obey the teacher simply because she is the teacher, African American children often obey the teacher because she constantly demonstrates the ability to control the class and pushes the students to succeed (Delpit, 1995).

Toward Cultural Continuity in the Classroom

Recognizing that learning styles may differ across cultures, we are still faced with the problem of how to bridge the gap between students' native culture and the culture of the classroom. It is not possible to duplicate every student's home background in the classroom. Nor is it possible, or even desirable, to assimilate every student into the mainstream culture—doing so would deny the importance of cultural diversity. Instead, we might follow a "model of mutual accommodation" (Villegas, 1991). According to this model, both teachers and students adapt their actions to the common goal of academic success with cultural respect. Thus, the Trackton teachers, mentioned previously, adjusted their questioning strategies to correspond to the type of questions Trackton parents asked. These questions drew many more responses from the children. Then, as the children became more engaged in learning, the teachers taught them how to respond to traditional question-answer routines.

Helping students to accommodate their actions to the culture of the classroom means that teachers must make that culture explicit (Delpit, 1995, 1996). The classroom culture is understood and taken for granted by students who share the teacher's cultural background. For students outside that background, however, the classroom culture is often implicit—invisible. Just as traveling in another country is much easier if someone tells you appropriate ways of acting, dressing, and speaking, so too students find it much easier to adapt to the classroom culture if the teacher explains classroom rules and expectations.

Accommodating the classroom to the students' culture, on the other hand, requires that the teacher know something about that culture. There is no one way to teach culturally diverse students—attempting to do so would be inconsistent with the very idea of cultural diversity. Teaching must be adapted to local circumstances. Just as traveling in another country is the best way to learn about another culture, so too teachers should visit their students' homes, attend events in their students' communities, and talk with parents and community leaders. Through these efforts, teachers become able to ground learning in students' personal cultural experiences and guide the activities and experiences that help students to learn in a culturally sensitive classroom (Diamond & Moore, 1995; Ladson-Billings, 1995).

Assessment

Culturally responsive instruction demands culturally responsive assessment. For a number of years, educators and researchers have acknowledged that standardized, norm-referenced tests are culturally biased. (See Chapter 10 for a discussion of purposes and types of assessment.) Culturally biased tests reflect, and thus favor, the dominant culture. Again, as with traditional instruction, students from a white, European, middle-class background tend to perform better on these tests than do students from other ethnic and socioeconomic backgrounds. Results of standardized tests have been used to place poor and minority students in lower-track classes, where instruction typically focuses on decontextualized subskills and bypasses higher-level cognitive skills which, of course, does not lead to improved academic performance (Allington, 1995).

Norm-referenced tests are culturally biased in several ways. First, culturally diverse students are often not represented in norming populations. Students' test scores on norm-referenced tests only have meaning if their background is similar to the background of the student population on which the test was normed. Second, test topics and vocabulary tend to be unfamiliar to students from nonmainstream cultures. Although publishers have attempted to make their tests more objective and authentic, no test can escape being influenced by the values and experiences of its writers and developers. Third, culturally diverse students tend not to be as testwise as mainstream students; that is, they are not as experienced in the characteristics and formats of tests, such as answering multiple-choice questions, nor are they as experienced in the test-taking situation. For example, working within time limits, especially if they must code switch, is difficult. These same criticisms can be applied to commercially produced criterion-referenced tests as well. Even typical end-of-the-unit or end-of-the-chapter teacher-constructed tests are frequently culturally biased.

Because of the bias inherent in formal standardized tests, informal testing that is flexible and ongoing may be more appropriate for culturally diverse students (DeLain, 1995). The primary purpose in assessing all students should be to determine their strengths and weaknesses and to tailor instruction to meet their needs. The following methods provide qualitative information about student achievement that can be used to make instructional decisions.

Culturally Responsive Assessment Techniques

- Performance-based testing. Have students demonstrate their knowledge or mastery of a skill. They might conduct a science experiment, solve a math problem, or draw a picture. You might even use drama as a means of assessing students' understanding.

Continued

- Open-ended responses. Use probing questions rather than multiple-choice questions. Have students write essays. Allow students to respond in their first language if you have access to interpretation.
- Teacher/student interaction. If culturally appropriate, dialogue with students.
- Teacher observation. Simply watching students' reactions to your instruction—a puzzled look, a frown, or a smile—will tell you whether or not you need to adjust instruction.
- Portfolios. Portfolios are collections of students' work over time. They might include essays, reports, daily work, artwork, audio tapes—almost anything that indicates learning. Various stages of a project, such as rough drafts of an essay, should be included and not just final products. Both students and teachers can select items for the portfolio.
- Anecdotal records. Briefly record when individual students accomplish a certain skill or show understanding of a certain concept. Anecdotal records focus on what students can do.

In summary, the following principles should be useful as a guide in implementing a model of mutual accommodation.

Principles for Creating an Inclusive Classroom Culture

1. Be explicit with students about the culture operating in the classroom. Don't assume that students possess the same cultural framework as you.
2. Learn about the cultures of the students in order to expand the classroom culture as a whole.
3. Develop a repertoire of teaching styles so that you can teach students in culturally appropriate ways. For example, use cooperative learning groups for students who learn better through peer interaction.
4. Ask questions of students and listen to their answers. Instead of making assumptions about why students react or behave or answer as they do, ask them "Why?" or say, "Tell me more about that."
5. Provide assessment that is situational—informal, flexible, ongoing practices that help you adjust your instruction to students' needs. Establish a risk-free environment so that students feel at ease in trying new skills, asking questions, or expressing their ideas and opinions.

PRACTICE ACTIVITY 8.4

Read the following anecdote adapted from Garcia (1978). Tell what you would have done if you were the teacher.

Mary Walking Tall, a student from the White Pine reservation, returned to her social studies classroom after lunch. She and her best friend,

Leslie, were busy talking as they took their seats next to each other. The teacher began to prepare the class for the weekly quiz on current events.

"Okay, class, it's time to get started," he announced. "Take out a piece of paper and number from one to ten. I'm only going to read each question once, so listen carefully."

After reading the third question, the teacher noticed that Mary was whispering to Leslie. "No talking during exams, Mary. If you talk to Leslie again, I'll assume you're cheating and throw your paper in the waste-basket."

After reading the fourth question, the teacher saw Mary pass a note to Leslie. "Mary, what's in that note you're passing to Leslie?"

"I'm just giving Leslie the answers to the questions."

"You're what! You're not supposed to cheat."

"I'm not cheating," exclaimed Mary. "Leslie doesn't know the answers so I'm just helping her out."

"I'll bet you are," said the teacher, grabbing Mary's paper and tossing it in the wastebasket.

PRACTICE ACTIVITY 8.5

Reread the teachers' lounge conversation at the beginning of this section. Using your understanding of learning styles, communication styles, attitude toward teacher authority, and assessment, list suggestions for helping the teachers to work with Dwayne, Mai, and Choua.

▼ ▼

A MULTICULTURAL CURRICULUM

Curriculum refers to the topics studied in the classroom and the materials used to present those topics. This last section describes a multicultural curriculum in more detail. It also examines the degree to which current textbooks reflect multiculturalism and discusses the value of multiethnic literature.

A Multicultural Perspective

As mentioned in the first section of the chapter, multiculturalism should be an integral part of the curriculum and not an additive. According to Banks (1993), multiculturalism is not merely adding ethnic minority heroes such as Martin Luther King, Jr., or Cesar Chavez to the curriculum. The "hero" approach does not describe the total experience of the cultural group. Nor is multiculturalism simply studying the customs and behaviors of ethnic groups. Activities such as building teepees and igloos and preparing ethnic foods that are not tied to broader discussions of the cultures they emanate from does not represent a multicultural teaching perspective. Nor is multiculturalism African American studies for African Americans, Native American studies for Native Americans, or Puerto Rican studies for Puerto Ricans. This approach tends to separate groups further.

A multicultural curriculum goes beyond these approaches to examine issues, events, and concepts from the perspective of more than one culture. In 1992 the United States observed the 500th anniversary of the arrival of Christopher Columbus in America. This quincentennial event provides an example of a multicultural perspective. As might be expected, in many classrooms across the country teachers led their students in honoring Columbus for his achievement in discovering the New World. According to the traditional viewpoint, Columbus was a hero because he opened the way for the settling of the continent. In other classrooms, however, teachers led their students to see another side to this event—the side of the Native American. To them, Columbus's arrival meant disease, death, and the destruction of their societies. After reading about the quincentennial event in tradebook selections and newspaper and magazine articles, students took the roles of Europeans and Native Americans and debated the pros and cons of Columbus's voyages.

As much as possible, teachers should incorporate a multicultural perspective into reading and writing activities. Social studies teachers will have many opportunities to help students examine historical events from a variety of viewpoints. For example, the colonial period in American history is usually studied from the viewpoint of the English colonists; but Native Americans, African Americans, Spaniards, and other groups were living in America at the time, and students should also research and write about their experiences. In studying feudalism in Europe, students might read about the feudal system in Japan as well as in Europe. English teachers can have students read the stories, poems, and plays of various cultural groups. They can use literature to discover how diverse groups have interpreted themes such as creation or power. Examples of multicultural reading and writing activities for other subject matter areas include the following.

Examples of Multicultural Reading and Writing Activities in Various Content Areas

- Science—In studying environmental issues, have students research and report on the ecological perspective of Native Americans.

- Civics—Have students find out how many people of color serve in the U.S. Congress, their state legislature, and their local government. They might display their findings in a graph. Discuss reasons for underrepresentation of minorities in governmental bodies and the effect the lack of a minority perspective may have on legislation.

- Health—Have students find alcohol and tobacco advertisements featuring racial minorities and blue-collar workers. Discuss issues related to targeting these products to minorities and working-class people.

- Home economics—Have students research the attitude of various cultures to food and hospitality. They might compile their information in a class chart.

Textbooks and Multiculturalism

Textbooks have a tremendous impact on what is taught in the classroom. In many instances, they determine the structure and content of a subject matter course. Thus, it is important to examine how well current textbooks support a multicultural perspective.

During the past twenty years, textbook publishers have done a better job of incorporating cultural diversity. More attention is being paid to the achievements of ethnic and racial minority groups, and there is more sensitivity toward the stereotyping of these groups. Much still needs to be done, however. Textbooks, by and large, are still predominantly Eurocentric or Americentric; that is, they are written from the perspective of the white, middle-class American of European descent. Inaccuracies regarding other cultures are not uncommon; for example, Chinese and Korean cultures are often treated as one and the same. Little space is given to describing the impact of historical events on various groups, such as the Civil War on African Americans. The examples used often do not reflect the students' experiences—word problems in a math textbook might talk about people traveling around the world in jet planes when problems about taking the subway might be more meaningful. In many instances, cultural diversity in textbooks is only cosmetic—photos and artwork might show people of color, but the text itself does not include these groups. The checklist in Figure 8.3 is designed to help you evaluate subject matter textbooks for their treatment of cultural diversity.

Checklist for Evaluating Textbooks for Use in a Multicultural Classroom

Does the textbook. . .	Yes	No
1. Acknowledge and reflect multiple perspectives where appropriate?		
2. Allocate adequate space for discussing the experiences of all ethnic and racial groups involved in an event (e.g., the slave trade or the detainment of Japanese Americans during World War II)?		
3. Include the achievements of a variety of ethnic groups?		
4. Portray ethnic and racial groups accurately and avoid stereotyping?		
5. Use examples that reflect the experiences of culturally diverse students?		
6. Contain photos and artwork showing people of color?		
7. Lend itself to accommodating ESL students (e.g., including photo essays, graphs, and other pictorial aids)?		
8. Include other resources for further reading in specific areas?		
9. Have a clear glossary of terms for nonnative speakers?		
10. Portray cultural diversity in an interesting and exciting way?		

Figure 8.3
Checklist for Evaluating Textbooks for Use in a Multicultural Classroom

The following list suggests ways you can supplement or correct your text to make it more appropriate for your classroom.

Ways to Supplement Text Information for Multiculturalism

1. Supplement the text with information from other resources such as films, filmstrips, tradebooks, magazines, and newspapers. Newspapers and magazines are excellent sources of updated information in all content areas.

2. Ask parents, members of the local community, and the students themselves to comment on or add to information presented in the text. Give students an opportunity to bring their community to the classroom.

3. Take the topic of study and brainstorm ways of applying it to students' experiences. For example, have students relate the structure of a Shakespearean sonnet to the structure of a rap song or have them find examples of various geometric figures in their everyday environments.

4. Have students use their notebooks as a forum for responding to their reading in a more personal manner. They might draw correlations between the reading and their own lives, state their feelings about the reading, think how a historical event impacted them, and so on.

5. Address stereotyping. Make students aware of the subtle stereotypes contained in the text. This will facilitate an examination of their own values. The class does not need to come to consensus on a particular value, but students do need to learn the consequences of stereotypical information and how it affects our society.

6. Encourage class discussion of what is read. This allows for sharing of multiple perspectives. Always ask students to think about who wrote the text and what that person's perspective might be. Help them see that they should not blindly accept everything they see in print, rather they should engage in critical reading.

7. Have students read about a specific topic in several sources. You might divide the class into cooperative learning groups and assign a different resource to each group. Then have the groups come together and discuss similarities and differences in the information presented. Students should see how information can vary across sources.

8. As you use a particular textbook, keep track of inaccuracies, omissions, or offensive statements. Note students' reactions to the material and whether they think particular groups have been treated fairly. Comments might be written on index cards and kept in a file box in the school library for other teachers' reference. Positive characteristics of the text should also be noted.

Technology and Multiculturalism

Diamond and Moore (1995) point out that the computer can be a powerful motivator for thinking, reading, researching, discussing, listening, and writing about one's own culture and the cultures of others. They suggest that hypermedia technology is particularly helpful for second-language learners because it is multimodal (integrating sound, text, and graphics), allows for the acquisition of information through semantically related networks, and displays information both spatially and visually. This versatility allows for a good match between learner characteristics and characteristics of the learning environment.

Of course, the Internet and the World Wide Web can also be used to enhance students' understanding and interest in other cultures. Through these channels, students have access to information from throughout the world and can communicate with students from other parts of the world. *MayaQuest* (Buettner, 1996; Thurston, 1995) represents an innovative use of the Internet. In February 1995, a team of cyclists and archeologists set out on a three-month expedition to southern Mexico, Belize, Guatemala, and Honduras in an exploration of the mysterious collapse of the Maya civilization in the ninth century. Using laptop computers and sophisticated satellite equipment, the team communicated online two times each week with students in 42,000 schools around the world. As the team cycled over 3,000 miles of treacherous terrain, students studied about their locales and advised them on which direction to go, where to dig for artifacts, and what to make of their discoveries. Thus, students became a part of this historic event as it unfolded.

However, it is important to note that technology in and of itself is not sufficient to contribute to a multicultural classroom. It is valuable only if students are supported as they use it with keyboarding skills, regular feedback, and frequent opportunities for guided learning, if it is integrated into the curriculum, and if all students—regardless of race, proficiency in standard English, and socioeconomic status—can use the computer for higher-order thinking activities rather than basic skills (Griffin & Cole, 1987; Sutton, 1991).

Multicultural Literature

Multicultural literature refers to tradebooks, both fiction and nonfiction, that portray individuals belonging to nonmainstream ethnic, racial, and socioeconomic groups. Reading about their own culture helps students develop positive attitudes and a sense of dignity and self-worth. It is also academically motivating when students see themselves in their reading. Reading about other cultures helps students gain understanding and appreciation for diverse groups and also paves the way for higher-order thinking and viewing events from multiple perspectives. Style (1988) suggests that an inclusive curriculum provides students with a balance of windows—through which they see and understand the experiences of others—and mirrors—in which they see their own reality validated.

English and social studies teachers in particular might use multiethnic literature to build a sense of community in culturally diverse classrooms. The following suggestions are among Diamond and Moore's (1995) guidelines for evaluating multiethnic books.

Guidelines for Evaluating Multiethnic Books

1. Do the characters authentically reflect the distinct cultural experiences, realities, and world view of a specific group?
2. Are the characters portrayed in a realistic, balanced manner?
3. Are specific language characteristics used as a natural part of the story, or are they contrived to reinforce a stereotype?
4. Is the culture treated respectfully or portrayed as inferior?
5. Are themes developed within the story or selection consistent with the values and beliefs, customs and traditions, needs, and conflicts of the specific culture?
6. Are the settings representative of an environment consistent with a historical/contemporary time, place, or situation of the specific culture?

For help in identifying and using multicultural tradebooks, consult the following resources. Keep in mind that second-language learners who are not yet proficient in English may benefit from reading books dealing with appropriate content but written at an elementary or intermediate grade level.

Books

Bishop, Rudine Sims. (1994). *Kaleidoscope: A multicultural booklist for grades K–8.* Urbana, IL: National Council of Teachers of English.

Harris, Violet J. (Ed.). (1992). *Teaching multicultural literature in grades K–8.* Norwood, MA: Christopher-Gordon Publishers.

Lindgren, Merri V. (Ed.). (1991). *The multicolored mirror: Cultural substance in literature for children and young adults.* Fort Atkinson, WI: Highsmith Press.

Minnesota Humanities Commission. (1991). *Braided lives: An anthology of multicultural American writing.* St. Paul: Minnesota Council of Teachers of English.

World Wide Web Sites

http://199.95.184.10/Instructor/hot/multicultural.html

http://www.bnkst.edu./library/multi.html

Journals and Newsletters

Council on Interracial Books for Children. *Bulletin.* New York: Council on Interracial Books for Young Children.

Multicultural Publishers Exchange Newsletter. Madison, WI: Praxis Publishers.

National Council for the Social Studies. *Notable children's trade books in the field of social studies.* In *Social Education* (April issue, annually). Washington, D.C.: National Council for the Social Studies.

CONCLUDING REMARKS

Good teaching is student centered. As the United States becomes even more culturally and linguistically diverse, teachers will need to be cognizant of the variety of values, experiences, and learning styles that students bring to the classroom. This chapter has not presented a single formula or recipe for teaching subject matter content to diverse groups. Instead, it has attempted to increase your sensitivity to the needs and achievements of diverse students so that you can make wise instructional decisions for your situation. This chapter has also encouraged you to establish a multicultural classroom—a classroom that accepts a variety of cultural perspectives and encourages students to express their cultural identity. Teaching in a culturally diverse classroom will require careful preparation, but then good teaching has always required this.

Good teaching also involves the teacher, as well as the students, in learning. A culturally diverse classroom presents exciting opportunities for you to grow in your teaching skills. First, however, you will need to open yourself up to and be receptive of the different cultures in your classroom and allow your students to teach you. Each year your skill will increase and you will find yourself spiraling to higher levels of confidence and competence.

REFLECTIONS
▼▼

1. Interview an ESL teacher. Discuss materials and methods used to instruct second-language speakers. Ask how subject matter teachers can help ESL students learn content as well as improve their language skills.

2. Visit a culturally diverse classroom. Observe whether or not the teacher's instructional style and communication patterns differ from those of the traditional classroom. Discuss your findings with your classmates.

3. Read about Marva Collins and Jaime Escalante, two teachers famous for their ability to motivate culturally diverse students. Write a report describing the characteristics and teaching style of these successful teachers.

▼ Collins, Marva, & Tamarkin, Civia. (1990). *Marva Collins' way: Returning to excellence in education*. New York: Putnam Books.

▼ Collins, Marva. (1992). *Ordinary children, extraordinary teachers*. Charlottesville, VA: Hampton Roads Publishing Company.

▼ Mathews, Jay. (1988). *Escalante: The best teacher in America*. New York: Putnam Books.

4. Research current educational programs or models of instruction that seem to be meeting the needs of culturally diverse students. Share your findings with your classmates.

5. Along with two or three of your classmates, pretend to be the textbook selection committee for your local school district. Using cooperative learning techniques,

evaluate textbooks currently on the market for their treatment of diverse cultures. If possible, serve on an actual textbook selection committee. Such committees can exert pressure on publishers to produce more culturally appropriate texts. (Note: Textbook selection committees should include teachers, administrators, and parents representing various ethnic groups and various areas of expertise.)

6. Design a multicultural reading/writing activity for your subject matter area. Share your activity with your classmates.

7. Read one or more fiction books featuring a minority character or culture. Write a book review for the class to read.

8. Explore your own cultural perspective on topics such as the organization of the family, interaction between adults and children, the role of women in society, the importance of work, attitude toward material possessions, or attitude toward the environment. Discuss your perspective with others in your class.

9. Explore the World Wide Web for current postings related to cultural diversity. Look for projects such as MayaQuest, sites at which teachers have posted multicultural content area lesson ideas, and other resources to help you to expand the culture of your classroom.

10. Begin an e-mail pen-pal program between your class and a similar class in another region of the country or the world. Students can share their understandings of subject matter while simultaneously building a relationship with students from another part of the world.

REFERENCES
▼▼

Alexander, C. F. (1980). African American English dialect and the classroom teacher. *The Reading Teacher*, 33, 571–577. A discussion of African American English and appropriate responses for classroom teachers.

Allen, V. G. (1991). Teaching bilingual and ESL children. In J. Flood et al. (Eds.), *Handbook of research on teaching the English language arts* (pp. 356–364). New York: Macmillan. A thorough review of research on teaching second-language learners.

Allington, R. L. (1995). Literacy lessons in the elementary schools: Yesterday, today, and tomorrow. In R. L. Allington & S. A. Walmsley (Eds.), *No quick fix: Rethinking literacy programs in America's elementary schools* (pp. 1–15). New York: Teachers College Press. An argument against traditional approaches to teaching students who experience difficulty with literacy learning.

Au, K. H., & Mason, J. M. (1983). Cultural congruence in classroom participation structures: Achieving a balance of rights. *Discourse Processes*, 6, 145–167. Discusses the nature of cultural

incongruity and ways to work toward cultural congruence in the classroom.

Banks, J. A. (1977). *Multiethnic education: Practices and promises*. Bloomington, IN: Phi Delta Kappa Educational Foundation. A concise report outlining the goals of multiethnic education and characteristics of the multiethnic school.

———.(1993). Multicultural education: Characteristics and goals. In J. A. Banks & C. A. McGee Banks (Eds.), *Multicultural education: Issues and perspectives* (2nd ed.) (pp. 3–28). Needham Heights, MA: Allyn and Bacon. A description of the goals and characteristics of multicultural education.

———.(1995). Multicultural education: Historical development, dimensions, and practice. In J. A. Banks & C. A. McGee Banks (Eds.), *Handbook of research on multicultural education*. New York: Macmillan. Comprehensive summary of research related to the development of multicultural education in this country.

Bean, T. W. (1978). Decoding strategies of Hawaiian Islands dialect speakers in grades 4,

5, 6. *Reading World*, 17 (4), 295–305. A presentation of decoding strategies used by a group of
Hawaiian children.

Bernhardt, E. B., & Kamil, M. L. (1998). Literacy
instruction for non-native speakers of English.
In M. F. Graves, C. Juel., & B. B. Graves, *Teaching
reading in the 21st century*. Needham Heights, MA:
Allyn & Bacon.

Buettner, D. (1996). *MayaQuest*. White Bear Lake,
MN: Nash/Onion Press. Chronicles the
MayaQuest journey through brilliant photos
and artful prose.

Cahape, P. (1993). *Blueprints for Indian education:
Research and development needs for the 1990s*.
Charleston, WV: ERIC Clearinghouse on Rural
Education and Small Schools (ERIC Document
Reproduction Service ED 357 908). A report
highlighting directions for much-needed
research on the education of Native American
children.

Cummins, J. (1980). The cross-lingual dimensions
of language proficiency: Implications for bilingual education and the optimal age issue.
TESOL *Quarterly*, 14 , 175–187. Differentiates
between the type of language proficiency
needed for academic communication and that
needed for social communication.

Cummins, J. (1994). The acquisition of English as a
second language. In K. Spangenberg-Urbschat
and R. Pritchard (Eds.), *Kids come in all languages:
Reading instruction for ESL students*. Newark, DE:
International Reading Association. Overview of
various aspects of second-language development written by a prominent figure in the field.

DeLain, M. T. (1995). Equity and performance-
based assessment: An insider's view. *The Reading
Teacher*, 48 (5), 440–442. Brief discussion of the
strengths and limitations of performance-based
assessment as it relates to teaching diverse
students.

DeLain, M. T., Pearson, P. D., & Anderson, R. C.
(1985). Reading comprehension and creativity
in African American language use: You stand to
gain by playing the sounding game! *American
Educational Research Journal*, 22, 155–173. This
study found that African American students'
abilities to comprehend figurative language in
text was influenced by their sounding skill as
well as their general verbal ability.

Delpit, L. D. (1995). *Other people's children: Cultural
conflict in the classroom*. New York: New Press. Well-
written book providing insight into the nature of
and solutions for this problem.

———. (1996, December). *Other people's children*. Paper
presented at the meeting of the National
Reading Conference, New Orleans, LA.
Thoughtful discussion of the characteristics of
successful teachers of diverse students.

Diamond, B. J., & Moore, M. A. (1995). *Multicultural
literacy: Mirroring the reality of the classroom*. New
York: Longman. Powerful book with concrete
ideas for integrating literacy development with
multiculturalism.

Educational Research Service (1995). Demographic
factors in American education. Arlington, VA:
Author. Presents demographic characteristics of
education in this country.

Erickson, F., & Mohatt, G. (1982). Cultural organization of participation structures in two classrooms of Indian students. In G. B. Spindler
(Ed.), *Doing the ethnography of schooling: Educational
anthropology in action*. New York: Holt, Rinehart &
Winston. Compares the academic behavior of
Native American students in two different classroom settings and identifies classroom characteristics that lead to the greatest student participation in academic events.

Fillmore, L. W. (1986). Research currents: Equity or
excellence. *Language Arts*, 63, 474–481. Points to
the need for teachers to promote higher-level
learning, rather than basic skills learning,
among students who are not yet proficient in
English.

Fitzgerald, J. (1995). English-as-a-second-language
reading instruction in the United States: A
research review. *Journal of Reading Behavior*, 27,
115–152. A thorough review of research on this
topic.

Flores, B., Cousin, P., & Diaz, E. (1991).
Transforming deficit myths about learning, language, and culture. *Language Arts*, 68 , 369–379.
Dispels common misconceptions about the
relationship between cultural and linguistic
characteristics and student learning.

Garcia, E. E. (1992). *The education of linguistically and
culturally diverse students: Effective instructional practices*. Santa Cruz, CA: National Center for
Research on Cultural Diversity and Second

Language Learning. This handbook provides information about instructional methods that have been effective with diverse learners.

Garcia, E. E., & Padilla, R. V. (Eds.). (1985). *Advances in bilingual education research*. Tucson: University of Arizona Press. A compilation of readings addressing critical issues of language and culture and their implications for bilingual education.

Garcia, R. L. (1978). *Fostering a pluralistic society through multi-ethnic education*. Bloomington, IN: Phi Delta Kappa Educational Foundation. Focuses on the role of education in the creation of a truly pluralistic society.

Goodman, K. S. (1969a). Analysis of oral reading miscues: Applied psycholinguistics. *Reading Research Quarterly*, 5 , 9–30. Describes the process of miscue analysis.

Goodman, K. S. (1969b). Dialect barriers to reading comprehension. In J. C. Baratz & R. W. Shuy (Eds.), *Teaching African American children to read* (pp. 14–28). Washington, DC: Center for Applied Linguistics. Presents an early hypothesis on the relationship between spoken dialect and reading comprehension.

Goodman, K. S., & Buck, C. (1973). Dialect barriers to reading comprehension revisited. *The Reading Teacher*, 27 (1), 6–12. Goodman revises his initial hypothesis regarding dialect and reading comprehension, asserting that dialect differences have a minimal impact on reading comprehension.

Griffin, P., & Cole, M. (1987). New technologies, basic skills, and the underside of education: What's to be done? In J. A. Langer (Ed.), *Language, literacy, and culture: Issues of society and schooling* (pp. 199–231). Norwood, NJ: Ablex. Suggests ways to use computers so that *all* students are engaged in higher-order thinking.

Heath, S. B. (1983). *Ways with words: Language, life, and work in communities and classrooms*. London: Cambridge. Describes the differences between discourse patterns in homes and schools in two working-class American communities.

Hudelson, S. (1984). Kan yu ret an rayt en Ingles: Children become literate in English as a second language. TESOL *Quarterly*, 18 , 221–238. Points to the relationship among reading, writing, listening, and speaking in the development of English speaking and reading proficiency.

Krashen, S. (1981). *Second language acquisition and second language learning*. Oxford: Pergamon. An often-cited reference on the difference between language learning and language acquisition.

Ladson-Billings, G. (1995). Toward a theory of culturally relevant pedagogy. *American Educational Research Journal*, 32, 465–491. Presents the results of a study of successful teachers of African American students.

Lewis, A. C. (1991). Washington news. *Education Digest*, 56, 51–53. Provides information about the state of education at this time.

Means, B., & Knapp, M. S. (1991). Cognitive approaches to teaching advanced skills to educationally disadvantaged students. *Phi Delta Kappan*, 73, 282–289. Presents ways to promote higher-order thinking among students who may be perceived as "at risk."

Moll, L. C., & Diaz, S. (1987). Changes as the goal of educational research. *Anthropology and Education Quarterly*, 18, 300–311. Discusses ways to incorporate students' cultural understandings into instruction.

National Education Goals Panel. (1995). *National education goals report: Building a nation of learners*. Washington, DC: Author. Reports the status of the nation's progress toward Goals 2000.

Nieto, S. (1996). *Affirming diversity: The sociopolitical context of multicultural education* (2nd ed.). New York: Longman. A thoughtful, readable book with in-depth discussions of a conceptual framework for multicultural education and implications of diversity for teaching and learning.

Peregoy, S. F., & Boyle, O. F. (1993). *Reading, writing, and learning in ESL: A resource book for K–8 teachers*. New York: Longman. A book filled with concrete teaching ideas for enhancing the literacy development of second-language learners.

Philips, S. (1983). *The invisible culture: Communication in classroom and community on the Warm Springs Indian Reservation*. New York: Longman. An in-depth study of the communication patterns of these Native American students at home and in school.

Reyes, M., & Molner, L. (1991). Instructional strategies for second-language learners in the content areas. *Journal of Reading*, 35 , 96–103. Describes several ways to teach subject matter to second-language learners.

Reynolds, R. E., Taylor, M. A., Steffenson, M. S., Shirey, L. L., & Anderson, R. C. (1982). Cultural schemata and reading comprehension. *Reading Research Quarterly*, 17, 353–366. Highlights the role of culturally relevant prior knowledge and schemata in the comprehension of text.

Richard-Amato, P. A., & Snow, M. A. (1992). *The multicultural classroom: Readings for content-area teachers.* New York: Longman. This com prehensive resource provides both general and subject-specific instructional strategies for teachers.

Rigg, P. S. (1974). A psycholinguistic analysis of the oral reading miscues generated by speakers of a rural African American dialect compared to the miscues of speakers of an urban African American dialect. Unpublished doctoral dissertation, Wayne State University. *Dissertation Abstracts International*, 35 (1975), 7624A. Reports that no significant difference was found between African American English dialect miscues and reading comprehension for urban and rural students.

Rigg, P. S. (1981). Beginning to read in English the LEA way. In C. W. Twyford, W. Diehl, & K. Feathers (Eds.), *Reading English as a second language: Moving from theory.* Bloomington, IN: Indiana University. Discusses using the language experience activity approach with second-language learners.

Russell, S. (1995). Sheltered content instruction for second language learners. *Reading Today*, 13 (2), 29–31. Suggests instructional techniques that increase understanding of subject matter while promoting language development.

Schlosser, L. K. (1992). Teacher distance and student disengagement: School lives on the margin. *Journal of Teacher Education*, 43 , 128–140. Reports on the learning experiences of students likely to drop out of high school.

Shade, B. J. (1994). Understanding the African American learner. In E. R. Hollins, J. E. King, & W. C Hayman (Eds.), *Teaching diverse populations: Formulating a knowledge base.* Albany, NY: SUNY Press. Focuses on the classroom climate, teacher-student interaction patterns, and learning styles related to African American students.

Sims, R. (1972). A psycholinguistic description of miscues generated by selected young readers during the oral reading of text material in African American dialect and standard English. Unpublished doctoral dissertation, Wayne State University. *Dissertation Abstracts International*, 33 (1972), 2089A. This study found that speakers of African American English made the same types of miscues whether reading text written in African American English or text written in standard English.

Sleeter, C. E. (1992). Restructuring schools for multicultural education. *Journal of Teacher Education*, 43, 141–148. A description of the types of changes needed to create schools that are truly multicultural.

Smitherman, G. (1994). *African American talk: Words and phrases from the hood to the Amen corner.* Boston: Houghton Mifflin. A dictionary of African American English accompanied by a description of its linguistic characteristics.

Style, E. (1988). *Listening for all school voices: Gender balancing the school curriculum.* Summit, NJ: Oak Knoll. Provides insight into ways of making school curricula more inclusive.

Sutton, R. E. (1991). Equity and computers in the schools: A decade of research. *Review of Educational Research*, 61(4), 475–503. A summary of the differential educational uses of computers based on race/ethnicity, gender, and social class.

Thurston, B. (1995, February 1). Maya by modem: On-line explorers dictate the archaeological journey. *USA Today*, p. 5D. Brief description of MayaQuest.

Tinajero, J. V. (1994). Are we communicating? Effective instruction for students who are acquiring English as a second language. *The Reading Teacher*, 48, 260–264. Suggests ways to maximize instructional opportunities for second-language learners.

Urzua, C. (1987). "You stopped too soon": Second language children composing and revising. TESOL *Quarterly*, 21, 279–304. A study of second-language learners engaged in process writing.

U.S. Bureau of the Census. (1995). *Statistical abstract of the United States: 1995.* Washington, DC: Author. A comprehensive report of the nation's demographic features.

U.S. Department of Education (1995). *The condition of education: 1995.* Washington, DC: Author. A report of the characteristics of educational programs in this country.

Villegas, A. M. (1991). *Culturally responsive pedagogy for the 1990s and beyond*. Princeton, NJ: Educational Testing Service. A discussion of what it means to be culturally responsive in your teaching with guidelines for practice.

Walker, C., & Tedick, D. (1996). *Strategies for working with non-native English speaking students*. Unpublished paper. University of Minnesota. A brief list of the characteristics of effective instruction for second-language learners.

Walmsley, S. A., & Allington, R. L. (1995). Redefining and reforming instructional support programs for at-risk students. In R. L. Allington and S. A. Walmsley (Eds.), *No quick fix: Rethinking literacy programs in America's elementary schools*. New York: Teachers College Press. Suggests ways to better meet the needs of students experiencing difficulty in literacy.

Watts, S. M. (June 24, 1992). Personal communication.

Wolfram, W. (1991). *Dialects and American English*. Englewood Cliffs, NJ: Prentice-Hall.

C H A P T E R

9

Technology and Literacy

CHAPTER OVERVIEW

This chapter will focus on the integration of technology into your classroom instruction. Our emphasis will be on the use of several elements of the Internet. This chapter is divided into four major sections. In the first section we discuss the challenges of learning from hypertext and strategies to facilitate learning from hypertext. The second section centers on the issue of evaluating content on the Internet and presents guidelines for selecting this content for classroom use. The third section of the chapter discusses how the Internet can be used to promote learning through the use of e-mail and ways for teachers to locate information on the Internet. Activities discussed throughout this book can be used to assist students' learning on the Internet.

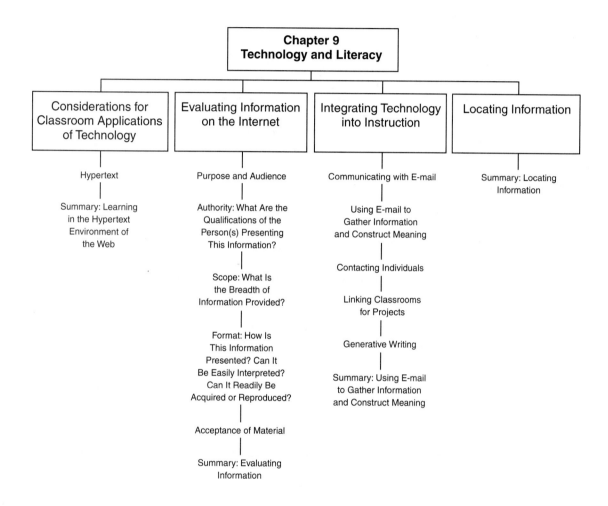

Chapter 9
Technology and Literacy

Considerations for Classroom Applications of Technology

Hypertext

Summary: Learning in the Hypertext Environment of the Web

Evaluating Information on the Internet

Purpose and Audience

Authority: What Are the Qualifications of the Person(s) Presenting This Information?

Scope: What Is the Breadth of Information Provided?

Format: How Is This Information Presented? Can It Be Easily Interpreted? Can It Readily Be Acquired or Reproduced?

Acceptance of Material

Summary: Evaluating Information

Integrating Technology into Instruction

Communicating with E-mail

Using E-mail to Gather Information and Construct Meaning

Contacting Individuals

Linking Classrooms for Projects

Generative Writing

Summary: Using E-mail to Gather Information and Construct Meaning

Locating Information

Summary: Locating Information

C onsider the following scenario.

In a small town located on the sparsely populated sandhill area of western Nebraska, a group of middle school students have just entered their classroom to begin a new day at school. Illuminating the back of the room are a half dozen computer screens, a printer, a scanner, and a small video and digital camera all connected to a network allowing students to communicate with other classrooms in the school as well as on the Internet. Already a number of students are busily huddled around a computer displaying files of material downloaded automatically overnight. One of these files contains photos taken the previous day in China displaying the art work of a group of ninth-grade students in Beijing. Another contains the morning edition of the *New York Times* and *The Wall Street Journal* as well as a half dozen newspapers from around the world. And yet another file displays results of a database search conducted to locate sources of information on the outbreak of mysterious viruses around the world. Soon a group of students gathers around another computer with a very small camera attached to it. Within a few minutes the students are conducting a video conference with students in Georgia and Brazil and a group of scientists at the South Pole to discuss their science project involving the movement of pollutants in the atmosphere.

No doubt just a few years ago this scenario would have been viewed as beyond the realm of possibility. Today, educational applications of technology such as these are becoming commonplace as a result of opportunities brought about by the availability of the Internet, CD-ROM, fiber optics, cable modems, powerful desktop computers, and thousands of powerful software programs. The availability of this interactive technology presents the potential for rather dramatic changes in the form of classroom instruction. Students can now actively explore ideas and issues through a medium that provides diverse content, instant access, and a global perspective. At the same time, technology allows students to engage in meaningful problem-solving tasks using a cost-effective tool for obtaining information (Means & Olson, 1994). With this emphasis comes the recognition that technology should no longer be viewed as a subject of study by itself, a position reflected in a Department of Education position paper on technology and educational reform:

> At the high school level it is still the case that technology is most often available in classes designed to teach computer programming or word processing (Becker, 1994). Our concept of authentic uses of technology does not deny the importance of obtaining facility with computer software or other technologies, but places the emphasis on the use of technology within the context of accomplishing authentic tasks. (National Academy of Sciences, 1995, p. 2)

This chapter focuses on the integration of technology into your classroom instruction. Our emphasis will be on the use of several elements of the Internet. We assume that you have a basic knowledge of the World Wide Web (the Web), e-mail, and browser programs such as Netscape (Netscape Corporation) or Microsoft Explorer (Microsoft Corporation). Our focus will be primarily on the use of the Web and several other components of the Internet. Please note that because the content of the Internet changes so rapidly, and because it is our desire to provide you with current information, addresses to specific web sites and other related information can be found on a Web site we have created specifically for this chapter. The address for this site is http://www.uwm.edu/~randall. We suggest that you connect to this site, then print its contents. As you read the chapter you will periodically see the following: (*). This symbol means that up-to-date information on this source can be found on our Web site. The site's content will be updated on a regular basis to ensure that you obtain timely information.

CONSIDERATIONS FOR CLASSROOM APPLICATIONS OF TECHNOLOGY

In this section we discuss two general topics. First, we discuss the role of hypertext in reading and learning and some challenges it presents to educators. Second, we examine the issue of evaluating the quality and accuracy of information on the Internet and present specific guidelines for selecting materials for classroom use. We begin with a discussion of hypertext—what it is, how it impacts learning, and strategies to assist students learning with hypertext.

Hypertext

Hypertext is a computer application that acts as a navigational tool, linking and organizing information and presenting the user the opportunity to imagine and create new organizations and patterns that reflect the user's knowledge (Callister, 1996). While the initial applications of hypertext were limited to written text, the term has been expanded to include computer applications involving text, graphics, video, and audio information. Hypertext is nonlinear, has no predefined sequences in its order of presentation, and allows the user to organize information that is relevant to the user's objectives (Rouet & Levonen, 1996). Because it is nonlinear, students generate novel pathways through the content of cyberspace according to the mental association in the student's mind (Nyce & Kahn, 1991). Reading in a hypertext environment is not a page-by-page, line-by-line approach, but one in which the user connects information in an intuitive, associative manner. Often this is characterized by the reader switching from one text or display to another based on individual intuition and association (Heim, 1993).

As displayed in Figure 9.1, the hypertext environment of the Web allows the user to click the mouse on text, graphics, or special icons to jump or link to other sources of information. In this case, the main menu for the Library of Congress presents the user with links in the form of text and graphics. The user is also provided navigational tools in the Web browser (in this case Netscape 3.1). Once screens have been displayed, the user can return to the previously displayed screen by using the Back button on the browser. Another navigational option is displayed in Figure 9.2. This option allows the user to select from a list of previously viewed screens. By clicking on the name listed in the menu the browser then redisplays the selected item.

While the numerous navigational options provided by hypertext are considered essential for reaching the goals of advanced knowledge acquisition (Spiro, Feltovitch, Jacobson, & Coulson, 1991), they also present the user with several barriers. Among

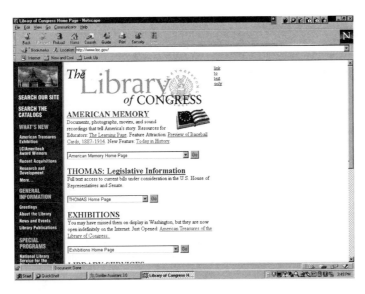

Figure 9.1
Example of a Hypertext Screen

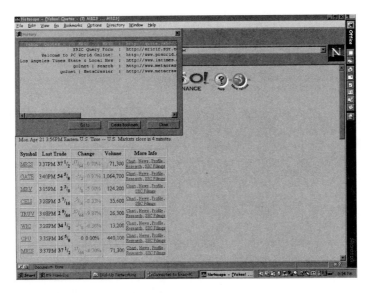

Figure 9.2
Example of Using the History Option on a Web Browser

the problems experienced by learners when using hypertext are the following cited by Gray (1990):

1. Difficulty in remembering what had or had not been viewed or read.
2. Inability to effectively navigate when organizational clues are absent.

3. Inability to find the needed information.

4. Inability to effectively make use of search options when available.

Reducing these obstacles appears to be a matter of generating structure for the hypertext medium (Rouet & Levonen, 1996). Providing students with a hierarchical index displaying the structure of the hypertext content (Dee-Lucas & Larkin, 1992; Simpson & McKnight, 1990) and providing links to hierarchical content (Mohageg, 1992) improve students' navigational skills. The use of concept maps, for example, increases students' ability to generate a meaningful representation of the text and their use of effective study strategies (Dee-Lucas, 1996).

While descriptions of hierarchical structures facilitate navigational efforts, making sense of the information located requires a clearly defined purpose and strategies for sorting through potentially large amounts of information. As students engage in hypertext, they must be mentally active and purposeful. Lacking that level of mental attention and purpose, students will readily become lost and frustrated in their attempts to navigate through various sorts of information. It would seem apparent in recognizing these challenges that students will need continued assistance and support with learning activities that involve the use of hypertext. Remember that the Web and its hypertext environment are still in their early stages of development and even seasoned users experience certain barriers to learning. Here, for example, are some comments obtained from three teachers who had been using the Web for nearly a year. Their comments focus on the obstacles they encountered when learning involved use of the hypertext environment of the Web.

Jan: I am amazed at the potential to move so quickly between different sites. As a result, I sometimes find that I have trouble keeping track of where I am. This is a significant problem when a site contains numerous links to content outside of the site. Sometimes I will be reading, follow a link, read a small portion of text, and come upon another link. Eventually I have no idea where I am, or where I have been. I finally learned a strategy that seemed to help. I would either finish looking at a site before I followed a link, or I would write down the address of the site and build a map showing where I had been. I hope they will soon be able to build a visual map of where we are, where we have been, and where we are going.

Armando: There is so much out there. So much to look at. My problem is keeping track of where I have been. Often I will be reading something, follow a link or two, then realize I need some information that I found at the beginning of my work. If I have access to my own computer I can usually examine the history of my session and then go back to a site. But when I am using the computers at school it is a problem because the history of sites on the browser contains other peoples' sessions. I am starting to paste the URLs (a site's address) into a word processing file along with notes on that site so I have a record of where I can find certain types of information.

Continued

> **Pauline:** I find that I become distracted by the numerous advertisements that I find on the search engines. I will be examining a number of sites from a search, then I see an advertisement for a product or a piece of software that I think might be useful in my classroom. I click on that link and get caught in all this information from a company. Sometimes I never find the free stuff they were advertising. On other occasions I find a link on that advertiser that leads me to another. This can continue for a very long time. Some of the products are really interesting to look at, though.

Comments such as these are typical and reflect some of challenges faced by individuals of all ages who are inexperienced users of hypertext. However, with the appropriate assistance and guidance, students can become more proficient in their ability to navigate and learn in a hypertext environment (Rouet & Levonen, 1996). Here are some suggestions to promote more effective learning from hypertext.

1. **Establish clearly defined goals and identify what is needed to reach these goals.** As we discussed in Chapter 3, establishing a goal increases the likelihood that learning will be purposeful and selective. This is particularly important in a hypertext environment where students can be directed in countless directions from various links and menu options. Whether goals are provided by the teacher or generated by the student, they serve an important role in assisting students navigating through hypertext. When it becomes necessary for students to navigate through several sites or follow multiple links, it may be useful to present goals that are site specific. This will ensure that students acquire the necessary information before they proceed to additional content.

2. **Provide students with navigational maps to establish a "route" for learning and exploration.** Providing students the addresses of Web sites and the order in which they should be viewed will save time, increase the students' ability to focus their attention to relevant information, and will reduce the likelihood that students become lost. There are several possible ways to address this issue and both require you to select sites prior to students engaging in the learning activity. One is to create a list of bookmarks on the Web browser that automatically takes students to the appropriate sites. Another option is to provide a diagram or flowchart on paper or the chalkboard listing the addresses of sites and their viewing order.

3. **Provide conceptual clues.** Recognizing relationships (e.g., cause-effect, problem-solution, time-order) can be a difficult task when dealing with hypertext. Students benefit from clues or prompts that draw their attention to these relationships. These clues may take the form of a flow chart showing logical relationships or may be simple diagrams whereby students insert information according to the type of relationship presented. Examples of the use of conceptual clues in a flowchart and a diagram are shown in Figure 9.3.

4. **Provide a mechanism for note taking and reflection as students navigate.** The hypertext environment of the Web poses a different type of challenge for students who desire to take notes, retain certain bits of information, or add information to that which exists on the screen. Using a textbook, students can highlight,

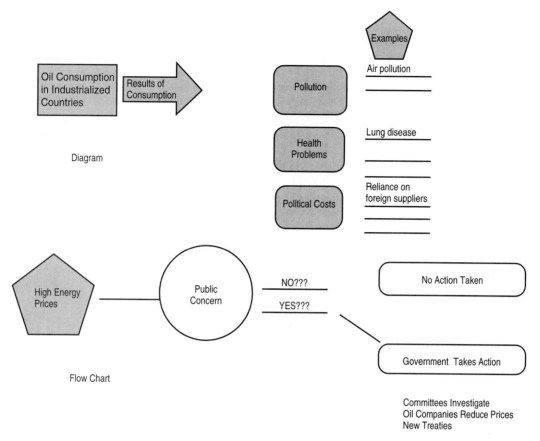

Figure 9.3
Use a Flow Chart to Signal Conceptual Clues

underline, write margin notes, or mark pages or entire sections of a chapter. Unfortunately, unless the student can print all screen images, the same note-taking and study behaviors cannot readily be applied to the Web. There are, however, some rather powerful note-taking techniques that are possible.

One is the "copy-paste" process. This is easy to learn, involves little effort, and results in a product that is permanent and easily reproduced. This process allows the user to "click and drag" with the mouse to highlight text displayed on the screen. Once the text is highlighted, the Edit menu on the Web browser is displayed and the Copy option is selected. The user (while still connected to the Internet) switches to a word processing program. The Edit menu on the word processor is selected, the Paste option is selected, and the text is automatically inserted into a word processing document. The user can then generate anecdotal comments by the inserted text, highlight important information, or generate a written summary of important points.

A second note-taking technique involves the use of a note-taking chart that is completed as the student is interacting with information on the Web. The format of this chart is shown in Figure 9.4.

Purpose   To examine the effect of the welfare reform on a national basis.

Possible Sites   U.S. Senate and U.S. House of Representatives, Department of Health and Human Services, Library of Congress, Department of Housing and Urban Development

Information Sought, Sites Used, and URLs

1. What are the challenges to welfare reform?
(http://www.handsnet.org/handsnet2/welfare.reform/Articles/art.824756291.html)
Developing preimplementation plans, phase-in strategies, and computer systems capable of tracking the time limits:

- Implementing eligibility changes, and tracking JOBS participation is demanding.
- Assuring recipient and worker understanding of the system is difficult.
- Revamping JOBS programs to maximize the number of recipients who find work before exhausting their time limits presents a huge challenge.

2. What is the President's position on welfare reform?
(http://www.os.dhhs.gov;80/cgibin/waisgate?WAISdocID=7997927728+1+0+0&WAISaction=retrieve)
Incentives and resources to reward states for moving people from welfare to work, not cutting them off:

- Work requirements for recipients and the child care people need to go to work and stay off welfare;
- Protections for states in the event of population growth, disaster, or economic downturn;
- Requirements and incentives for states to maintain their stake in welfare reform; and
- The toughest possible child support enforcement.

3. What positions do governors have on the issue of welfare reform?
(http://www.handsnet.org/handsnet2/welfare.reform/Articles/art.824961643.html)
The NGA proposal repeals the federal guarantee for Aid to Families with Dependent Children (AFDC) benefits; allows states the option to block grant child welfare programs; cuts food stamp funding for non-immigrant programs; maintains the federal guarantee for children in the school lunch program but block grants the administrative costs; adopts the Senate's Supplemental Security Income (SSI) provisions; and accepts a state option for family cap.

Figure 9.4
Note-Taking Chart for Navigating the World Wide Web

Summary: Learning in the Hypertext Environment of the Web

Technology has and will continue to have a profound influence on curriculum, instruction, and policies in our schools. For those teachers who have begun to use the Web, the potential this technology offers our schools is readily apparent. The degree to which this technology has a long-lasting effect on the nature of instruction, however, will depend in part on our ability to modify the way we teach and what we view as the best way for students to learn. For students, the hypertext environment provides tremendous opportunities. But it also presents some challenges for those beginning to use the Web or other hypertext tools such as CDs. Many of these challenges, however, can be met by acknowledging and addressing the issues we have raised in this section. Assisting students in these efforts will allow students to acquire strategies for dealing with the demands facing citizens and workers in an ever-growing information society.

PRACTICE ACTIVITY 9.1

Select any four sites on the Web. Examine each site, filling in the information in the frame that follows. Once you have visited each site and completed the entire frame, answer the questions that appear below.

	Size and Length of Text	Number of Links	Use of Graphics	Ease of Use
Site One http://_____				
Site Two http://_____				
Site Three http://_____				
Site Four				

1. Considering the factors you noted in the frame, what makes a site attractive or easy to use?
2. Now that you have explored these four sites, how does hypertext make acquiring information more active than it would otherwise be in a textbook?

▼▼

EVALUATING INFORMATION ON THE INTERNET

The Internet offers a rich multimedia environment for exchanging and obtaining information in the form of graphics, text, sound, and video. Contrasted with the content of a textbook, the content of the Internet is dynamic, extensive, and accessible.

These characteristics present unique challenges to the teacher. The first characteristic of information on the Internet is its dynamic nature. New sites are added daily, information on existing sites can change within minutes, and some types of information (such as video and audio) are real-time and thus cannot be retrieved at a later date. To accommodate this dynamic medium, the teacher must be capable of adjusting to an evolving source of information. A second characteristic of information on the Internet is its extensive nature. On any given topic, the problem is not the inability to find information, but how to select from the multitude of sources available on that topic. Teachers must not only consider the complexity and length of a given source, but also if the source is credible and suitable for the learning objectives. The third characteristic is that of accessibility. This includes the ease of obtaining information, the speed at which it is obtained, and the cost of access. Using powerful search engines or agents, you can obtain hundreds of sources of information on a given topic within seconds at no cost. At the same time, this ease of access can be daunting as you attempt to selectively locate appropriate sources. The dynamic, accessible, and extensive characteristics of the Internet provide an unparalleled source for learning and discovery. Yet this dynamic medium also presents some major challenges for the selection of materials for classroom use. Thus it becomes important for teachers and students to make judgments as to the quality and appropriateness of materials available on the Internet. In what follows we present a number of considerations for selecting and evaluating information on the Internet.

Due to the ease of obtaining and placing information on the Internet, it has been labeled as a great democratizer. As we have mentioned, students and teachers have immediate access to a wealth of information on any given topic. Yet the diversity of sources also presents the dilemma of determining which source may contain the most up-to-date, accurate, and appropriate information for your learning objectives. To us, the greatest challenge for teachers is determining the merit of the information contained on a given site. Unlike textbooks, which generally undergo a rather extensive process of review and editing, there is no commonly accepted process for reviewing materials on the Internet. Anyone with an account with a service provider and a few hours of instruction on the use of a Web authoring program can create a site on the Internet. As a result of this ease of constructing a site, information from credible and noncredible sources can often have the same professional appearance. In recognition of these issues, we present the following guidelines adapted from Ryder and Hughes (1997) on evaluating information on the Internet.

Guidelines for Evaluation of Information

Purpose and Audience — What is the intent of this information? Why is it being communicated?

Authority — What is the level of expertise or experience of the individual(s) or group(s) who generated this information?

Scope — What is the breadth, detail, of the information provided?

Continued

> **Format** — How is this information presented? Can it be easily interpreted? Can it readily be acquired or reproduced?
>
> **Acceptance of Material** — What is the opinion that others have of this material? To what extent has this material gained widespread acceptance?

A more complete description of these factors and their importance for classroom instruction follows.

Purpose and Audience

Well-designed sites make their purpose and their intended audience obvious to the user. Lacking a thorough description, you can devote considerable time exploring a site only to find that it is not appropriate. Similar to the information contained in the introduction of a textbook, information on the Internet should contain a description of its purpose, its design, and its audience. Unfortunately many Internet sites lack this sort of information. As an alternative, you may want to consider some of the sites that have descriptive links to educational materials (*) or search engines that provide a short description of targeted sites' content (*). Finally, consider placing a posting on an educational newsgroup indicating the type of material you are seeking, the purpose of using the material, and the grade level and subject matter for which the material is intended. A list of educational newsgroups can be found on our home page (*).

Authority: What Are the Qualifications of the Person(s) Presenting this Information?

Most classroom texts and instructional materials are written by individuals who possess considerable knowledge or expertise in their field. This helps to ensure the accuracy and timeliness of the material. This expertise, combined with the assistance of an editorial staff and a team of reviewers who are experts themselves in the field, results in an authoritative product. The content of the Internet, on the other hand, does not necessarily undergo this same process, so it is crucial to gain a sense of the qualifications of the individual(s) who wrote or created the information. For example, let's compare two examples of information on the treatment of cancer obtained from the Internet to determine the role of authority when assessing information.

Comprehensive Therapy for Cancer via Herbal Medicine

(Translation from *People's Daily*, overseas edition)

By Comprehensive Therapy for Cancer via Herbal Medicine, it is meant to use the cancer treatment of cleansing heat and clearing poison within the body, smoothing the qi and blood, so that the balance of the patient's bodily mechanism is restored, the resistance against the proliferation of cancer cells improved, and the cancer part in the body controlled or cured . . . . . The aim at improving the capacity of the patient's immune system is not only the distinctive difference between this therapy and that of operation of modern medicine, and that of traditional herbal therapy of "combating poison with poison," but also the key to its high efficacy.

http://www.generation.net/~cathay/infoherb.html#chronicleukemia

CancerNet from the National Cancer Institute

Information from PDQ for Patients: Myeloproliferative disorders
—How myeloproliferative disorders are treated—
There are treatments for all patients with myeloproliferative disorders. Usually the diseases cannot be cured, but the symptoms can be controlled and the number of blood cells can be reduced with treatment. Sometimes there are few symptoms and no treatment is needed.
Chemotherapy uses drugs to kill extra blood cells in the body. Chemotherapy may be taken by pill, or it may be put into the body by a needle in the vein or muscle. Chemotherapy is called a systemic treatment because the drug enters the bloodstream, travels through the body, and can kill cells throughout the body.

http://cancer.med.upenn.edu/pdq/201983.html

In the first example dealing with the use of herbs to treat cancer, there is no information as to the source of the information, the author of the article, or data to indicate the degree of success with herbal treatment. In the second example, taken from the National Cancer Institute, the individual providing the information is identified, the source of the information is identified, and in the article we find information on the success rates of chemotherapy and radiation treatment for specific types of cancers. Students need to be able to distinguish between sources such as these in order to determine the authority of the text.

Scope: What Is the Breadth of Information Provided?

The breadth of the information refers to how extensive the content is for a given topic or theme. Taking a few moments to examine the degree of coverage in a textbook by examining the textbook's table of contents and index is a simple task. Determining the degree of coverage of information on the Internet is more difficult because size is normally described in terms of the size of the file (in bytes). Here, for example, are two sources listed from a search on socialism using the Lycos (*) search engine:

INTRODUCTION:THE CRISIS OF SOCIALISM
INTRODUCTION:THE CRISIS OF SOCIALISM. SOCIALISM TODAY is in crisis. Once the banner under which millions of working people resisted the . . .
http://www.anu.edu.au/polsci/marx/contemp/pamsetc/socfrombel/sfb_int.htm (6k)
[94% relevant] 1 page of text
Guild Socialism Reconsidered Contents Preface
Date: Sunday, 26-May-96 13:00:34 GMT Last-Modified: Monday, 21-Aug-95 10:47:15 GMT
Content-type: text/html Content-length:
10044 Guild Socialism Reconsidered Contents Preface Reconsidering. . .
http://william-king.www.drexel.edu/top/personal/wkpaps/gildf/gildpref.html (10k)
[90% relevant]

Examining these two sources one could assume that the breadth of coverage would be greater in the second source because the size of the file is 10k, whereas the size of the file for the first source is 6k. Unfortunately, the size of the file can be misleading because the content of the site may not be entirely devoted to the topic or concept you are examining. At present, the best procedure for assessing the breadth of coverage for a given source of information is to access the site and examine its contents. Hopefully as search engines become more powerful and descriptive in their presentation the task of assessing this factor will become less time consuming.

Format: How Is this Information Presented? Can It Be Easily Interpreted? Can It Readily Be Acquired or Reproduced?

These criteria are based on commonly accepted practices for the design of hypertext documents. A poorly designed Web site can be tedious to navigate and is likely to produce frustration for the user. However, a user can distinguish well-designed Web sites based on the following characteristics defined by Ryder and Hughes (1997):

1. **Minimal graphics.** Because in-line graphics can take considerable time to download, the size of the graphics should be kept to a minimum. Additionally, when a graphic is presented as a distinct screen (that is, the user has an option to examine the graphic), the size of the file should be indicated so the user can opt not to download large files.

2. **A table of contents.** A clearly presented overview should precede the content, allowing the user to obtain a sense of the breadth or diversity of the content covered. Users should be provided options to link directly with each distinct section of the content.

3. **Citations and credits.** The creator(s) of the information should be acknowledged on the home page. Where a site has established links to other sites, that link should take the user to the home page to acknowledge its creator/author.

4. **Information on links.** The content of links should be described to avoid unproductive browsing.

5. **Absence of dead-end pages.** Pages should always allow the user to return to the home page or to another part of the site.

6. **Pages should present consistent options.** Each page should contain consistent options and format. For example, links should be presented in the same color and font, and graphics used for symbolic notation should be consistent.

7. **Statements of reproduction.** Each site should indicate its policy for reproducing information contained at that site. Many sites will allow reproduction only for educational or noncommercial purposes. Educators should make certain that if a site allows reproduction of its materials for educational purposes that a copy of that statement is placed on file and is included in any copies that may be distributed to students, parents, or staff.

Acceptance of Material

With the lack of widely accepted criteria for defining the quality of material on the Internet, one of the best procedures for selecting materials is to seek the opinion of colleagues, professional organizations, or agencies. As with materials in print, one of the best indicators of "quality" is widespread acceptance of material by your peers. The use of discussion groups and listservs provides a useful mechanism for obtaining information on sites or to request assistance from other professionals. Not only will this save valuable instructional time, but it will also allow you to obtain additional information on useful sites and will generate an awareness of the importance of well-designed hypertext documents. Here, for example, is a posting from a teacher seeking assistance with an open learning environment.

Subject:
       Seeking opinions on Open Classrooms
Date:
       Tue, 05 Nov 1996 05:33:38 GMT
From:
       stonewal@voicenet.com (jackson)
Organization:
       Voicenet - Internet Access - (215)674-9290
Newsgroups:
       k12.chat.elementary

       I teach in a building that has grade levels in pods without walls
       between the individul classes. Does anyone have any experience with
       this physically open "learning environment"? Is this a successful
       experiment in education? How have you worked with or changed this
       situation?

       If you have an opinion, learned or otherwise, please drop a line. We
       are very interested.

       Thanks,

Summary: Evaluating Information

While evaluating information on the Internet would seemingly be no different than selecting books, visuals, or audio and video tapes in a library, there are some important distinctions. One is the matter of the frequency with which information on the Internet changes and the ease of modifying that information. As the Internet increasingly becomes a global repository of information, its diverse content is constantly being modified by individuals representing the interests of various groups, organizations, cultures, and agencies throughout the world. The size and content of a school's library or curriculum center, on the other hand, is restricted by the cost of acquisitions and the decisions of a relatively small group of individuals. On the Internet, the flow of information is controlled by the teacher or the student. It is their decision to determine what to access, how credible that information is, and whether that information may be used to solve problems or answer specific questions. With the opportunity to select from such a vast array of information, an essential strategy is to learn how to select information appropriate for the user's intended purpose. We urge you, therefore, to consider how the criteria we have outlined in this section may assist you and your students in evaluating and selecting materials found on the Internet

▼ PRACTICE ACTIVITY 9.2

Select a chapter from a textbook or an article that would be suitable for use in your classroom. Next, using a Web search engine, conduct a search on the same topic. Once you have obtained the results of this search, compare any two of the sources using the criteria discussed in this section (purpose and audience, authority, scope, format, acceptance of material). Finally, reflect upon and note how these two sources varied on the basis of these criteria.

▼▼

INTEGRATING TECHNOLOGY INTO INSTRUCTION

In this section of the chapter, we will examine ways of applying instructional strategies or concepts presented throughout this book to instructional applications of the Internet. Two types of applications will be examined. The first is the use of the Internet for communications. Here we will address the use of e-mail. The second type of application we will explore is how to search and filter information on the Internet to gain meaning and solve problems. Our efforts here will be directed toward the use of search engines to locate specific information and to gather information to respond to tasks involving higher levels of thinking.

Communicating with E-mail

E-mail has become an indispensable component of daily communication in our personal and professional lives. With the number of e-mail messages passing across the Internet exceeding one billion a month, it is clear that e-mail has become a primary mechanism for communication. The advantages of using e-mail in an educational setting are speed and access. Messages submitted via e-mail can be received around the world in minutes. Thus, inquiries or correspondences can often be answered within minutes or hours rather than the days or weeks required for surface mail. With such a dramatic increase in the speed of acquiring information or sharing ideas, e-mail is likely to become commonplace in classroom instruction. The second advantage of e-mail is its ability to access individuals throughout the world. Recently, for example, one of us was teaching a content area reading course in a multimedia classroom on our campus. While discussing a particular instructional strategy, a number of issues were raised by the students as to the rationale for the use of the strategy. Rather than attempt to presume the intent of the author of this particular strategy, connection was made to the Web, the home page of the author's university was displayed, and the name and e-mail address of the faculty member was obtained. The class then put their questions to the author in the form of an e-mail message, and before the end of the class (which lasted two hours) the author had provided a response to the inquiry. In the past, questions such as these could have been presented in the form of a letter transported by surface mail, but by the time a response was received the issue was no longer vital to the discussion at hand. E-mail has certainly increased our ability to make contact with people in our schools, community, nation, and our global community. Two tools make the task of locating people and educational institutions particularly easy. First is the use of e-mail address locator services (*). These are locations on the Web where you can enter an individual's name and other pertinent information, and the program searches for the individual's e-mail address. An example of the e-mail address search function available on the search engine Lycos is shown in Figure 9.5.

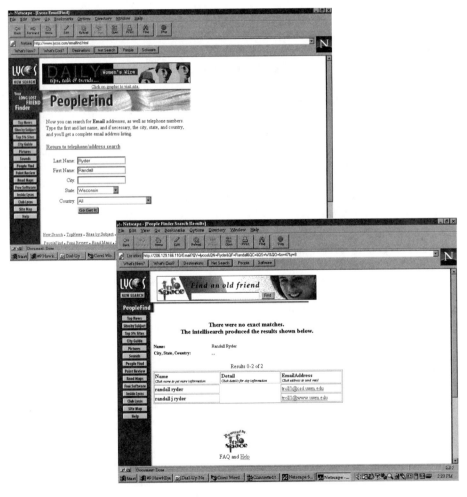

Figure 9.5
E-mail Address Locator Service on Lycos

A second useful e-mail tool are locator services for classroom e-mail partnerships. One of these, Intercultural E-mail Classroom Connections (IECC) at St. Olaf College in Minnesota (*), provides a convenient subscription process for locating students nationally or internationally to participate in your classroom projects. Here is an example of a posting from a teacher seeking assistance in having students respond to a survey.

Time Survey to Maywood Center

Date: Tue, 21 May 1996 07:55:36 -0700
From: Diane Smith <dianes@halcyon.com>
Subject: Time Survey to Maywood Center

The Math Pen Pal class at Maywood Center in SeaTac, WA would like to request answers to this survey for our contribution to Math Pen Pals this year. We would like to see how kids around the world spend their time.

Please keep track of how you spend your time for one week using the following categories:(please record in hours and use decimals for parts of an hour—.1 hour = 6 minutes)

Reading books -
At the movies -
Using the computer -
Playing sports -
Watching TV -
Studying for school -
Total hours logged -

Other information requested:

Name of your school? (or you if homeschooler) -
City, State, Country -
Teacher's name -
How old are you? -
What grade are you in? -
How many are in your class? -

Please send us your answers by May 21, 1996 to:
Kidproj list or to mcenter@directnet.net(Diane Smith)

Put "Time Survey" in the subject line.

We will be putting the answers in a computer spreadsheet and totaling up the hours. We will then compare the different categories. At the end of the survey, we will summarize the information and post it to Kidproj.

Classroom applications of e-mail provide a rich forum for the exchange of information and ideas. Here are some general types of activities for several subject matter areas. These are followed by a discussion of how specific strategies presented in this book can assist in e-mail projects.

Using E-mail to Gather Information and Construct Meaning

In the classroom, e-mail has two general applications. One is its use as a means of contacting an individual to obtain some sort of information or assistance. Generally this application of e-mail is a person-to-person action with no intention of long-term back and forth communication. The second is class projects that involve e-mail as a means of linking classrooms together to serve as partners in learning. Generally this requires groups of people and is likely to require numerous back and forth communications, sharing of responsibilities, and the eventual production of a learning product. Each of these types of e-mail applications, coupled with activities discussed in this book, provide powerful tools for engaging students in meaningful learning experiences.

Contacting Individuals

E-mail is an efficient and easy way to contact individuals for information or assistance. This application can involve the use of experts to assist in classroom learning activities, requests for obtaining materials or supplies, or providing individual homework assistance to students. Contacting experts is becoming increasingly popular. The U.S. Geological Survey, for example, has an "Ask-A-Geologist" service (*) that allows K–12 students to submit questions to USGS earth scientists. Once questions are submitted to the site, they are routed to various scientists who then provide a response within a few days. Another example of using e-mail for obtaining classroom expertise is the Electronic Emissary (*), a service of the School of Education at the University of Texas at Austin. This service matches subject matter experts around the world with classrooms who draw upon these experts' knowledge to complete classroom projects. This is an exciting service that provides access to individuals with unique qualifications. Consider the potential of having access to the resources of Anita Cohen-Williams, whose expert listing from the Electronic Emissary is described below.

Name:	Anita Cohen-Williams
Institution:	Center for Spanish Colonial Archaeology (a non-profit research center)
Description:	Doing archaeological excavations at the Spanish Colonial Presidio of San Diego (1769-1835).
City,St,Zip:	San Diego, CA, 92117
E-Mail per week:	4 - 5 times a week
Area of Expertise 1:	Spanish Colonial history and archaeology of the United States and Northern Mexico

Continued

Description of Area 1:
I am trained as a historical archaeologist which includes the study of history and archaeology. My particular subject is the period of the Spanish settlers in what is now the United States and northern Mexico. This includes Texas, New Mexico, Arizona, and California. I am quite interested in what is called material culture, the artifacts that they have left behind. What did these people use when they lived here? Where did they get their pottery from? Who did they trade with? How did they live? I am also interested in the military history of the area.

In addition to drawing upon the expertise of individuals, e-mail also serves as an important link between the school and the community. Here are a number of these applications.

▼ **Parent newsletter.** With computers in over 50% of all homes, e-mail provides a fast and convenient way to keep parents up to date on class projects, school events and issues, and policies of interest to parents. A newsletter can also serve as a useful educational resource for parents. Articles on topics such as helping your child with homework, dealing with the stress of adolescence, and numerous issues centered around students' physical and emotional health can readily be located on the Internet, then attached to the electronic newsletter.

▼ **Parent-teacher communication.** With so many parents working, e-mail becomes an efficient way for teachers and parents to communicate. This allows teachers and parents to be readily accessible, but it also allows the teacher to provide parents examples of students' written work by transferring electronic files of their work.

▼ **Community tutorial projects.** E-mail provides a convenient way to establish a community-based tutorial program. Students can readily be paired with volunteers who then are available to answer questions on homework assignments, provide feedback on students' writing, or advise students on school-to-work initiatives. Tutors may be located from area businesses, service organizations, or the ever-growing group of senior citizens who are using the Internet.

Linking Classrooms for Projects

Groups of students or classrooms located in distinct geographical areas collect data on a common problem or topic, then solve a problem or reach conclusions by using their aggregate data. The general process for this project involves (1) defining a learning objective that is the product of the data collection, (2) locating various geographical areas from which you would like to collect information, (3) locating participating schools/individuals, (4) clearly articulating lesson objectives, expectations, and anticipated contributions from project participants, (5) defining a project time line, and (6) communicating how the results of the project will be shared with all participants. Here are two examples of this e-mail cooperative learning effort that can be used with students in grades 6–9. The first involves a lesson in science, and the second a lesson in social studies.

Science Project

Objective: Students will examine the effect of personal income and population density on the waste stream.

Geographical Areas Represented: Large cities and rural areas in the United States, Europe, Asia, Australia, and South America.

Lesson Expectations: Students will monitor the waste stream in their homes. For one week, students will weigh the amount of paper, plastic, etc., placed in the homes' "garbage" containers. Separate weighings will be conducted for plastic, paper products, glass, cans and containers, and other disposable items. Material set aside for recycling will be included. Total weighings will be divided by the number of inhabitants to determine a weekly average waste flow per person. Population density and personal income of each location will be provided by the participating teachers.

Project Time Line: One week.

Sharing of Project Results: Data from each location will be shared with the originating teacher, whose class will summarize the data and provide copies of this data to all participating schools. Each class will produce a report specifying generalizations they reach regarding the distribution of waste in various geographical/cultural areas and the relationship between the production of waste and population density. Final reports will be circulated to all participants one week following the collection of data.

Social Studies Project

Objective: Students will examine the nature of neighborhoods in cities throughout the United States.

Geographical Areas Represented: School districts in various geographic regions of the U.S. located in medium and large size and urban communities.

Lesson Expectations: Students will tour and examine three neighborhoods in their respective city. In each neighborhood they will select approximately one square block. Within this area they will note the distance to public transportation, parks and greenbelt areas, and libraries. Additionally, they will note if the neighborhood has alleys and driveways, sidewalks, and streetlights. Finally, they will

Continued

calculate the percent of residences that have fences, and the percent of homes, condominiums, and apartments in the neighborhood.

Sharing of Project Results: All participants will share information and each will summarize the results of the survey. On the basis of preliminary results, participants will be encouraged to conduct follow-up e-mail messages to ask specific questions regarding the neighborhoods in specific cities. Following summarization of information, students will summarize the nature of regional variation, provide reasons for this variation or consistency, and share their findings with project participants.

In each of the preceding examples, e-mail is used to gather information, share ideas, and help generate conclusions to a higher-level comprehension question. Several strategies discussed earlier in this book could effectively be used in these e-mail activities to (1) prepare students for learning, (2) engage them in the learning task, and (3) facilitate their ability to summarize and reach conclusions.

Prior to communicating with their peers by e-mail, the use of anticipation guides, concept maps, frames, and previews would enhance students' background knowledge and actively involve them with the lesson objectives. Anticipation guides have the advantage of drawing students' attention to general concepts they will address in their e-mail project. This is particularly important because this type of project is not based on existing materials. Thus the presentation of statements that engage students in relevant concepts will enhance their ability to focus on the lesson objectives as they engage in the e-mail activity. Similarly, the use of frames and concept maps prior to using e-mail could focus on some of the information students will gather while using e-mail as well as providing them with essential background information. The concept map displayed in Figure 9.6, for example, could be used prior to the lesson on the waste stream. As a class, students could draw upon their prior knowledge to add information to the three major factors identified. Additional information could then be presented by the teacher.

As students are engaged in e-mail projects, the numerous instructional activities discussed in Chapter 3 could be used to enhance students' learning. These include question sequencing, discussion webs, concept maps, and frames. Question sequencing is particularly useful in allowing students to focus on key concepts and information necessary to draw conclusions, generalizations, or inferences. The discussion web can be used in a similar manner, but has the advantage of allowing the teacher to carefully monitor and assist students in constructing a response or attaining a certain level of understanding. For example, if students are asked to generate responses to the statement "we have more disposable items in this country because of our busy lifestyle," they could examine various elements of the statement by gathering information from a number of countries via e-mail. Once acquired, this information would be incorporated into the discussion web. Eventually students would use this information in generating a response to the question. This approach has the advantage of first exposing students to an idea, allowing them to discuss it on the

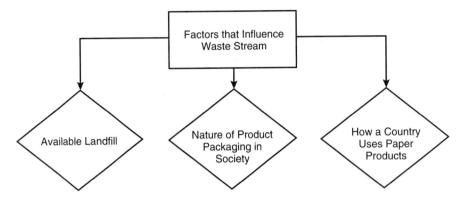

Figure 9.6
Example of the Use of a Concept Map for an E-mail Lesson

basis of their prior knowledge, then allowing them to generate specific questions to individuals by e-mail to formulate a response. Finally we come to the use of the concept map and frame. Both of these types of graphic organizers are effective in focusing students' attention as they gather information and seek answers to the lesson objective. Use of the frame, for example, in the lesson on the waste stream would serve as a focal point of students' attention as they were gathering information via e-mail. Note how the following frame would provide students with cues to tailor their e-mail communications.

	Availability of Landfills	Purchasing Power of Citizens	Incentives to Conserve Natural Resources
Chicago			
Tokyo			
Calcutta			

Following the use of e-mail, students should be provided the opportunity to consolidate information, reach conclusions, and reflect on their learning. Constructing written summaries is a natural outcome of using e-mail to pool information. Use of graphic organizers, questioning, discussion webs, and the like organizes information much along the lines of the GRASP procedure discussed in Chapter 4. Students can then draw upon this information to generate sentences, then summaries, in the manner outlined in GRASP. Another natural outcome of using e-mail to pool information is establishing a context for engaging students in Socratic questioning. The ability of the teacher to direct students to the relationships that are addressed in the four directions of questioning in the Socratic strategy is assisted by the information students acquire through their e-mail activity. Furthermore, students can discuss and evaluate the views and information provided by their peers and the information they acquire from the Internet.

Generative Writing

E-mail is an excellent tool to promote writing activities involving students of various geographical, cultural, and socioeconomic backgrounds. The underlying assumptions of generative writing are that students can gain a better understanding of the writing process through cooperative efforts, and that writing can reflect the product of a problem-solving process whereby students draw upon various sources of information to generate a conclusion. Generative writing involves the following steps:

▼ The teacher presents a problem or task to the students that involves higher-level learning. Students are told that the activity involves two stages. In the first stage they will construct a written response to a portion of the problem using information they have gathered as a group and information provided to them from their e-mail cohorts. In the second stage students revise their written response on the basis of feedback provided by their e-mail cohorts.

▼ Students, in cooperative groups, outline their response to the question or problem to provide justification, evidence, and related information. These outlines are shared with the e-mail cohort group, who in turn provide their portion of the task to their counterparts.

▼ On the basis of the feedback and information obtained from their cohorts, each group drafts a written response to the task. Once completed the writing is submitted to the e-mail cohorts. Each cohort group now engages in a formal peer review of the writing using the procedures we have outlined in the section on evaluating writing in Chapter 6. Again, students exchange their evaluations of each other's writing, the writing undergoes a final revision, and the products are exchanged between the e-mail cohorts.

Generative writing is a flexible activity that provides students an opportunity to gain insight into the process of writing and to share ideas, information, and cultural knowledge. Conducting the writing activity by e-mail is likely to promote students' active involvement and interdependence and to engage students in tasks with groups of individuals of various cultures and perspectives. As a result, students are likely to gain a deeper understanding of the importance of writing, of engaging in cooperative efforts, and of the process of solving problems and engaging in higher-level thinking. Here is a sixth-grade teacher's observations on the use of this activity.

My students enjoy the generative writing activity. We have used it on two occasions this year. The first dealt with the prevalence and causes of violence in this country and involved five classrooms around the country. The second addressed the impact that television has on our lives from the global perspective of four classrooms located in different countries. I feel there are three distinct advantages to this activity. First, it provides students a great deal of ownership. I was surprised with the level of involvement my students displayed and the interest they expressed in communicating with their peers via e-mail. A second advantage is relevancy. Perhaps it was the topic of our writing assignments, but many students expressed the view that this activity provided them the opportunity to do something meaningful to them and allowed them to feel they could express their point of view. And a third advantage was the breadth of knowledge students learned. Not only did they gain a better understanding of the topics and the process of writing, but they also gained a better understanding of different cultures, different geographical and regional perspectives, and most importantly, they learned a great deal about the common interests of sixth graders throughout the world. The main drawback I see with the activity is the time the projects required. Students sent much more e-mail to one another than I anticipated, and they made more revisions than I had anticipated. In the future I intend to deal with this problem by narrowing the topic.

Summary: Using E-mail to Gather Information and Construct Meaning

In this section we have examined numerous ways to use e-mail in an educational setting. We have also described how various instructional strategies discussed throughout this book can be applied to the use of e-mail. Certainly the potential of e-mail as an educational tool is substantial. Its successful application, however, requires careful planning and delivery. The use of e-mail in and of itself does not ensure that learning will be more effective, interesting, or authentic. Teachers will need time to plan and prepare for the use of e-mail in classroom instruction. People, institutions, and agencies will need to be located on the Internet, objectives will need to be clearly defined, and instructional strategies will need to be integrated into the use of e-mail to enhance students' learning. There is also the issue of making certain that students understand and adhere to e-mail netiquette and acceptable use (*). Recognize that students are responsible not only to their peers in the classroom, but their peers on the Internet.

▶ PRACTICE ACTIVITY 9.3

Connect to the Internet and select one of the educator discussion groups that we have listed on our home page (*). Generate a posting in which you request feedback from teachers as to their success in using e-mail in the manner we have discussed in this section. Specifically, determine what success teachers are having with projects involving collaborative efforts on e-mail as well as how they make use of e-mail in their classroom.

▼▼

LOCATING INFORMATION

In this final section of the chapter, we discuss ways to locate information from a number of sources on the Web. Our focus will be on the use of the Web as a tool to promote understanding, through the use of strategies to locate, select, and examine information obtained from multimedia sources.

The Web contains numerous tools for locating various types of information. Some are rather straightforward in their use and produce results that are related to the topic being searched. Others require more effort and often generate results that bear little relationship to the topic you are searching for. Gaining a better understanding of their strengths, limitations, and uses in a classroom setting will allow you to understand the potential of these tools and increase the likelihood that they will become part of your day-to-day instruction. We will explore the use of Web indexes, search engines, and agents. Again, we assume that you have basic knowledge of browser programs and some experience in navigating the hypertext environment of the Web.

A Web index is a subject-based categorization scheme for sites on the Internet. Most of these follow a structure proceeding from general categories to subcategories, and finally subcategories containing individual listings. An example of Yahoo, one of the most popular Web indexes, is shown in Figure 9.7. Here we see the general categories, followed by a screen displaying the educational K–12 subcategories. Finally, the resources listed on the K–12 subcategory, which are a series of links of various educational sites, are displayed.

Search engines are powerful tools for locating information on the Web. Within a matter of minutes a descriptor of the information you want to locate can be entered. Sites throughout the world containing potentially relevant information can be located, and finally, as seen in Figure 9.7, a list of these sites and descriptions of their content are displayed on-screen. These sites can then be accessed by simply clicking on the name or site address displayed in the search results. Although search engines can have a database of millions of sites, results of a search on the same topic will vary from one search engine to another. For example, entering "Korean War" in four widely used search engines produced 60,000 documents in AltaVista, 7,815 in Excite, 19 in Yahoo, and 12,857 in Lycos. Thus conducting a search must frequently involve the use of multiple search engines to obtain comprehensive results. For this reason, a search engine hybrid has been developed that combines the results of a number of search engines.

One of these, MetaCrawler (shown in Figure 9.8), doesn't maintain any internal database. Rather, it draws upon the databases of nine different services, producing a composite of the results. Our search on "water pollution," for example, resulted in 45 sites compiled from nine different search engines. Regardless of whether a search engine or one of the hybrid engines is used, the process can consume considerable time. Any given search can result in 50 or 100 possible sites. Obviously, examination of individual sites, under these circumstances, would be an overwhelming task. Recognizing this problem, several agent-based software programs are now available (*). Agent programs automatically search and locate documents on the Web, then save the results to a file that can be viewed while the computer is not connected to the

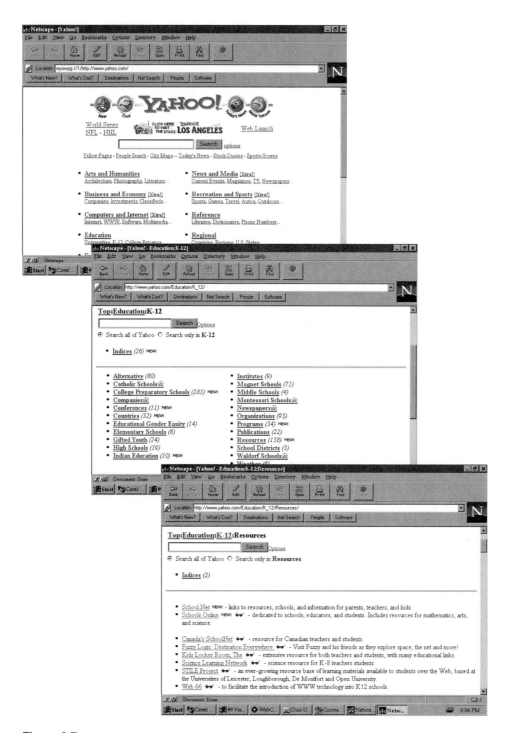

Figure 9.7
Example of a Search with Yahoo

Figure 9.8
Example of Results from the MetaCrawler Web Search Engine

Internet. Many of these agents also allow the user to schedule the search automatically, a particularly attractive feature for schools with limited access. The teacher or student can specify the search topic, schedule the search to be conducted overnight, then examine the results the next day. An example of the results of an automated search on Crohn's disease using WebCompass (Quarterdeck Corporation) is shown in Figure 9.9. In this example, 114 sites on Crohn's disease were located. For each site specified in the results, WebCompass identifies the number of links and images in a document, the search engine that provided the listing of the site, the address of the site, and a summary of its contents. Certainly the use of a hybrid search engine is more efficient than conducting an identical search with a number of individual search engines.

It is also important to recognize that the results of this search are rather comprehensive. Reading the summaries requires an understanding of the content and descriptors being examined. And when this information is inadequate, a considerable

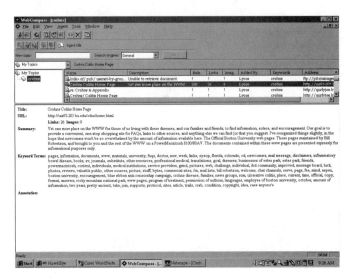

Figure 9.9
Example of a Search Agent

amount of time can be misdirected by examining individual web sites provide in the search results. To minimize these problems we suggest the following:

1. Searches should be conducted, in most instances, by the teacher. Unless students are already proficient in the use of search engines and have knowledge of the topic being searched and the skills to determine valid sources, browsing through the results of a search may actually lead students to acquire incorrect information or become overwhelmed with information. By selecting the sites in advance, students' energies can be directed at learning objectives rather than searching for information.

2. Carefully examine the results of your search. There are a number of useful tips to determine which sites may contain useful information. First, examine the Web address or URL of the site. If it contains a .com, it is a commercial site. Other designations include .gov for government sites, .org for organizations, and .edu for educational institutions. Pay particular attention to commercial sites that may use phrases or terminology for product advertising. A second consideration is to examine the description or summary of the site contained in the search results. Many listings will contain summaries of personal postings on discussion groups or home pages constructed by individuals who may wish to make a personal statement rather than provide objective information. Here, for example, are two of the listings from the search on Crohn's disease. The first is a commercial site promoting advertising, the second is a site at Boston University.

Title:	MedSurf Diseases and Conditions Crohn's Disease
URL:	http://www.medsurf.com/Diseases_and_Conditions/Crohns_Disease/
	Links: 15 **Images:** 0
Summary:	Click here, for information on how to spice up or add your advertisement to MedSurf!

Title: Crohn's Colitis Home Page

URL: http://qurlyjoe.bu.edu/cduchome.html

          Links: 26   **Images:** 9

Summary: Yet one more place on the WWW for those of us living with
          these diseases, and our families and friends, to find information,
          solace, and encouragement. Our goal is to provide a conve-
          nient, one-stop shopping site for FAQs, links to other sources,
          and anything else we can find (or that you suggest). I've reorga-
          nized things slightly, in the hope that newcomers won't be so
          overwhelmed by the amount of information available here. The
          Official Boston University web pages.

  3. Show students how to use the results of a search. Over time, it is to the
students' advantage to learn how to conduct and evaluate the results of a search
engine. Consider modeling this process with the students. Note the importance of
learning how to examine the results and point out the problems they will encounter
when randomly examining sites listed from the results of a search.

  4. Consider other means of locating sites of interest. While search engines
provide resources from a huge database, don't overlook other sources for locating
information. One is to post a notice on an educational discussion group (*) that
expresses your need for information on a topic. Another option is to refer to sites
designed specifically for educators (*).

Summary: Locating Information

As we have noted, finding information on the Internet is not a problem. But finding
information that is appropriate for your needs and suitable for your students can be
a lengthy process. Fortunately the tools we use for searching the Internet are constantly being improved to make them more efficient and accurate, and tailored to
the needs of the user. However, until they become more readily adaptable to the
needs of diverse learners, it is important to consider their role in the classroom and
their potential to provide students with resources previously limited to a select
group of people.

▼ PRACTICE ACTIVITY 9.4

Select three search engines and conduct a search on all three using the same search
term. Compare the number of "hits" you receive from each engine and the thorough-
ness of the description of each site. Also consider if the listings proceed from those
sights that have the greatest relevance to your search. Finally, using the same evaluation criteria, conduct the same search using MetaCrawler (*).

▼▼

CONCLUDING REMARKS

This chapter began with a discussion of the characteristics of learning from hypertext. We also noted ways to enhance the use of hypertext in the classroom. The central issue is that hypertext provides tremendous opportunities for students to become active learners and have access to enormous amounts of information. It is also important to recognize that hypertext presents certain difficulties for the learner. Teachers should, therefore, make special efforts to define goals, provide navigational maps and conceptual clues, and develop activities for note taking and reflection.

The next section of the chapter discussed ways to evaluate information on the Internet by examining its purpose and audience, authority, scope, format, and degree of acceptance. Evaluating information on the Internet is central to effective classroom instruction. Failing to acknowledge a procedure for evaluating Internet information is likely to lead students to the use of inaccurate or unreliable sources.

In our discussion of the integration of the Internet into classroom instruction, we focused on two major topics: the use of e-mail and the methods of locating information on the Internet. E-mail can be used to contact individuals, link classrooms in cooperative learning activities, and promote generative writing activities. These applications can literally extend the classroom to a global audience through authentic activities conducted in a culturally diverse setting. We also discussed the use of search engines, Web indexes, and hybrid search engines to locate information. These powerful tools provide access to text, videos, graphics, software, and audio information.

In closing our discussion of technology, we would emphasize two points. First, technology by itself is not likely to promote learning. We must learn how to modify our instruction, our view of the role of teacher and student, and remain receptive to modifying our instruction as new technological tools become available. Instruction involving technology requires thorough planning, clearly articulated goals, and constant attention to the needs of the students. The role of teacher and student often becomes blurred as students discover and share new sources and approaches to the use of technology and teachers acquire greater insight into the process of generating meaning in a fluid and dynamic environment. Finally, we would note that the blazing pace at which technology changes will require a professional commitment to remaining current in its applications to the classroom.

Our second point is that the integration of technology in the classroom is consistent with the guiding principles of content area reading instruction we discussed in Chapter 1. The importance of functional learning tasks that acknowledge the dynamic social and intellectual environment of the global classroom will continue to focus on the importance of using technology to assist students in their construction of knowledge. This type of learning emphasizes active learning—learning that allows students to control the flow of information, define personal objectives, and gain a level of understanding that is shaped by multiple sources and points of view.

Reflections

▼▼▼

1. To gain a better idea of the multiple options provided by hypertext, examine the home page of the Library of Congress. The Web address for this site is: http://www.loc.gov/. Once you have brought up the home page of the site, examine the number of links (text appearing in color and graphic images that you can "click"). Also note the number of graphics displayed on the page. Now compare the information and options on this home page to the table of contents of a book. Consider the differences and similarities between these two sources of information.

2. Using the guidelines for evaluating information on the Internet discussed in the first section of this chapter, evaluate a web site. For your source of information, conduct a search on tobacco and find a site that supports the use of tobacco, then apply the evaluation criteria to that site. Summarize your observations as to the overall validity and quality of the material on this site.

3. Examine the achieved e-mail projects presented at the IECC Web site (http://www.Stolaf.edu/network/iecc/). Select three or four of the projects listed and determine (1) the clarity of the objectives, (2) the defined responsibility of the participants, (3) the product of the project, and (4) the extent to which the project made use of Internet resources. Once you have gathered this information, determine the overall quality of this project and modifications you would suggest to enhance its effectiveness.

4. Select a subject matter textbook or curriculum guide. From this source, find a topic for a unit of classroom instruction. Now use MetaCrawler (*) to conduct a search on this topic noting the number of documents provided in the results of the search. Examine four or five of the documents to determine how well they address the topic you have selected. Finally, using the criteria in Chapter 10 for assessing text difficulty, determine whether the materials located on the Web would be appropriate for classroom use.

5. Select one of the Web indexes provided by Yahoo (*) or AltaVista (*). Select the education category and examine the web sites included as links on the index. From this list of sites, determine how many sites contain (1) instructional materials, (2) information on professional organizations or agencies, (3) individual school sites, or (4) resources that may be of interest to educators. Once you have examined one of these indexes, define how they might be used in an educational setting for staff development, curriculum development, and as a professional resource.

6. Select a topic that you might teach to your students. Now enter keywords for that topic into a Web search engine. Once you have obtained the search results, select three or four sites that appear to have useful information. As you find information that is relevant to your lesson, highlight that information by holding down the mouse key and dragging the cursor over the text. Next go to the Edit function in your web browser, click on that function and select the Copy option. Now switch to a word processing program, again select the Edit function, and "paste" the highlighted text into the word processor document. Repeat this process several times until you have created your own custom tailored document. Now list ways you can use this process to generate instructional materials that are tailored to the needs and interests of your students.

References

▼▼

Becker, H. J. (1994). *Analysis and trends of school use of new information technologies.* Irvine, CA: University of California, Irvine, Department of Education. A comprehensive report detailing classroom observation of the use of computers in school settings.

Callister, T. A. (1996). Knowledge at the crossroads: Some alternative forms of hypertext learning environments. *Educational Theory,* 1996, 562–571. Reviews the use of hypertext to enhance learning.

Dee-Lucas, D. (1996). Effects of overview structure on study strategies and text representations for instructional hypertext. In J. E. Rouet & J. J. Levonen (Eds.), *Hypertext and learning.* Mahwah, NJ: Lawrence Erlbaum. Examines problems the learner encounters when learning from hypertext.

Dee-Lucas, D., & Larkin, J. H. (1992). *Text representation with traditional text and hypertext* (Tech. Rep. H.P. #21). Pittsburgh: Carnegie Mellon University, Department of Psychology. Examines the distinction between learning with traditional text and hypertext.

Gray, S. H. (1990). Using protocol analysis and drawing to study mental model construction during hypertext navigation. *International Journal of Human-Computer Interaction,* 2, 359–377. Examines how learners process information when learning from hypertext.

Heim, M. (1993). *The metaphysics of virtual reality.* New York: Oxford University Press. A thorough discussion of the applications of virtual reality and how it may impact on learning.

Means, B., & Olson, K. (1994). The link between technology and authentic learning. *Educational Leadership,* 51, 15–18. Addresses some of the current ideas regarding the importance of technology in generating authentic learning tasks for students.

Mohageg, M. F. (1992). The influence of hypertext linking structures on the efficiency of informational retrieval. In R. McAleese & C. Green (Eds.), *Hypertext: The state of the art.* Oxford: Intellectual Books. Examines the problem of learners becoming lost when switching between hypertext documents and the role that linking structures may have in assisting the learner.

National Academy of Sciences (1995), Reinventing schools, the technology is now. Http://www.nap.edu/readingroom/books/tech-gap/media/aclarke.html. An extensive report examining the use of technology in our nations' schools.

Nyce, J. M., & Kahn, P. (1991). *From Memex to hypertext: Vannevar Bush and the mind's machine.* Boston: Academic Press. Reviews the work of Vannevar Bush, the father of the hypertext revolution.

Rouet, J. F., & Levonen, J. J. (1996). Studying and learning with hypertext: Empirical studies and their implications. In J. E. Rouet & J. J. Levonen (Eds.), *Hypertext and learning.* Mahwah, NJ: Erlbaum. A thorough review of our knowledge of how we learn from hypertext.

Ryder, R. J., & Hughes, T. (1997). *Internet for educators.* Upper Saddle River, NJ: Prentice-Hall. Provides an overview of the tools of the Internet and their use in the classroom setting.

Simpson, A., & McKnight, C. (1990). Navigation in hypertext: Structural cues and mental maps. In R. McAleese & C. Green (Eds.), *Hypertext: The state of the art.* Oxford: Intellectual Books. Reviews our knowledge of ways to enhance learning in the hypertext environment.

Spiro, R. J., Feltovitch, P. J., Jacobson, M. J., & Coulson, R. J. (1991). Cognitive flexibility, constructivism and hypertext: Random access instruction for advanced knowledge acquisition in ill-structured domains. *Educational Technology,* 31, 24–33. Discusses how hypertext may provide a useful way of promoting a constructivist approach to learning environments.

Assessment

CHAPTER OVERVIEW

This chapter is divided into four sections. The first section presents an overview of the need for classroom assessment, focusing on the characteristics of assessment and the concept of authentic assessment. The second section describes two types of classroom assessment, formal and informal tests. In the third section we discuss two methods for constructing informal assessment for the subject matter classroom. The fourth and final section considers factors that affect text difficulty and concludes with strategies to assess textbooks and text readability.

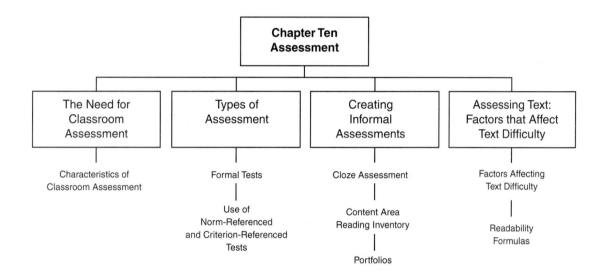

THE NEED FOR CLASSROOM ASSESSMENT

Educational assessment typically involves gathering information about students, educational programs, or educational products. Mehrens and Lehmann (1991, p.4) assert that the term assessment "is used broadly, like evaluation; or it is often used to indicate the use of both formal and informal data gathering procedures and the combining of the data in a global fashion to reach an overall judgment." Although assessment is often associated with formal measures like norm-referenced tests, it also involves less formal measures such as teacher observations, in-class questioning, student portfolios, or student self-reports. Formal assessment often is used as a measure of how well students in a school or district perform on certain academic tasks. These tests are often required by local or state agencies. Informal assessment is the day-to-day evaluation conducted by teachers to determine how well students perform on given objectives or to evaluate what students know about elements of the curriculum.

The process of gathering information about an individual or groups' performance or response to an activity is entrenched in our everyday lives. Whether it is our ability to drive a manual transmission automobile, to engage in a sporting activity, to prepare various types of foods, or to build or create an object, we all want some sort of feedback on our performance. For some, a personal evaluation will suffice; others seek the advice of peers or colleagues to define the level of performance or degree of satisfaction that was achieved. Most frequently we engage in assessment to provide ongoing feedback about our success in reaching an objective. Consider, for example, a home improvement activity. While painting the interior walls and trim of a room, we gather information about existing conditions as well as our performance in the task of painting. Initially we define our goal in terms of the color we want the walls and trim painted, and the finish we want the paint to display (flat, gloss, or semigloss). We examine the existing walls and trim to gather information that could affect the outcome of our efforts (whether the paint is blistered, scaled, or alligatored), then begin the process of preparing the surface and painting. As we continue painting, we continually monitor our work to determine if the new paint covers the existing paint, if there are visible brush marks, or if paint is splattering on adjacent surfaces. Based on feedback from this ongoing assessment, modifications may be necessary to accomplish our defined goal. An improperly sanded surface is resanded to allow the paint to adhere. Once the painting job is completed, we again assess the total impact of the effort and encourage others to provide verbal feedback on the finished product, trusting they focus on our craft rather than the blobs of paint on ourselves.

Characteristics of Classroom Assessment

The painting analogy highlights three important characteristics of classroom assessment—it is *ongoing*, *flexible*, and *valid*. First, classroom assessment is a process that occurs over an extended period of time. While it is important to evaluate a student's performance on a task at a given point in time, it is equally important to observe and note changes in performance or behaviors throughout the year to optimize instruction and provide meaningful feedback. A second characteristic of classroom assessment is flexibility. Different types of assessment can be used for a variety of purposes: to meet accountability measures defined by a local school district or state educational agency, to assess students' in-class performance on oral discussions and written assignments, or to collect students' individual work to create portfolios that represent the diversity and growth in their learning. A final characteristic of classroom assessment is validity. In order for an assessment to be meaningful and relevant to the nature of the activities and social context of the classroom, what is assessed must mirror what actually occurs in the classroom. Assessing students with a multiple-choice test, for example, in a mathematics course stressing problem solving and hands-on applications would not be a valid measure of the nature of classroom learning. As Glaser and Silver (1994, p.26) note:

> As assessment and instruction are more closely linked, achievement measurement will be integral to learning rather than imposed by some external shaper of students' fates. Assessment will be tied to the curriculum, so that it examines what has been taught and practiced and is thereby more representative of meaningful tasks and subject matter goals. Assessment tasks will increasingly provide worthwhile instructional experiences that illustrate the relevance and utility of the knowledge and skill that is acquired and its application to different settings.

Authentic Assessment

Recently there has been an emphasis on assessment that includes more essays, open-ended problems, real-to-life hands-on problem solving, computer simulations, and students' evaluation and assembling of their own work over a period of time. Collectively these forms of assessment are called "authentic assessments" (Archibald & Newman, 1988; Resnick & Resnick, 1992; Wiggins, 1989) because they evaluate tasks that students encounter in their day-to-day learning. Authentic assessments can, according to Calfee (1996), include the teacher's subjective judgment of students' understanding of concepts and their ability to transfer skills to more general learning tasks. Authentic assessments can involve both teacher assessment of students' performance on class activities and students' evaluation and selective presentation of their own work. This movement toward assessment that more closely matches the content, social context, and cognitive tasks of the classroom may have a significant impact on our view of how we measure educational outcomes (Blum & Arter, 1996).

Assembling the efforts of the teacher and student in a portfolio similar to those used by artists and architects has been suggested as a framework for both individualization and self-assessment (Flood & Lapp, 1989; Tierney, Carter, & Desai, 1991; Valencia, 1990; Wolf, 1989). Use of portfolios at the beginning of an instructional year can define a student's baseline of performance on a given instructional objective. Periodic assessment thereafter is useful to determine if the student **can maintain** that level of performance and whether the student **can transfer** the newly acquired knowledge to various contexts. The teacher can then modify instruction based on the information provided. Administration of tests that do not address a specific educational need or that fail to provide information that directs curricular or instructional decisions is of little value to the teacher. All too often tests are given and individual scores are placed in cumulative folders that are seldom examined by the teacher.

TYPES OF ASSESSMENT

This section addresses two types of assessment: formal and informal. The discussion of formal assessment focuses on two measures: norm-referenced tests and criterion-referenced tests. This is followed by a supplementary section providing a detailed look at characteristics of formal tests. The section concludes with an examination of the use of informal tests in the subject matter classroom and descriptions of procedures for administering two types of informal reading assessments.

Formal Tests

Formal tests sample students' behavior using uniform or consistent procedures for administering and scoring the tests (Mehrens & Lehmann, 1991) in an attempt to obtain accurate and reliable results. For example, if the directions of a test instruct the teacher to present a sample test item to students followed by class discussion of the process needed to solve the item, it would be reasonable to assume that omission of the sample item could have an adverse effect on students' test performance. The administration of a timed test also may affect test performance. If a teacher allowed one group of students fifteen minutes to complete a set of problems and another group was allowed thirty-five minutes, it would be reasonable to assume that the students provided additional time would have higher test scores. The clarity of directions can also affect student performance. Consider, for example, the following question:

Directions: Circle the word that is not a noun.

> (A) flog
> (B) medallion
> (C)convalescence
> (D) fragrance

Most likely you had little difficulty recognizing that *flog* (to flail or beat) is a verb, and thus does not have the same grammatical function as the other three words. Now consider the following question:

Directions: Circle the best response from the following.

> (A) rendezvous
> (B) summit
> (C) parlance
> (D) rebuttal

Ambiguous directions make this question more difficult. You may have assumed the answer was derived from a comparison of the word's meanings. If so, you would select the fourth response alternative, *rebuttal*, believing that the other terms dealt with people drawing together for the purpose of discussion, whereas *rebuttal* dealt with opposing views during debate. Your response would be incorrect, however, if the intent of the question was to select the term that is derived from a foreign word (*rendezvous*).

Formal tests can be either norm referenced or criterion referenced. Norm-referenced tests compare the performance of an individual with that of other individuals in what is termed the *norm group*. Generally, norm-referenced scores provide information on what percent of individuals performed above and below the level of the individual tested. Scores are often expressed in terms of percentiles (the percent of individuals who scored below a given point). A percentile score of 78 on the Iowa Test of Basic Skills (Hieronymus, Hoover, & Linquist, 1986) indicates that a student scored as well as or better than 78% of the individuals at that grade or age level. A distinctive characteristic of a norm-referenced score is the comparison of an individual's score to those of other individuals.

Criterion-referenced tests do not compare students' scores; rather, they report a student's performance on a specified domain of educational or behavioral outcomes. For example, a criterion-referenced test may present a series of problems to determine if students have learned to add and subtract mixed fractions. These problems may present a wide range of difficulty to determine how well a student performs over the range of problems presented. Often called mastery tests, criterion-referenced tests provide information about a student's performance relative to the criterion of performance desired. Results of criterion-referenced tests, therefore, are reported on the basis of whether the student scored at the criterion level of performance. No comparisons are made between an individual's score and that of some norm group. Test results, therefore, are examined on the basis of how well individual students or students as a whole perform on a test item. Consider, for example, a criterion-referenced test assessing students' ability to multiply mixed fractions. A teacher may receive results indicating that 89% of the students in a given class correctly multiply mixed fractions. No information is provided as to how well students in other schools performed, nor are scores reported as percentiles or grade equivalents.

Uses of Norm-Referenced and Criterion-Referenced Tests

Student assessment is often conducted to compare an individual student's performance to that of others, or to compare the performance of a school district to other districts or the national average. Under these circumstances, a norm-referenced test may be the best choice. Norm-referenced tests are often used to predict students' potential to succeed and thus are frequently used as a criteria for admission to educational programs or institutions. They are also widely used by school districts to measure a district's performance in comparison to national, regional, or local norms. These comparisons not only provide some measure of how well a school district stacks up to other districts, but provide, over a period of time, a measure of the students' level of achievement. Formal, norm-referenced tests have been a fixture in our schools for over 100 years and account for approximately 71% of all school-wide testing (U.S. General Accounting Office, 1993). During the past decade, the use of these tests has increasingly been questioned. In particular, it has been noted that formal, norm-referenced tests (1) provide false information on the status of learning in the schools, (2) are biased against students of a minority group, those with limited English proficiency, and those students of low income, (3) tend to reduce teaching to the preparation for test taking, and (4) emphasize lower rather than higher-order thinking skills (Chambliss & Calfee, in press). More recently the validity of formal achievement tests has been questioned on several grounds. First, the most widely used achievement tests assume that learning can be examined by identifying isolated skills assessed outside the context of the classroom and the situations in which those skills are used (Paris, Lawton, Turner, Roth, 1991). Many educators believe that tests direct what is taught (O'Day & Smith, 1993), and often the emphasis on multiple-choice, true-false tests leads teachers to emphasize the acquisition of skills and memorization of details rather than the types of cognitive tasks that are required in the real world. Contrary to our understanding of how students learn, many assessments—particularly traditional multiple-choice and true-false assessments—test facts and skills in isolation (Corbett & Wilson, 1991; Shepard & Smith, 1988; Smith & Cohen, 1991), seldom requiring students to apply what they know and can do in real-life situations involving active learning. Achievement tests generally do not consider the learner's motivation or the content or setting of the task, factors that have strong effects on learning. Second, achievement tests do not present tasks typically encountered in the classroom curriculum (Linn, 1987; Wiggins, 1989). Tasks that require students to read extended selections of text, to synthesize information drawn from various sources, or solve problems through cooperative efforts with their peers are seldom evident on achievement tests.

Criterion-referenced tests tend to measure more specific objectives; therefore, it may be possible to draw conclusions regarding an individual's performance on the objectives measured (Mehrens & Lehmann, 1991). This is an important consideration in subject matter areas where students must master certain fundamental information before they can be presented with higher-level concepts. In mathematics, for example, students need to master the concepts of circumference and radius before they can acquire concepts to determine the area of circles. Criterion-referenced tests are used to measure students' mastery of specific instructional objectives taught in the classroom, to assess those skills that are defined as minimal competencies for high school graduation, or to identify students who may require compensatory or accelerated instruction.

The decision of whether to use a norm-referenced test or a criterion-referenced test depends on the desired educational outcome. Criterion-referenced tests often assess a minimum level of performance. All practicing dentists, for example, must pass a criterion-referenced test to become licensed; yet among any group of dentists there are differences in how well they have mastered dentistry. Norm-referenced tests generally are more sensitive to individual differences and include items to indicate how well students learn defined skills.

CREATING INFORMAL ASSESSMENTS

This section presents a brief discussion of the use of informal assessments in the subject matter classroom, followed by three forms of informal assessment: the cloze assessment, the content area reading inventory, and portfolios. As you read this section it may be useful to consider the advantages these three types of informal assessment have over standardized tests and the applications they may have in your classroom.

Informal assessments have the advantage of being highly sensitive to students' performance, beliefs, and reflections on the content addressed in a given classroom. The tasks students engage in, the material they use for the tasks, and the cognitive strategies these tasks may require are determined by the teacher. If, for example, a social studies teacher emphasizes students' ability to draw generalizations from multiple sources, an informal assessment can be constructed with perhaps five different reading selections to assess students' ability to construct generalizations. Informal assessments can be administered at various times throughout the school year. At the beginning of the year, an informal assessment may be used to assess students' knowledge of the content presented in a class. Results can be used to identify individual's abilities, to form cooperative learning groups, to aid in the selection of supplemental reading material, and to determine the pace of instruction. Informal assessments are also useful in gaining an understanding of a group's performance.

By examining the average score of a class, the teacher can determine the general level of students' background knowledge and their ability to engage in cognitive tasks required in the curriculum.

What follows is a description of two types of informal assessments suitable for classroom use: the cloze assessment and the content area reading inventory.

Cloze Assessment

The cloze assessment was first developed by Taylor (1953), who surmised that the concept of closure, a term referring to the tendency to make meaning of incomplete information, was a fundamental element in the reading process. To maintain coherence and understanding as we read, we tend to fill in those "vacuous slots" caused by words or concepts that may be unknown. In the following sentence, for example, it takes little effort to insert a word in the blank that is semantically and syntactically appropriate.

The horses entered the final turn on the dirt covered _____ as they sped toward the finish line.

It is likely that you made closure by filling in the term *track* or *racetrack* due to the familiarity of the content and the word itself. Sentences are not always this easy to understand. When the content of a passage or sentence is unfamiliar, the ability to supply the appropriate word can be difficult as is evident in the following sentence.

The body is capable of producing its own opiate-like compounds through a process where neurotransmitters bind to opioid _____, thus producing a sensation of pleasure similar to that obtained from opium.

Lacking a background in pharmacology or neurology, it is difficult to reach closure with this sentence to produce the word *receptors*.

Noting that the ability to attain meaningful closure is a function of the reader's background knowledge and ability to draw upon cues in the text, Taylor proposed a form of reading assessment that draws upon the reader's ability to interact with the text as it is being processed rather than testing one's understanding at the completion of the reading. The cloze procedure was later described by Bormuth (1968, 1969) as a method to assess comprehension. The cloze assessment is constructed, administered, scored, and interpreted by the teacher.

Constructing the Cloze

Constructing a cloze test is easy. The first step is the selection of several passages from your classroom reading materials. Each passage should be approximately 200 to 300 words in length. The passages should be selected from the beginning of the text or a chapter to reduce the likelihood that students' understanding of the passages will be affected by concepts addressed in earlier portions of the text. Once a passage has been selected, the cloze test can be constructed. First, the first sentence or two of the selection is left intact. Next, every fifth word is deleted and replaced by a blank. This blank should be of an equal length for each of the deleted words to remove clues as to the word's length. A total of fifty deletions are made. Once the fifty deletions are made, the last sentence or two of the passage is left intact.

Administering the Cloze

Many students are unfamiliar with the cloze procedure. It is advisable, therefore, that you model the process of selecting words to be placed in the blanks. Modeling can begin by presenting a simple example containing five to ten deleted words. The content of this example should be familiar to students to ensure their attention is directed to the process of completing the cloze rather than attempting to determine the meaning of the passage. Stress to students that in formulating their answers they should attempt to select the word used in the original text by considering the author's style and choice of words. Following the initial teacher modeling, students should be provided with another passage that contains familiar content consisting of ten or fifteen deletions. This example should be completed by each student without time limits. Once completed, you can discuss the answers, provide a short discussion of the purpose of the cloze, then request individual students discuss their rationale for their responses. This example of the cloze should also be administered without time limits. Once the sample cloze tests are completed, the cloze test can be administered. Administration of two or three cloze passages will increase test reliability and the accuracy of the procedure's results.

Scoring the Cloze

As mentioned previously, correct responses are limited to the exact word appearing in the original passage. Spelling errors are acceptable. Synonyms or changes in the words' tense or inflection are not acceptable. While the acceptance of synonyms would increase students' scores, the relative difference between the scores would remain constant (Bormuth, 1968). Additionally, scoring of synonyms has been shown to reduce test reliability (Henk & Selders, 1984), and exact replacement scoring has shown to correlate significantly with informal reading inventories as well as standardized reading tests (Smith & Zinc, 1977). Therefore, it is recommended that to maintain the objectivity of scoring (McKenna, 1976), and to reduce the time necessary to determine if a synonym is acceptable, only the exact word should be accepted. Once the number of items scored correctly is totaled, that sum is multiplied by two, providing a percentage of items scored correctly.

Cloze scores are reported as indicating one of three reading levels: independent, instructional, and frustration. These scores were derived by Bormuth (1968) in an analysis comparing the cloze scores with those of a standardized reading test and a multiple-choice comprehension test. According to Bormuth a score of 57% on the cloze corresponded to a comprehension score of 90%, and a cloze score of 44%

corresponded to a comprehension score of 75%. Accordingly, Bormuth suggested the following scoring criteria:

Reading Level	Cloze Test Scores
Independent	**58%–100%**
Instructional	**44%–57%**
Frustration	**<44%**

Students scoring at the *independent* level are assumed to be capable of comprehending the text at a level that will not require instructional assistance from the teacher. Students scoring at the *instructional* level will require some instructional assistance from the teacher. And students scoring at the *frustration* level will require either considerable assistance from the teacher or a less difficult text.

Commentary: Cloze Assessment

The cloze assesses students' ability to comprehend reading material used in the classroom. It is easy to construct, administer, and score. Results of the cloze have been shown to correlate highly with other measures of reading comprehension; thus one can assume that it measures some of the same aspects of the reading process that are found in standardized reading tests. Because it measures students' ability to read classroom material, its results should be a good predictor of students' ability to learn from subject matter materials. Like any assessment, the cloze also has limitations. Among these is the likelihood that it measures comprehension only at the sentence level (Shanahan, Kamil, & Tobin, 1982) and that it requires students to search for information to fill in the blanks rather than read for a more general understanding (Johnston, 1983). Finally, the cloze will not describe how well students will apply higher-level thinking strategies.

▼ PRACTICE EXERCISE 10.1

Now that you have read about the procedures for constructing, administering, and scoreing your own cloze test, complete the following sample assessment. Your objective is to write in each of the fifty spaces the exact word that you believe appeared in the text. Once you have completed the cloze sample, score your responses using the answers found at the end of the chapter.

Sample Cloze Assessment

Suntan: Your Skin's Natural Protection

Until relatively recent times, displaying one's suntan was not an attribute widely accepted by the population. In fact, for many years having a suntan was a label denoting one as a laborer. Over time, however, a _____ became fashionable as those _____ could afford to travel _____ maintain their tan by _____ in distant locations. More _____ however, many individuals in _____ medical community have warned _____ excessive sun can cause _____, premature aging of the _____ and wartlike growths. _____ individual's resistance to the _____ of sun is determined _____ the thickness of your _____ and the amount of _____. Individuals who have thicker _____ are less likely to _____. The extent of your _____ color is determined by _____, a skin pigment. _____ skin pigment is made _____ skin cells called melanocytes. _____ is these cells that _____ melanin, the pigment that _____ your skin from the _____ rays of the sun. _____ who have large concentrations _____ melanin are less likely _____ be affected by the _____ rays. Suntan as well _____ sunburn is caused by _____ invisible ultraviolet rays of _____ sun. These UV rays _____ the most intense between _____ A.M. and 2:00 P.M., _____ which time the sun's _____ are less likely to _____ deflected by the Earth's _____. The effects of the _____ are particularly strong the _____ time one is outdoors _____ a prolonged period of _____ indoors such as the _____ months. For those individuals _____ burn quickly, the first _____ to the sun should _____ limited to no more _____ fifteen minutes a day. _____ subsequent exposures the duration _____ exposure can be increased _____ increments of fifteen minutes. _____ from the sun's UV rays can be obtained from sunscreens. These products contain chemicals to screen out portions of light in the UV spectrum to prevent the skin from burning.

▼▼▼

Content Area Reading Inventory

The second informal reading assessment presented in this section is the content area reading inventory (CARI). It can be used to (1) measure students' ability to use the learning aides in a textbook as well as more general reference aides, (2) assess students' vocabulary knowledge as well as their ability to acquire word meanings from context, and (3) assess students' understanding of literal and inferential comprehension of text materials and their ability to understand the organizational structure of text. Listed below are the skills and content assessed by the CARI. While this is a rather comprehensive list, it is not necessary that the CARI contain all of the follow components. Being an informal test, you can construct the CARI to assess learning behaviors you believe will be valuable to you and your students. As stated at the beginning of this chapter, assessment should be flexible to meet the needs of your particular classroom.

Part 1: Components of a Textbook

1. Table of Contents
2. Index
3. Glossary
4. Chapter/Section Previews
5. Preview/Review Questions
6. Graphs and Statistical Charts
7. Pictures

Part 2: Reference Skills

1. Locating information from library sources
2. Locating information from classroom references

Part 3: Vocabulary Knowledge and Strategies

1. Recall of word meanings
2. Determining word meanings from context
3. Determining word meanings from morphological analysis
4. Obtaining word meanings from dictionary

Part 4: Comprehension and Strategies

1. Locating and recalling literal information
2. Constructing inferences from text information
3. Constructing knowledge from multiple text sources

The CARI is constructed from the types of materials students generally read and the reading tasks that students generally engage in while reading subject matter material. Like the cloze test, the CARI is designed to be constructed and administered by the teacher, and many of its results are intended to reflect students' performance on tasks unique to a specific area of study. Use of classroom reading material and the presentation of questions typical of classroom instruction contribute to the CARI's validity. Similarly, presentation of several questions for each of the three parts of the test contribute to its reliability; a greater number of text reading tasks are measured. Construction, scoring, and interpretation of the CARI are conducted as follows:

Construction

1. Select a text passage three to five pages in length. This passage should be obtained from materials typically read in the classroom and should not contain concepts presumed to have been covered in other portions of the text.

2. It is recommended that a total of twenty to thirty questions be constructed. Of these, six to ten questions should be constructed for Part 1, six to ten for Part 2, and six to ten for Part 3.

3. Questions should assess the same types of tasks required in the classroom, or those skills that you presume students must possess to acquire or construct meaning from a subject matter classroom. If, for example, most of a teacher's activities focus on tasks that apply information from the text to everyday problems, questions assessing students' comprehension should reflect these sorts of cognitive skills. Examples of the types of questions you may desire to ask for Parts 1, 2, and 3 are presented in Figure 10.1.

Administration

1. The CARI is given to the entire class. It should be administered over two sessions. Parts 1 and 2 are presented in the first session, and Parts 3 and 4 in the second session.

2. Students should be provided directions informing them of the purpose of the CARI and how the results of the assessment will be used.

3. As noted previously, the CARI should reflect the types of questions and materials the teacher generally presents in class. While it has been suggested that students be provided ample time to complete the test (Baumann, 1988), the time limits for Part 4 can reflect classroom practice. If, for example, students generally engage in comprehension activities outside of class, then they should be allowed ample opportunity to complete this section of the inventory. However, if students commonly engage in comprehension activities in class under defined time limits, then this section of the inventory should adhere to classroom practice.

Scoring

1. Scoring the CARI should reflect criteria of what you consider acceptable performance. It is recommended that these criteria follow your practice in assessing students' performance and what you consider to be acceptable performance on the types of tasks presented in the inventory designed for your students. It may be useful to examine individual items or groups of items that assess certain types of learning, then calculate a percentage of correct responses. For example, if you emphasize in your class tasks that require students to construct inferences, yet results of the CARI indicate that only 30% of your students demonstrate this ability, additional attention should be directed to this form of learning as you design your instruction. Similarly, examining individual student scores for these items will assist you in identifying students that may benefit from some additional assistance or who may benefit from group tasks that focus on cooperative efforts to discuss ways to draw inferences with the subject matter material presented in your class.

Interpretation of students' performance is determined from the scores obtained on each of the four parts of the test. Take, for example, the following class averages for two groups of students.

Class	Part 1	Part 2	Part 3	Part 4
Hour 4	23%	29%	67%	64%
Hour 7	21%	27%	87%	88%

Part 1: Components of a Textbook

Directions: *Use the following table of contents to answer these questions.*

1. If you wanted to know more about fats and oils that you use in your kitchen, what page in the text would you turn to read about this topic?

2. Does the text provide a distinct chapter describing weight reduction methods for those people who are overweight?

3. If you were interested in including a lot of carbohydrates and fiber in your diet, with particular emphasis on breads and cereals, what page would you turn to to read about this topic?

CONTENTS

PREFACE vii

Part I   FOODS, NUTRITION, AND CONSUMER CHOICES   1
    1. What Is Nutrition?   3
    2. Why We Eat What We Eat   23
    3. The Confused Consumer   57

Part II   ENERGY AND BODY WEIGHT   75
    4. Our Need For Energy   77
    5. The Challenge of Maintaining Ideal Weight   89
    6. Underweight   109

Part III   THE NUTRIENTS AND THE FOODS THAT SUPPLY THEM   115
    7. Carbohydrates and Fiber   117
        Supermarket Nutrition: Choosing Foods in the Bread and Cereal
                        Group,   133
                        Choosing Sugars and Sweeteners,   145
    8.   Fats   151
        Supermarket Nutrition: Choosing Fats and Oils,   162
    9.   Proteins   169
        Supermarket Nutrition: Choosing Foods in the Meat Group,   186
                        Choosing a No-Meat Diet,   202

From D. A. Wenck, M. Baren, and S. P. Dewan, *Nutrition.* VA: Reston, 1980.

Part 2: Reference Skills

Directions: *List three standard reference sources you could use to learn more about nutrition.*
    1. _____
    2. _____
    3. _____

Figure 10.1
Example of Content Area Reading Inventory

Part 3: Vocabulary Knowledge and Strategies

Directions: *Select the best definition for the following words.*

1.**heredity**
   a. one's relations
   b. one's genetic makeup
   c. one's physical appearance
   d. one's mental abilities

2.**malfunction**
   a. not working correctly
   b. not thinking appropriately
   c. not operating at best levels
   d. not producing enough

Read the following sentence, paying particular attention to the underlined word. After reading the sentence, select the best definition of the underlined word.

"To say that <u>obesity</u> is caused by overeating and inactivity is an oversimplification of a much more complex problem." (Wenck, Baren, & Dewan, 1980, p. 93)

obesity
a. being without exercise
b. being overweight
c. being malnourished
d. being underweight

Examine the following words. For each word write the word's prefix and root and provide a meaning for each.

noncaloric
   prefix:
   root:

undernutrition
   prefix:
   root:

Read the underlined words in the sentences below, then examine the dictionary entries for those words. Write the dictionary definitions that apply to the context of the sentence.

The crisp, fibrous foods provide lots of chewing action for the dieter or nervous eater who needs constant mouth motion, but this may stimulate the <u>appetite</u> rather than satisfy hunger. Thus the <u>diet</u> that is based on large amounts of low-calorie, watery, fibrous foods may soon be discarded by the dieter.

appetite: 1. a desire for food or drink. 2. a desire to satisfy any bodily craving. 3. a desire for some taste.

diet: 1. food and drink considered in terms of nutritional qualities. 2. a particular selection of food, especially to improve one's looks or health. 3. the foods habitually eaten by a group of people or animals. 4. to feed

Figure 10.1
Continued

Part 4: Comprehension

Directions: *Read the following selection on diets. When you have finished, answer the questions at the end of the reading.*

WEIGHT LOSS DIETS

A person can lose weight on just about any diet if calories consumed are less than calories expended. But many fad-type diets are not nutritionally well balanced, may be unhealthful, and offer but a temporary solution to a permanent problem. An effective diet plan is one that will maintain a healthful level of nutrients and will teach new eating habits that can continue to be followed, with modification, after weight is lost.

A weight control diet that includes a variety of foods will not become monotonous and is more likely to be followed than one that severely restricts the kinds of foods that can be eaten. The diet needs to be low enough in calories so weight can be lost on it, but not so low that a person will be undernourished or hungry all the time.

An important criterion for choosing foods for a weight control diet is the caloric content. The energy values of food depend on their composition, that is, the relative amount of fat, protein, and carbohydrate they have in proportion to the noncaloric components of water and fiber. Watery, fibrous foods such as vegetables and fruits have fewer calories per portion than such foods as fatty meats, whole milk, cheese, ice cream, and nuts, which have proportionately large amounts of fat, protein, sugar, and starch.

Another factor to consider in choosing foods for a diet, in addition to their energy value, is their satiety value–their ability to keep you feeling satisfied for a period of time. Fats and protein have the greatest satiety ability.

From Wenck, Baren, & Dewar, 1990, p.97.

1. What types of food will satisfy your hunger for the longest period of time? (literal recall question)

2. Why do diets that contain a balance between carbohydrates, proteins, and fats seem to be best for most people? (constructing inferences)

3. Refer to the reading above and the following excerpt from Jane Brody's *Good Food Book* to answer this question: Once you have lost weight on a diet, why is it so difficult to keep that weight off? Can you maintain a lower body weight by diet alone? (product or hypothesis)

According to one prevalent theory of weight control, your normal (that is, usual) body weight is like water—it constantly seeks its own level. The weight at which you stabilize when you make no special effort to gain or lose is called your body's *set point*. When your weight drops below that set point, chemical signals of starvation seem to trigger a corrective system into action to bring you back to "normal", even though normal by your definition means fat. This may be a major reason behind the failure of diets to produce long-lasting weight loss for most people.

From J. E. Brody, *Jane Brody's Good Food Book*. New York: Norton, 1985, p. 217

Figure 10.1
Continued

Scores in Parts 1 and 2 draw attention to the difficulty both groups are experiencing with common reference materials and text structures. Scores on vocabulary and comprehension items indicate sizable differences between the two groups, thus requiring different instructional approaches to each class. While the performance of the fifth-hour class would suggest a less difficult text may be in order, the seventh-hour class may be better served with a text that is more difficult. If no alternate text materials are available, the fifth-hour class will require considerable assistance from the teacher. Text could be presented in small chunks, prereading activities such as those described in Chapter 3 could serve to provide additional background information, and the teacher could provide questions prior to reading small portions of the text to allow students to obtain a surface-level understanding of the material.

Before concluding the discussion of the CARI, it is important to call attention to its use in establishing cooperative learning groups. Because the CARI is constructed from text materials used in the classroom, the results provide a useful measure for creating the sort of cooperative learning groups described in Chapter 7. The type of grouping arrangement will depend on the nature of the learning task and the objectives of the teacher. For learning activities involving greater cooperative thinking, and those requiring one to take a perspective obtained from the reading material, a heterogeneous grouping arrangement is advisable (Johnson & Johnson, 1991). Homogeneous groups are recommended when it is required that students master specific skills or instructional objectives (Johnson & Johnson, 1991). Because the CARI may provide one of the more accurate assessments of students' ability to learn from text materials, its results provide a particularly useful measure for assigning students to cooperative learning groups.

Commentary: The CARI

The CARI offers a useful assessment of students' ability to use a textbook and reference materials and their ability to learn vocabulary and to comprehend text information. Because the reading material presented in this informal assessment is the same as the material students read in class, and the questions or tasks reflect those presented in your class, the results of the CARI provide a good indication of students' ability to learn from your subject matter text. Moreover, the CARI can highlight both the individual needs of students and the overall ability of a class or grade level. Results can be useful in planning instructional activities that are best suited to the needs of the students, in establishing cooperative learning groups (discussed in Chapter 8), or in estimating the overall ease or difficulty of text material. While the CARI can be a valid measure of those learning tasks presented in the classroom, its construction will require considerably more time than a cloze. Additionally, care must be exercised in writing questions that reflect the various types of thinking required in the classroom to ensure they are valid and reliable.

▼ PRACTICE EXERCISE 10.2

Take a few minutes to examine and complete the CARI displayed in Figure 10.1. As you examine this sample, note the variety of tasks presented and the variety of sources of information the reader is required to use in the various parts of the inventory. Now consider how this form of assessment differs from norm-referenced assessments.

▼▼

Portfolios

A relatively new and promising form of authentic and informal classroom assessment is the portfolio. Broadly defined, a portfolio is an artifact of the learning process that may include how students go about the process of learning, how they reflect upon that learning process, and how students may interact within the context of the classroom, and assembles products of the learning process. Examples of these artifacts comprise writings, journals, videos, interviews, graphic representations, photos, computer projects, audio tapes, and a myriad of physical objects (art work, musical scores, woodworking projects, etc.). Key elements of portfolios adapted from those identified by Tierney et al. (1991) and Valencia and Place (1994) include the following:

▼ Assess students' progress over a range of learning activities students are engaged in
▼ Align themselves with the curriculum
▼ Document authentic instances of students' reading and writing
▼ Represent learning and progress over time
▼ Include multiple modes of documenting student ability (samples of work, interviews, observations)
▼ Provide meaningful opportunities for students to develop ownership in their learning and evaluation of that learning; students assess their own learning

From this list, it is evident that portfolios assess a very wide range of student learning behaviors, products, and attitudes. Unlike traditional testing practices that tend to focus on what students learn about the content, portfolios examine how students learn and how they view their own learning. But portfolios are much more than a collection of artifacts placed in a folder or on a computer. The portfolio provides an assessment of intentional, purposeful learning situations, activities, and tasks. The teacher and student have clearly defined objectives for the construction and development of the portfolio as well as the learning activities reflected in the portfolio. Four types of portfolios have been identified by Valencia and Place (1994): showcase, evaluation, documentation, and process. The showcase portfolio exhibits a high degree of student ownership. In effect, it is the product of the students' effort, reflecting what they feel to be their favorite work. Generally, the content, use, and presentation of the showcase portfolio is directed by the student as described by Tierney et al. (1991, p. 45):

Each portfolio consists of a large folder for each student that is placed in a key location in the classroom so that the students have easy access to them. Students sort through them, select materials to go in and out of them, share them with their parents, class-mates, and visitors and use them to help them decide upon future learning goals. These portfolios represent the work students do across time and serve as the catalyst and basis for self-assessment.

The evaluation portfolio is more teacher directed and provides for both a defi-nition of the elements of the learning process and an evaluation of students' perfor-mance on these elements. This form of portfolio stresses students' progress in accor-dance with criteria established by the teacher, but the teacher and students are involved in evaluation of the portfolio.

The documentation portfolio is an archive of student products that reflects progress in the context of classroom learning. Products placed in the documentation portfolio by either the teacher or the student are not scored or evaluated.

The process portfolio contains ongoing products of a student's work, which are chronicled and described by the student. This type of portfolio is an ongoing effort to assess students' progress over extended periods of time. As such, students are encouraged to reflect on their learning, to observe and comment on changes in their performance, and to attempt to define or describe the nature of their learning.

Implementation of portfolios in subject matter classrooms does have a positive effect on student learning (Koretz, Stecher, & Deibert, 1993) and teachers' instruc-tional practices (Aschbacher, 1993). In planning for the implementation of their use, the following considerations are worth noting.

1. Effective use of portfolios is a long-term commitment. Because portfolios are an informal assessment requiring novel ways to reflect upon and document the process of learning, it is not unusual for the process of implementation, refinement, and adoption to take several years.

2. Generate student ownership. Students should come to realize that portfo-lios are expressions of their personal growth and performance. Unlike tests created by the teacher, the portfolio is an artifact of learning produced by the student. Ownership is increased when the teacher involves students in the planning, con-struction, and implementation of portfolios. By making this a team effort, students are more likely to recognize the relevance of portfolios and understand how the port-folio can reflect their insights, values, and educational achievements.

3. Provide modeling. Both teachers and students will benefit by others mod-eling the planning, construction, and evaluation of portfolios. This may require a for-mal presentation from a colleague and students who have experienced the use of portfolios, or it may require the presentation of completed portfolios so both teacher and student have a better understanding of their use in the classroom.

4. Build consensus. Teachers and students are more likely to accept the use of portfolios when provided the opportunity to engage in ongoing reflections of their use and potential benefits. These discussions not only clarify the use of portfolios, but they also allow teachers and students to gain some common ground in terms of expectations, structures of the portfolios, and the strengths and weaknesses of vari-ous forms of portfolio assessment.

5. Consider and define the nature of the portfolio and its content. Carefully consider the purpose of using portfolios and how they may facilitate students' learning. Not all learning experiences may be suited for portfolio use. If, for example, students in a geometry class are calculating areas of various geometric shapes as a way of applying formulas, there would be little reason to have students engage in portfolios. If, however, the learning objective is to allow students to apply their ability in calculating areas of geometric forms to solve everyday problems, then a portfolio may indeed be a useful form of assessment. When portfolios are used, students and the teacher should have a mutual understanding of their purpose, their form, and how the portfolios should be evaluated.

Portfolios can provide students a framework for exploration and discovery, for reflection, and tools for monitoring their performance and learning. Here is an example of an activity used in a high school science class from a town in Iowa located on the Mississippi River. Note that the teacher begins the lesson by presenting the students with a checklist of competencies she will observe when the students present their portfolios.

Checklist for Your Portfolio Presentation

1. Ability to locate and present relevant information.

   __ Rudimentary __ Emerging __ Accomplished __ Exemplary

   Comments:

2. Ability to draw upon and use relevant concepts.

   __ Rudimentary __ Emerging __ Accomplished __ Exemplary

   Comments:

3. Ability to predict consequences.

   __ Rudimentary __ Emerging __ Accomplished __ Exemplary

   Comments:

4. Ability to apply concepts of environmental science and political science.

   __ Rudimentary __ Emerging __ Accomplished __ Exemplary

   Comments:

5. Ability to summarize pertinent findings.

   __ Rudimentary __ Emerging __ Accomplished __ Exemplary

   Comments:

6. Ability to understand and communicate how pollution may affect our society.

   __ Rudimentary __ Emerging __ Accomplished __ Exemplary

   Comments:

The Problem: We will be touring a three-mile stretch of the Mississippi by boat to locate sources of pollution that flow into the river. At issue here is the pollution of our major waterways. Your task is to identify where this pollution is coming from, how serious this pollution might be, and what steps you can take to see this comes to the attention of government officials. When you complete this project, you will be asked to make a presentation to the class making use of your notes, reflections, information you gathered from people or other sources, and photos or videotapes. You will be asked to submit a documentation portfolio at the completion of this project.

Things to Examine Before Our Trip

▼   What is considered to be pollution and where does it come from?

▼   What government agencies (state, local, federal) are responsible for monitoring the pollution of our waterways?

▼   Contact the above agencies for information on laws and regulations and what citizens can do to report or monitor pollution.

▼   Read, interview individuals, or contact experts on the Internet to determine the effects of pollution on our waterways.

For My Portfolio: Notes and information about what I have learned about pollution, who monitors it, what the laws and regulations are, and what effects it might have.

Things to Examine and Note on the River

▼   Take water samples at the source of the pollution (these will be analyzed and compared to samples of water taken from different locations on the river).

▼   Make notes of your reaction to the pollution you located. Consider where it came from, how serious it may be, and how you located this source.

▼   What steps do you think should be taken to reduce this pollution?

▼   Note wildlife, vegetation, and activities of people that may be affected by this pollution.

For My Portfolio: Notes on what I observed on the river, my reaction to it, and what consequences this may have on our environment, our health, and our lifestyle.

After the Trip—What Did You Discover?

▼   Note your reflections on the usefulness of laws and regulations intended to address pollution of our waterways.

▼   What thoughts do you have on the seriousness of the pollution you found and its consequences on our city and the cities downstream?

▼   How easy was it dealing with governmental agencies?

For My Portfolio: Notes and reflections that I have for the above questions.

From the preceeding example it can be seen that students are asked to document their reflections in a learning task involving the use of portfolios. This type of reflection may require assistance and most likely will develop only after long-term practice. Students experiencing difficulty engaging in reflective behaviors may benefit from prompts such as the following:

▼　What steps did you follow in this problem or task?

▼　What did you understand to be your goal in this problem or task?

▼　What thoughts or information did you use from what you already knew?

▼　How well did you accomplish the goal?

▼　What would you do differently next time?

▼　Consider making a list of things you learned from this task, then put those ideas in words to describe the process you used in addressing this problem.

Use of portfolios will no doubt provide teachers and students with a distinctive perspective on the nature of learning in the subject matter class. This form of informal assessment has advantages for teachers and students. Teachers gain more valid insight into the process as well as the products of learning. With its emphasis on the process of learning, teachers are likely to gain a better understanding of not only what students think as they progress through problem-solving tasks, but they also gain a better understanding of the extent to which students possess the requisite skills or knowledge to engage in classroom learning tasks. Understanding this information allows the teacher the opportunity to supplement and modify instruction to more appropriately meet the needs of students. For students, portfolios provide an opportunity to gain insight into their own learning, but they also provide students the opportunity to gain a sense of ownership and pride in the various elements of learning.

ASSESSING TEXT: FACTORS AFFECTING TEXT DIFFICULTY

This section focuses on factors that influence students' understanding of textbooks, with the goal of providing some reasonable criteria for assessing classroom reading material. The first part of the section presents a list of factors that affect text comprehension, followed by a checklist for adopting or selecting text for classroom use. The second part of the section discusses readability formulas with an emphasis on their use and limitations.

Factors Affecting Text Difficulty

The discussion of text difficulty that follows focuses on six factors that are largely inherent in the text itself. The factors considered here are *vocabulary, sentence structure, length of text, elaboration, coherence and unity,* and *text structure.* Two of these, vocabulary and sentence structure, are the two factors considered in readability formulas discussed later in this chapter. While these two factors are important, they cannot serve as the sole criteria for determining text difficulty. As has been pointed out by a number of authorities (Kintsch & Vipond, 1979; Ryder, Graves, & Graves, 1989; Zakaluk & Samuels, 1988), features of text other than vocabulary and sentence structure are certain to make a much greater difference than the combined effects of these two factors. The discussion of text difficulty begins, then, with a description of how vocabulary can affect text difficulty.

Vocabulary

Vocabulary is one of the most easily identifiable characteristics of text difficulty. While there is sizable evidence pointing to the fact that texts containing difficult vocabulary are likely to present problems in comprehension (Anderson & Freebody, 1981), simply replacing difficult words with easier ones may not simplify a text; in fact, it may make a text even more difficult. If, for example, the term *herculean* is used, the simpler substitution "requiring a lot of strength" does not convey the same meaning. Replacing "The man lifted the car to free the woman. His *herculean* effort warranted a medal from the mayor" with "The effort that took a lot of strength warranted a medal from the mayor" leads to a sentence that conveys a much different meaning.

Knowledge of vocabulary aides comprehension. But reading text that contains few new words does have its limitations. A reasonable number of words should be unfamiliar to students to provide the opportunity to learn new words. Lacking these new words, students' ability to increase their word knowledge is reduced.

Sentence Structure

The effect of sentence structure is relatively easy to assess. Very long and complex or convoluted sentences make text more difficult to read. While it may seem reasonable to deliberately select a text because it has short and simple sentences, sentences in a text need to be complex enough to convey the meaning of the text clearly (Irwin & Pulver, 1984; Pearson, 1974–1975). If the intended meaning of a sentence is "Having lost his job, Ted had to return the new sports car to the dealer who would now lose his sales commission," breaking the sentence into something like "Ted lost his job. He had to return his car to the car dealer. The car dealer would now lose his commission" is not going to result in more comprehensible text. Text that includes only short, simple sentences may lack logical connectives, thus placing the demand of inferring relationships upon the reader. This added burden can cause problems for some students.

Length of Text

Often overlooked as a factor influencing the likelihood that a student will complete a selection with full understanding is the factor of length. For students with reading problems, length alone can be a very formidable obstacle (Graves & Graves, 1994). Although longer text can, at times, provide elaboration that may enhance understanding, longer text per se is not always better. In some cases, summaries or much reduced versions of complete text may produce better comprehension than longer versions (Carroll, Smith-Kerker, Ford, Mazur-Rimetz,1988; Reder & Anderson, 1982). Fortunately the amount of material students are required to read is under the teacher's direct control. Sometimes short summaries may be more effective than longer selections. Similarly, the teacher may limit the amount of text read by directing students' attention to key concepts.

Elaboration

Elaboration is providing explanatory information behind the "bare-bones" information presented. It extends thought, provides greater description, and qualifies statements. Because elaboration makes information more meaningful and understandable, it becomes more memorable. Reading that "Jason bought a new car" is certainly understandable, but it is not a very memorable sentence. Yet the elaborated sentence, "Maria bought a new car that had a top speed of 140 miles per hour and was used in a James Bond movie" is more memorable.

While it has been shown that elaboration facilitates comprehension and recall (Bransford & Johnson, 1972), it has also been noted that shorter texts sometimes produce better comprehension and memory than longer ones. The matter of under which circumstances elaborated text hinders or aids the reader is not yet resolved. It appears, however, that shorter texts may be more effective if one needs to remember material, while elaborated text may be more effective if one needs to understand material thoroughly (Charney & Reder, 1988).

Coherence and Unity

Coherence refers to the clarity of each topic or subtopic and how well the various topics of a text relate to each other (Anderson & Armbruster, 1984; Beck & McKeown, 1988). For the young and inexperienced reader, text needs to be coherently written; each piece of information should fit with another.

Unity is the text's focus on a single purpose. Well-written texts do not wander in their presentation of topics, nor do they contain chunks of irrelevant material. Text that abruptly shifts topics or themes or provides nonessential or unrelated illustrations or examples can be difficult to follow.

Text Structure

Text structure refers to the organization of the text. The majority of texts students encounter in school can be categorized as belonging to one of two broad categories: narrative or exposition. These two types of text are organized quite differently (Chambliss & Calfee, in press). Narratives (literature having characters, themes, plots, and events) are stressed throughout students' primary grade years, and students do fairly well with this type of text structure. Exposition (text that informs the reader through explanation, compare-contrast, definition-examples, and problems-solutions) presents the reader with several problems. First, exposition does not provide the cues that narratives do. While narrative text generally has predictable sequences of problems-actions-resolutions, expository text generally lacks direct cues. A second problem with expository text is that very little of children's literature is exposition; parents read primarily narrative text to their children, and basal readers primarily contain narrative text selections. As a result, many students find expository text particularly difficult. Procedures for teaching students the various types of expository text structures are discussed in Chapter 4.

Text difficulty, as noted, can be affected by a number of factors within the text. Vocabulary, sentence structure, length, elaboration, coherence and unity, and text structure contribute to our understanding as we read. There are, however, factors outside the text—factors involving the reader—that also affect text difficulty. Briefly considered here are familiarity of content and background knowledge, and interestingness.

Familiarity of Content and Background Knowledge Required

Reading a selection on which we have little familiarity is a difficult task, and attempting to read a selection that is totally unfamiliar is an impossible task (Adams & Bruce, 1982). As was discussed in Chapter 1, understanding text involves more than a degree of familiarity with the content, it requires whatever background knowledge that is assumed by the author (Armbruster, 1986). Generally we can understand most short stories and novels with the knowledge that we acquire from day-to-day experiences. However, many social studies, science, and mathematics texts require extensive background knowledge for comprehension. Lacking this information, reading becomes a laborious and frustrating task.

Interestingness

This is a subjective factor referring to the degree of attention and intrinsic attractiveness of the reading. Although anecdotal information may sometimes lead attention away from important parts of the text (Hidi & Baird, 1986), interestingness seems to have a significant effect upon students' comprehension (Anderson, Shirley, Wilson, & Fielding, 1986; Graves et al., 1988). In general, it appears that texts that are intrinsically interesting are likely to facilitate comprehension, but texts that exhibit interesting, lively voice are limited in their effect if the text lacks coherence (Beck, McKeown, & Worthy, 1995).

Assessing Text Difficulty: Concluding Remarks

The criteria for assessing text difficulty have addressed six factors inherent in the text (vocabulary, sentence structure, length, elaboration, coherence and unity, and text structure) and two factors involving the reader and the text (familiarity of content and background knowledge, and interestingness). Note that this list is not a checklist in the sense that you can quickly tally these factors and arrive at a score reflecting text difficulty. Instead, the list represents a set of factors to consider carefully, to contemplate, as you consider if a particular text is to be used for a given group of students. Moreover, a factor critical in one text situation may not be important in another. Sentence length, for example, may be important in the circumstance where the text is not interesting, requires considerable background knowledge, and is required reading for students who are less-than-average in reading ability. Conversely, sentence length would be unimportant when considering an interesting narrative selection that presents highly familiar themes and characters in a familiar style.

Matching students and texts requires careful attention to the factors outlined here, factors related to the students themselves, factors in the text, and the teacher's objectives in using a textbook. While assessing these factors through some sort of numerical scale is inappropriate, they play an important role in how well students learn from text selections. In an effort to address the points raised in this section, the following procedure should be helpful in assessing text difficulty in the subject matter classroom. This procedure is outlined in Figure 10.2. Please note that factors of the text as well as factors of the students are addressed. While having students complete Part 2 of the text survey will require some additional effort, their evaluation of the text can provide a valuable perspective in your efforts to assess a text's difficulty. Often text that may appear to the teacher to be interesting and of an appropriate level of difficulty is viewed in an entirely different manner by the students. Assessing potential problems in advance of students' reading allows the teacher to make modifications in the use of the text or obtain alternate selections that may be more appropriate for the students' ability, background knowledge, and interests. If the text contains numerous new words that cannot be defined from context, then it may be advisable to teach these words prior to reading. A variety of strategies for teaching words are presented in Chapter 2. Similarly, if portions of a text selection contain numerous new concepts, an absence of detail, or content that may seem uninteresting or irrelevant to students, then it may be advisable to engage students in activities that prepare them to learn the material. These types of activities are presented in Chapter 3. If sentences are excessively long to the point that they may interfere with learning or if, on the other hand, they are excessively short, fragmented, or convoluted, then it may be advisable to obtain a different selection altogether.

Readability Formulas

The term readability has been used to describe a text's legibility, interestingness, or comprehensibility. However, readability is most often associated with formulas that provide grade level estimates of text difficulty. These formulas were originally designed under the assumption that text difficulty can be predicted by limiting text analysis to measures of sentence length and word difficulty. Assessment of the reader's background knowledge or interestingness of the material were not considered. The following contains a short explanation of how these formulas were derived, a discussion and examples of the use of two readability formulas, and a discussion of the limitations and use of the formulas.

One widely used and easily administered readability formula is the Fry Readability Graph (Fry, 1977). This graph, shown in Figure 10.3, was designed to provide a grade level estimate of text used in grades one through college. The grade level estimate is based on two factors: word difficulty and sentence length. Calculation of readability begins with the sampling of three, 100-word selections obtained from different parts of the text. For each 100-word sample, the total number of sentences and total number of syllables for all words, including proper

Part 1: Factors Inherent in the Text

Directions: *Examine three or four parts of the text in answering each of the following questions. It is recommended that you first read each of these parts of the text, then respond to the questions.*

	Yes	No

Vocabulary

1. Does text allow students the opportunity to learn new words?   ___ ___
2. Can words be learned through context clues?   ___ ___
3. Does text provide definitions for new vocabulary in content or in glossary?   ___ ___
4. Does text contain a large number of new vocabulary in a given passage?   ___ ___

Sentence Length

1. Are sentences of a reasonable length?   ___ ___
2. Are meanings of sentences clearly conveyed?   ___ ___
3. Are there excessive numbers of short, fragmented sentences or long convoluted sentences?   ___ ___

Coherence and Unity

1. Do ideas presented in text fit together logically?   ___ ___
2. Does text contain irrelevant material?   ___ ___
3. Does text contain, where appropriate, summaries and transitional or linking sentences?   ___ ___

Length

1. Are topics or sections of text of an appropriate length?   ___ ___

Part 2: Student Factors

Directions: *Provide students with passages or sections of the text examined in Part 1, and direct them to read the text. Then direct students to respond to each of the following questions.*

	Yes	No

1. Is the text interesting to read?   ___ ___
2. Does the text contain many concepts or ideas that are new to you?   ___ ___
3. Does the text provide enough detail, or examples so you can understand the information being presented?   ___ ___
4. Can you understand most of the individual sentences in the text?   ___ ___
5. Is this the sort of text that students in your grade could read and understand?   ___ ___

Figure 10.2
Procedures for Examining Text Difficulty

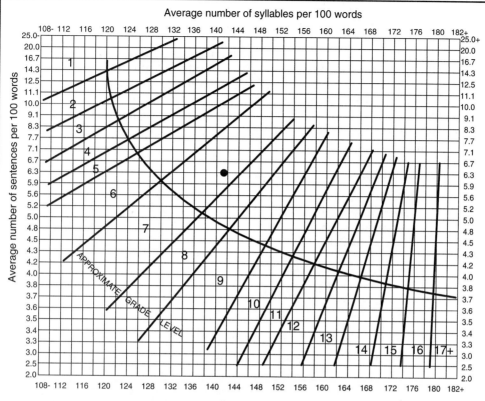

Average number of syllables per 100 words

Average number of sentences per 100 words

APPROXIMATE GRADE LEVEL

1. Randomly select three (3) sample passages and count out exactly 100 words each, beginning with the beginning of a sentence. Do count proper nouns, initializations, and numerals.

2. Count the number of sentences in the 100 words, estimating the length of the fraction of the last sentence to the nearest one-tenth.

3. Count the total number of syllables in the 100-word passage. If you don't have a hand counter available, an easy way is simply to put a mark above every syllable over one in each word, then when you get to the end of a passage, count the number of marks and add 100. Small calculators can also be used as counters by pushing the numeral 1 then pushing the + sign for each word or syllable.

4. Enter the graph with the *average* sentence length, and *average* number of syllables; plot the dot where the two lines intersect. The area where the dot is plotted will give you the approximate grade level.

5. If a great deal of variability is found in syllable count or sentence count, putting more samples into the average is desirable.

6. A word is defined as a group of symbols with a space on either side; thus, *1945* is one word.

7. A syllable is defined as a phonetic syllable. Generally there are as many syllables as vowel sounds. For example, *stopped* is one syllable and *wanted* is two syllables. When counting syllables for numbers and initializations, count one syllable for each symbol. For example, *1945* is four syllables.

From Edward Fry, "Fry's readability graph: clarifications, validity, and extension to level 17." *Journal of Reading, 21* (1977): 242–252. Reproduction permitted— no copyright.

Figure 10.3
Fry Readability Graph

nouns, are tallied. Initializations and numerals are counted as a syllable for each symbol. For example, 1993 would be counted as four syllables and IBM would be counted as three syllables. The average number of sentences for the selection and the total number of syllables are then plotted on the graph. For example, a selection of 142 syllables and 6.3 sentences (indicated by the filled-in circle on the graph) would fall within the mid-range of seventh grade. Once the grade level estimates are obtained for each of the three text samples, these values are averaged to provide a composite estimate of the text's readability. Shown below is the first sample that is plotted on the graph, two additional samples, and the composite readability estimate.

	Sample 1	Sample 2	Sample 3
Average Sentences	5.9	7.1	7.0
Average Syllables	142	136	144
Readability Estimate	7.75	7.0	7.5

$$\text{Composite Readability} = \frac{(7.75 + 7.0 + 7.5)}{3} = 7.4$$

According to Fry (1977), the readability graph is designed to provide an estimate of a instructional grade level. In other words, the Fry grade level estimate assumes that the teacher provides students assistance with the reading. Fry also notes that the formula is accurate within 1.0 grade level of measuring text difficulty. If scores fall within the shaded areas of the graph, they are considered unreliable, and it is recommended that an additional 100-word sample be examined.

While the Fry graph is relatively simple to use, computing readability estimates can be accomplished through most word processing programs. Programs such as Word (Microsoft Corporation) and WordPerfect (Corel Corporation) automatically calculate readability estimates by using the grammar checker functions of the program.

As noted, readability formulas are limited to the assessment of a few factors within the text. The level of a student's background knowledge, interestingness, and density of concepts of the material, the abstractness of the text, or the individual's motivation to engage in the reading are not considered. As a result, the estimates of text readability reported by these formulas may not accurately reflect the true ease or difficulty of the material. To provide an example of the importance of various factors in the text and factors within our background knowledge that affect the difficulty of text, and to provide you with the opportunity to apply the Fry formula, conduct a readability analysis of the following piece written by Plato. Rather than analyze three samples of the text, as directed by the guidelines for the Fry graph, the calculations here will be limited to a single sample. To allow for a better appreciation of Plato's style of writing, the sample included exceeds 100 words. The 100-word sample is noted by the slash we have placed in the text. Limit your analysis to the 100-word sample. Spaces have been provided at the end of each line so you may note the number of syllables per line for the Fry graph. The line-by-line tally of syllables and words having more than three syllables and calculations of the readability estimates of these two formulas can be found at the end of the book. It is important that you complete this exercise before you continue reading the discussion of readability formulas.

Excerpt from *The Republic* by Plato

And do you not suppose, Adeimantus, that a single boxer who was perfect in his   _____
art would easily be a match for two stout and well-to-do gentlemen who were not   _____
boxers? Hardly, if they came upon him at once. What, not, I said, if he were   _____
able to run away and then turn and strike at the one who first came up? And   _____
supposing he were to do this several times under the heat of a scorching sun,   _____
might he not, being an expert, overturn more than one stout personage?   _____
Certainly, he said, there would be nothing wonderful/ in that.   _____
And yet rich men probably have a greater superiority in the science and practise
of boxing than they have in military qualities.
Likely enough.
Then we may assume that our athletes will be able to fight with two or three times
their own number?
I agree with you, for I think you right.
And suppose that, before engaging, our citizens send an embassy to one of the two
cities, telling them what is the truth: Silver and gold we neither have nor are
permitted to have, but you may; do you therefore come and help us in war, and take the spoils
of the other city: Who, on hearing these words would choose to fight against lean wiry
dogs, rather than, with the dogs on their side, against fat and tender sheep?

(*The Works of Plato*, (1937) Translated into
English with Analyses and Introductions. By B. Jowett
Tudor Publishing Company, New York. p. 135–136.)

According to the Fry formula, this excerpt from *The Republic* has a readability of 7.0. Recognize that this estimate is not an aberration we used the formula on two additional samples taken from this work and found similar results. While conducting a readability analysis on a piece of Plato's writing was intended to be illustrative of the process of using readability formulas, it may also have made you aware of some of the formulas' limitations. Undoubtedly material written at the seventh- or eighth-grade level would be easier to understand than this selection of Plato's writing, even though the words are familiar and the sentences are not particularly long. What makes this a difficult piece of text to understand? It is Plato's style of writing. The use of phrases like "before engaging, our citizens send an embassy," and the excessive use of colons and semicolons in the last sentence are uncommon stylistic features. Also you may have noted that the thematic elements addressing states rights, individual responsibilities, and the virtues and excesses of wealth are presented in a rather obscure manner. Readability formulas are further limited in their inability to account for the reader's background knowledge or the density of concepts presented in the text.

As noted previously in this chapter, readability formulas have been used to write text that is presumed to be more easily understood. The outcome of writing to a readability formula is the production of material that is actually more difficult to understand (Davidson, 1984; Pearson, 1974–1975) because the writer attempts to omit logical connectives and construct short, simple sentences containing frequently appearing words. For this reason, writing text solely on the basis of factors assessed by a readability formula is discouraged (Giles, 1990; Marshall, 1970). When selecting text materials, attention should be directed at the sentence and word length. If you find sentences that are consistently short and unnatural or the continued use of short words, consider the following alternatives:

Criteria for Assessing Text Difficulty

1. Complete the criteria for assessing text difficulty (presented on page 352).

2. Compare the text selection to other text presenting the same content. Note and compare the length of sentences, use of short words, and the clarity of the writing.

3. Administer a cloze assessment on the selected text.

4. Collect four or five samples from a given textbook or reading selection and direct students to read and evaluate the relative ease of the text.

Readability formulas are only approximations of text difficulty. Because they assess a small number of the factors that affect text difficulty, no single formula will provide an accurate estimate. As noted by Bruce, Rubin, and Starr (1981), readability formulas do not address discourse cohesion, number of inferences, number of items to remember, complexity of ideas, rhetorical structure, dialect, and background knowledge required. Additional factors not directly assessed by readability formulas include density of concepts, style of the author, motivation of the learner, contribution of graphic aides to text understanding, and the grammatical correctness of the text.

CONCLUDING REMARKS

This chapter began with a discussion of standardized and informal assessments and the uses of these two types of assessments. We then discussed two types of standardized tests: norm referenced and criterion referenced. We discussed in some detail the construction, administration, and interpretation of two types of informal reading assessments: cloze and the content area reading inventory (CARI). Finally, we discussed text difficulty by first pointing out those factors that make text difficult, then presenting procedures for assessing text difficulty.

In concluding this chapter, we emphasize two points. First, assessment involves much more than creating quizzes and tests. Assessment can direct learning. The procedures we have outlined for reading assessment provide both teacher and student with information to attend to certain behaviors. As you consider the use of the assessment techniques we have presented in this chapter, remember that assessment is an integral element of our ability to engage in those everyday learning tasks encountered outside of school. We believe that assessment should take on the same level of importance in your classroom.

Second, assessment should be ongoing and flexible. Assessing textbooks and or students' reading are not one-shot matters. Classroom learning is often uneven. To monitor students' progress and to direct their attention to certain learning behaviors you will need to draw upon a variety of assessment tools during the course of the year. Initially, use of the cloze procedure or CARI will identify students' level of understanding of your content and it will identify individual's knowledge of that content. Later on, as you begin to engage students in learning activities, you may need to have students engage in peer-mediated holistic writing assessments or monitor cooperative learning, which are discussed in Chapters 7 and 8, respectively. The form and frequency of assessments will vary according to the task at hand and the need to consider the social and intellectual factors in your classroom and your instructional objectives. Implementing and maintaining effective assessment techniques may require substantial effort on your part. If you feel somewhat overwhelmed by the numerous assessment techniques we have presented, consider adopting one of the techniques each semester or one each year. Over time, the advantages of making these techniques part of your teaching will outweigh the initial effort.

REFLECTIONS
▼▼

This section of the chapter provides you with activities that allow you to reflect on some of the major topics of the chapter and how these topics apply to decisions you will make on the role of assessment in your class.

1. Interview a subject matter teacher to determine the various types of assessment used to measure students' ability to learn from reading material. Inquire about the use of formal and informal assessments, those assessments that are required by the school district or state government, and which assessments are designed or used by the teacher. Finally, inquire about the teacher's perception of how the reading ability of students has changed during the course of the teacher's career.

2. Obtain the aggregate test score data on a norm-referenced achievement test from a school district. Examine and summarize the mean (average) reading performance at the various grade levels tested and report on how these results compare to national averages. If possible, break down the district test score data by school and comment on factors that may account for any differences observed between schools.

3. Construct a CARI from reading materials in your subject matter area. Administer the device to several colleagues, then score and interpret the results. Summarize your colleagues' comments on the validity of the test and your own views on the strengths and limitations of this form of assessment.

4. Obtain several types of reading materials (textbooks, periodicals, newspapers) that you might read during the course of a year. Select two 100-word samples from each source, then using your own judgment, estimate the grade level of each

text sample. Next, obtain a readability estimate of each text sample by applying a readability formula. Comment on any discrepancies between your estimate and that obtained from the formula.

5. Construct, administer, and score a cloze test using text selected from your subject matter area. Comment on what you perceive to be the strengths and limitations of this assessment device.

6. Obtain a copy of a formal, norm-referenced achievement test from a library, testing center, or from your instructor. Complete the test as if you were the test taker. Write a summary of the validity of this form of assessment, paying particular attention to the following questions:

▼ Does the test present the type of questions one typically encounters in school?

▼ Is the reading material itself similar in style to that encountered in the material written for your subject matter area?

▼ Does this test seem to measure tasks similar to those commonly presented in your subject matter area?

▼ Are passages long enough to obtain an accurate assessment of one's ability to learn from text?

7. Working with a group of your peers, apply the procedures for examining text difficulty (Figure 10.2) to a sample of text used in your subject matter area. Summarize your views on the qualitative aspects of the text's vocabulary, sentence length, coherence and unity, and length. Next, present the text selection to another group of your peers and ask them to complete Part 2 of the text difficulty assessment (Figure 10.2). Compare your groups' views of the text with those of the group completing Part 2.

REFERENCES
▼▼▼

Adams, M. L., & Bruce, B. (1982). Background knowledge and reading comprehension. In J. A. Langer & T. M. Smith Burke (Eds.), *Reader meets author: Bridging the gap* (pp. 2–25). Newark, DE: International Reading Association. Thorough description of the importance of prior knowledge in the comprehension process.

Anderson, R. C., & Freebody, P. (1981). Vocabulary knowledge. In J. Guthrie (Ed.), *Reading comprehension and education*. Newark, DE: International Reading Association. Thorough description of the role and importance of vocabulary knowledge.

Anderson, R. C., Shirley, L. L., Wilson, P. T., & Fielding, L. G. (1986). Interestingness of children's reading material. In R. Snow & M. Farr (Eds.), *Aptitude, learning and instruction: Cognitive and affective process analyses*. Hillsdale, NJ: Erlbaum. Addresses the concept of interestingness in materials commonly read by younger students.

Anderson, T. H., & Armbruster, B. B. (1984). Content area textbooks. In R. Anderson, J. Osborn, & R. Tierney (Eds.), *Learning to read in American schools: Basal readers and content texts*. Hillsdale, NJ: Erlbaum. Interesting review of the nature of textbooks used in subject matter classes.

Archibald, D. A., & Newman, F. M. (1988). *Beyond standardized testing: Assessing authentic academic achievement in secondary schools.* Washington, DC: National Association of Secondary School Principals. Extensive presentation of the role and importance of authentic assessment.

Armbruster, B. B. (1986). Schema theory and the design of content-area textbooks. *Educational Psychologist,* 21, 253–267. Discusses the role of schema and the limitation of text in facilitating schema development.

Aschbacher, P. R. (1993). *Issues in innovative assessment for classroom practice: Barriers and facilitators* (Technical Report no. 359). Los Angeles: University of California, CREEST; Center for the Study of Evaluation. Useful discussion of some of the difficulties inherent in authentic classroom assessment.

Baumann, J. F. (1988). *Reading assessment.* Columbus: Merrill. Discusses both formal and informal, group, and individual reading assessment.

Beck, I. L., & McKeown, M. G. (1988). Toward meaningful accounts in history texts for young learners. *American Educational Research Journal,* (August–September), 31–39. Examines informal assessment of textbook comprehension.

Beck, I. L., McKeown, M. G., & Worthy, J. (1995). Giving a text voice can improve students' understanding. *Reading Research Quarterly,* 30, 220–238. Explores the effects of stylistic elements of text construction and their influence on understanding.

Blum, R. E., & Arter, J. (Eds.). (1996). *A handbook for students' performance assessment in an era of restructuring.* Alexandria, VA: Association for Supervision and Curriculum Development. Thorough presentation of performance assessment issues.

Bormuth, J. R. (1968). Cloze test readability criterion reference scores. *Journal of Educational Measurement,* 5, 189–196. A rather comprehensive review of the cloze procedure.

Bormuth, J. R. (1969). Empirical determination of the instructional reading level. In J. Figurel (Ed.), *Reading and realism* (pp. 716–721). Newark, DE: International Reading Association. A useful discussion on instructional reading levels and their use in instructional practice.

Bransford, J. D., & Johnson, M. K. (1972). Contextual prerequisites for understanding: Some investigations for comprehension and recall. *Journal of Verbal Learning and Verbal Behavior,* 11, 717–726. Reviews text and stylistic features that affect students' understanding.

Bruce, B., Rubin, A., & Starr, K. (1981). Why readability formulas fail. IEEE *Transactions of Professional Communications,* 24, 50–52. Explores problems with readability formulas and provides suggestions for alternatives to their use.

Calfee, R. C. (1996). Assessing critical literacy: Tools and techniques. In M. F. Graves, P. van den Broek, & B. M. Taylor (Eds.), *The first R: Every child's right to read.* New York: Teachers College Press. Presents an overview of the need for assessment of higher-order thinking skills.

Carroll, J. M., Smith-Kerker, P. L., Ford, J., & Mazur-Rimetz, S. A. (1988). The minimal manual. In S. Doheny-Farina (Ed.), *Effective documentation: What we have learned from research.* Cambridge, MA: MIT Press. Reviews our understanding of factors that enhance comprehension and elements of text structure.

Chambliss, M. J., & Calfee, R. C. (In press). *Today's textbooks: Tomorrow's minds.* London: Blackwell. Description of the nature of textbooks, their role in promoting learning, and suggestions for enhancing text construction.

Charney, D. H., & Reder, L. L. (1988). Studies in elaboration of instructional texts. In S. Doheny-Farina (Ed.), *Effective documentation: What we have learned from research* (pp. 47–72). Cambridge, MA: MIT Press. Reviews the influence of text elaboration on comprehension.

Corbett, H. D., & Wilson, B. L. (1991). *Testing, reform and rebellion.* Norwood, NJ: Ablex. Outlines many of the concerns with traditional assessments and presents suggestions for alternatives.

Davidson, A. (1984). Readability formulas and comprehension. In G. G. Duffy, L. R. Roehler, & J. Mason (Eds.), *Comprehension instruction: Perspectives and suggestions.* New York: Longman. Overviews the value of readability formulas and their value as a measure to predict students' understanding.

Flood, J., & Lapp, D. (1989). Reporting reading progress: A comparison portfolio for parents. *The Reading Teacher,* 42, 508–514. Discusses the use of portfolios for communicating student progress.

Fry, E. (1977). Fry's readability graph: Clarifications, validity and extensions to level 17. *Journal of Reading*, 21, 242–252. Discussion of the Fry graph for postsecondary assessment.

Giles, T. D. (1990). The readability controversy: A technical writing review. *Journal of Technical Writing and Communication*, 20, 131–138. Overview of the use and limitations of readability assessment.

Glaser, R., & Silver, E. (1994). Assessment, testing and instruction: Retrospect and prospect (CSE Technical Report 379). Pittsburgh, PA: University of Pittsburgh, CRESST/Learning Research and Development Center. Provides a succinct review of assessment devices and provides a view of issues that will lead toward changes in the nature of classroom assessment.

Graves, M. F., & Graves, B. B. (1994). *Scaffolding reading experiences: Designs for student success*. Norwood, MA: Christopher-Gordon. Addresses numerous instructional strategies designed to facilitate independent reading.

Graves, M. F., Slater, W. H., Roen, D., Redd-Boyd, T., Duin, A. H., Furniss, D. W., & Hazeltine, P. (1988). Some characteristics of memorable writing: Effects of revisions by writers with different backgrounds. *Research in the Teaching of English*, 22, 242–265. Examines the effects of various versions of a text on students' comprehension.

Henk, W. A., & Selders, M. L. (1984). A test of synonymic scoring of cloze passages. *The Reading Teacher*, 38, 282–287. Examines the effect of scoring synonyms on the cloze assessment.

Hidi, S., & Baird W. (1986). What children remember: A study of school textbooks. *Orbit*, 17, 10–11. A useful source for an insight into the effect of textbooks on student learning.

Hieronymus, A. N., Hoover, H. D., & Linquist, E. F. (1986). *Iowa Test of Basic Skills*. Chicago: Riverside. Manual for one of the nation's most popular achievement tests.

Irwin, J. W., & Pulver, C. J. (1984). Effects of explicitness, cause and order and reversibility on children's comprehension of causal relationships. *Journal of Educational Psychology*, 76, 399–407. Examines a number of variables affecting students' comprehension, including sentence length.

Johnson, D. W., & Johnson, R. T. (1991). *Learning together and alone: Cooperative, competitive, and individualistic learning*. Englewood Cliffs, NJ: Prentice-Hall. A comprehensive text on implementing cooperative learning in the classroom.

Johnston, P. H. (1983). *Reading comprehension assessment: A cognitive basis*. Newark, DE: International Reading Association. Provides a thorough overview of the nature of reading and its assessment.

Kintsch, W., & Vipond, D. (1979). Reading comprehension and readability in educational practice and psychological theory. In L. Nilsson (Ed.), *Proceedings of the conference on memory*. Hillsdale, NJ: Erlbaum. Discusses factors related to text difficulty.

Koretz, D., Stecher, B., & Deibert, E. (1993). The reliability of scores from the 1992 Vermont portfolio assessment program (Technical Report no. 355). Los Angeles: University of California, CRESST; Center for the Study of Evaluation. Examines reliability of the use of an ongoing portfolio assessment program.

Linn, R. L. (1987). Accountability: The comparison of educational systems and the quality of test results. *Educational Policy*, 1, 181–198. Examines the role of tests and their value in measuring educational programs.

Marshall, N. (1970). Readability and comprehensibility, *Journal of Reading*, 22, 542–544. Explores the relationship between readability assessments and the degree that a text can be understood.

McKenna, M. C. (1976). Synonymic versus verbatim scoring of the cloze procedure. *Journal of Reading*, 20, 141–143. Explores scoring synonyms as correct responses on the cloze procedure.

Mehrens, W. A., & Lehmann, I. J. (1991). *Measurement and evaluation in education and psychology*. Fort Worth, TX: Holt, Rinehart and Winston. A comprehensive text on the use of evaluation and measurement devices.

O'Day, J. A., & Smith, M. (1993). Systemic school reform and educational opportunity. In S. Fuhrman (Ed.), *Designing coherent educational policy: Improving the system* (pp. 250–311). San Francisco: Jossey-Bass. Explores school reform and change.

Paris, S. G., Lawton, T. A., Turner, J. C., & Roth, J. L. (1991). A developmental perspective on standardized achievement testing. *Educational Researcher*, 20, 12–20. Examines the validity of standardized test instruments and alternative measures.

Pearson, P. D. (1974–1975). The effects of grammatical complexity on children's comprehension, recall, and conception of certain semantic relations. *Reading Research Quarterly*, 10, 155–192. Explores the effect of sentence complexity on students' comprehension.

Reder, L. M., & Anderson, J. R. (1982). Effects of spacing and embellishment on memory for the main points of a text. *Memory and Cognition*, 10, 97–102. Examines the influence of summaries and adjuncts to main ideas.

Resnick, L. B., & Resnick, D. P. (1992). Assessing the thinking curriculum: New tools for educational reform. In B. R. Gifford & M. C. O'Connor (Eds.), *Changing assessments: Alternative views of aptitude, achievement, and instruction*. Boston: Kluwer Academic. A revealing discussion of the importance of higher-level thinking and its assessment.

Ryder, R. J., Graves, B. B., & Graves, M. F. (1989). *Easy reading: Book series and periodicals for less able readers*. (2nd ed.). Newark, DE.: International Reading Association. An annotated bibliography of high-interest, easy-reading texts.

Shanahan, T., Kamil, M. L., & Tobin, A. W. (1982). Cloze as a measurement of intersentential comprehension. *Reading Research Quarterly*, 17, 229–255. Review of the usefulness of the cloze procedure for comprehension assessment.

Shepard, L. A., & Smith, M. L. (1988). Escalating academic demand in kindergarten: Counterproductive policies. *Elementary School Journal*, 89(2), 135–45. A thoughtful discussion of skills and assessment of knowledge.

Smith, M., & Cohen, M. (1991, September). A national curriculum in the United States? *Educational Leadership*, 49(1), 74–81. Revealing discussion of the impact of a national educational curriculum.

Smith, N., & Zinc, A. (1977). A cloze-based investigation of reading comprehension as a composite of subskills. *Journal of Reading Behavior*, 9, 395–398. Use of the cloze procedure as an indicator of various comprehension skills.

Taylor, W. L. (1953). Cloze procedure: A new tool for measuring readability. *Journalism Quarterly*, 30, 415–433. The original discussion of the use of the cloze assessment technique.

Tierney, R. J., Carter, M. A., & Desai, L. E. (1991). *Portfolio assessment in the reading and writing classroom*. Norwood, MA: Christopher-Gordon. Text discusses the advantages and use of various portfolio assessment techniques.

U.S. General Accounting Office. (1993). *Student testing: Current extent and expenditures with cost estimates for national examination*. Washington, DC: U.S. General Accounting Office, Program Evaluations and Methodology Division. Review of issues pertaining to a national assessment.

Valencia, S. W. (1990). A portfolio approach to classroom reading assessment: The whys, whats, and hows. *The Reading Teacher*, 43, 338–340. A brief overview of the use and implementation of portfolio programs.

Valencia, S. W., & Place, N. A. (1994). Literacy portfolios for teaching, learning, and accountability: The Bellevue literacy assessment project. In S. W. Valencia, E. H. Hiebert, & P. P. Afflerbach (Eds.), *Authentic reading assessment: Practices and possibilities*, Newark; DE: International Reading Association. Discusses the portfolio program in a school district.

Wiggins, G. (1989). A true test: Toward more authentic and equitable assessment. *Phi Delta Kappan*, 70, 703–713. Advances the role and importance of alternative assessment devices.

Wolf, D. P. (1989). Portfolio assessment: Sampling student work. *Educational Leadership*, 46, 35–39. Overviews various forms of portfolio assessments.

Zakaluk, B. L., & Samuels, S. J. (1988). Toward a new approach to predicting text comprehensibility. In B. L. Zakaluk & S. J. Samuels (Eds.), *Readability: Its past, present, & future*. Newark, DE: International Reading Association. Presents alternatives to traditional readability formulas.

Answers to Practice Activities

CHAPTER ONE

Answers to Practice Activity 1.1

There are a number of instructional techniques and activities to facilitate students learning. Here is a partial list of activities to prepare students for learning, to assist them while they are engaged in the learning task, and activities that extend students thinking after the lesson.

Preparing to Learn

▼   instruction of key vocabulary used in the lesson

▼   presentation of key ideas or concepts in order to enhance students' background knowledge

▼   creating discussion groups where students identify from their prior knowledge information that relates to the lesson, and possibly allowing students the opportunity to generate a written summary of their ideas

▼   presenting a film, videotape, or other form of visual display that will acquaint students with concepts contained in the lesson

▼   asking students to respond to a series of statements that address concepts, values, or beliefs that are contained in the lesson

As Students Are Learning

▼   presenting students with questions that direct their attention to the lesson content

▼   directing students to work in cooperative groups to examine and respond to questions they may generate as they engage in the lesson

▼   asking students to generate their own questions as they engage in the lesson—these questions can then be examined and discussed by the class as a whole at the completion of the lesson

▼   presenting students with higher-level thinking questions that force them to go beyond the literal information in the lesson

At the Conclusion of the Lesson

▼   having students write written summaries of what they have learned

▼   initiate a classroom discussion to clarify lesson objectives and extend students' understanding

▼   direct students to obtain additional information on the lesson content from sources they believe to be useful—this information can be used to extend students' understanding through discussions, demonstrations, or writing activities

▼   apply the lesson content to real-world activities or events

Answers to Practice Activity 1.2

Responding to the stated goal, your attention should have been directed to information pertaining to influenza vaccinations. As you encountered information on influenza vaccinations, that information was localized and examined to determine if it aided you in accomplishing your goal. You may also have noted voids in your understanding of mutations and vaccine strains at the conclusion of the reading. To obtain additional information, it may have been necessary to reread. It is likely that you drew upon prior knowledge before, during, and after reading. Prior to reading you may have attempted to note the effects of having a virus, particularly if you live in an area of the country that has extremes in weather. During reading, you most likely constructed a better understanding of the risks and benefits of vaccines and those who are at particular risk if they fail to obtain a vaccination. After reading, you may have realized that many people have determined not to have influenza vaccinations because they feel it is not effective—only to find out that they had mistaken the onset of influenza for some other illness. You also noted that influenza mutations make it difficult to develop strains of a vaccine in time for the beginning of flu season.

There is one more mental scheme you may have experienced in the preceding example of metacognition, noncompliance. If you have not experienced influenza, the content of this selection would have little meaning, and reading the selection may have proceeded without much relevance.

Answers to Practice Activity 1.3

This example demonstrates the importance of automaticity in the reading process. By inverting the words, your automatic recognition of words was reduced; as a result your fluency and comprehension were likely reduced. In fact, you may have sounded somewhat like a remedial reader. You also may have noticed that on the first reading you had little recall other than a few isolated facts; your understanding of the "gist" of the reading was likely to have been limited. Due to the inverted text, you may have found that certain words were processed at the level of individual letters or letter clusters to construct a pronunciation. Again, when this occurred, your processing of the text was slowed and your comprehension of the sentence was most likely fragmented. By the third trial, the context had become more familiar, as had the rather unique "shape" of the words. You most likely doubled your rate from the first trial, and by the conclusion of the third trial you may have constructed a relatively sound understanding of the passage.

CHAPTER TWO

Answers to Practice Activity 2.1

Words for Eighth Graders

fling (a wild time)	____a new meaning
rationale number	____a new word for a known concept
pneumonia	____a word in students' oral vocabularies
finite	____a new concept

Words for Eleventh Graders

fluke	____a new word
languish	____a new word for a known concept
fugue	____a new concept
taxonomy	____a new concept

Answers to Practice Activity 2.2

Words for Junior High Students

harmony is likely to be at the acquainted level.
languid is likely to be at the unknown level.
fast food is almost certainly at the in-depth level.
triangle is likely to be at the established level.

Words for Senior High Students

examinations is almost certainly at the in-depth level.
pi is likely to be at the established level.

erstwhile is likely to be at the unknown level.

aerobic is likely to be at the acquainted level.

Answers to Practice Activity 2.4

Reactions	*Fearful Places*
terror	cemetery
fainting	forest
screaming	haunted house
shaking	cave
running	dark alley
freezing	deserted island

FEAR

Antonyms	*Synonyms*
certainty	horror
courage	fright
boldness	dread
confidence	alarm
assurance	panic

CHAPTER THREE

Answers to Practice Activity 3.2

The Effects of Oil Spills on Society

Economic Costs	*Environmental Costs*	*Health Costs*
Clean up	Destruction of animals and plants	Polluted water supply
Polluted water supply		
Reduction in tourism		

Answers to Practice Activity 3.3

___ ___
A   D

The increased awareness of violence has changed how people live, where they go, and the level of concern they express about violence.

(This statement is clearly written and most people could easily respond to it.)

___ ___
A   D
It would seem that watching violent acts on television and hearing about them constantly could make some people think that violence is acceptable in our culture.
(This is a clearly written statement and most people could readily respond to it.)

___ ___
A   D
There is some evidence that violent behaviors are inherited.
(While an interesting statement, it is not likely that most people would have the level of background knowledge required to respond to the statement.)

___ ___
A   D
In 1989 there were 1200 people on death row in state penal institutions. (This statement is much too specific.)

CHAPTER FOUR

Answers to Practice Activity 4.1

Question 1 is a level 2 question because you need to combine information in the reading with background knowledge. In this case one must infer that fewer calories are used because one becomes less active as they become older.

Question 2 is a level 1 question because the answer (decreased activity) is found directly in the text.

Question 3 is a level 3 question because one must recognize the relationships between high caloric intake, sedentary activity, and few nutrients in one's diet. This question also requires considerable background knowledge.

Question 4 is a level 3 question as an active adult may or may not require more calories depending on the level of activity in their life. This question requires considerable background knowledge and will likely produce a wide variety of answers depending upon the information used in response to the question.

Answers to Practice Activity 4.2

Discussion

Purposes	*Uses With Text*	*Characteristics*
Stimulate exchange of ideas	Verification	No right answers
Consider counterarguments	Indirect reference	Requires trust
Sharpen students' conceptual understanding	Refocusing	Students share and justify responses
	Paraphrase	
	Closed book	

Answers to Practice Activity 4.4

Mr. Smith's explanation of summarizing focused on *what* strategy the students were learning and *how* to use the strategy. The explanation did not include *why* summarizing is helpful and *when* to use it.

Answers to Practice Activity 4.5

While Ms. Anders designed questions that matched her goal of application of the material, she did not focus on the characteristics of the text or her students that would help or hinder her students achieving this goal. Her instruction does not seem likely to result in the students' successfully applying the concept of sets. Ms. Trujillo, on the other hand, carefully considered her text in relation to the goals and what she knew about her students. From this she was able to design instruction that provided the support they needed, as well as actively engage them, in the reading process as they worked toward successfully meeting the goal. She attended carefully to the needs of her students with reading difficulties. Her plan to use alternative sources, study questions, and discussion, as well as her cooperative grouping considerations, provided the means for these students to comprehend and apply the material.

CHAPTER FIVE

Answers to Practice Activity 5.1

In this example, the first question is relatively easy to answer if you have the requisite background knowledge: acid rain would fall without pollutants produced from fossil fuels. Lightning and the decomposition of organic matter contribute to the production of acid rain. According to our definition, answering this question requires critical thinking because the reader must understand the definition of fossil fuels, know that burning fossil fuels contributes to acid rain, and must understand what sources other than fossil fuels contribute to the production of acid rain. Some of this information must be accessed from prior knowledge, while other information can be obtained from the paragraph. The second question, also requiring critical thinking, is more difficult. The reader must be selective in gathering a greater amount of information from prior knowledge (the density of the population is greater in the eastern part of the country, more industries in the east burn fossil fuels, climatic differences, etc.), and the reader must be able to relate that knowledge to information in the reading (factories contributed to the increase in acid rain, the burning of fossil fuels increases acid rain). Note how both questions require much more than the recognition or retrieval of literal information.

Answers to Milk Container Problem

In this problem the amount of liquid in the two containers is identical. To solve this problem you need to determine the volume available in each container and the actual volume of the milk. If the container's volume is greater than the milk's, then space is wasted. Note that the top of the milk container (the fold-out spout) is empty space. Another factor in this problem is the packing of the containers. The pyramid-like containers fit neatly together with no wasted space.

Answers to Practice Activity 5.2

The following elements of everyday problems were found in the stereo problem:

1. *In everyday problem solving, it is not clear what information will be needed to solve a given problem.* In this case, the seventh grader was not certain the existing cassette and headphones could be used with a component system. Not recognizing this the students faced the problem of either buying the affordable system or delaying the purchase.

2. *The solutions to everyday problems depend upon the information you know and strategies you use to solve the problem.* Again, the student was not aware of the potential to use the cassette with the integrated system, or postpone the purchase of speakers while using the headphones.

Answers to Practice Activity 5.3

There are several possible solutions to this problem. One involves separating the balls into groups of four. The first two groups are placed on the scale (four balls on each side). If the scale balances, the oddball is not among the eight balls being weighed. If on the first weighing the scale does not balance, remove one group and place another on the scale. If the scale now balances, the oddball is in the group set aside. If the scale still does not balance, the oddball is on the side of the scale where the balls have not been replaced. The group containing the oddball can now be halved, as can the group on the other side (which now serves as the "standard" weights). The balls in the oddball group can now be weighed against the standard, and through a process of elimination the oddball will be identified.

Answers to Practice Activity 5.5

Outline of an Understanding Unit for ninth-grade physical science designed by a science teacher (Schmidt, 1996).

Generative Topic: Energy

Understanding Goals:

▼ Students will understand that energy is the ability to cause change.
▼ Students will understand that energy can be converted from one form to another.
▼ Students will understand the principle of conservation of energy.

Understanding Performances (These are two of many students will engage in.):

▼ Students in groups of three will answer four questions on energy on large sheets of paper, paste these around the room, and discuss their responses with the class and the teacher.

▼ Students will fill out energy crossfire maps, check them with each other, and turn them in to the teacher to get feedback.

▼ Each of five groups of students will complete a design conversation worksheet on one of the five forms of energy, post their worksheets in the front of the room, and receive feedback from other students and the teacher.

How the Unit Includes Frequent Understanding Performances:

▼ The unit lasts two to three weeks and includes ten understanding performances. The first one noted above comes on day 1, the second on day 6, and the third on day 8.

Answers to Practice Activity 5.6

▼ Generative learning activities that could be used with the section on generative learning include paraphrasing, writing summaries, giving demonstrations, making comparisons, making predictions, and a number of others.

▼ One prediction that could be made based on the text is that students who engaged in generative learning in studying a topic would learn and remember more than students who just read about it.

Answers to Practice Activity 5.7

Content area reading instruction would, of course, be a very appropriate topic for a design conversation in the class in which you are using this text. In the design conversation, we would discuss the purposes of content area reading instruction, its structure, some examples of it, and some arguments for and against it. One purpose, for example, is to assist students in constructing meaning from what they read in all content areas. One structure, and the typical one, is to have reading instruction integrated into the ongoing activities of a classroom. One example is a science teacher soliciting students' background knowledge on velocity and building a semantic map of that knowledge on the chalkboard before students read a chapter on velocity. One argument in favor of content area reading instruction is that it increases students' learning from what they read. One argument against it is that it does take time.

CHAPTER SIX

Answers to Practice Activity 6.2

Some Processes We Go Through When Writing

Thinking	Rethinking
Jotting down notes	Making an outline
Writing a partial draft	Finishing the draft
Revising the outline	Revising the draft
Starting over	Revising more
Revising again	Setting it aside
Revising and editing	Spell checking
Checking references	

The Extent to Which Our Writing Process Differs

Our writing process differs tremendously from one writing task to another. The above list represents a lot of the things we do for papers we are submitting for publication. However, the logical order of the above activities is not always followed in our writing. Most of the time, we jump around a lot more than this. Also, when we do informal writing, perhaps writing a note to a friend, we may do a single draft. Conversely, when we write something very important, a letter recommending a colleague for promotion, we may go through many more activities than are listed above, with one of the major ones being to have someone read and respond to our various drafts and rewrites.

Answers to Practice Activity 6.4

Here we are responding to guideline 3: Give students varied audiences to write for. Advantages—They get a feel of what it is like to write for various audiences. They come to realize that there are various audiences for their writing and that the audience affects both what they write and how they write. They are forced to adapt their writing to various audiences. They come to appreciate differences in such matters as vocabulary, syntax, formality, and freedom from errors that make a piece of writing appropriate or inappropriate for different audiences. Disadvantages—Writing for many different audiences may be too difficult for some students. Finding different audiences to write for takes time and effort.

Our position after considering the advantages and disadvantages of writing for varied audiences is that the advantages far outweigh the disadvantages. Of course, we cannot expect students to write for audiences they know nothing about, and we cannot expect them to quickly become adept at writing for virtually any audience. But we do believe that we do them a real service by giving them opportunities to discover that different audiences require different sorts of writing.

Answers to Practice Activity 6.9

Strong	Typical	Weak	
	X		Ideas, insights, thinking
	X		Organization, structure, guidance for reader
X			Language, sentences, wording
X			Mechanics: spelling, grammar, punctuation, proofreading
X			Overall

Comments:
On the positive side, this eighth-grader's theme shows competent use of language, sentences, and wording. It is mechanically very clean for something written by an eighth grader. And it has a clear topic—Midwest farms and farmers. At the same time, the writing lacks a clear thesis. It also lacks tight organization; there are no glaring twists or turns, but it rather rambles on. All in all, it is far from great writing, but it is strong for an eighth grader.

CHAPTER SEVEN

Answers to Practice Activity 7.1

1. *Positive interdependence.* The two of us writing this book constitute a definite instance of positive interdependence. Neither of us has the expertise to do the book alone, and neither of us had the time to get the book done by the target date. Together, though, we did it; and we both know that we could not have done it alone.

2. *Interpersonal skills.* There are probably a number of jobs in which small-group skills are not needed a lot, but interpersonal skills are almost always needed. We certainly need them in our work as teachers. Administrators need them, whether they are school administrators or administrators in business and industry. Barbers and beauticians need them. Sales people certainly need them. Travel agents need them. And executives of all sorts and at all levels need them. There are not, in fact, many jobs in which interpersonal skills are not needed.

3. *Group processing.* In our jobs as university teachers, we do a lot of group work. It is not unusual to have three or four small-group meetings a day. And how often do we process our group work? In our collective total of over 50 years as university teachers, neither of us can remember a time when group processing was a part of our group work. On reflection, we think this is a real shame. Obviously, without processing our group work, the chances that it will become more effective are much reduced, and we would like the groups we work with to be more effective.

Answers to Practice Activity 7.2

Theoretical support for cooperative work comes from Vegotsky's notion of the zone of proximal development, the notion that teaching something is an excellent way to learn it, and the notion of metacognition. Areas in which students working cooperatively have outperformed others include academic achievement, self-esteem, accommodation to others, attitudes toward school, interpersonal relationships, and higher-level skills.

Answers to Practice Activity 7.4

Forming skills are the beginning or prerequisite skills that students need just for groups to function, such as talking in quiet voices. Functioning skills are skills that students use as they work in groups, such as paraphrasing others' responses. Formulating skills are the roles or functions that group members have in their groups, including roles such as summarizing the group's learning.

Answers to Practice Activity 7.5

▼ Show students the need for cooperative skills.

▼ Make sure that students thoroughly understand each skill.

▼ Have students practice the skill.

▼ Make certain that students process their group work.

▼ Ensure that students continue work on their skills over time.

Our belief is that these guidelines are broadly applicable for teaching in situations in which we as teachers know the answer to the question we are asking, understand the concept we are teaching, or know how we want the skill performed. They are less widely applicable when the answers to the questions are unclear, the concepts are fuzzy ones, or the skill can be performed in a variety of ways.

CHAPTER EIGHT

Answers to Practice Activity 8.1

There are no right or wrong answers. The purpose of the exercise is to help you think about your own response to culturally diverse students. If you were able to rank these students, then consider the attitudes, values, and perceptions underlying your decisions. For example, you might feel most uncomfortable having a homeless student in class because of the instability you perceive in this child's life or the difficulty this child might have fitting in with middle-class children. Another teacher might not see having a homeless child in class as a problem.

Answers to Practice Activity 8.2

Answers will vary. You might introduce the topic by demonstrating photosynthesis or by asking students to describe their experiences with growing flowers or vegetables. Hispanic students might read about the process in simplified texts. The one who is the most proficient in English could explain the concept to the others. The class could work in linguistically heterogeneous cooperative learning groups to discuss the text and answer questions. They could work in cross-language pairs to draw diagrams of the photosynthetic process.

Answers to Practice Activity 8.3

Vignette 1. This is a risk-free environment where the student feels free to speak in her nonstandard dialect. It's also an environment where the teacher has been explicit about the difference between standard and nonstandard dialects. The teacher and student have developed a rapport—the student knows the teacher is not making fun of her.

Vignette 2. This interaction takes place within the context of instruction, whereas the preceding interaction takes place spontaneously. In Vignette 2 the teacher is more interested in assessing the student's understanding of content.

Asking the student to rephrase his answer in standard English might discourage him—and others—from responding. If the teacher wants students to practice standard English, he should state this at the outset of discussion.

Answers to Practice Activity 8.4

The teacher should have considered Mary's cultural background before judging her actions. As a Native American, Mary has probably been taught to share her things and put others ahead of herself. Competition and individual accomplishment are foreign to many native cultures. The teacher might have ignored Mary's whispering and later spoken to her privately about her actions.

Answers to Practice Activity 8.5

The teachers in this scenario should consider cultural perspectives other than their own. Dwayne, Mai, and Choua may have styles of learning and communicating that are different from those expected by their teachers. For example, while Ms. Wilson views Dwayne's rapping as disruptive and unrelated to learning, she could view it as an alternate way of learning—a way of learning that is meaningful to Dwayne—and she could incorporate this learning style into her classroom culture. Similarly, Ms. Blair could view Mai and Choua's desire to work independently as a way of learning rather than a way of disobeying her. From an assessment standpoint, Ms. Wilson's "simple" multiple-choice test may not provide all students with the opportunity to display their knowledge of the subject matter. And the statements that students do not respect their teachers or value learning are based on the faulty assumption that everyone demonstrates respect and value in the same way. All of the teachers should be encouraged to create classroom cultures that are mutually accommodating and to be explicit about their expectations rather than assuming that all students understand their implicit cultural rules.

CHAPTER TEN

Answers to Practice Activity 10.1

Until relatively recent times, displaying one's suntan was not an attribute widely accepted by the population. In fact, for many years having a suntan was a label denoting one as a laborer. Over time, however, a *suntan* became fashionable as those *who* could afford to travel *could* maintain their tan by *sunning* in distant locations. More *recently* however, many individuals in *the* medical community have warned *that* excessive sun can cause *melanoma*, premature aging of the *skin* and wartlike growths. An individual's resistance to the *amount* of sun is determined *by* the thickness of your *skin* and the amount of *melanin*. Individuals who have thicker *skin* are less likely to *burn*. The extent of your *natural* color is determined by *melanin*, a skin pigment. *The* skin pigment is made *of* skin cells called melanocytes. It is these cells that *produce* melanin, the pigment that *protects* your skin from the *harmful* rays of the sun. *Individuals* who have large concentrations *of* melanin are less likely *to* be affected by the *sun's* rays. Suntan as well as sunburn is caused by *the* invisible ultraviolet rays of *the* sun. These UV rays *are* the most intense between 11:00 A.M. and 2:00 P.M., *at* which time the sun's *rays* are less likely to *be* deflected by the Earth's *atmosphere*. The effects of the *sun* are particularly strong the *first* time one is outdoors *after* a prolonged period of *time* indoors such as the *winter* months. For those individuals *who* burn quickly, the first *exposure* to the sun should *be* limited to no more *than* fifteen minutes a day. O*n* subsequent exposures the duration *of* exposure can be increased *by* increments of fifteen minutes. P*rotection* from the sun's UV rays can be obtained from sunscreens. These products contain chemicals to screen out portions of light in the UV spectrum to prevent the skin from burning.

Answers to Practice Activity 10.2

Part One: Components of a Textbook

1. Page 162
2. No. It only addresses the problems of maintaining the ideal weight.
3. Page 133

Part Two: Reference Structures

1. Encyclopedias
2. Databases that provide references on nutrition
3. Government publications
4. Card catalog or computerized card catalog

Part Three: Vocabulary Knowledge and Strategies

1. *heredity*: (b). one's genetic makeup
2. *malfunction*: (a). not working correctly

   obesity: d. being overweight

   noncaloric: *prefix*: non = not *root*: caloric = having calories

   undernutrition: *prefix*: under = less than *root*: nutrition = available vitamins, minerals fats, proteins

   appetite: 1. a desire for food or drink

   diet: 1. food and drink considered in terms of nutritional qualities

Part Four: Comprehension

1. Fats and protein have the greatest satiety value.
2. Diets that have a balance of carbohydrates, proteins, and fats are the best for most people because this type of diet is less likely to become monotonous and provides a level of nutrients to maintain health and weight.
3. Losing weight involves more than watching what you eat. If your body has a set point, you must lower the set point. This means that you must burn more

calories through exercise. Many diets don't work for long periods of time because once one has lost weight they will go back to their normal weight established by the set point.

Answers to Fry and SMOG Readability Calculations

Excerpt from *The Republic* by Plato

	Fry	FOG
And do you not suppose, Adeimantus, that a single boxer who was perfect in his	22	0
art would easily be a match for two stout and well-to-do gentlemen who were not	21	0
boxers? Hardly, if they came upon him at once. What, not, I said, if he were	19	0
able to run away and then turn and strike at the one who first came up? And	19	0
supposing he were to do this several times under the heat of a scorching sun,	20	1
might he not, being an expert, overturn more than one stout personage?	18	1
Certainly, he said, there would be nothing wonderful/ in that.	13	0

SMOG

    1. Number of verbs with three or more syllables   2

    2. Average sentence length   20

        $22 \times .4 = 8.8$ grade level

FRY

    1. Total number of syllables   132

    2. Number of sentences   4.9

        From graph = 7.0 grade level

INDEX

About the Authors

Randall Ryder received his Ph.D. from the University of Minnesota in 1978. Prior to this he was a Title I reading teacher in the Poudre R-1 School District in Fort Collins, Colorado. He currently is a Professor in the Department of Curriculum and Instruction at the University of Wisconsin—Milwaukee where he teaches courses in content area reading and secondary developmental reading. His research interests include vocabulary development, staff development, and comprehension instruction. He has worked extensively in professional development schools in the Milwaukee Public School District and is presently a member of a school board in suburban Milwaukee. He has published *High Interest Easy Reading: Book Series and Periodicals for Less Able Readers* for the International Reading Association and has published widely in journals such as the *Journal of Reading, Elementary School Journal, Journal of Educational Research, Journal of Educational Psychology*, and *Reading, Research and Instruction*.

Michael Graves is a professor in the Department of Curriculum and Instruction at the University of Minnesota, where he chairs the Literacy Education program and teaches courses in content area reading, reading research, and secondary remedial reading. Prior to receiving his Ph.D. from Stanford in 1971, he was a composition instructor at Long Beach State College and a secondary English teacher in the Long Beach and Fountain Valley School Districts in California. His research and development interests include vocabulary development, comprehension development, and effective instruction. He is the former editor of the Journal of Reading Behavior, the former associate editor of *Research in the Teaching of English*, and the coauthor of two forthcoming books—*Scaffolding Reading Experiences* and *Essentials of Classroom Teaching: Elementary Reading*. His articles have appeared in such journals as *American Educator, Child Development, Elementary School Journal, English Journal, Journal of Educational Psychology, Journal of Educational Research, Journal of Reading, Reading Research Quarterly*, and *Review of Research in Education*.